MATTHEW PRIOR

» «

Poet and Diplomatist

» «

NUMBER 144 OF THE COLUMBIA
UNIVERSITY STUDIES IN ENGLISH
AND COMPARATIVE LITERATURE

Matthew Prior as Plenipotentiary to France

From painting by Belle

MATTHEW PRIOR

» «

Poet and Diplomatist

By

CHARLES KENNETH EVES

OCTAGON BOOKS

A DIVISION OF FARRAR, STRAUS AND GIROUX

New York   1973

Copyright 1939 by Columbia University Press

Reprinted 1973
by special arrangement with Columbia University Press

OCTAGON BOOKS
A DIVISION OF FARRAR, STRAUS & GIROUX, INC.
19 Union Square West
New York, N. Y. 10003

Library of Congress Cataloging in Publication Data

Eves, Charles Kenneth, 1888—
    Matthew Prior, poet and diplomatist.

    Originally presented as the author's thesis, Columbia.

    Original ed. issued as no. 144 of Columbia University studies
in English and comparative literature.

    Bibliography: p.
    1. Prior, Matthew, 1664-1721.   I. Series: Columbia University
    studies in English and comparative literature, no. 144.
PR3643.Eq   1973   821'.5   [B]   73-1151
ISBN 0-374-92646-8

Manufactured by Braun-Brumfield, Inc.
Ann Arbor, Michigan

Printed in the United States of America

To Lavinia

Preface

THE WRITING of a new biography of Matthew Prior requires no justification. Son of a joiner and nephew of a vintner, he became a specialist in diplomatic affairs, a master of light verse, a celebrated wit, living a varied and eventful life. Yet he has been patronized by his biographers, who have admitted his accomplishments but have been repelled by aspects of his character which they have been prone to attribute to his humble origin and his upbringing in a tavern. His origin, however, was not so humble as they have assumed.

The present volume owes its existence to Professor William P. Trent, who once suggested that a biography of Prior could be written without disparaging either Prior's character or achievements, and I wish to acknowledge my gratitude to Professor Trent for his kindly advice and wise guidance. I am further indebted to all who have written about Prior and the period in which he lived, particularly to Mr. Francis Bickley and to Mr. L. G. Wickham Legg, but I have drawn from manuscript material unutilized by previous biographers.

Thanks are due to many persons who have generously aided me in my research: to His Grace, the Duke of Portland, who placed at my disposal the Prior papers at Welbeck Abbey; to Sir Thomas Hare, who kindly lent me the Bolingbroke Letter Books, a possession of his family since the time of Thomas Hare, Lord Bolingbroke's secretary; to Mr. R. B. Adam, who gave me photostat copies of four of Prior's letters from his collection of rare eighteenth century manuscripts; to Miss Belle da Costa Greene, Director of the Pierpont Morgan Library, who allows me to print an hitherto unpublished letter of Prior's; to an anonymous benefactor who permitted me to examine letters from Prior to Lord Lexington, not included in the *Lexington Papers* and to the firm of Bernard Quaritch, Limited, who had custody of these letters. The greater number of previously unused documents, however, are in public institutions. To the managers of these institutions, I offer sincerest thanks: the Harvard College Library, the British Museum, the Public Record Office, Somerset House, the Bodleian Library, the Bibliothèque Nationale, and the French Foreign Office. Thanks are also extended to the Syndics of the Cambridge University Press for permission to quote not only from Prior's poems in the *Cambridge English Classics* but also from Prior's letters and manuscripts as printed in Mr. Wickham Legg's study of Prior; to the librarians of St. John's College and Trinity College, Cambridge for kindly sending me photographs of the portraits of Prior and for granting permission to reproduce them. It is a pleasure to acknowledge the grant of the William Bayard Cutting Traveling Fellowship by the officers of Columbia University which enabled me to continue my research in England and in France.

Professors Ernest Hunter Wright, Emory Neff, George Sherburn, J. L. Gerig, and J. P. S. Tatlock and Dr. Henry W. Wells read my manuscript and gave helpful and critical advice. My friend, Professor August H. Mason, made many valuable suggestions as to selection and arrangement of material. Appreciation is also due to Professors Minnie Clare Yarborough and Adeline Courtney Bartlett, and to Miss Helaine Newstead for reading the manuscript; to Miss Constance Southard Veysey and to my sister, Miss Mildred Eves, for reading proof. The greatest debt of gratitude I owe to my wife, whose aid and encouragement have been unfailing.

References to Prior's writings (unless otherwise noted) direct the reader to the standard edition of Prior's works, edited by A. R. Waller for the *Cambridge English Classics: Poems on Several Occasions*, 1905, and *Dialogues of the Dead and Other Works in Prose and Verse*, 1907. The two volumes of papers of the Marquis of Bath, preserved at Longleat, Wiltshire, and published by the Historical Manuscripts Commission, are designated as *Longleat Papers*.

CHARLES KENNETH EVES

NEW YORK, N. Y.
MAY, 1939

Contents

Illustrations

Matthew Prior as Plenipotentiary to France   *Frontispiece*
*Portrait, c. 1714–1715, by Alexis Simon Belle, in the Hall of
Saint John's College, Cambridge, England, to which college
it was bequeathed by Prior himself*

Mathew Prior, c. 1700   150
*Portrait by Sir Godfrey Kneller, in the Old Combination Room,
Trinity College, Cambridge, England*

MATTHEW PRIOR

» «

Poet and Diplomatist

CHAPTER I

Channel Row Days

THE DARK curtain lowered by the Commonwealth at the close of the Civil Wars had risen once more on an English royal setting. The dour Cromwell was gone, and Charles II was the center of a brilliant new social and literary scene in London. Four years had elapsed since he had been restored tranquilly enough to the throne of the Stuarts; and although the heads of the Regicides still scowled down from their pikes on Tower Hill, reminding passersby that the return of Maypoles and mince pies could only be accomplished with a measure of vindictiveness, it was none the less true that the pleasure-loving king was not so much determined upon revenge as he was loath to resume his travels. Memories of Barebone Parliaments might still haunt the halls of Westminster, but life in the new régime flowed about Whitehall, where Charles, the laziest, the merriest, the most amorous of men, led his band of reckless youths "flown with insolence and wine" in a mad whirl of

> . . . . court amours
> Mix't dance or wanton mask or midnight Bal,

or discoursed with them upon the merits of the latest madrigal or comedy produced in the convivial Restoration atmosphere.

Certainly it was a new world that the suave monarch ushered in upon his return from France, a world that laughed heartily at Hudibras and all fanaticism, and affected cynicism toward sobriety, religion, and morals. Even the dire events of the next three years, the Plague, the Great Fire, and the disgraceful burning of the English fleet on the Thames by the Dutch scarcely disturbed the Merry Monarch and his circle of Wits in Whitehall, given over to frolics and gallantries, and exchanging brilliant literary quips inspired by the swiftly flowing cup.

In this careless and indulgent atmosphere, and almost within sight of the straggling buildings of Whitehall, was born on July 21, 1664, the poet and diplomat, Matthew Prior—destined to play no mean part in the life of his time. Matthew was the next to the last of six children[1] born to his parents, and it is quite probable that he was the only one of them to survive infancy. Stephen's Alley, Westminster, Matt's birthplace, was described by a contemporary historian[2] as a "pretty handsome street, it being a passage for coaches . . . leading from King Street into Channel Row."

His father, George Prior, came from the small village of Godmanstone in East Dorset, about five miles from Dorchester. Here, where the ancestral home was situated, it is believed that George was born, one of a large family of seven children. Christopher Prior, Matthew's grandfather, was a farm laborer, so poor that all the sons but the eldest were compelled to leave home and seek their fortunes elsewhere. The description of George Prior as *generosus*, given by Matthew on his admission to St. John's College, Cambridge, and at other times, has generally been attributed to schoolboy pride; yet public records concerning Arthur Prior, Matthew's uncle, and Samuel Prior, a cousin, invariably designated them as gentlemen, a circumstance com-

[1]Their names and dates of baptism as taken from the parish registers at St. Margaret's Westminster are as follows:

Oct. 10, 1650, Lucretia Pryor, d. of Geo. and Elizabeth
Aug. 21, 1653, George Pryor, s. of Geo. and Elizabeth
July 27, 1656, Katherine Pryor, d. of Geo. and Elizabeth
September 21, 1662, Elizabeth Prior, d. to Geo. and Elizabeth
August 2, 1664, Matthew Pryor, s. to Geo. and Elizabeth
Nov. 29, 1668, Thomas Prior, s. to Geo. and Elizabeth.

[2] John Stow, *A Survey of the Cities of London and Westminster, brought down from 1663 to 1720 by J. Strype*, Vol. II, Book VI, chap. v.

patible with their rise in the world. The coat of arms, engraved on Matt's bookplate in books willed to his college, is one which appears on a sixteenth-century Roll of Arms as belonging to a family of Peres or Perrers, and has, in more recent times, been used by families of the name of Prior.[3] At a comparatively early age George was bound as apprentice to a joiner at Fordington, a hamlet on the outskirts of Dorchester, whence he went up to London and settled near his brother Arthur, who owned the Rhenish Tavern on Channel, now Cannon, Row.

Matthew's mother has remained practically anonymous all these years. It was not until 1918, when Canon Westlake discovered Matthew's baptismal entry in the parish registers of St. Margaret's Westminster, that her given name, Elizabeth, was made known. There is a strong likelihood that she was the daughter of Abraham Pennefather of Hanbury-on-the-Hill, Staffordshire. The Pennefather family is an old one, having received charters of lands in Warwickshire as early as 1340, and having settled in Staffordshire by the end of the fifteenth century. The will of Thomas Pennefather, son of the aforesaid Abraham, dated July 14, 1649, mentions his wife Lucretia, a brother Matthew, and a sister Elizabeth.[4] Although no legal documents have been found which record the marriage of Elizabeth Pennefather to George Prior, the baptismal records of the children of Elizabeth and George Prior reveal a repetition of the names Lucretia, Elizabeth and Matthew—a recurrence which is surely more than a coincidence. Furthermore, Matthew Prior kept in touch in later life with Matthew Pennefather the Third, whom he referred to as a "cousin german" and whom he once spoke of as his only relation of "any virtue or merit."[5]

For many years it was uncertain where Matthew was born, a

[3] Records of the College of Heralds.

[4] Somerset House, Prerogative Court of Canterbury: 158 Pembroke, Will of Thomas Pennefather.

[5] P. R. O., *State Papers, France*, 105/28, fo. 225, Prior to the Duke of Shrewsbury, Paris, Nov. 30/Dec. 11, 1713.

matter about which he himself seems to have been confused in his youth. A charming tradition, still cherished by the people of Wimborne, Dorset, is that he was a native son. Some nine years after Prior's death, Conyers Middleton, the librarian at Cambridge, became curious and wrote to his cousin, Conyers Place, the headmaster of the Dorchester Grammar School, to make inquiry about Matt's ancestry.[6] Place interviewed one Christopher Prior, "an honest laboring man," who was then living in the "mansion-cottage" at Godmanstone but who was so poor that he was a charge upon the parish. Christopher enjoyed indulging in reminiscences about happier days and his famous relative. He remembered especially "his cousin Matthew coming over to Godmanstone when a boy and lying with him." This statement convinced Place that Matthew was born "at or near Wimborne," and so he reported to Middleton. For the spread of the Wimborne tradition, Matt was partly responsible. On entering college, he told the registrar that his birthplace was Wimborne, Dorset, and on the following day, when his admission blank as a scholar was filed, he again gave his county as Dorset. The original entries were corrected subsequently so that the county now reads as Middlesex.

That no record of Matt's birth, or of his parents' marriage, or of his mother's death (she was erroneously reported to have been buried at Wimborne) was to be found at Wimborne was attributed by those who claimed Prior for Dorset to the fact that the Dorsetshire Priors were Dissenters. Indeed Prior himself wrote:

> So at pure Barn of loud Non-Con
> Where with my *Granam* I have gone,
> When Lobb had sifted all his Text,
> And I well hop'd the Pudding next.[7]

---

[6] *Portland Papers*, VI, 33, Conyers Place to Conyers Middleton, Dorchester, Dec. 7, 1730.
[7] "An Epistle to Fleetwood Sheppard," *Poems on Several Occasions*, p. 13 (unless otherwise indicated references to this volume are to the 1905 edition, ed. by A. R. Waller). Stephen Lobb was a nonconformist divine who came to London in 1681 as pastor of the independent congregation in Fetter Lane.

There is the possibility that George Prior left London during the Plague year and returned to Dorsetshire for a time when Matthew was quite young; hence the confusion in Matthew's mind as to his native county. The above lines, however, more probably recall summer holidays spent in Godmanstone with his grandmother, when he and young Christopher indulged, no doubt, in the less godly pursuits of boyhood, as well as in attending the Nonconformist chapel with the "Widdow Prior." It is known that the kindly Uncle Arthur was wont to return to his native county every summer to visit relatives and to renew acquaintances. Young Matt may have accompanied him and visited around in the three villages—Godmanstone, Wimborne, and Dorchester—endearing himself to his relations by the humor and ready wit which distinguished him in maturity. The townspeople of Wimborne recalled Matt with affection, and in the old Minster, where, as a little boy he used to watch with wonder the mechanical soldier beating out the hours on the historic astronomical clock, a bronze plate has been erected in his memory bearing the motto *perennis et fragrans* beneath the inscription.

In spite of this linking of Matt with Wimborne—the street on which he was supposed to have been born was even named in some nineteenth-century annals of the parish—there is no mention in his writings of any connection with that delectable county, which His Majesty Charles II called the loveliest in all England. In later life Prior neglected the humble kinsfolk living on in their few acres in Godmanstone. Cousin Christopher Hunt, a seaman, once applied for help to Matt in the days of his "diplomatic glory," but Matt put him off with "some ready money," promising that he, as a bachelor, would remember his kinsfolk when he died.[8]

Much capital has been made of Prior's lowly origin. About his early life he was undoubtedly reticent, but in view of the Pennefather connection, his ancestry cannot be considered so

[8] See footnote 6, above.

humble as has generally been assumed. The relatives on his mother's side, however, were too far away to be of any service to Matthew, since the one surviving male member of the family, presumably the uncle for whom Matthew was named, had taken up vast tracts of land in Ireland. But there were always the Dorsetshire Priors to remind Matt of his social status. The members of that family, however, who migrated to London were not lacking in enterprise. There are records to show that George Prior prospered, as did his brother Arthur, although the craft of the joiner was not yet appreciated as it was to be in the days of the great eighteenth-century cabinet makers. The hearth tax returns for 1664, the year of Matthew's birth, show that George Prior of Stephen's Alley paid a tax on five hearths.[9] Records of eleven years later (1675) indicate that he paid taxes on eleven hearths in two houses in Stephen's Alley.[10] Furthermore, a schedule of payments for the parish of St. Margaret's in 1674 names George Prior as one of the collectors for "a fourth part of the payments coming from ye 4th of November 1673 and to be pay'd to the Receiver General by the sub-collector on or before the 25th of February 1673/4."[11] Thus we see that Matthew's father held a position of trust in the community, and that he had accumulated a little property.

» 2 «

Matthew, meanwhile, was growing up into a tall, thin, sickly lad, shy and sensitive, and addicted to his books. From the Priors he inherited his high cheek bones and the hectic flush, indicative of the consumptive tendencies that plagued him throughout his life. From his mother he probably derived his keen blue eyes, the long flaxen curls of childhood, his enter-

[9] Middlesex Guildhall, Hearth Tax Accounts, 16 Charles II, City and Liberties of Westminster, No. 7. The hearth tax or chimney tax was a payment to the King of two shillings on every hearth "in all houses paying to church and poor."
[10] P. R. O., Subsidy Rolls, E 179: 253/25.
[11] *Ibid.*, 143/366.

prising nose. Where he got his early schooling or whether he had any is not known, but as a child he wrote verses. Referring once to his early impulse to write, he said that he could remember nothing further back in his life. The romantic legends of his native land furnished his earliest inspiration. For the hero of his first verses he chose Guy of Warwick, whose vanquishing of Colburn the Giant captured his childish imagination. In later life Matt claimed this deed for himself, proudly declaring, "I . . . killed Colburn the Giant before I was big enough for Westminster School."[12] When Matt was ten, he sent as a New Year's gift to his Uncle Arthur a poem, for which he was perhaps rewarded with the combination Bible and Prayer Book, dated 1633, which bears the inscription: Matthew Prior his Book, 1674/5.[13] This poem, with its image of the Nile, was written after he had become a student at Westminster School, and represents the dawning of his interest in the classics. Yet the classical training of the public school never completely obliterated his fondness for the early literature and history of his own country. Although he has been called an Augustan of the Augustans,[14] it was he who started the vogue for imitating Spenser. Horace proved to be the lucky stroke to success, yet Spenser was Matt's first love, and it was his last wish that he be buried at the feet of that great poet.

It must have been bewildering to the Stephen's Alley joiner, a man of little education, to find this fifth child of his lisping in numbers. But, proud of his prodigy, and being, as it is said, "of generous temper," the father decided to give Matt an education. As Stephen's Alley was within sound of the low-toned bell of Westminster School, it was there that the boy was sent.

The years at Westminster were happy ones for Matt, who throughout his life retained a sentimental loyalty for the school.

---

[12] *Dialogues of the Dead*, p. 185.
[13] Strong, *Letters . . . at Welbeck*, p. 103.
[14] William Lyon Phelps, *The Beginnings of the English Romantic Movement*, Boston, 1893, p. 49.

Once when he wished to commend in highest terms Lord Jersey's young son, he declared: "The boy has behaved like a true Westminster scholar; which your Lordship [Lord Oxford] knows I take to be the sum of all perfection in a person of his age."[15] Nowhere among his writings can be found any criticism of the curriculum similar to that made by a more famous Westminster, John Locke, who said that mines of gold and silver are not to be discovered on Parnassus.[16] Matthew did not claim to have found either gold or silver, but he never felt, as did Locke, that his school had offered no practical preparation for life. In after years when Prior had opportunity to form an opinion of French *lycées*, he compared them unfavorably with Westminster. They were effeminate, he thought. The French masters spared the rod, and the boys were too saving of their fists. One English boy, he bragged, was the equal of three French boys when it came either to boxing or to construing Latin.[17]

The rigorous discipline of Westminster was beneficial to the growing Matt. It sharpened his wits, developed the competitive instinct, and encouraged self-reliance. Every morning the courtyard echoed with the sound of shrill voices and the clatter of sturdily shod feet upon the cobblestones. The cry, "——s coming," from a Junior King's Scholar posted on guard, announced the arrival of the headmaster. Shouting and wrestling would cease, and the lads would file indoors to chant their Latin prayers, drone their Latin prose, sweat over their Latin verses, spout their Latin declamations. On Sundays and Saints' Days they marched solemnly into the Abbey for worship, where they listened attentively to the sermons which must be summarized for a class exercise the following day. But school was no mere round of prose and prayers. Twice a week there was instruction in music by the master chorister of the Abbey. Once a year the school presented a play of Terence. The games, dear to English

[15] P. R. O., *State Papers, France*, 105/29, fo. 70, Prior to Lord Oxford.
[16] *Some Thoughts Concerning Education*, London, 1693, p. 311.
[17] *Longleat Papers*, III, 306, Prior to Lord Buckhurst, Paris, Dec. 16/27, 1698.

boys for generations—knuckle-taw, racket, shuttlecock, and football—offered release for healthy animal spirits. Every Shrove Tuesday was dedicated to the mighty pancake rush, which always ended in one great melee of squirming, kicking boys heaped knee-deep in the courtyard. At night smoking torches flirted with the darkness of the cloisters, where, it was whispered, the ghost of Queen Elizabeth still walked.

Outside the walls of the old school the city seethed with plots, panics, trials, executions. It was an age of violence and terror. Conflict raged between Whig and Tory, between Court and Party, between Catholic and Protestant, between Anglican and Dissenter. The King in Whitehall made secret treaties with Louis XIV and sold his country for hard cash in order to support himself and his seraglio independently of Parliamentary grant. William of Orange visited England and carried his cousin, the slim princess Mary, back to Holland as his wife, much to the chagrin of Louis, who had designed that she should marry the Dauphin. Titus Oates and his "popish plot" threw panic into the hearts of timorous citizens, quaking at the fear of being burned or massacred. Shaftesbury's power rose and declined. Russell and Sidney were executed. Statesmen like Halifax and Temple were above reproach, but most politicians were rogues. The King was not only a rogue but finally turned despot and ruled without Parliament.

In Westminster School there was also a despot, a pedantic despot, Dr. Busby, who had ruled for forty years without interference—through Civil War, Roundhead Parliament, and Restoration. In spite of the fact that the rigidly classical curriculum had remained the same since the days of Queen Elizabeth, the school grew in fame and named among its graduates Dryden, Cowley, Wren, Locke, South, and Smalridge. Zealously Dr. Busby trained the boys to be scholars and orators, and sent them forth to be statesmen and divines.

Not yet dreaming of the career of statesman that lay ahead of him, little Matt, whose mind was nimble, slipped easily through his lessons and won a reputation for precosity. Unfortunately, just as he reached the middle of the third form, his father died. The widowed mother, unable to pay the Westminster School fees, placed her son in the care of his Uncle Arthur. How long Elizabeth Prior survived her husband is not known, for, shadowy as has been her appearance thus far, she drops out of the story completely at this point. Did she go to live with her sister in Staffordshire or with her brother in Ireland, or did she remain in Stephen's Alley until death claimed her a few years later? One conjecture is as good as another. Uncle Arthur, finding that Matt was good at figures, made the boy his assistant at the Rhenish and gave him a seat behind the bar. Keeping accounts at the tavern seemed at first a poor exchange for Sallust and Cicero and the other delights of the third form at Westminster, but Matt soon adapted himself to the change, and in after years acknowledged deep gratitude to his uncle, whose care proved "paternal."

From this time on, Matt's life was closely identified with that of the Arthur Prior family, who occupied spacious quarters above the tavern. Arthur had married a comely German girl, Katherine Young, the daughter of Jacob Young of Hamburg, from whom he probably imported much of his stock of Rhine wine.[18] Their children, Anne, Katherine, and Lawrence, were near enough to Matthew in age to be companionable. Among the earliest festivities that Matthew attended was the wedding, in June, 1674, of Anne, the elder daughter, then a charming girl of seventeen, to John Thompson, Gentleman, a large land-owner in Hertfordshire.[19] Katherine, less than two years older than Matt,

[18] *Letters of Denization . . . 1603-1700.* Publications of the Huguenot Society of London, XVIII, 118, 120n. "Katherine Pryor, born in the city of Hamburgh, wife of Arthur Pryor of Westminster, vintner, and daughter of Jacob Young."

[19] *Allegations for Marriage Licenses . . . 1558-1699.* Publications of the Harleian Society, XXIII, 229. Although Anne died in 1685 and her husband remarried, he maintained his friendship with Matthew, remembering in his will his "good friend and kinsman, Matthew Prior." See *ibid.*, 247.

was his favorite cousin, as his correspondence shows. Something of a madcap, she had those qualities that Prior admired in his "Cloes" of later years. If we may believe Christopher Prior's reminiscences, Katherine was a flirtatious miss and not to be trusted in a tavern. According to Christopher, she was a young beauty, so captivating that her worried father sent her down to Dorchester to "secure her virtue" from his predatory guests. The father's precautions were of no avail: one "Guy of Yorkshire," no doubt Henry Guy, Charles II's cupbearer, pursued the girl to Dorchester and carried her off in true cavalier fashion with his coach and six. So much for Christopher's story. Records reveal that Katherine later became the respected wife of Colonel George Villiers, son of the Earl of Grandison, a neighbor in Channel Row.[20] Matt celebrated the marriage with a poem in which he hailed the couple as "So great a Hero and a Bride so fair."[21] About Lawrence we know little except that he, not caring to follow in his father's business, became a searcher in the customs service, and that when he died in 1690 he left his cousin Matthew a legacy of fifty pounds.

Prior's early biographers were confused by the circumstance that at the same time that Arthur Prior was the landlord of the Rhenish another Prior, Samuel, kept the Rummer—a well-known tavern between Whitehall and Charing Cross, just two doors from Adam Locket's famous eating house. There is good reason for believing that the owner of the Rummer was a son of another of the Godmanstone Priors,[22] and hence a cousin of Matthew's. It is obvious that the similarity in the names of the two tavern keepers led to the misstatement that Samuel of the Rummer was the uncle who befriended Matt. The relationship of Samuel Prior is not simply a matter of conjecture, for when Samuel was drafting his will,[23] Matthew displayed the avid in-

---

[20] Somerset House, Will of Col. George Villiers, executed June 15, 1695.
[21] *Dialogues of the Dead*, p. 315.
[22] Presumably the Samuel Pryor of St. Martins in the Fields, who died in 1662.
[23] There is a copy of his will in Somerset House.

terest of a poor relation in the doings of a rich kinsman. Attacked by a severe illness soon after his retirement from business,
Samuel called in a lawyer and four friends to witness his will
which would dispose of his fortune, a considerable one for those
days. Matthew's curiosity about this document is betrayed by
two entries in his diary:

The 31 Dec^r: 1704 or New Years day 1704/5.

Mr. Sam: Prior told M^r. Mason that He had not made any alteration
in his Will. M^r. Biggs who made that Will told Me some time before.

The 2^d or 3^d of Jan.

M^r. Lan: Burton carryed from me a letter to M^r. Sam: Prior, to which
M^r. Prior promised M^r. Burton He would in a day or 2 return Me an
answer, but did not.[24]

Matthew's uneasiness was justified, for when the will was pro-
bated in March, 1705, it was found that he had not been remembered by his relative.

Pepys's *Diary* furnishes the earliest references (1660–1661) to
Arthur Prior and the Rhenish Tavern. Often in the company of
his cousin Roger, or with Mr. Creed, Pepys would repair to the
Rhenish and there, over a pint of wine or two and a dish of
anchovies, discuss politics or gossip about the ladies. By the
time that Matthew went to live with his uncle, the Rhenish was
one of the most popular taverns in London. Its location near
Westminster and Whitehall made it a convenient meeting place,
not only for members of Parliament and government officials but
also for the Court Wits. A vivid passage from *The Character of a
Tavern*, published in 1675, would indicate that a Restoration
public house was far from being a wholesome place for a boy:

A Tavern is an Academy of Debauchery, where the Devil teaches the
seven deadly sins instead of Sciences, a Tipling-School a degree above
an Ale-house, where you may be drunk with more credit and Apology,

[24] Strong, *Letters . . . at Welbeck*, App. V, p. 266.

'tis the Randevous of Gallants, the Good Fellowes' Paradice, and the Miser's Terrour . . . . 'Tis a *Bedlam* of Wits, where men are rather *mad* than *merry*, here one breaking a Jest on the Drawer, or perhaps a *Candlestick* or *Bottle*, over his Crown, there another repeating scraps of Old Plays or some Bawdy Song . . . whilst all with loud hooting and laughing confound the noise of *Fidlers* who are properly called a *Noise*, for no Musick can be heard for them.

Matt from his seat behind the bar had ample opportunity to observe the free, easy manners and conversation of the patrons. Much that came out in his own life and verse afterwards is plainly traceable to the tavern, proving, said Dr. Johnson, the truth of the Horatian aphorism, "The vessel long retains the scent which it first receives." Unfortunately the apprenticeship at the tavern handicapped Prior in later life. Whereas his descent from the lowly Dorsetshire forebears might be hidden from public knowledge, the association with the Rhenish could not be lived down. During the more circumspect reign of Queen Anne, taverns lost in prestige. In 1709 the Queen ordered the continuance of the salaries of all of her late husband's servants provided they kept no public houses. Whenever Matt's enemies in later life wished to taunt him, they would spread the pages of their pamphlets with such nicknames as "Matthew, the Pint Boy" and "Matthew Spindleshanks, the Tavern Boy"—a bitter reminder that his hold on public office was precarious. Certain of Matt's characteristics may be traced to the atmosphere of the Rhenish—the impulse to quote from the *Rehearsal* on all occasions, the tendency to use the easy meters of the tavern ballads in his own verse, the fondness for barmaids. Surely the Rhenish in the sixteenth-seventies boasted a barmaid as fetching as the "lilly at the bar" of the Rose, for whom Sir George Etherege sighed when in far-off Ratisbon. Yet it is to be questioned whether Prior's coarseness, his love of drink, his ribaldry, are to be attributed so much to the influence of the tavern as to that of the times.

But tavern life had its better side. Ever since the days of Shakespeare and Ben Jonson the taverns had been the meeting places for men of literary ambitions, as well as for those dilettantes of less serious aim who foregathered to sharpen their wits over their wine. The Rhenish was no exception. That the fashionable men of letters frequented it, we know from so reliable an authority as Sir James Montague, who as a boy lived directly across from the tavern and who was one of Matt's closest friends:

That public house was the place of meeting of persons of the greatest figure in those days; for the Earl of Dorset, and such as he most commonly kept company with, generally came to this eating-house, and the approbation that noble lord gave to the entertainment he met with there made it to be accounted the meeting-place of the men of learning and parts, to whom that noble lord was always a patron.

While the inn drowsed during the quieter hours of the day, Matt applied himself to his books. Then one afternoon the Earl of Dorset found him reading Horace, a happening which marked a turning point in the boy's fortunes. Again we quote from Sir James Montague's memorandum:

And it happened that this noble lord, coming into the bar of this house to inquire if Mr. Fleetwood Sheppard, his constant companion, was come, he surprised this youth, Matthew Prior, with a Horace in his hand, which taking from him to see what book he had got, he asked him what he did with it. Young Matthew answered he was looking upon it. How, said Lord Dorset, do you understand Latin? He replied, a little, upon saying which the noble lord tried if he could construe a place or two, and finding he did, Lord Dorset turned to one of the Odes, and bid him put it into English, which Mat did in English metre, and brought it up to the company before they broke up, and the company was so well pleased with the performance, and the oddness of the thing that they all liberally rewarded him with money; and whenever that company met there, it was certainly part of their entertainment to give Odes out of Horace, and verses out of Ovid to translate.[25]

[25] "Memorandums concerning the late celebrated poet & statesman Mr. Matthew Prior," by Sir James Montague, quoted by Austin Dobson from a transcript of the original,

From this moment, Matt became Dorset's protégé. How old he was when this incident occurred, it is not easy to determine. A sentence from a letter written in 1694—"My Lord Dorset has been pleased to favour them [Matt's affairs] since I was ten years old"[26]—would make 1674 the date of the meeting. We know, however, that his father was still living in that year and that Matthew had not yet gone to work for his uncle. A more probable date is obtained from a communication to George Stepney, also in 1694, in which Matt speaks of having been acquainted with Fleetwood Sheppard for eighteen years; in other words, since 1676, at which time Matt was twelve years old— still a very early age for any boy to display such proficiency in Latin verse.[27]

Dispensing favors with a lavish hand, Matthew's patron, Charles Sackville, sixth Earl of Dorset, moved among the companions of the King, adored for his faults as much as for his virtues. Where Dorset was, there was the center of London's merrymaking. Leader in his youth of the riotous escapades of his set, he and Sir Charles Sedley once startled respectable folk by running stark naked through the streets after midnight. Yelling like demons, they frightened belated pedestrians and reproved them for keeping late hours. Among the Earl's hilarious companions were Henry Savile, Fleetwood Sheppard, George Etherege, and the Earl of Rochester—all members of that society of Wits with whom Charles II was accustomed to spend his evenings.

But, fascinated by the brilliance of his conversation, the breadth of his sympathy, the munificence of his patronage of letters, men forgot the Earl of Dorset's pranks. He was indeed the acknowledged arbiter of the arts and literature of his age.

---

in *Selected Poems of Matthew Prior*, p. 210. The memorandum must have been written between Sept. 21, 1721, the date of Prior's death and October, 1722, the date of Montague's death.

[26] *Longleat Papers*, III, 32, Prior to Dorset, Hague, Sept. 10, N. S., 1694.

[27] *Longleat Papers*, III, 37, Prior to Stepney, Hague, Dec. 11/21, 1694.

As a poet he was much admired by his contemporaries. Prior's tribute to the originality of the Earl's thought, his felicity of expression, the "lustre" and inimitability of his verse is too flattering. The small number of published poems ascribed to the Earl—the best known being *Bonny Black Bess* and *To all you Ladies now at Land*—indicate that his verse was overrated. He has been aptly characterized by a modern critic as "a very complete and entirely charming minor poet."[28]

Fleetwood Sheppard, who lived with Dorset and was the dispenser of his favors, was one of the noisiest of the coterie of Wits and generally kept the company in an uproar of mirth. He often served as an intermediary for Prior with the Earl. Prior wrote two "Epistles" to Sheppard, conducted a correspondence with him, and recorded many anecdotes concerning the untoward accidents which befell him—to pursue the story of how Sheppard "broke his head" and became "a man of blood"[29] would, however, be a digression. Sheppard had a slight talent for verse-making, but it was his good nature and boisterous humor that won him a place with the Wits.

It was not long after Matthew's brilliant acquittal of himself with his Horace that Dr. Sprat, the Dean of Westminster, Mr. Knipe, the second master of Westminster School, and Lord Dorset surprised the boy by asking if he would like to resume his studies under Dr. Busby. Matthew was eager to learn, and with his uncle's consent returned to school, the Earl paying for his tuition and Uncle Arthur furnishing board and clothing. The routine of study was dull in comparison with the gaiety of the tavern, but Matt threw himself into it heartily and enjoyed his first excursions into Greek. Among the newcomers at Westminster were the Montague boys, who lived in Manchester House, across the street from the Rhenish, and with them Matt formed a warm friendship. Since the elder of the brothers,

28 Kerr, *Restoration Verse*, p. 385.
29 See *Longleat Papers*, II, 160, Henry Savile to the Earl of Rochester, Dec. 17, 1677.

Charles, was three years Matt's senior, it was James, nearer to Matt in age, who became a closer friend, at least in the early years.

Another lad, George Stepney, who lived in near-by Charing Cross with his widowed mother and his two sisters, likewise attended Westminster School, and became another of Matt's intimates. His career, as we shall learn, forms almost a parallel to Matt's. George, the Montagues, and Matt began a friendship that lasted, with ups and downs, throughout their lives.

The Montagues and Stepney seem to have met Matt on equal terms despite the difference in their social status. The Montagues, though poor, were well born, being the grandsons of the Earl of Manchester, and might naturally have snubbed a joiner's son. Stepney's forebears had served in the royal household, his grandfather, Sir Thomas Stepney, as cupbearer to Charles I, and his father as groom to Charles II. Yet there was no thought of rank when George was dubbed "Catt," when James became "Jemmy," when Charles was tagged "Chamont." As for Matthew, his nickname was foreordained.

The boys were practically inseparable outside of school hours. On almost any holiday one tall boy and three chubby ones might have been seen racing through the streets of Westminster on mischief bent. Channel Row doubtless echoed with their shouts, and harassed mothers and aunts must have wished the boys confined again within the cloisters. Aunt Katherine, of frugal German temper, never forgave Charles for one boyish mishap, which probably sent all four youths supperless to bed. Matt recalled the incident years later in a letter to Charles: "Really, Master, I am mightily satisfied to see you in the place where you are; as I should have been to . . . have kept my aunt tight to your interests, who I think does not heartily forgive you . . . the breaking of her windows in former days."[30]

[30] Bodleian Library, sc. 25427, *MS Montague*, d. 1. p. 100 b., Matthew Prior to Charles Montague, Paris, July 30/Aug. 9, 1698.

Matthew's habit of addressing Charles as "Master" dates, we believe, from their schooldays. In 1677 Charles became a King's Scholar and Captain of his election. By far the most brilliant boy at Westminster, he won distinction by his extempore epigrams made upon the theses delivered by the King's Scholars at the time of his election, and received more gifts upon the occasion than any of his classmates. Matthew, always a hero-worshipper, was filled with admiration for the Captain of the King's Scholars, and Charles, vain beyond measure, accepted the tribute of the younger boy both in and out of school as a matter of course.

After three years of happy association the four "inseparables" realized that their circle was to be broken. Charles finished at Westminster in 1679 and entered Trinity College, Cambridge, where his uncle, Dr. John Montague, was a tutor. Matthew, following in Charles's footsteps, was elected a King's Scholar at Westminster in 1681. This meant that he had passed a thorough examination in Latin and Greek literature and grammar; that he was entitled to instruction and residence without charge; that he drew an allowance for livery and commons and an extra sum for luxuries on festivals and holidays. Moreover, he was privileged to wear a cap and gown and a college waistcoat and to listen to debates in the House of Commons. To provide for the time when he should go to the university, he might become a "little tutor" to one of the young town boys, who paid small fees for such instruction.

As Matt passed his eighteenth birthday, he became concerned about the choice of a university. The usual destination of Westminster King's Scholars was Christ Church, Oxford, which bestowed studentships upon the chosen few. This was the most valuable preferment a candidate might obtain. More than half the expense of his undergraduate career was granted him, and, if he chose an academic life, the grant was made permanent. The Westminsters at Christ Church, moreover, held themselves aloof from the rest of the student body and looked haughtily down at the poor unfortunates who had not been bred to the "genius of Westminster." But all these privileges failed to tempt Matthew, who could not bear the thought of separation from his friends. In 1682 Stepney, taking advantage of a vacancy at Trinity, joined Charles Montague there, and Matt knew that James was also planning to go to Cambridge.

The spring of 1683 found Matt in a quandary. Lord Dorset intended that he should go up to Oxford; Dr. Busby, that he should stay on at Westminster for another year to pursue the study of Hebrew and Arabic. Matt, however, thought it high time to quit grammar for the logic and divinity of the university. Therefore, when the opportunity came in April, he applied for and received one of the five scholarships lately established at St. John's College, Cambridge, by the Duchess of Somerset. By his quixotic behavior, he displeased both Dr. Busby and Lord Dorset. Even James Montague, who would be entering Trinity the following year, was disgusted with Matt's obstinacy. Subsequently the fact that Matt was the only Westminster boy at St. John's brought him into more prominence than he would have attained at Christ Church, a fact which, to some extent, vindicated his choice. Dr. Humphrey Gower, master of the college, the son of a Dorchester vicar, "did cast an eye," it is said, on Matt from the day of his matriculation. Thus Matthew's entry into college was propitious.

CHAPTER II

"Fast by the Banks of Cam"

» 1 «

PRIOR entered St. John's College, Cambridge, as a pensioner on April 2, 1683, and on the following day enrolled as one of the five Somerset Scholars. By the terms of the deed establishing the Somerset Scholarships,[1] the college would not only provide him tuition but would pay him the sum of five shillings a week for his subsistence and give him a chamber—to be shared with the other four boys—and a private study. His garb was to be a gown with open sleeves, such as was worn by the students at Christ Church, Oxford, and a square cap without tassels. Who the other lucky holders of the scholarships were, the college records do not tell us; but the five boys must have applied directly to the Duchess herself, they must have received the awards from her own hands, and, since they were the very first to hold the Somerset Scholarships, they must have created some stir among the undergraduates when they first appeared at St. John's.

Matt was jubilant over his good fortune and his reunion with Charles and George, who as neighbors at Trinity initiated him into university life. The new scholar settled himself in his quarters overlooking the plum-colored court that Ruskin was to think so beautiful, and soon felt almost as much at home as he had at Westminster. In April the old buildings still bore their winter chill, but spring had come outdoors, and Matthew explored the town and the fields, reveling in the new-found beau-

[1] *Liber Scholasticus*, pp. 400–403.

ties of Cambridgeshire. In the long afternoons, he would call for Charles and George, and they would stroll along the sacred Backs, there to sprawl lazily upon the banks of the Cam in the shade of the low-hanging willows, conversing or not, as good friends may.

When in convivial mood the trio might repair to a public house to indulge their thirst and overspend their allowances. Often there would be too many rounds of drinks, a townsman would call a gownsman an "insolent puppy," or vice versa, a free-for-all brawl would ensue, and, provided there were no casualties, all would go home feeling happier for the diversion. Young Matt, being bred to tavern ways, rarely overstepped the limits at such encounters, but one serious case for discipline is recorded against him at the college. For this offense Master Gower put him on short rations and forbade him to dine in the Hall with his comrades. Having no liking for bread and water, Matt immediately sent such a humble but tactful petition to the Master that he was reinstated promptly.[2] One of the few surviving anecdotes of these early Cambridge days gives a glimpse of the habits of Prior and Stepney; it may even indicate Matt's need for discipline. During one of his holidays spent in London, Matt called on Mrs. Stepney, who inquired anxiously about her son's physical and moral well-being. To a query about George's drinking, Matthew discreetly answered that Catt drank with moderation. But the mother was not satisfied and pressed the question, asking, "Mr. Prior . . . did you ever see him drunk in your life?" Matthew, with quick wit, replied, "No, madam, for I was always drunk before him."[3]

Towards the end of July, 1683, the whole university burst into song to celebrate the marriage on St. Anne's Day of the Princess Anne to Prince George of Denmark. Charles Montague, Stepney, and Prior each contributed to the volume of prothala-

[2] See letter and poem addressed to Dr. Gower in *Poetical Works of Matthew Prior*, ed. R. B. Johnson, I, 302, 303.

[3] Longleat MSS, XXI, fo. 136b, quoted by Francis Bickley, *Life of Matthew Prior*, p. 48.

mia which bore the title *Hymenaeus Cantabrigiensis*. Matt's brief
poem of fourteen lines is an excellent sample of his Latin verse.

The death of Charles II in February 1684/5 and the accession
of James II called forth from the university poets the customary
valedictory and salutatory verses. The merriest of monarchs had
been popular at St. John's, where on a royal visit he had been
greeted with Latin speeches, entertained at dinner, and presented with an English Bible. All the town and the university
had turned out to welcome him, and the conduits had flowed
with wine. Upon the King's death Prior wrote another short
Latin poem and like his brother poets succumbed to the obvious temptation to apostrophize the royal brothers as Castor
and Pollux.[4] Stepney and Montague also composed appropriate
poems for the Cambridge volume. Montague, by this time a
Master of Arts and a Fellow of Trinity, wrote his poem in
English. His fulsome praise of Charles II attracted the attention
of the Earl of Dorset, who, always ready to encourage promising
young poets, invited Montague, and Stepney as well, to London
to introduce them to the literary circle of the town. Stepney
declined the invitation, it is said "out of his love for a retired
life"—a strange remark, considering his love of pleasure and
his sociable nature.[5] Charles, grasping this opportunity to advance himself, accepted the Earl's hospitality, and thus made
his debut into the society of the Wits.

A few days after the death of Charles II, Cambridge proclaimed James as King—somewhat precipitately, even before
the arrival of any orders from London. Bells rang throughout
the day, and each college enjoyed a feast. At night bonfires were
lighted in the courts, and pledges of loyalty were drunk in Hall
and tavern. Prior wrote a hosannah for James,[6] which has assumed entirely too much importance in the minds of certain

[4] *Moestissimae ac laetissimae Cantabrigiensis affectus decedente Caroli II succedente Jacobi II*,
Cambridge, 1684/5, see leaf T 4 r.
[5] C. Montague, *Works and Life*, p. 7.
[6] *Dialogues of the Dead*, p. 279.

critics who maliciously point to Prior's later derogatory remarks about the unfortunate monarch. It should be remembered
that the poem was no more than a conventional panegyric
written in a burst of enthusiasm. Stepney followed the tide in
writing a poem on the same occasion, and if Charles had not
been absent on the visit to Lord Dorset, he doubtless would have
indited the most glowing effusion of the three.

Prior, we may note, had not been invited with his friends to
London, probably because he was not as yet within sight of his
degree, and not because he was still out of the Earl's good
graces, as has been surmised. Soon after arriving at college, he
began to make overtures to the jolly, soft-hearted Earl, who,
"charitable to a fault," readily accepted them. A Latin poem
written for Lord Dorset at the beginning of 1684 may have been
a petition piece; it is definitely a birthday offering:

And do thou, O Janus, be kind to my song—he will come on his natal
feast to thy altars, O Lord of the opening year. Oh! to the very gods
above may this day hallowed be, and with a white stone in the calendar
be marked—this day on which his illustrious mother bore this noble
son and brought forth for me a patron, for his people a great lord, and
to the creative mind and impulse, an inspiration almost divine.[7]

Such adulation was not to be ignored, and it seems certain that
the Earl forgave Matt for his boyish hardheadedness.

Matt rapidly turned out other pieces of this kind, seizing upon
any important happenings in the Earl's life that might be
versified. He made the Earl's marriage to Lady Mary Compton
in March, 1685, the subject of a pastoral dialogue, casting the
bride and groom as Dorinda and Daphnis, respectively.[8] Another poem, "A Journey to Copt Hall," was occasioned by a
visit to the Earl's seat in Essex. On this visit Prior may first
have met Lady Mary, whose striking beauty he afterwards
celebrated in the verses, "To the Countess of Dorset, walking
in a Garden":

[7] *Poetical Works of Matthew Prior*, ed. R. B. Johnson, I, 307.
[8] *Dialogues of the Dead*, p. 283.

Yes, I did stubbornly believe
The place no added Beauty cou'd receive
'Till bright Dorinda's passing by
Convinc'd my infidelity.[9]

Back at Cambridge, the "small beer and college mutton" failing to inspire the Muse, Matt wrote in prose to thank the Earl for the "kindest entertainment" of his life.[10] The birth of a son to the Earl and the Countess again stimulated Matt to verse; this time his offering was a Pindaric ode, containing lines that bear a familiar ring:

But Oh! what Clouds of glory, clouds of light
Roll round the noble Babe, and mock my drowned sight![11]

The Earl, delighted with the complimentary verses, encouraged Matt to pursue seriously the writing of poetry, but Matt modestly disclaimed talent, declaring: "If I ever had any Wit 'twas when I had the Honour to be with your Lordship, and then it was not mine by Nature but inspiration."[12]

Besides the poems already mentioned Prior wrote many others during his undergraduate days at Cambridge, poems which he preserved in manuscript throughout his life. Pope and other eighteenth-century writers knew of this early verse of Prior's, but it was never published until Mr. Waller assembled all available Prior manuscripts in 1907. A few of these early pieces have either an academic or a religious note. In two of them Prior hymned the praises of Lady Margaret Tudor,[13] foundress of St. John's. Two others—"God is Love"[14] and "A Hymn to Spring"[15] suggest their themes in their titles. In lighter poems, like "To a Lady Sleeping,"[16] we find Matt successfully matching the ease and smoothness of Waller, but in none of them is there promise of the light-hearted, laughing Muse of his later years. Nor is the anapaestic measure, a favorite with the Earl of Dorset and one which Prior later used so admirably, employed in the Cam-

[9] *Ibid.*, p. 282. [10] *Ibid.*, p. 288. [11] *Ibid.*, p. 296. [12] *Ibid.*, p. 305.
[13] *Ibid.*, pp. 276, 378. [14] *Ibid.*, p. 294. [15] *Ibid.*, p. 298. [16] *Ibid.*, p. 274.

bridge occasional pieces. The chief forms used are the Pindaric ode and the pastoral dialogue.

Despite the encouragement of Lord Dorset, Prior had no more intention than did either Stepney or Montague of making the writing of poetry a sole means of livelihood. Stepney, as soon as he got his bachelor's degree, entered the diplomatic service and forsook verse except when occasion demanded a public panegyric. Montague dallied with the question of a career longer than Stepney, but immediately after obtaining a public office he dropped verse writing altogether. Prior continued to write verse after public life had claimed him; nevertheless he was always apologetic about his "Muse, who in her perfect liberty was but indifferent, though my Lord Dorset's kindness brought her up, and his example taught her." He once laid the blame for not giving himself wholeheartedly to the Muse partly to the fact that prose rather than verse was in fashion in the college where he was bred, and partly to the fact that he was sent as King's Secretary to The Hague soon after he left the University. "So that poetry," he explained, "which by the bent of my mind might have been the business of my life was by the happyness of my education only the amusement of it."[17]

This comment upon the trend of his university education is clarified if we recall that when Prior came to Cambridge the conflict between the old and the new philosophy, between scholasticism and experimental science, had been decided in favor of science. Bacon and Descartes had replaced Aristotle. Mathematics and natural science took their places in the curriculum. The Royal Society had been chartered. The influence of Hobbes was to be felt not only in the realms of psychology and political science but in literature as well. The new scientific thought inhibited the imaginative creation of the poets.[18] The

[17] "Essay upon Learning," *Dialogues of the Dead*, p. 185.

[18] Kerr, *Restoration Verse*, p. xvi. See also Vivian de Sola Pinto, *Rochester: Portrait of a Restoration Poet*, London, 1935, Chaps. II and VII, and Basil Willey's *The Seventeenth Century Background*, London, 1934.

greatest of them was, towards the end of the decade, to seek for "erring judgments an unerring guide" in the arms of an absolute and authoritative church.

At neighboring Trinity, Charles Montague was winning honors in mathematics and beginning a lifelong friendship with Isaac Newton. Though the atmosphere at St. John's, where the strict and devout Gower held sway, was far more conservative, Matt did not escape the influence of the scientific spirit. Just how keen the impact was, we do not know, but it is on record that Matt's spiritual adviser, the Reverend Francis Turner, Bishop of Ely and Visitor to the Somerset Scholars, urged him to translate Prudentius. Prior promised to send the Bishop the translation but only the promise has been found.[19] Prudentius, that early Christian apologist who dealt with themes Lucretian in language Virgilian, may well have been deemed a good corrective for wavering faith. Evidently any religious doubt that Prior may have had as an undergraduate was promptly dispelled, for as a newly elected Fellow at Cambridge he wrote an ode ridiculing the attempts of the scientists to explain the universe. Throughout the rest of his life he was skeptical of scientific theory. In "Alma" he scoffed at all philosophical systems and in "Solomon" he gravely avowed:

> Forc'd by reflective Reason I confess,
> That human Science is Uncertain Guess.

Prior's second excuse for not choosing poetry as a vocation is somewhat misleading. During the four years that elapsed between graduation and the appointment at The Hague, he experimented further with poetry, he served as a tutor, and he even contemplated taking holy orders. The real reason he could not devote himself wholly to writing poetry was the practical necessity of earning a living. St. John's was an expensive college, and he was deeply in debt.[20] The general de-

---

[19] *Dialogues of the Dead*, p. 168.
[20] In a letter in the R. B. Adam Collection, March 2, [1688/9?], Prior wrote: ". . . I am also sorry (for all Vexations come together) that the Steward has so little Patience when

cadence of the arts during Prior's youth gave no promise of a profitable career as a poet. The decade of 1680 shows a decline in the arts all over Europe. Mr. Kerr remarks: "Bernini dies in Italy, Calderon in Spain, and a century of great artistic achievement dies with them; the Dutch painters are going or gone; the brief summer of French classicism is over already; and for a time too there is a decline in the birth-rate of ability."[21] Mr. Kerr goes on to say that Purcell, the only great artist born in England in the sixteen-fifties, only partially retrieved the period between Rochester and Prior for the arts. Rochester died in 1680 at the age of thirty-three, and Oldham in 1683 in his thirtieth year. Thus the two most talented young poets of the age just before Prior's were cut off in their prime. There was little to serve as a flame to the imagination of the fledgling poet in the verse published in England during these years, it being for the most part criticial or satirical. Verse reached its highest level in Dryden's satires against Shaftesbury and Shadwell; its lowest in the many critical treatises in rhyme, mere paraphrasings of the commonplace maxims of Horace and Boileau on the art of poetry. There was also the flood of new translations from the ancients by Dryden and his collaborators that the enterprising young publisher, Jacob Tonson, was gathering up in his Miscellanies. Such was the poetic output in England during the years that Prior was at College.

The translations so annoyed Prior that he composed in 1685 a "Satire on the Modern Translators of Ovid's Epistles."[22] Although Dryden was the chief object of the satire, Mulgrave,

---

I've so little money. Why did he dunn Mr. Wigley? I fancied I was excused from anything of acts, or else in 3 year (for so long at least I shall be out of the College) I shall be over head and Ears in debt. Pray advise with the Learned in that Point, and send me word if I should not write to the Master about it." Quoted by kind permission of Mr. R. B. Adam.

[21] Kerr, *Restoration Verse*, p. xiv.

[22] *Dialogues of the Dead*, p. 47. Recent critics who have disputed Prior's authorship of the poem have failed to notice his letter to Dr. Gower (*Longleat Papers*, III, 2) in which Prior enclosed a copy of the poem and in which he said, ". . . thus Sir, I humbly throw this trifle at your feet, hoping the product of my vacant hours may prove the diversion of yours."

Tate, Rymer, Mrs. Behn, and Dryden's other collaborators shared in the attack. The ridicule is somewhat heavy and ill-mannered. Mulgrave's "Essay upon Satire," which Prior labeled as a "spiteful satire" on the Wits, is attributed to Dryden, and there is mention of the Mulgrave-Dryden alliance and the consequent "Rose Alley Ambuscade."

Again, in the following year (1686), Prior attacked Dryden and his fellow poets in an avowed imitation of the Seventh Satire of Juvenal. Here the language is more restrained than in the former satire, but the "Rose Alley" affair is not overlooked. More important, however, than Prior's spite against Dryden, is his attitude toward the state of poetry and of poets in the beginning of the second year of the reign of James II. Matt admired the Court Wits Rochester and Sedley and, of course, his patron Dorset; but they, he points out, were men of fortune who were not dependent upon their writings:

> *Sedley*, indeed, and *Rochester* might write
> For their own Credit, and their Friends Delight,
> Shewing how far they cou'd the rest outdo,
> As in their Fortunes, in their Writings too.[23]

Young Matt had no intention of dancing attendance in "slow Mulgrave's hall," of becoming a "hireling drudge," or of starving in a garret "to dream of Dinner, and curse Poetry." And taking yet another dig at Dryden, the poet declared:

> But should Drudge Dryden this Example take
> And *Absaloms* for empty Glory make,
> He'd soon perceive his Income scarce enough,
> To feed his nostril with inspiring Snuff;
> Starving for Meat, not surfeiting on Praise,
> He'd find his Brains as barren as his *Bayes*.

Matt had only to look about him to realize that poetry was

[23] *Dialogues of the Dead*, p. 52. The last seventeen lines (see *ibid.*, p. 390), of the Longleat copy of the poem are addressed to "my satyrist and angry Friend," presumably Dr. Gower, and promise in the future to "sing of wondrous piety and you."

uncertain as a profession. It was not a lucrative trade for Dryden, and none of the other poets were faring so well under James II as they had under the Merry Monarch—even Dryden's butt of canary, a perquisite of the poet laureate, had been discontinued. Wisely or not Prior distrusted his creative impulse, which though irresistible did not amount to poetic fury.[24] His talent, he thought, might help him secure public employment; it might prove the amusement of his idle hours, but it could never be depended upon for a livelihood. A man in his financial position, who must look to himself and his own wits to make a fortune, could not afford to dally too much with the "tuneful trade."

» 2 «

If poetry as a profession was out of the question, to what else could Matt turn? Conditions in England were generally unsettled, owing to James's attempt to Catholicize the realm, and there was widespread unrest, which naturally enough penetrated to the universities. Those young men who must choose careers might at a moment's notice be called upon to change their religion or politics or both. Prior's uncertainty as to his future lasted for a number of years. Records of his undergraduate days are meager, but by piecing together the poems that he continued to write even after he had definitely decided against a career as poet, we discover that he was looking ahead toward public employment and hence declaring himself on the right side politically and that he was unwillingly contemplating the church as an alternative.

The rebellion staged by the Duke of Monmouth in July, 1685, gave Matt opportunity to express himself politically. Cambridge was indignant over the insurrection, and a portrait of the Duke was taken from the walls of Convocation House and burned. Upon the suppression of the rebellion, a general holiday was

---

[24] See "Epistle to Lord [Dorset?]," *Dialogues of the Dead*, p. 305, and conclusion to "[Inspired Wit]," *ibid.*, p. 399.

declared at the university. Carried on by the wave of patriotism, Matt composed a poem breathing loyalty to the King and condemnation of Monmouth's followers.[25] The poem also indicates that Prior thought it wise to stand well with the churchmen, for it contains a compliment to Bishop Turner, the "sacred prelate," whose persuasive tongue, the poet said, might have won any man save "the haughty harden'd Absalon" to confession. If this poem was only shared by the bishop, Prior addressed four others—two in English and two in Latin—to him alone.[26] In Marvell's coarse satire "The Divine in Mode," the pompous but fashionable Turner is represented as a man surpassing in vanity even Sir Fopling Flutter himself. Nevertheless, he was a powerful churchman and by virtue of his office— Visitor to the Somerset Scholars—one whom it behooved Prior to cultivate. Matt's offerings to the bishop therefore abound in obvious compliment. Another churchman, and one much more likable than Turner was Dr. Sprat, newly appointed Bishop of Rochester, whom Prior lost no time in congratulating.[27]

It may be that this flattery of the churchmen does not necessarily imply that Matt was considering holy orders, but that he was simply looking forward to a day when he would be in need of favors. In support of the theory, however, that Matt might be angling for a church living, it may be pointed out that the church was a very natural haven for a young man who had little money, social position, or influence. Even Charles Montague toyed with the idea of taking orders, perhaps because his uncle was Master of Trinity.[28] Addison, too, considered the church

[25] "Advice to the Painter, upon the Defeat of the Rebels in the West and the Execution of the late D. of Monmouth," *Dialogues of the Dead*, p. 289. A more independent attitude was struck by Stepney, who in his poem, "On the University of Cambridge burning the Duke of Monmouth's picture" ridiculed the university for her fickleness. See *Celebrated Authors*, II, 4.

[26] For the poems in English, see *Dialogues of the Dead*, pp. 168, 169; for the poems in Latin, see *Poetical Works of Matthew Prior*, ed. Johnson, I, 305, 306.

[27] *Ibid.*, 304, 305, and *Dialogues of the Dead*, p. 293.

[28] The Reverend John Montague, who was a tutor at Trinity when Charles matriculated, became Master of the College in 1683.

as a possible career. It is quite clear that, although Matthew faced for several years the prospect of entering the church, he always regarded orders with aversion. Even as late as 1695 he wrote from The Hague that if he must go home to his college, he would never take orders until hunger or thirst compelled him to do so.

It is difficult to visualize Matt as a clergyman. Exiled to a remote country parish, he might perhaps have been a second Herrick, celebrating rustic Cloes and solemnizing other Solomons. Prior and Herrick were much alike in their indulgence in dissipation, their fondness for women, their skill with light verse, their love of the world. Herrick took orders as a last resort, and so Prior would have done; Herrick made up his mind to be a good parson, and we imagine that Prior would have made a similar resolve; Herrick was discontented with his lot for years, and we believe that Prior would have found the life of a divine even more uncongenial.[29]

More important, however, than the choice of a career was Matt's need for money. The weekly allowance from his scholarship was inadequate, and the Earl of Dorset evidently was giving his protégé no more substantial aid than encouragement in verse-writing. Consequently in July, 1685, Matt appealed to his Uncle Arthur for assistance:

If my necessity, Sir, encourages my boldness, I know your goodness sufficient to excuse one and relieve t'other. I am very sensible what expences my education puts you to, and must confess my repeated petitions might have wearied any charity but yours; but since I have no advocate, no patron, no father but yourself, pardon that importunity which makes me seek the kindness of all these in you, which throws me at your feet to beg at once your blessing and assistance, and that, since your indulgence has set me safe from shore, you would not let me perish in the ocean.[30]

---

[29] For an interesting comparison between Prior and Herrick see Oswald Doughty, *The English Lyric in the Age of Reason*, pp. 49–53.

[30] *Longleat Papers*, III, 1, Prior to his Uncle Arthur, July 18/28, 1685.

The letter is dignified, restrained, and appreciative, but it did not bring results. A few weeks later, Matt approached his Aunt Katherine in an amusing way. He took the dialogue written for the pompous Bishop Turner, made some slight revisions, and told himself that it was now an appropriate offering for his aunt, to whom he had neglected to write. Prior was only twenty-one at the time, and although he modestly proclaimed the effort as "bad verse," perhaps he was naïvely proud of it and eager for his aunt's approbation. By the same post, he sent a letter penned in the formal, florid style of the time, yet a happy example of his tact and wit in begging indulgence:

My neglect, Madam, is but a new occasion for you to exercise your goodness on. You, like heaven, can as often return a pardon as I give up my repentance; the truth of which, Madam, be pleased to accept as well in honest prose as in bad verse; though, Madam, this afflicts my zeal, that the oracle never answers. My religion depends much upon faith, and I can tell no more news from my heaven than the astrologers from theirs, unless like them I fairly guess at it. I should really be afraid to write did I imagine your silence proceeded from your anger. I am extremely willing to attribute it to your hatred which you said you had to writing. That was in your last letter dated a considerable time ago. I'll swear to show both how your Ladyship abhors pen and paper and what reason I have to complain. If your own goodness will allow me one letter a year, after the great satisfaction of hearing how you do, let me know if Jenny does fill out grains in ivory pails; if Mrs. Wilson be not still out of humour because her house is not burnt; if Mrs. Watson thinks her windpipe secured by this time, and that cribbage of a Sunday night is not Popish doctrine. Now to be serious, Madam, with ten thousand thanks for all your favours and as many prayers that you would renew them by a letter, wishing you as much health as a country parson in the dedication of his sermon to his patron, I am etc."[31]

Since no other letters to the Channel Row relatives have been preserved, we do not know whether or not this appeal brought

[31] *Ibid.*, Prior to Mrs. Katherine Prior, Aug. 11/21, 1685.

the desired response. In September of this year Uncle Arthur made his will,[32] bequeathing to Matthew one hundred pounds, a much larger sum than he left to any relative other than his wife and children. Undoubtedly he considered Matt a member of the immediate family. After Uncle Arthur's death in 1687, Aunt Katherine carried on the business of the Rhenish until she died in 1698. During these years "Dame" Prior, as the boys affectionately called her, acted as banker for Matt and George Stepney while they were abroad.[33] She often complained that Matt did not write to her and worried over his carelessness about his debts. Nevertheless, she remembered him in her will.[34]

The college terms and vacations came and went, and all too soon the quartet of Westminster boys was beginning to break up, never to be united again except when vacations from business might bring them together in London. Stepney was the first to leave the academic life. Soon after graduating with high honors in 1685/6, he departed for Hamburg to take up a secretaryship secured through the influence of Lord Middleton, Secretary of State. James Montague began to study for the bar at the Middle Temple, while Charles continued as a Fellow at Trinity. In the spring of 1686 Charles and Matt evidently went to London for a holiday. While there they put their heads together and sent Stepney some "extempore epigrams." Charles concluded an accompanying letter by saying, "There are some others which are fitter to create mirth over a glass of wine than to be put into writing, so will trouble you no further." Since most of the specimens enclosed are more vulgar than witty, we shall likewise spare the reader and pause to quote only one, a comment on a most exciting piece of literary news:

[32] Wickham Legg has published the will in his *Matthew Prior*, App. A, p. 282.

[33] See letters from Richard Powys to Prior, *Longleat Papers*, III, 53, and *passim;* also a letter from George Stepney to his sisters, P. R. O., *Stepney Papers*, 105/54, Hague, Oct. 26, 1694. "Mrs. Prior of Channel Row will pay you ye other 50 lbs. at sight of yr. Bill here enclosed."

[34] There is a copy of her will, executed July 6, 1695, in Somerset House, 62 Pitt.

> The Church of Rome on us reprisal makes
> For turncoat Oates, she turncoat Dryden takes.[35]

Events were now taking a turn quite contrary to the predictions made by Bishop Turner in his coronation sermon before King James. The bishop's text had been: "Solomon sat on the throne of the Lord as King instead of David his father, and prospered; and all Israel obeyed him." Israel was not obeying; the bigoted and inept King was not prospering; in fact the growing restiveness of the nation was soon to culminate in the King's downfall. Dorset, who had been out of favor with the Court since James's accession, now sat in the inner councils of the Whigs, and vigorously opposed in Parliament some of the King's pet projects. He was therefore soon deprived of his commission as Lord Lieutenant of Sussex.[36]

All the events of the day were being watched by our bright young men, about to embark upon their careers. The revocation of the Edict of Nantes by Louis XIV, the efforts of James to swing his people to his faith by filling the offices of the realm with Catholics, the sudden conversions of those desirous of royal favor were topics of the greatest interest. From Hamburg, Stepney sent Charles Montague a satire upon Dryden and other new converts and an epigram on Louis XIV. These pieces were passed around among the young Wits in London, and when Dorset saw them, he approved them heartily. The fact is significant. All of "my Lord Dorset's boys," as Stepney, Montague, and Prior were later designated, were attacking Dryden's conversion. Their final impudence was the parody on the *Hind and the Panther*.

» 3 «

During the early winter months of 1687 Prior took his bachelor's degree, the eleventh in the *Ordo Senioritatis* of the univer-

[35] P. R. O., *Stepney Papers*, 105/82, Charles Montague to George Stepney, April 14, 1686.
[36] *Trumbull Papers*, I, 259.

sity for that year.[37] Shortly afterwards, in the latter part of April or May, he went to London, perhaps having been summoned there during his uncle's last illness. While calling upon Charles Montague at James's quarters in the Middle Temple, Matt collaborated with Charles in an undertaking which was to bring him more credit than anything he had hitherto written, namely the parodying of the *Hind and the Panther*, which had only recently appeared. Sir James Montague, who witnessed the composition of the parody,[38] told entertainingly the story of the birth of the *jeu d'esprit:*

Dryden's poem being very much cried up for a masterpiece of that great poet, it created great dissatisfaction to all who opposed the bringing in of popery by King James, and it was the wish of many that the same should be answered by some ingenious pen, but it is not certain that either Mr. Montagu or Mr. Prior, at first, resolved to undertake the doing it, but the book which came afterwards out by the name of the City Mouse and the Country Mouse, which was allowed by all persons to be the most effectual answer to that poem of Mr. Dryden's and which was composed by Mr. Montagu and Mr. Prior jointly together, happened to owe its birth more to accident than design; for the Hind and the Panther, being at that time in everybody's hands, Mr. Prior accidentally came one morning to make Mr. Montagu a visit at his brother's chambers in the Middle Temple, London, where the said Mr. Montagu lodged when he was in London, and the poem, lying upon the table, Mr. Montague took it up, and read the four first lines in the poem of the Hind and Panther, which are these:

> A milk white Hind immortal and unchanged
> Fed on the lawns, and o'er the forest ranged
> Without unspotted, innocent within,
> She feared no danger, for she knew no sin.

Where stopping, he took notice how foolish it was to commend a four-footed beast for not being guilty of sin, and said the best way of

---

[37] Cambridge University, *Historical Register*, p. 417.

[38] While the exact title of the parody is "The Hind and the Panther Transvers'd to the Story of the Country-Mouse and the City-Mouse" (*Dialogues of the Dead*, p. 1) we have in this chapter and elsewhere used the abbreviated form of the title by which Prior and his friends always referred to it.

answering that poem would be to ridicule it by telling Horace's fable of the City Mouse, and the Country Mouse in the same manner, which being agreed to, Mr. Prior took the book out of Mr. Montagu's hands, and in a short time after repeated the four first lines, which were after printed in the City Mouse, and the Country Mouse, viz:

> A milk white mouse, immortal and unchanged
> Fed on soft cheese, and o'er the dairy ranged,
> Without unspotted, innocent within,
> She feared no danger, for she knew no gin.

The repeating these lines set the company in laughter, and Mr. Montagu took up the pen by him, and wrote on a loose piece of paper, and both of them making several essays to transverse, in like manner, other parts of the poem gave a beginning to that work, which was afterwards published to the great satisfaction of many people, and though no name was set to the book, yet it was quickly known who were the authors of it. . . ."[39]

The intention, design, and method of the writers were clearly set forth in a preface to the parody.[40] They took their motto, "Much Malice mingled with a little Wit," from the *Hind and the Panther* and borrowed the form and the machinery for their piece from Buckingham's *Rehearsal*. In the new burlesque, Bayes takes "those languishing gentlemen," Smith and Johnson, to hear his new poem in praise of Popery, just as in *The Rehearsal* he had taken them to witness his newest heroic tragedy. One wonders whether in the haste of the moment the youthful satirists realized the merits of the poem they were ridiculing—its grace, its wit, its vigorous argument. The obvious defect which made it easy prey, that of having animals conduct a theological polemic, was readily seized upon by the impetuous young men. Nor did they refrain from personalities. They twitted Dryden about his "pampered paunch," accused him of "Billingsgate manners," and impugned the sincerity of his conversion.

---

[39] "Memorandums concerning the late celebrated poet, & Statesman Mr. Matthew Prior," quoted by Austin Dobson in *Selected Poems of Matthew Prior*, pp. 214, 215.

[40] *Dialogues of the Dead*, p. 3. See also Prior's letter on "The Occasion of Writing the Country-Mouse, and the City-Mouse" addressed to Dr. Gower (?), *ibid.*, pp. 385, 386.

Undoubtedly Sir James's account contains the most fair and accurate statement of the part each of the young men had in the piece. In later days Tory partisans sought to minimize the share that Montague had in the work. Lord Peterborough, on being asked if Montague had not written the satire with Prior replied, "Yes, just as if I was in a chaise with Mr. Cheselden here, drawn by his fine horse, and should say,—'Lord how finely we draw this chaise!'"[41] On the other hand, we cannot accept Matt's own attempt, some years later, to give all the credit to Charles, since at that time Matt was desperately in need of political influence and was seeking a renewal of the former friendship.[42] Most probably Montague wrote the preface, Prior the verses, and both together, the prose passages.

Not since *The Rehearsal* had an attack upon Dryden made such a stir. The Wits declared that the "City-Mouse and the Country-Mouse" had gnawed such an ugly hole "in Bayes's jacket that it could only be mended by applying a patch as scandalous as the flaw." No Wit, it was said, had a title to open his mouth in company for six months unless he could demonstrate by quotation that he had "blest his eyes with a sight of the prodigy."[43] According to Dean Lockier, Dryden was "greatly pained" by the parody: "I have heard him say; 'for two young fellows that I have always been very civil to; to use an old man in misfortune, in so cruel a manner.' And he wept when he said it."[44] Whether or not we take the latter statement seriously, we know that Dryden long bore the authors of "The Country-Mouse and the City-Mouse" a grudge, for when he had occasion to invite the promising young poets of the town to assist him with his translations from Juvenal, he passed Montague and Prior by.[45]

[41] Spence, *Anecdotes*, p. 102.
[42] Brit. Mus., *Add. MSS*, 7121, fo. 49, Prior to Halifax, Feb. 4/14, 1707.
[43] Ned Ward, *The Secret History of Clubs*, p. 364.
[44] Spence, *Anecdotes*, p. 47.
[45] Dryden invited Stepney to furnish a translation of the Eighth Satire, having forgiven Catt for his Satire "on Dryden and the new Converts," because he wrote it in a place [Hamburg] "where civility and good manners were a sin." See P. R. O., *Stepney Papers,*

After sharpening his wits in London, Prior returned to Cambridge and applied for a fellowship at St. John's; his way, however, seemed barred, there being already two Fellows from Middlesex. One of the Keyton fellowships, founded in 1532 by Dr. John Keyton, once chorister of Southwell Minster, was vacant, but Prior had never been a chorister. In default of candidates from the Southwell choir, however, "persons . . . most singular in manner and learning" might be elected. There being no doubt that Prior was qualified as a scholar to hold such a fellowship, he made bold to journey up to Southwell to apply for a choristership. A recently discovered document among the records of the Southwell Chapter shows that he was duly examined and received into the choir on February the first, 1687/8.[46] This indicates that the musical training Matt had acquired at Westminster bore some fruit, but, as Sir Robert Scott says, "it would be interesting to know whether he acted as a chorister even for one day." Two months later, in April, 1688,[47] he was granted a Keyton fellowship and took up his residence in the Fellows' quarters of his college. In assigning him to one of the two "medical fellowships," the authorities again favored him, and the immediate prospect of taking the dreaded holy orders was averted.

Little is known of Prior's activities as a Fellow except that as Linacre Lecturer, from July, 1706, to July, 1710, it was his duty to lecture on the works of Galen. Prior, of course, knew next to nothing about medicine, but a hastily prepared paper, enlivened with wit and read with assurance, must have sufficed. He held this fellowship until his death.

Prior owed his first employment outside his college to a much

---

105/82, James Montague to Stepney, Middle Temple, Feb. 14/24, 1690. For Alexander Pope's notes on Dryden's corrections of Stepney's translation before publication, see Hist. MSS. Com., Fifth Report App., p. 294.

[46] See Sir Robert Scott's article in *The Eagle*, XLIV, 57ff.

[47] The entry in the College Register is as follows: *Ego Matthaeus Prior, Middlesexiensis, juratus et admissus sum in perpetuum socium hujus Collegii pro Doctore Keyton decessore Magistro Roper*, 3 April 1688.

less sensational piece than "The Country-Mouse and the City-Mouse." Some time during 1688 he composed the annual poetic tribute which the college paid to one of its benefactors, the Earl of Exeter. This poem (previously referred to) which stands first in all collections of Prior's verse, is an ode on Exodus 3:14 —"I am that I am." Here Prior states that reason alone cannot explain the universe and asserts that faith in the mysterious God who revealed himself to Moses is a necessity. In his long poem, "Solomon," he reiterated the very same beliefs. The Exodus poem, as Mr. Dobson says, "with its careful and perspicuous art, must have been far above the usual average of the votive verses which went annually to Burleigh house by Stamford town."[48] It is the most finished of Prior's efforts thus far:

> Why does the constant Sun
> With measur'd steps his radiant Journeys run?
> Why does he order the Diurnal Hours
> To leave Earth's other Part, and rise in Our's?
> Why does He wake the correspondent Moon,
> And fill her willing Lamp with liquid Light,
> Commanding Her with delegated Pow'rs
> To beautifie the World, and bless the Night?
> Why does each animated Star
> Love the just Limits of it's proper Sphere?
> Why does each consenting Sign
> With prudent Harmony combine
> In Turns to move, and subsequent appear
> To gird the Globe, and regulate the Year?

When Lord Exeter, a few months later, was looking for a tutor for his son, Gower reminded him of Prior's creditable tribute. Consequently, young Mr. Prior packed his boxes and was soon on his way to Burleigh. Would he feel exiled at this great house, remote from London and his friends? Perhaps, for it was a stirring time in the nation's history, when William's victories over James were being heralded by all the young poets.

[48] *Selected Poems*, ed. Dobson, p. xxvii.

Montague's celebration of the battle of the Boyne had gained the applause of London. Since his friends were stepping into larger positions, Matt might well feel that his appointment was tame and unpromising. The experience, however, proved profitable.

At Burleigh he enjoyed a mode of living quite different from that of Channel Row or St. John's College. Lord Exeter was a gentleman of learning and culture, a patron of artists and poets. He had traveled extensively and had collected many valuable paintings and other works of art. Life at Burleigh was leisurely, gracious, and good-mannered. Prior's duties as tutor were not strenuous. He employed his free time in studying the art treasures, strolling in the spacious gardens, or listening to Lady Exeter play on the lute. He acquired an ease of manner which was an asset to him in his diplomatic services later on.

The poems of the year 1689, reminiscent of Prior's new interests, are the best records of his stay at Burleigh. Lady Exeter's music inspired a short poem after the manner of Waller, marked by ease, clarity of diction, and graceful compliment:

> What Charms You have, from what high Race You sprung,
> Have been the pleasing Subjects of my Song:
> Unskill'd and young, yet something still I writ,
> Of CA'NDISH Beauty joined to CECIL's Wit.[49]

The paintings stimulated several less important occasional pieces, among them "A Picture of Seneca dying in a Bath" and "Verses to the Countess Dowager of Devonshire on a Piece of Wissin's." Since Wissing's portrait shows the Countess surrounded by her seven grandsons, Prior was moved to stage a contest between nature and the painter:

> WISSIN and *Nature* held a long Contest,
> If She *Created* or He *Painted* best.[50]

---

[49] *Poems on Several Occasions*, p. 5.
[50] *Dialogues of the Dead*, p. 31.

The most important of the Burleigh poems, to the biographer, is the *Epistle to Fleetwood Sheppard*, dated May 14, 1689. This poem, written in an easy, familiar style and in Hudibrastic couplets, is the first example of Prior's skill at *vers de société*, a genre of which he was to become master. In the Horatian lines, given below, we find a description of the leisurely life of the young tutor:

> For me, whom wand'ring Fortune threw
> From what I lov'd, the Town and You;
> Let me just tell You how my Time is
> Past in a Country-Life.—*Imprimis*,
> As soon as PHOEBUS' Rays inspect us,
> First, Sir, I read; and then I Breakfast;
> So on 'til foresaid God does set,
> I sometimes Study, sometimes Eat.
> Thus, or your Heroes and Brave Boys,
> With whom old HOMER makes much Noise,
> The greatest Actions I can find,
> Are, that They did their Work, and din'd.
>
> The Books of which I'm chiefly fond,
> Are such, as You have whilom con'd;
> That treat of CHINA's CIVIL LAW,
> And Subjects Rights in GOLCONDA:
> Of Highway-Elephants at CEYLAN,
> That rob in Clans, like Men o' th' HIGHLAND;
> Of Apes that storm, or keep a Town,
> As well almost, as Count LAUZUN,
> Of Unicorns and Alligators,
> Elks, Mermaids, Mummies, Witches, Satyrs,
> And twenty other stranger Matters;
> Which, tho' they're Things I've no Concern in,
> Make all our Grooms admire my Learning.
>
> Criticks I read on other Men,
> And *Hypers* upon Them again;
> From whose Remarks I give Opinion
> On twenty Books, yet ne'er look in One.
> Then all your Wits, that flear and sham,

Down from Don Quixote to Tom Tram
From whom I Jests and Punns purloin,
And slily put 'em off for Mine:
Fond to be thought a Country Wit:
The rest,—when Fate and You think fit.

Sometimes I climb my Mare, and kick her
To bottl'd Ale, and neighb'ring Vicar;
Sometimes at Stamford take a Quart,
'Squire Sheppard's Health—With all my Heart.

Thus, without much Delight, or Grief,
I fool away an idle Life;
'Till Shadwell from the Town retires
(Choak'd up with Fame and Sea-coal Fires)
To bless the Wood with peaceful *Lyric;*
Then hey for Praise and Panegyric,
Justice restor'd, and Nation's freed,
And Wreaths round William's glorious Head.[51]

Especially significant is the last stanza, which suggests discontent with this pleasant but idle existence and contains a jesting prophecy that the author might one day succeed the newly appointed poet laureate, Shadwell—not as the Prince of Dulness, we hope—and likewise employ his pen in doing honor to "William's glorious Head."

But this congenial life did not last long. Lord Exeter, who was opposed to the Revolution and who had refused to take the oath of allegiance to William III, was no longer happy in England. It is said that on one occasion when King William visited Burleigh, the Earl absented himself. The King was much pleased with the place and returned on the following day, only to find the master still away. When an attendant asked King William how he liked Burleigh, he replied that the house was too large for a subject. The friction between William and the Earl resulted in Exeter's resuming his travels on the continent. As his son accompanied him, Prior was out of employment.

[51] *Poems on Several Occasions*, p. 14.

» 4 «

Matthew returned to Cambridge in a mood of dejection, which he voiced in a most dolorous paraphrase of the Eighty-eighth Psalm.[52] He soon shook off this mood, and we next see him in the role of a mural painter; that is, if we accept the conjectures of Dr. Previté-Orton, librarian at St. John's, about the pictures recently uncovered at the college in a room presumably occupied by Fellows in the seventeenth century. Only a summary of Dr. Previté-Orton's article[53] can be given here. The partly obliterated decorations are no more than sketches, executed in tempera. There are two small scenes and a large rather complicated one. The latter shows a bit of undulating countryside with two "eminences" to the left and right, and a valley between. An enormous hawk occupies a vantage point on the left "eminence," while in the foreground are two other creatures—a tawny animal, presumably a panther, is lying on the ground; a white wolf is standing beside him. On the right "eminence," is a fawn-colored deer couched within a circle of musical instruments. The deer's expression is timid, yet smirking. Farther to the right, traces of reddish buildings remain. Above are swifts in flight, and a sun with a cheerful human countenance sheds its rays upon the scene.

Since Prior was a Fellow at St. John's, and may have been living in these very rooms during the years 1688 to 1690 (except for his short absence at Burleigh), the conjecture that he enlivened some dull hours by illustrating *The Hind and the Panther* seems entirely plausible. Evidence in support of this theory is found in his interest in paintings. A surprising number of his poems were prompted by admiration for various pictures, and the collection at Burleigh may have awakened a latent talent for drawing.

The other two wall paintings need but a word. One shows a

[52] *Dialogues of the Dead*, p. 83.
[53] *The Eagle*, Vol. XLIV, No. 193, December, 1924.

church, while the other portrays an impudent looking monkey, chained to a large basket of fruit and nibbling an apple. "It would not have been unlike Prior," Dr. Previté-Orton suggests, "to consider taking orders as submitting to the chain for the sake of provender, and this would agree with the neighboring picture of the church [? a college living]." In view of Prior's frequent use of the beast fable theme in reference to his own experiences, it looks as if he was again faced with the problem of taking orders.

But the road to preferment by way of politics was shorter and more attractive, Prior thought, than the route by the church; he therefore applied to Dorset, Lord Chamberlain in the new regime in place of the odious Mulgrave. It is true that the grave, phlegmatic William looked askance at poets, regarding them as a profane and licentious lot. The "Glorious Revolution," however, offered opportunities for ambitious young men in other activities than verse-writing. Matt has left his own amusing account of the besieging of Lord Dorset by eager office seekers.[54] He "stood among the crew"

> When Crowding Folks, with strange Ill Faces,
> Were making Legs, and begging Places,

but his "patience vext and legs grown weary," he decided to go home and make his plea by letter. The part that Dorset had played in taking Matt away from the Rhenish and giving him his early education is then recalled:

> All this you made me quit to follow
> That sneaking Whey-fac'd God *Apollo*.
> Sent me among a Fidling Crew
> Of Folks, I 'ad never seen nor knew,
> *Calliope*, and God knows who.
> To add no more Invectives to it,
> You spoil'd the Youth to make a Poet.

---

[54] It appears to be the second of the two epistles to Fleetwood Sheppard. See *Dialogues of the Dead*, p. 45.

He set forth his claim to further patronage in the lusty language of the tavern—

> In common Justice, Sir, there's no Man
> That makes the Whore but keeps the Woman.

And he concluded with a mischievous postscript:

> My friend CHARLES MOUNTAGUE's preferr'd,
> Nor would I have it long observ'd,
> That one *Mouse* eats while t'other's starv'd.

The last three lines suggest that Mouse Montague had run away with the bacon. Contemporary gossip about the unequal fortunes of the two Mice bore out Prior's contention; moreover, the Wits about town flayed the greedy mouse in their epigrams:

> Since one industrious Mouse took all the Pains
> 'Tis hard the other should ingross the gains;
> But smooth Tongu'd Confidence will still prevail
> When Wit, eclips'd with Modesty, shall fail.

Ned Ward's chatty *History of the Kit-Cat Club* furnishes many similar epigrams and makes clear the disparity of the fortunes of Lord Dorset's protégés:

About the same time that one of the celebrated Mice was happily crept into the High Road of Preferment, here at Home, another of the Witty Triumvirat, who had the Honour to be call'd my Lord D——'s Boys, was put in a fair way to make his fortune Abroad; so that the Third who had given much better testimonies of his Wit than any of 'em, was the only growing Genius of the Three that was left unprovided for.[55]

As we know, Stepney was the one who had gone abroad. Charles Montague was the one on the high road of preferment, having abandoned all thoughts of entering the church to identify himself with the Revolution by joining the rising in Northamptonshire and signing the letter of invitation to William of

[55] Ward, *Secret History of Clubs*, p. 364.

Orange. Lord Dorset, when introducing him to King William, aptly remarked that he had "brought a Mouse to kiss His Majesty's hand." The King replied, "You will do well to put me in the way of making a man of him," and thereupon bestowed upon this lucky mouse a pension of five hundred pounds.[56] In January, 1689, Montague was returned to the Convention Parliament for Malden, and three years later was appointed Commissioner of the Treasury. Another instance of Charles's climbing was his extraordinary marriage, at twenty-seven years of age, to a widow who had first been married six years before his birth. She was the Countess Dowager of Manchester, a cousin of the Montague family, and had borne nine children by her first husband. The marriage of "Chamont," Prior celebrated duly in a very uneven poem, which indicates that he indulged himself in a fit of extreme sensibility over losing his boyhood friend to love—if love it was.[57]

Fortunately for our story, the other mouse was not left to starve. Events soon took a turn by which Prior, likewise, embarked upon a public career. Charles Montague wrote to Stepney in October, 1690, "We are endeavoring to get Mr. Prior to be secretary to my Lord Dursley in the room of Dr. Aglionby."[58] While the appointment was pending, Prior, as befitted an aspirant for political preferment, wrote a Pindaric ode for the celebration of King William's birthday. A long, dreary, stiff poem it was, but it was sung before Their Majesties at Whitehall on November 4, 1690. The poem is significant because it is not only the first poem which Prior published singly but it is also the first panegyric that he offered up to William:

[56] Montague, *Works and Life*, p. 17.

[57] Brit. Mus., *Add. MSS*, 7121, fo. 47, "To Charles Montague on his Marriage to the Honble. Countess of Manchester." Mr. Waller also published it from a copy at Longleat, in *Dialogues of the Dead*, pp. 301-5, with the title of "To a Friend on his Marriage." The opening line "Chamont was absent, and remembrance brought" reveals the identity of the friend.

[58] P. R. O., *Stepney Papers*, 105/82, Charles Montague to George Stepney, Oct. 6/16, 1690.

And on Seine's Banks the Hero well renews
The glories of the Boyne.[59]

We next see Prior, a few days later, in his first public office, as secretary to Lord Dursley, the English Ambassador to The Hague, where he spent the next seven years of his life.

[59] "A Prophecy by Apollo, A Pindarique on His Majestie's Birthday, Sung before their Majesties at Whitehall, the Fourth of November 1690." In the Catalogue of the Ashley Library, the poem is published in full from a unique copy in Mr. Thomas J. Wise's collection, Vol. V, pp. 68–70.

CHAPTER III

"Secrétaire du Roy"

» 1 «

WHEN MATTHEW arrived at The Hague in November, 1690, he found the small city astir with an air of importance, for it was the center of the recently formed alliance against Louis XIV, William having chosen it as the meeting place of the Grand Congress. It was no mean position for which Dorset and Montague had recommended their protégé. In all the diplomatic service there was no other post which would bring a raw recruit into closer contact with the statesmen of the world. During the next seven years, King William and his ministers, as well as the representatives from the German and Austrian states, from Denmark, Sweden, Spain, and Portugal passed in and out of the Dutch capital on business for the League of Augsburg.

Even before the formation of the League, The Hague had acquired a reputation as the diplomatic center of Europe, the place where was to be found the "greatest accumulation of diplomatists and near diplomatists, inventing secrets or detecting them, or giving them away."[1]

The English diplomatic secretaries liked The Hague and envied young Matt. One of them called it "a sweet place," and Prior's predecessor, Dr. William Aglionby, pronounced it "the delicatest borough in the world."[2] It was a clean, quiet little town of broad, shady streets, bordered by noble lime and elm trees, of

---

[1] G. N. Clark, *The Dutch Alliance*, App. I, p. 143.
[2] A[glionby], *The Present State of the United Provinces of the Low Countries.*

imposing buildings, and of picturesque canals. Brick paved paths led to pleasant woods on the north, across flowery meads to Delft on the south, and on the west to Scheveningen and the sea. The principal canal to the east was bordered by the residences of the prosperous Calvinistic burghers—substantial Dutch houses, set in the midst of tiny gardens, wherein Louis hoped to billet his dragoons free of charge.

But the young secretary was filled with a nostalgic longing for his beloved England. He felt himself an exile in this strange country. Even an entertainment given by Lord Dursley in celebration of His Majesty's birthday failed to cheer him. All the foreign ministers and representatives of the states had been invited to the splendid affair. Lord Dursley's house was one great illumination; in front of it stood three enormous tables laden with trophies of King William's conquests and honors. Since noon wine had been flowing to the people through the mouths of a lion and a unicorn, and would continue to flow all night, we learn from the homesick Matt, to whom the party was nevertheless "all a very solemn affair," and who slipped away alone while it was still in progress.[3]

For a time there is little news of Prior. In his first official letter to Richard Warre, under-secretary to Lord Nottingham, Senior Secretary of State, Matt carelessly omitted the inside address, an oversight which would have annoyed the businesslike Montague had he known that his protégé had begun so badly: "Dear Sir," Prior wrote, "I succeed Dr. Aglionby as Secretary to his Exc^ce my Ld Dursley. I have sent you the *Gazette* as usual, and when anything extraordinary occurs, I shall be sure to advise you of it. . . ."[4]

Thus Prior began his routine duties. One of his tasks was the issuance of passports—certainly a humdrum business, but it required shrewdness to detect the motives of persons who applied

---

[3] P. R. O., *State Papers, Holland*, 84/221, Prior to Richard Warre, Hague, Nov. 4/14, 1690.

[4] *Ibid.*, fo. 271. Prior to Warre, Hague, Nov. 10, 1690 (N. S.).

for them. He must also watch for spies going from France via Holland and notify the port authorities at Harwich and London of suspects. One such problem concerned a foreigner in Rotterdam, called Clerck, who pretended to be an Italian, but was more probably a Frenchmen. Prior believed that Clerck would attempt to slip into England surreptitiously. The secretary communicated his suspicions to Vander Poole, Master of the Port at the Briel, and to the postmaster at Harwich, asking them to watch for the man. Further, Prior asked Richard Warre to have the suspect examined at Westminster, where he intended to go if successful in eluding the port authorities.[5] Before Prior was through with Clerck, he learned that his man was none other than the Scots Jesuit Clark, or Father Cosmo, a famous Jacobite engaged in regular errands between St. Germain and the Jacobites in London. So many of his sort slipped by port authorities that Prior drew up a little scheme for remedying the abuses in the granting of passports, which won the approval of Secretary Trenchard, Nottingham's colleague as one of the two principal Secretaries of State.[6]

Still less exciting than issuing passports and hunting spies was the semiweekly dispatching to Whitehall of the news letters which arrived from the various strategic towns in the League and which contained news of the War of the League of Augsburg then in progress. The news was not very thrilling, nor were Prior's comments upon it. Even letters to Dorset are deadly factual recitals of battles, too dull to quote. As time went by, and Prior grew more familiar with his correspondents, he learned to enliven his letters with such small talk as the rivalry between the Allies and the French over the election of the Bishop of Liége, the discord between the wife of the Swedish Envoy and the wife of the Imperial Resident over the purchase of a splendid equipage by the Imperial Resident, and the mar-

[5] *Longleat Papers*, III, 4, Prior to Warre, Hague, Feb. 3/13, 1692/3.
[6] *Ibid.*, 7, Prior to Adam Cardonnel, Aug. 19/29, 1693.

riage of the Elector of Bavaria to the Princess of Poland, who, although not extremely handsome herself, had a maid of honor who was.[7]

The gathering of all the Princes and the representatives of Princes at the Congress in February, 1691, brought a touch of color and gayety to the little town soberly hibernating among its ice-covered canals. King William was accompanied from London by a magnificent train of gentlemen, including Secretary Nottingham, the Earl of Dorset, the Earl of Devonshire, and the Bishop of London. In the complicated matters of the Congress, Prior could have played only a very humble part, made doubly so by the fact that not even Nottingham nor any of his colleagues knew much about the business of the Congress: William was his own minister for foreign affairs and remained so to the end of his life.

After many tedious deliberations and princely banquets, the Congress broke up, and the town was left to finish its winter sleep. The new English secretary had time to study his French and Dutch and to acquire a style of writing suitable for secretarial epistles, reports, memorials, and the like. He had had his first taste of the dull magnificence of a congress of diplomats. He had been noticed by the King and the appraising ministers. "In the solemn assemblies" of the Congress "he made his first appearance in public business." It was a disappointing affair.

It has been said that Matt was at first unwilling to accept the post at The Hague, partly because of his insufficient knowledge of French, partly because a subordinate position abroad might mean premature oblivion.[8] The first obstacle he so readily overcame that in time no Englishman of his day spoke or wrote better French than he did. The second objection was one that was to trouble him all during his diplomatic career, experience proving the truth of his saying that men abroad were forgotten.

Throughout his whole public life Prior was handicapped by

[7] *Ibid.*, 18, 35, 45.   [8] Bickley, *Life of Prior*, p. 33.

two disadvantages. He lacked what Stepney once termed "a character" and a private fortune of his own. When Stepney was being recommended for promotion and was asked for his credentials, he sent Charles Montague a full account of his pedigree from the Pembrokeshire Stepneys and the Lancashire Ancoats.[9] Matt had no such background. More embarrassing was his lack of private fortune. Diplomatic secretaries were not only poorly paid, but they were seldom paid promptly. The Treasury was an indifferent paymaster, and, as time went by and the War drained all the nation's resources, conditions grew worse. Secretaries like Stepney, who had some fortune of their own, could tide themselves over until the Treasury saw fit to send them part of their back salaries, but poor Matt, who spent his pay too freely, was often left with only a stick of peat in his hearth and was compelled to beg or borrow from whatever friend was willing to lend.

Still another serious difficulty, which he labored under along with his colleagues, was the inefficiency of the Secretaries of State. There were of course two principal Secretaries of State, one for the Southern Department, which embraced the Latin Countries and Turkey, and one for the Northern Department which embraced the rest of Europe. As a rule, the Senior Secretary took charge of affairs of the Southern Department. The post at The Hague was therefore in the province of the Secretary for the Northern Department, but in November, 1690, when Prior came to The Hague, the Secretary for the Southern Department, Nottingham, took charge of both Departments because his colleague was too indolent to perform the duties of the office. During the seven years Prior was in Holland, many changes took place in the State Department, but most of King William's choices were mediocre, and English diplomacy was ineffectual. The situation was well recognized by Louis XIV,

---

[9] P. R. O., *Stepney Papers*, 105/60, Stepney to Charles Montague, Dresden, Oct. 24/ Nov. 3, 1693.

who consistently took advantage of the inadequacy of the
English department of foreign affairs.[10] No one in England was
so much concerned over the problem of the diplomatic service as
Charles Montague. He was aware of all its shortcomings, but
realized fully the impossibility of improvement so long as
William remained his own minister and gave to the Secretaries
little authority or knowledge of his policies. In a very few words
Charles once characterized the situation to Stepney:

Formerly after a man had discharged a commission in foreign parts
. . . he was called home and made a Secretary of State, but that matter
is a good deal altered, and I believe we shall not see more instances of
that kind. This King is so much a master of all foreign transactions
that his choice is directed by some considerations at home more than
by their skill in business abroad.[11]

Quite often a Secretary was a mere figurehead, and if he was a
hypochondriac like Shrewsbury or an ineffectual like Trumbull,
he left the office routine to his under-secretaries. Men who stood
closer to William than his Secretaries of State were his Dutch
friends and advisers, and one Englishman, the Secretary of War,
William Blathwayt, who accompanied his royal master on the
battlefield.

As a consequence of this chaos in the State Department Prior
had too many taskmasters to whom he must bow and scrape.
Much of his correspondence during the early years at The Hague
is not only dull, as we have seen, but it is tiresome because it is
importunate and sycophantic. His correspondence with the
principal secretaries, the under-secretaries, the Secretary of War,
the Dutch favorites, and the Treasury officials is a lasting monument to his eagerness to please, to his feverish pleadings of his
cause, to his distressing financial embarrassments, and to his
shameful necessity of fawning upon the snobbish and inefficient

[10] For a comprehensive study of the State Department, see Mark Thomson's *The Secretaries of State, 1681-1782.*
[11] P. R. O., *Stepney Papers*, 105/82, Montague to Stepney, London, Aug. 7/17, 1694.

superiors, who delayed or refused to him the rewards of his labors and compelled him to beg continually for his pay.

To some extent the dullness of the correspondence was no fault of Matt's. The War of the League of Augsburg was an inglorious struggle between the hastily mobilized armies of the Allies, torn by jealousies and divisions among their leaders, and the perfectly organized forces of the Sun King. Even the diplomatic and military genius of William could not triumph over such heavy odds. When Prior came to The Hague, a thick gloom had settled over the whole Dutch front. There were no stirring scenes to fire the imagination of a young poet. The French were victorious in all land engagements—a circumstance which gave a French poet in the *Mercure de France* the opportunity of boasting with malevolent satisfaction in a satire on William III:

> Toujours vaincu, jamais vainqueur,
> Nassau va son chemin de Flandre en Angleterre,
> Laisse passer l'hiver, puis revient à la guerre,
> Quand les prés et les bois ont changé de couleur.[12]

The news from England was not more reassuring. The air was filled with stories of Jacobite intrigue, and even Whigs like Shrewsbury were believed to have opened communications with James, now a pensioner at the Court of Louis XIV. As Prior learned, the French, at the beginning of the year 1692, had an army of thirty thousand troops quartered in Normandy, eager to descend upon the English coast and put James back upon the throne. Transports were in readiness, and Tourville was ordered to protect them with a stout fleet. Contrary to rumors of defection, Russell attacked Tourville at La Hogue and burned his fleet under the very eyes of the French army encamped in Normandy. This naval battle was the one victory for the English in a year of defeats, and it moved the poet-secretary to compose a poem in praise of William in imitation of Horace's

[12] "Les Démarches du Prince d'Orange," *Mercure de France*, January, 1694, pp. 221-23.

Angustam amice pauperiem pati. In stirring verse, Matt called upon the nation to arouse itself from lethargy:

> How long, deluded *Albion*, wilt thou lie
> In the Lethargic Sleep, the sad Repose,
> By which thy close thy constant Enemy,
> Has softly lull'd Thee to Thy Woes,
> Or Wake degenerate Isle, or cease to own
> What thy old Kings in *Gallic* Camps have done;
> The Spoils They brought Thee back, The Crowns they won.[13]

This poem was the first of Prior's verse to be published by Jacob Tonson, that autocrat of printers, whose attention had been attracted by the success of "The Country-Mouse and the City-Mouse." For some time Tonson had little else to publish from Prior, whose secretarial duties claimed undivided effort. Lord Dorset's boys had exchanged poetry for business when they left Cambridge, and the stream of their college verse had been checked by prosaic matters. No one of the group regretted its decline more than Charles Montague. In moments snatched from Treasury affairs, he jotted down in his Commonplace Book lines which suggest a longing for the old days when nothing more serious than the composition of an occasional poem had occupied his mind and the minds of his friends:

> Stepney and Prior, alas, they have been Thine
> Indulged and cherished by the tuneful Nine
> Now Business they pursue and Poetry decline.[14]

Meanwhile the "tuneful Nine" must wait while Matt was serving his apprenticeship under Lord Dursley and was learning the tricks of the diplomatic trade.

» 2 «

As time went by, the gouty Dursley gave increasing responsibility to his secretary. Of Dursley, we hear but little. He

---

[13] "An Ode, in Imitation of the Second Ode of the Third Book of Horace," *Dialogues of the Dead*, p. 36.
[14] Brit. Mus., *Add. MSS*, 28,644, fo. 66.

was a kindly but ineffectual person, who, it is said, did not enjoy the confidence of his royal master. He was not a man to encourage a companionship such as later existed between Prior and his superiors. Dursley's young son, Charles, however, was one of Prior's friends—Prior was always fond of children. In the boy, the secretary took a tutorial interest, chiding him in Latin letters[15] for neglecting his studies. When Charles wished to come over to Holland on a visit, he counted on Prior's interceding with Lord Dursley, but Prior tantalized the lad for a while saying that progress in Latin would be the price of his influence. Charles evidently heeded the admonition, for later Prior recommended him for admission to Westminster School.[16] In appreciation of this solicitude for his son, Dursley made Matt a gift of English ale and cider.

Prior's conduct satisfied a greater man than Dursley—the King himself, who, when Dursley went to England on a sick leave in November, 1692, suggested half in earnest that Mr. Prior should be left behind as "secrétaire du Roy." Despite the royal disdain for poetry, the King and his secretary were somewhat alike. Both had frail constitutions; both were capable of tender and loyal friendships; both had a fondness for pictures, an interest in gardens. Both at times sought amusement with gay, convivial, or even vulgar companions. Prior, in consequence of his sovereign's favor, was made a Gentleman of the King's Bedchamber and was granted an annual pension of one hundred pounds by Queen Mary.[17]

Dursley's absence in England gave Prior the responsibilities of a minister. Through transacting business with the Grand Pensioner, Antonius Heinsius, one of the wisest and most capable of statesmen, Prior had the opportunity of learning more of statecraft than from Dursley. His duties now brought him

[15] *History of His Own Time*, p. 12.
[16] *Longleat Papers*, III, 22, Prior to Mr. Knipe, June 8/18, 1694.
[17] From March 6/16, 1692/3. See *Calendar of State Papers, Domestic, William and Mary*, XXXVIII, 310.

directly in contact with the principal secretaries in London to whom he sent his reports. He might find the little Dutch town dull, and the thrifty burghers and their "provident vroughs" uninteresting; nevertheless he was gaining in diplomatic skill and making himself known among men of political prominence.

In October, 1693, Dursley gave up his office. As his formal leave, however, did not arrive until the following June, Prior was placed in the meantime in a most uncertain position. Dursley had not provided for him, and whoever succeeded Dursley would probably bring over his own secretary. Scanning the field for secretarial vacancies, Matt found five possibilities and immediately wrote to Dorset, petitioning for his favor:

My having had the honour to be bred by your Lordship, and trailed a pen here onward of four years, makes some people flatter me that I may not be forgot in this great harvest with few laborers, since Aglionby, Cresset, and Stepney, who are already working, are journeymen as I am, have about the same estates at home, and are sent to preach politics as the Apostles were on a better errand, without purse or scrip. I take it for granted that your Lordship will mention me to Mr. Secretary Trenchard, if you think anything of this kind proper for me.[18]

Finally Lord Falkland was chosen to succeed Dursley. Prior, told to stay on until the new minister arrived, complained to Dorset that the order to remain was only a verbal one, and that, although he had been made a minister, he had received no commission to act as such. Moreover, the official letters for which he was obliged to pay the post were costing him many a pretty penny that he did not possess.[19] When Falkland unfortunately died of smallpox before assuming office, Prior was left in an awkward predicament. He did not know whether he would be retained at The Hague or recalled; he had no official title, and no money with which to meet the various obligations that devolved upon the one representative of the English government

---

[18] *Longleat Papers*, III, 15, Prior to Dorset, Hague, Nov. 14/24, 1693.
[19] *Ibid.*, 21, Prior to Dorset, Hague, May 23/June 1, 1694.

in Holland. At once he wrote to Blathwayt, deploring the uncertainty of his position, yet expressing every confidence in Blathwayt's consideration. He was no longer Dursley's secretary, and did not know whose to say he was if any situation should arise demanding the need of some such designation. The King's order, conveyed through Blathwayt, was that Prior should continue to serve as the English secretary with the annual allowance of 20 shillings *per diem*. Prior was in deep despair —he had been promoted but was not provided for financially. His expenditure for postage alone would amount to from eight to twelve pounds a week, which sum would not be refunded from the Treasury until a year later. Had his superiors, he wondered, ever heard of a "professed panegyric poet" possessed of enough money to "advance two guineas to the public?"[20]

Thus Matt had the duties and the expenses of a minister while he was given only the title and the pay of a King's secretary. He was afraid of seeming presumptuous if he assumed the relations with the Duke of Shrewsbury—now Secretary of State in place of Nottingham—that a minister should maintain. The advice of "Father" Vernon, Shrewsbury's under-secretary, on this point was that he should write to the Duke as often as did any of the other ministers. "Let him know in your own hand all that passes," Vernon advised, shrewdly adding, "Mr. Stepney does it with great exactness, and I don't doubt that you will make yourself as remarkable."[21] Accepting Vernon's timely counsel, Prior composed a letter of congratulation to Shrewsbury, thus beginning a friendly correspondence between the joiner's son and the "King of Hearts," the politest gentleman in England.

Presently it was agreed at Whitehall that Prior should have an allowance in keeping with his expenses. It was a long time, however, before he actually received anything beyond verbal

[20] *Ibid.*, 25, Prior to Dorset, Hague, June 12/22, 1694.
[21] *Ibid.*, 24, James Vernon to Prior, Whitehall, June 12/22, 1694.

assurance. Although Charles Montague was Chancellor of the Exchequer, the wheels of the Treasury moved so slowly that Prior declared, nearly three months after he was appointed, that the post had given him much credit, but, so far, not one penny of money. The sympathetic Vernon tried to encourage Matt by writing that Whitehall desired to reconcile the ministry with the minister.[22]

Prior resolved to ask for an increase in salary, and approached Blathwayt and Lord Portland about it while the King was holding Court at The Hague in October, 1694. Here is the first mention of William Bentinck, Earl of Portland, the King's faithful friend and unofficial prime minister, with whom Prior was to be closely associated later. Matt not only laid his distressing situation before the two ministers but also repeated the substance of his interview with them to Shrewbury. If the ministry wished him to remain at The Hague, he said, they ought to make it possible for him to live more comfortably. It was not fitting that he should scramble out to ordinaries along with Switzers and French Protestant exiles. It was unreasonable to expect him to support himself and his servants on the sum of twenty shillings a day, which tallies and the exchange reduced to an insignificant eighteen. He needed a coach and felt indignant that he had to go to the Pensioner and to other secretaries on foot, whereas even their clerks came to him in carriages. Soon it would be winter, and he knew the bitterness of the winds blowing in from the North Sea, making The Hague colder even than London. He had seen the storm clouds sweeping across the sky and breaking upon the town. A comfortable house of his own with warm fires would safeguard his frail constitution from the penetrating chill of the gales that howled around the corners of the old streets and churned the waters of the Vyver. Unless some satisfactory arrangements were made, there would be nothing left for him to do but to throw himself

[22] *Ibid.*, 32, Vernon to Prior, Whitehall, Aug. 28/Sept. 8, 1694.

and his servants into the next packet boat and return to England.[23]

Frugal Dutch sense would not permit Lord Portland to be easily swayed by the eloquent pleading of a young though efficient secretary. Nevertheless, Portland was willing to admit that Prior's appeal was founded on reason rather than on vanity and promised that he would bring the matter to His Majesty's attention before he should leave Holland. Yet when William sailed for England no action had been taken on Prior's appeal. Shortly afterwards, however, Shrewsbury, Portland, Blathwayt, and Vernon held a conference at Whitehall. They decided that it would be wiser to add the cost of a carriage and certain other expenses to Prior's extraordinaries than to ask for an increase in salary. Was there much difference between a hundred pounds by bill of extraordinary and a hundred pounds by privy seal? Prior thanked Vernon and the Lord Duke for their consideration. Was he not too old to cry for a coach and too young to have real want of one?[24] Seneca had taught him resignation.

It was now December, and vexed with the ministers who would not grant him an increase because they lacked a precedent for so doing, he poured out his troubles to Stepney, at the time on leave in London:

They have all sorts of weapons, I see, and keep us, as you advised me to keep my virago, at arm's length: and we must e'en arm ourselves in the Apostle's magazine with the helmet of patience and the sword of faith. There is certainly nothing more irregular than the last proposal of £200 in a lump: but that is an objection that I ought not to start, but that we are talking only of examples and precedents. . ."

The tone of their correspondence during these weeks is that o disillusionment—a note common to the youth of any time who are anxious about their future: "'Tis all a game, Catt, and we

[23] *Ibid.*, 34, Prior to Shrewsbury, Hague, October 30/November 9, 1694.
[24] *Ibid.*, 36, Prior to Vernon, Hague, Dec. 4/14, 1694.

that are partners are rather to hold up our cards than blame our adversaries for peeping into our hands, or endeavoring to trump the cards we hope to make our tricks by."[25] To this Stepney replied, "Believe me, Matt, there is nothing but roguery and double dealing in this world and to live upon the square is the certain way of being cheated."[26] Occasionally they were friendly rivals for a post. Stepney had the advantage over Prior of four extra years of service, a thorough knowledge of German affairs, and, above all, a shrewd wisdom that made him a valuable man for any diplomatic errand from Dresden to Vienna. Foreign service was now palling on both of the friends, and they were casting their eyes towards appointments in London. The pity was that there were no posts available at home so satisfactory as those they held. If only a friend of theirs should become Secretary of State, they reasoned, they might be given appointments in his office; from such a position it would be only a step to a plenipotentiary's post; they could cite precedents to bolster up their hopes. Idle speculations these, for King William insisted that Shrewsbury again take the office, and the young men's hopes were dashed to the ground. Another source of annoyance was the King's inclination to favor Dutchmen and French Huguenots for diplomatic service. Perhaps this preference was due to his belief, strange though it seems, that no Englishman could keep a secret. It would have been impolitic to air their grievances further, so Matt and "Catt" adopted "Patienza" for their motto and courted their patron, the Earl of Dorset, with letters and poems and gifts of books.

The permission to add various expenses to his bill for extraordinaries would relieve Prior to some extent. Cash to repay certain loans from his friends he must have, and in hope of receiving prompt reimbursements he laid his plight before Sir William Trumbull, then a commissioner of the Treasury. Sir

William was a mild, genial man, a moderate Whig and less a party man than Trenchard, whom he succeeded as Secretary of State the following year. Since Trumbull was something of a patron of poets, Prior might reasonably expect assistance from him:

Necessity, Sir, has as little manners as it has law; and when one is really starving, 'tis in vain to be told one is impertinent. Hitherto I have borrowed and done pretty well: those who lent me money and are not yet paid have had the trouble on't, but for want of more such civil persons I begin to be a little troubled myself. There is a great correspondence between the stomach and the heart: one is out of humour commonly when one is hungry; and it is time to think what friends I have at Whitehall when famine sits triumphant on the cheeks of my two footmen and the ribs of my two horses. You will be pleased to take this into consideration when Mr. Powys presents your Lordship my extraordinaries.[27]

The letter won Prior a new patron. From now on he frequently sent verses to Trumbull, who once paid him this high compliment: "You have found the secret of joining two things generally incompatible, poetry and business, and both in perfection."[28]

In response to all Matt's pleadings, the Treasury sent six hundred pounds in December. Temporarily at least, his difficulties were over; yet he was not altogether satisfied. He envied Stepney's four pounds a day and three hundred pounds for equipage. Grudgingly he admitted to the Lexingtons that he would not starve before April; in fact he was cutting such a figure that he had been taken for a president, and two or three gullible ministers had invited him to dinner.[29]

From other gossipy letters to Lord and Lady Lexington at Vienna, we catch a glimpse of the social life at The Hague in the closing years of the seventeenth century:

For news here I have no other than that the King was very merry on

---

[27] *Longleat Papers*, III, 39, Prior to Sir William Trumbull, Hague, Dec. 11/21, 1694.
[28] *Ibid.*, 78, Sir William Trumbull to Prior, Whitehall, May 15/25, 1696.
[29] *Lexington Papers*, 26, Prior to Lord and Lady Lexington, Hague, Dec. 21/31, 1694.

Monday night at Mrs. D'Odyck's ball, where he led in your sister Kaunitz, so bedaubed with diamonds, that one might mistake her for Mrs. Barry, in the 'Maiden Queen;' she danced, too, a little like Mrs. Barry, with her — up, her toes in, and her head below her shoulders, much to the satisfaction of the Envoyess of Lapland, who mended the matter well with my Lord Cutts, who had only the pretense of having his foot broke for dancing most exquisitely ill. Lord Selkirk lost a heart there, and one of the States a diamond buckle of greater value.[30]

By the beginning of 1695, there were rumors that Lord Villiers would be appointed as His Majesty's Plenipotentiary at The Hague; hence Prior pursued the search for another post with more diligence than ever. Trumbull, Montague, Dorset, Pembroke—in fact every one whom he had ever addressed as patron, father, or master was petitioned. Ratisbon was most discussed, although Florence, Venice, Berlin, and even the more northern posts of Sweden and Denmark were considered. For a time it seemed as if Matt would be sent to Ratisbon, although Vernon was dubious of his being content there: "I have heard how two of your predecessors spent their time there, Mr. Pooley [*sic*][31] in making love to the *fräuleins* and Sir George Etherege in making Lampoons upon them."[32] At both of these occupations Prior would have excelled, Vernon to the contrary.

As soon as the appointment of Villiers was confirmed, Prior sent him the customary letter of congratulation. He expected Lord Villiers within a fortnight, and wrote to Lady Lexington, "I do not know what will become of me. I have an ague in the bargain and owe £400."[33]

The summer passed with no change in Matt's fortunes. Villiers was slow in taking up his post, and Prior used the time to advantage by writing ingratiating letters to him. In July he confided that Stepney, although preferring Vienna, was to have the

[30] *Ibid.*, 14, Prior to Lord and Lady Lexington, Hague, Nov. 9/19, 1694.
[31] Sir George Etherege succeeded Edmund Poley at Ratisbon in March 1685. See *The Letter Book of Sir George Etherege*, ed. Sybil Rosenfeld, Introd., p. 15.
[32] *Longleat Papers*, III, 52, Vernon to Prior, Whitehall, May 17/27, 1695.
[33] Lexington MSS, Prior to Lady Lexington, Hague, June 19/29, 1695.

coveted post at Ratisbon, hence he (Prior) would become "le Ministre de la Fortune, et le très humble serviteur des événements."[34] Disappointed but still hopeful, he reconsidered the possibilities of Berlin and Florence. If the latter post were still open, he proposed to buy Veneroni's *Grammar*, and perfect his Italian. Villiers was a friend of Keppel, the dissolute young Dutch courtier who was gradually supplanting the faithful old Portland in the King's affections. Thinking that Keppel could be helpful, Villiers suggested that Prior appeal to him. Eagerly following this advice, Prior dispatched to the new favorite a long and unrestrained epistle. Cleverly enough he argued that, "though Ratisbon might not want a resident, the King's Secretary at The Hague would soon want a residence, and though his Majesty might have small use for a scribbling servant, he had great occasion for the bounty of a Royal Master." As might be expected, there was fulsome flattery of Keppel and of the King. But the best part of the letter was his drowning man's plea for help and his pledge of unremitting loyalty:

Wherever he [the King] pleases to send me, I am ready to go; where if there be not much business, I shall apply myself to those studies that may make me capable of doing his business when there is any; and when there is nothing, to be written for his service in prose, I will write his conquests and glories in verse. A resident or envoy may in some small time be sent to Venice, another to Florence; be it at either of these two places, at Ratisbon, Berlin, at Stockholm, Copenhagen, or even Moscow, it is well, provided I may serve my King, my hero, and my Master, but it is a sad reflection for me to think of going home as if I were disgraced, after having served here five years with some credit, and spent my little all in order to my being fit for something hereafter; and I take the boldness to protest to you I cannot think of returning to my College, and being useless to my country, to make declamations and theses to doting divines there, having drawn up memorials to the States General in the name of the Greatest King in Europe.[35]

[34] *Longleat Papers*, III, 59, Prior to Villiers, Hague, July 17, 1696.
[35] *Ibid.*, 60, Prior to Arnold Joost van Keppel, Hague, August 3, N. S., 1695.

For its forthrightness this letter surpasses any written to his own countrymen. Whether Keppel ever read it—it was in English—we do not know. The following year he wrote in French to Prior, who, taking the hint, ever afterwards addressed him in that language.

Villiers finally came to The Hague as Plenipotentiary in September, 1695, but Prior's fortunes were left undecided until the King held Court there during the following month. Upon the strong recommendation of Villiers, the King declared it his pleasure that Prior remain at The Hague until employment should be found for him elsewhere. William would not augment Matt's allowance by privy seal, but would double his salary by the addition of twenty shillings a day to the extraordinaries. For a time then, Prior's anxiety about his future was at rest, and he could dismiss the unpleasant thought of returning home with no prospects except his fellowship at Cambridge. "I am fixed to my secretaryship and The Hague," he told Vernon, "where I shall live very contented for the present, and endeavor to make myself useful for the future."[36]

From this time we may date the beginning of the extraordinary friendship between Prior and Lord Villiers (later Earl of Jersey), which continued until the Earl's death in 1711. Essentially sociable by nature, Prior readily formed friendships and clung tenaciously to them. Villiers was a man of but ordinary understanding and character. He was an affable, pleasure-loving person, quite unlike Prior's other superiors. Like Matt, Villiers was an alumnus of St. John's College, Cambridge—a circumstance that formed an added bond between the two men. His wife Barbara was daughter of the disreputable Will Chiffinch, keeper of the backstairs for the Merry Monarch. His own family were variously connected with the Court. His mother had been Princess Mary's governess, and his sister Anne had been her playmate at Richmond. Anne Villiers married Portland, but

[36] *Ibid.*, 66, Prior to Vernon, Hague, Oct. 15/25, 1695.

died in 1688, and the brothers-in-law afterwards were none too friendly, Villiers preferring the vain and frivolous Keppel to the more solid and reliable Portland. The other sister, Elizabeth, a remarkably clever and witty woman, was the King's mistress, a relationship which accounts for her brother's sudden rise in royal favor.

Prior's fortunes were now on the upswing. As Villiers attained one high office after another, Prior faithfully followed at his heels, receiving preferment as a result of his friend's ready commendation. Villiers's cousin, Colonel George Villiers, had married Matthew's cousin, Katherine Prior, a circumstance which may have made it easier for the Plenipotentiary to use his influence in Matt's behalf. With his relief from ministerial duties and with the forming of this congenial friendship, Prior's spirits rose. He continued to have occasional despondent moments, when he turned to verse as an outlet for his melancholy:

> In vain by Druggs and rules of Art
> Poor Ratcliffe wou'd my Lungs ensure
> They lye too near a wounded heart
> Whose sickness Death alone can cure.[37]

On the whole, however, Prior was content. He took a house, establishing as housekeeper "Flanders Jane," whose domestic virtues are celebrated in "Jinny the Just" and whose charms as a mistress are immortalized in the "Cloe" poems. Stepney was a frequent visitor at The Hague, stopping off between his diplomatic journeys from King William's camp in Flanders to the small German States. The two young secretaries enjoyed the comforts of Matt's new ménage and the indolent ease which the small town afforded. They found Lord and Lady Villiers "very good people to live withal"; there were "great doings" at their hospitable mansion—balls and masquerades, where matters of state gave place to dancing and coquetry.

---

[37] "In a Window in Lord Villiers House, 1696," *Dialogues of the Dead*, p. 337.

» 3 «

While the war pursued its devious course through seven campaigns on the fields of Flanders, Prior, from The Hague not far distant, sent regular reports of its progress to Dorset and to the secretaries in London. Unlike Stepney, who was an eyewitness to the siege of Namur in 1695, Prior never caught a glimpse of the fighting. At one time it looked as if he might have to join Blathwayt in camp if no other employment was available, but he put aside the thought of service with the Secretary of War as a last resort, for he did not like the "cold Mr. Blathwayt."

By 1696 persistent rumors of peace reached The Hague. The previous year had been a bad one for Louis. The loss of Namur put an end to the series of French victories which had clouded Prior's earlier dispatches with gloom. More serious to Louis was the loss of his greatest general, Luxembourg, whose place could not be filled by the incompetent Villeroy. Prior continued to send to Dorset throughout the summer of 1696 the latest gossip from the front. In June it was thought that Caillières, Louis XIV's veteran diplomat, was in Holland incognito, feeling out the sentiment of the Dutch.[38] A setback to the moves for peace occurred during the following month, and the talk of secret negotiations "cooled off extremely." This caused much speculation in diplomatic circles, and Prior was divided between two opinions—perhaps the English had refused the French terms, or perhaps the French had not yet made any proposals.[39] The question of a peace remained a matter of "guesses and wagers" until September, when it was made known that France would consent to one founded upon the basis of the treaties of Westphalia and Nimeguen. Prior passed this news on to Dorset, adding that he expected to hear shortly of the naming of plenipotentiaries to serve with Lord Villiers for the drawing up of a treaty. He expected to become the secretary for the Embassy,

[38] *Longleat Papers*, III, 80, Prior to Dorset, Hague, June 12/22, 1696.
[39] *Ibid.*, 82, Prior to Dorset, Hague, July 21/31, 1696.

and lost no time in asking Dorset to write a good word in his behalf that he might show to Lord Portland.[40]

In spite of diplomatic trifling, both England and France needed peace. The death of Queen Mary the previous year had taken from William all zeal for war. The treasuries of both countries were practically exhausted. Refugees from France furnished Prior with lurid stories of the distressful conditions among the poor there. In England the situation was bad, although not quite so desperate as it had been two years earlier, and there were signs of improvement. William had been able to borrow in the summer of 1696 from a new source—the Bank of England. Charles Montague was proving himself a great financial genius in founding the Bank and the National Debt and in reforming the currency. Such a reform, however beneficial in the end, was extremely hard at the outset. While the old coin was being called in and the new coin was being slowly circulated among the timid public, there was in fact a money panic.

Prior, as might be expected, was as hard hit as any one. In September he could not sell his tallies without a thirty per cent loss, and the rates of discount became even higher. Nor could Aunt Katherine send him a farthing. The chain and medal given him by the States-General on the retirement of Lord Dursley were in pawn, and he had but two pistoles in the house, or, what is more distressing, in the world. He painted a dismal picture of a levee every morning—"God be thanked for the respite on Sunday"—of postmen, stationers, tailors, cooks, and wine merchants who had not been paid since the previous December. He wrote at the end of a letter to Montague: "If you can get me any ready money, it would be more charity than to give an alms to the poorest dog that ever gave you a petition; if not, patience is a virtue and a scrap or two of Horace must be my consolation."[41] It is not likely that the busy Montague replied to this

---

[40] *Ibid.*, 83, Prior to Dorset, Hague, Sept. 4, N. S., 1696.
[41] *Ibid.*, 86, Prior to Charles Montague, Hague, Sept. 1696.

entreaty, for in December Prior wrote to Powys, "Some miracle may possibly mollify the hearts of the Treasury that we may get a little ready money for these bills and the ordinary appointments."[42]

Powys replied immediately "it must be a miracle indeed, as you say," for there was not a sixpence of disposable money to be had; all that was in the Exchequer, he said, was being appropriated either for the war or for the repayment of loans.[43]

» 4 «

The rumor of a marriage between King William and the Princess of Brandenburg came as a welcome relief from financial harassments, the details of war, and the wagers of peace. Secretarial pens busied themselves in passing the word along, and the poor young Princess was anatomized completely. Prior from the beginning thought there was little in the rumor, "for one of the parties only are resolved," meaning, of course, the Princess and her family.[44] The King planned a visit to Clèves, the seat of the Elector of Brandenburg. This visit, Prior thought, would offer an opportunity to distinguish between "love and civility." Trumbull was all agog with curiosity. He felt sure there was "something in all this noise," and he urged both Prior and Stepney to send him the most particular accounts and an exact character of the Princess, "as to her person, age, humour and everything."[45] So Prior, who was at Loo courting the King's favor and "briguing," as he called it, for the secretaryship to the Peace Congress, accompanied the King in his train to Clèves.

[42] *Ibid.*, 95, Prior to Richard Powys, Hague, Dec. 7, N. S., 1696.

[43] *Ibid.*, 97, Powys to Prior, Whitehall, Dec. 8/18, 1696.

[44] William's advisers were determined that he should marry again. With that aim in view, they drew up a list of all the eligible Protestant Princesses ranging in age from fourteen to twenty-five years. William refused to listen to these plans, saying on one occasion, "If you have forgotten your mistress, I have not." For the list and descriptions of the Princesses, see *Correspondentie van Willem III en van Hans Willem Bentinck*, The Hague 1927, II, 80.

[45] *Longleat Papers*, III, 83, Trumbull to Prior, Whitehall, Aug. 22/Sept. 1, 1696.

In his Journal, as well as in a letter to Shrewsbury, he recorded with relish the amusing incidents of the journey.[46]

The Elector of Brandenburg drove forth to meet King William, received His Majesty most respectfully, and the two drove back to Clèves in one coach. The exchange of the first greetings took place while the assembled company stood for about an hour. Afterwards the King, the Electrice, and the Duke of Zell played ombre for five hours in the Electrice's apartment. Matters of precedence were observed in the seating during the game: the King had an armchair; the Duke of Zell an ordinary one, as did also Mr. Cresset,[47] who was coaching the King; the Electrice sat upon the bed; the young Princess stood during the entire time. Prior found the Electrice talkative and civil, if not handsome: her face, he thought, was "not unlike [that of] our poor Queen, upon Queen Dowager's body." Few of the women were handsome, and all were "ill-dressed in old fashioned stiff-bodied gowns too big for them, with their breasts and shoulders naked." As for the sixteen-year old Princess, Prior described her as "not ugly but disagreeable; a tall miss at a boarding school with a scraggy lean neck, very pale." We learn from Stepney that she was slightly cross-eyed, fair complexioned, tow-haired and flat chested. "I suppose," he wrote, "her gown was plentifully quilted to make her appear full-chested, for she has little or no breasts; and large plumpers must have been used to help out the hips." Her conversation was dull, her bearing unregal, but she had "very good principles of religion"; she was modest and humble, and the King did not "much dislike her."[48] The young men were certainly not prepossessed with the Princess, who, finding this reconnoitering visit of the King's trying, appeared more gauche and timorous than she really was.

[46] For his Journal, see *Longleat Papers*, III, 508, 509. The letter to Shrewsbury is contained in *Buccleuch Papers*, II, 391.

[47] James Cresset, the English envoy at Zell.

[48] P. R. O., *Stepney Papers,*, 87/11, fo. 352, Stepney to Sir William Trumbull, Loo, Sept. 8/18, 1696.

The King and the Elector, Prior recorded, clashed over the matter of seating at meals. Armchairs, thought William, were for kings only, but, said the Elector, surely he could sit in an armchair in his own palace. The result was that they dined at different tables in the great hall, every one else being seated according to rank. It was a festive occasion, with good wine served so bountifully that most of the diners were drunk before the dessert. If the guests lost their bearings, it made no great difference, for each one was safely conducted to the castle gate by a servant with a flambeau, whence there were coaches to carry them to their lodgings. On Sunday the King and the Elector heard different sermons for the same reason that caused them to eat at different tables. The King took his departure at four o'clock Sunday afternoon, and the Elector conducted him back to the riverside. No match had been arranged. So far as we know, it was never mentioned again.

On the return journey, Prior and Stepney witnessed a quarrel between Portland and Keppel. Portland was in one of the Duke of Zell's coaches, and Keppel in one of the King's. Keppel overtook Portland and kept ahead all the way to Dieren, where Portland, getting out of the coach, threatened to beat the coachman, calling him and his master impertinent puppies, or words to that effect. The quarrel had its beginnings at Clèves, where, while Portland had been most of the time with the Elector and the Ministers, Keppel had sat with the King, a distinction which fretted the older man. Here we find a forerunner of that feud between William's two Dutch favorites which eventually resulted in Portland's surly withdrawal from Court, leaving the field to his young, handsome, and more amiable rival.

» 5 «

When Prior returned from Clèves, he found all peace affairs still unsettled. The three English ambassadors for the peace treaty were as yet unnamed. Fortunately Matt had made an early bid for the secretaryship, his six years in service having taught him that the pressing of one's interests was necessary, although it must be done with the utmost tact. As a result of his foresight, he was the first applicant, but there was a rumor that Sir William Trumbull would be one of the plenipotentiaries and that he would bring with him his own secretary, John Ellis. Not only were the prospects for peace slim, but alas, the secretaryship might fall to another.

The one great point which must be settled before any preliminary agreement could be reached was the recognition by Louis of William as King of England. To Louis XIV, James II was the lawful monarch. The decision of the House of Commons on October 20 to support William against all enemies fully dispelled from the mind of Louis any hopes of a Jacobite restoration, and the depleted state of his Exchequer finally forced him to acknowledge William. In December Prior sent Dorset word that although Caillières had been for some time chicaning about the "manner of owning the King," an order from Versailles had authorized him to yield to the English demand.[49]

To Trumbull, Matt imparted the same information. Trumbull was as curious about Caillières as he had been about the young Princess of Brandenburg and expected Prior and Stepney to furnish him with any inside facts they might learn about the crafty lawyer-diplomatist, who, in a burlesque account of the Parnassian war between the Ancients and the Moderns, had referred to the English people as barbarians with no literature or polite learning of their own. We have not Prior's estimate of Caillières, but Stepney told Trumbull that the French emissary was a "tall, lean black man," whose "chief excellency is speaking his own language politely."[50]

William appointed the plenipotentiaries in December, 1696. Again Prior and Stepney were disappointed when Lexington was

[49] *Longleat Papers*, III, 96, Prior to Dorset, Hague, Dec. 1/11, 1696.
[50] *Trumbull Papers*, I, 697, Stepney to Trumbull, Oct. 27/Nov. 6, 1696.

not named. "Lord L. and his beautiful lady at Vienna" were favorites with the two secretaries, who had hoped in 1694 that Lord Lexington would be made Secretary of State rather than the weak and sickly Shrewsbury. William considered Lexington for one of the places but decided that he was indispensable at Vienna and so gave the honor to Sir Joseph Williamson. The other two plenipotentiaries were, as Prior expected, Villiers and Pembroke. None was the equal of the experienced Caillières.

Williamson was a stranger to Prior and hence a man to be courted. Taking a hint from Blathwayt, Prior at once congratulated Sir Joseph on his appointment and begged to be retained at the post as secretary.[51] A correspondence ensued, Prior keeping Williamson informed of all the preliminary moves towards peace. The Allies named three possible places for the meetings of the Congress—Maastricht, Nimeguen, and Breda—from which the French were to choose. Caillières would have none of these, but held out for Ryswick, William's palace halfway between The Hague and Delft.[52]

England for the moment was in the throes of a trial for treason —the celebrated case of Sir John Fenwick and his accomplices— and the King's ministers in London gave no thought to the details of the coming Peace Congress. Growing impatient, Prior dashed off to England to clinch an appointment. He returned to The Hague with the privy seal as secretary of the Embassy in hand.

Notwithstanding the fact that his position at the Congress was a minor one, Prior here gained a knowledge of treaty making which led to more important posts. His *Memoirs Relating to the Treaty of Ryswick*, his Journal, and his letters to the ministers in London all testify to his ability as a secretary. Furthermore, they furnish a complete and readable account of the negotiations such as is not contained in any other single source.

[51] *Longleat Papers*, III, 99, Prior to Williamson, Hague, Jan. 1, N. S., 1696/7.
[52] *Ibid.*, 101, Prior to Williamson, Hague, Jan. 5/15, 1696/7.

There comes a break in the Journal from April 3 to May 9 and a lull in the correspondence with the home office. From a personal letter, we learn that Matt had contracted a violent head cold. The treatment of the ailment was severe in those days, but the patient's sprightly humor did not entirely desert him. He had "neither an eye nor a hand," he told Lexington, "one eye being civilly put out by a defluxion and the other weeping till it comes again, and the arm in a scarf having been let blood for abatement of salt humours."[53] And when on the mend he continued:

I cannot boast of my eyes. I have a great respect for the God of Love, but am not aspiring to divinity: a blind boy may turn Cupid; but at thirty, if the mischance falls on one, I know nothing but singing psalms upon Fleet Bridge that remains for one.[54]

Matt was unduly pessimistic while ill, and began to wonder what his employment would be when the Peace Congress—it was hardly under way yet—should be over. Ever since Dursley had left The Hague, Prior had felt that his position was impermanent; hence the forethought was not unwarranted. A vacancy at Lisbon prompted him to ask Montague for advice about making a bid for the post: "Your friend, Matt Prior might learn Portuguese, and get two thousand pounds in three years, and come home again to dedicate the rest of his life, *amicitiae aeternae*, and to the commands of my Master."[55] A week later a better opening presented itself. While the King was at The Hague, Villiers, who had been appointed one of the Lords Justices of Ireland, recommended Prior to His Majesty for the chief secretaryship to the Lords Justices. King William told Villiers that he was well satisfied with Prior's service, but thought that some one else had bespoken the position. If the other Lords Justices would agree upon Prior, however, the King

53 *Lexington Papers*, 253, Prior to Lord Lexington, Hague, April 2/12, 1697.
54 *Ibid.*, 264, Prior to Lexington, Hague, May 7/17, 1697.
55 *Longleat Papers*, III, 113, Prior to Montague, Hague, N. S., April 23/May 3, 1697.

would concur. Prior then asked Montague to use his influence with the other two Justices, the Marquis of Winchester and the Earl of Galway.[56] Deciding to court favor from every available source, he also wrote to Sunderland, now Lord Chamberlain in the place of Dorset, who had retired from Court.[57] His appeals were effective. The two other Justices were easily induced to accept him, and within a fortnight he was assured of the appointment.[58]

The Congress at Ryswick had opened by this time, the first meeting having taken place on May 9, 1697. The King's palace in which the sessions were held no longer stands, having been destroyed during the Napoleonic Wars, but we can picture the spacious old Dutch mansion with its large central hall and the twin wings on the right and left. Each wing conveniently had access to the central hall through its own gate and bridge. The Allies were segregated in one wing, the French in the other; while the Mediator occupied the hall between. Outside, the characteristic rectangular garden, bounded by canals and divided into formal woods and flower beds, lay serene in the spring sunshine. Inside, the peacemakers continually haggled over the question of precedence. So acute became their differences at one time that the gates of the courtyard had to be taken down in order that all the dignitaries might drive in abreast. Fortunately, when both factions met with the Mediator, an enormous round table made it possible for all the negotiators to be seated without regard for precedence.

The proceedings were so slow that it looked as if there would be a repetition of the Nimeguen meeting, which had lasted for nearly a year. The first day of the Congress was occupied with the exchange of credentials. Then it was decided that meetings would be held only on Wednesday mornings and Saturday afternoons. The whole method of transaction was clumsy and time-

[56] *Ibid.*, 114, Prior to Montague, Hague, May 10, N. S., 1697.
[57] Sunderland had been appointed Lord Chamberlain in April.
[58] *Longleat Papers*, III, 117, Prior to Montague, Hague, May 11/21, 1697.

wasting. The secretary for one group would solemnly hand a memorandum to the Mediator; he would solemnly hand it over to the Minister concerned, who might or might not be ready with an answer at the next session.

To Prior all this was discouraging. By May 24 he had little news for Trumbull:

The Imperialists gave in Saturday before an imperfect paper, and tacitly confessed their having done so by changing it on Wednesday—you see, Sir, how slowly we advance; I hear the French grow impatient at it and I take this to be a good argument that they are in earnest for a peace.[59]

William himself grew tired of these delays and decided to speed up the negotiations. The war, after all, had been his contest with Louis XIV; so the peace was an affair to be settled between them. King William therefore deputized Portland, ever his right-hand man, to hold a conference with Boufflers, marshal of France. Prior knew of their meeting, but did not know its import. He passed the news on to Sunderland with the surmise that a suspension of arms was designed. On the same day, by order from the English plenipotentiaries, he wrote Blathwayt, asking what answer the Lords Ambassadors were to make to the Imperialists, who were curious to know the occasion and result of the interview between Portland and Boufflers. Apparently nothing else was talked of in the "conferences, assemblies and coffee houses" for several days. Prior's reward for his pains was a curt note from Blathwayt saying that the King had already sent the Lords Ambassadors sufficient instructions in the matter, which need not be repeated.[60]

By the end of July, Lord Portland and Marshal Boufflers had held four conferences. For greater secrecy they transferred their meetings from the shade of the apple trees at Ryswick to conference rooms in Brussels. The tone of Prior's bulletins was now

[59] *Ibid.*, 119, Prior to Trumbull, May 24, N. S., 1697.
[60] *Ibid.*, 137, Blathwayt to Prior, Camp, July 5/15, 1697.

more cheerful: "His Majesty, with the greatest wisdom and calmness has let the French understand that he would have peace or war." Furthermore, the King deemed it inexpedient to protract the negotiations. Prior's report closes on a hopeful note: "I believe this declaration will do more towards the procuring a speedy peace than all the *factums* and musty papers which can be given in and transmitted by the Mediator here."[61]

The English and the French being thus resolved on peace, got together and settled their chief points of dispute. A separate article was drawn up whereby Louis was to promise to expel James II from France and to give no protection or support to him or to any of William's enemies, King James not being expressly named in the article.

The settlement of the respective claims of the English and French in America was given scant attention. The Cabinet was not well informed about American affairs and was waiting for the new Board of Trade and Plantations to furnish it with further facts. In 1690, at the outset of the war, Sir William Phips had taken Port Royal and Acadia from the French and had held them throughout the war. Yet there is no indication that the plenipotentiaries were alive to the significance of his conquest. Prior took the initiative in examining sheaves of documents about the Colonial possessions but found only one bundle pertaining to affairs in America since the signing of the Treaty of Breda in 1667. It was therefore impossible for him to ascertain the facts, and he accepted the current opinion that the American affairs would be settled on much the same basis as at the beginning of the war.[62] He protested, however, that such a settlement would retard the expansion of trade with the Colonies and he often reiterated his real concern for America in his correspondence with Lord Lexington and others during the summer of 1697.[63]

[61] *Ibid.*, 142, Prior to the Marquis of Winchester, Hague, July 21/31, 1697.

[62] *Ibid.*, 126, Prior to Trumbull, Hague, June 8/18, 1697.

[63] See especially the letters to Lord Lexington, Lexington MSS, June 1/11, 1697, and June 18/28, 1697.

In the drawing up of the treaty, a dispute arose over the possession of two unnamed forts on Hudson Bay. Just before the war the French had captured these forts from the Hudson's Bay Company, but during the war the English recovered them. Under the article of general restitution, the forts would be returned to the French. Blathwayt thought that restitution in this case would be unfair. He maintained that by an act of war the English had only recaptured their original possessions.[64] In accordance with Blathwayt's suggestion, Prior wrote into the treaty a clause which would except from restitution these two forts.[65] The French rejected this proposal, insisting on following the restitution clause to the letter. William decided to refer the dispute to a commission in the hope of inducing the French to give him certain other concessions.[66]

It was Prior's business to draw up an article which would empower the above named commission to meet.[67] Agents of the Hudson's Bay Company reached The Hague in September, too late to furnish the English treaty makers with details of the Company's grievances against the French. Prior pledged his help when their affairs should come up for final discussion.[68] For some inexplicable reason this commission never met. Hudson Bay, Newfoundland, and Acadia were all left in French hands until the Treaty of Utrecht—Matt's Peace—turned them over to England sixteen years later.

When the great day fixed for the termination of the negotiations arrived (August 31, 1697) everything was still in a state of confusion. The French had raised their terms, as King William had predicted they would. Barcelona was on the point of surrendering to the French; it might therefore serve as a hostage for Strassburg, so an offer was made to restore Barcelona if

[64] *Longleat Papers*, III, 124, Blathwayt to Prior, Cockleberg, June 8, N. S., 1697.

[65] For correspondence between Prior and Blathwayt concerning the Hudson's Bay dispute, see *ibid.*, 122, 124, 129, 130, 137, 148, 156, 179.

[66] *Ibid.*, 148, Blathwayt to Prior, Loo, August 9/19, 1697.

[67] *Lexington Papers*, 302, Prior to Lexington, Sept. 7/17, 1697.

[68] R. B. Adam Collection, Prior to Blathwayt, Hague, Sept. 7, N. S., 1697.

Strassburg might remain French. Count Kaunitz replied for the Allies that they had no new terms to offer. The exasperated Mediator took his leave, protesting before God and man that it would not be his fault if the negotiation broke up.

Prior was plunged into gloom. "God send us peace," he exclaimed to Lexington, "and a little respite from mémoires, journals, resultas, responses and the Devil and all."[69] Sir Joseph Williamson's untimely attack of gout that made him "complain very much and eat very excessively" added to Prior's burdens.[70] Matt took hope, however, when he learned that Portland was renewing the conferences with Boufflers at Brussels. Once more the negotiations got under way, and the conclusion of the treaty seemed imminent. At the eleventh hour the English and the French disagreed over the language of the preamble to the treaty, which was finally settled when a model prepared by the French was accepted by the English Ambassadors. Prior's translation of this preamble into Latin—the language of treaties in those days—is a dusty testament to his share in the wording of the document.

The tedious heckling and bargaining eventually came to an end: the peace was signed. At three o'clock on the morning of September 21, 1697, the English Ambassadors dispatched Prior with a message to their King notifying him that England, Spain, and Holland had signed the treaty with France. The Imperialists had refused to sign, but they were given an extension of time.

Prior left for England immediately on a ship hired for the occasion, and landed at Lowestoft on September 23. On the following day he reached Whitehall, left a copy of the treaty with Secretary Vernon, and then went to pay official calls. King William was absent in Flanders, there having been no cessation of fighting during the sessions of the Peace Congress. Prior

---

[69] Lexington MSS, Prior to Lord Lexington, Hague, Sept. 9, N. S., 1697.
[70] *Longleat Papers*, III, 162, Prior to Blathwayt, Hague, Sept. 4/14, 1697.

therefore paid his respects to all the Lords Justices—those gentlemen of high degree who looked after the realm when the King was away. The *Postman* announced Prior's arrival in England with the "welcome news of the peace," and the event was an occasion of much rejoicing by a people tired of war.[71] The guns at the Tower were fired, flags displayed, bells rung, bonfires lighted, and a general celebration declared.[72] On September 26, the Lords Justices—the Archbishop of Canterbury, the Lord Chancellor, Lord Romney, and Lord Sunderland—made Prior a gift of two hundred guineas and put the man-of-war *Centurion* at his service for the return to Holland.

Prior made the round trip to London in less than eight days. He returned to attend to certain minor details and to exchange the usual round of complimentary visits with the plenipotentiaries. He was to leave his post for the new one as soon as the King arrived from Flanders to set his hand to the treaty—the final formality. Yachts were riding at anchor in the harbor, ready to bear the royal party home. The public in the Dutch capital was planning a great demonstration.

Seven years to the month after he had come to The Hague, Prior was ready to return to London, whence as an inexperienced young Cantabrigian he had set out to make his fortune. Fortune he had none except a sum of twelve hundred pounds, and that was owing to him by the worst of debtors, the Treasury. But he had acquired friends, if not riches, and had won the esteem of his superiors—best of all, of William himself, a man not given to hasty flattery, yet quick to recognize faithful service. His work had not been mere routine; he had learned the ways of diplomacy and had mastered the intricate art of treaty making. Melancholy and cynical though many of his private reflections had been during this period, he had exhibited re-

[71] Sept. 14-16, 1697.

[72] Luttrell, *A Brief Historical Relation*, IV, 278. See also *Correspondentie van Willem III en van Hans Willem Bentinck*, The Hague, 1927, II, 79, Romney to Portland, Sept. 14/24, 1697.

markable cheerfulness in the face of ill health, unpaid salaries, and disappointments in preferment. He now turned his mind towards his new employment, the Irish secretaryship, for which he had already drawn several months' salary. The chill salt winds might blow through the streets of The Hague and the gray mists might gather over the quaint old town, but Prior need have no further worry about securing sufficient turf to keep his fires burning.

CHAPTER IV

"The Englishen Heer Secretaris"

» 1 «

NOTWITHSTANDING Charles Montague's lament that Matt had forsaken the Muse for business, the secretary found some time from his routine duties to devote to poetry, as quite a number of amorous songs, political panegyrics, and other verses testify. After he had acquainted himself with his responsibilities at The Hague, he needed no prodding from Dorset or Montague to have poems ready to inclose in his letters to them. Of his inclination to write poetry, he spoke with conviction later in life. One who had ever felt this impulse, he declared, could not be turned from it, do what he would. Of his own experience, he said, "I found this impulse very soon and shall continue to feel it so long as I can think."[1] He might complain that secretarial duties were an "encumbrance on an English Muse," but he was not to be deterred from addressing the fair ones or celebrating King William's "conquests and glories" in verse.

The first of the poems which Matt wrote during his diplomatic apprenticeship is the ode "To the Honourable Charles Montague, Esq." Like a number of his other pieces it appeared in the *Gentleman's Journal*, a monthly paper published in London by Peter Motteux, enterprising French Huguenot and Jack of all literary trades. Containing as it does Pindaric odes, pastoral dialogues, verse epistles and prologues, amorous songs, enigmas, fables, and "characters" in verse, the *Journal* is an interesting revelation of the verse forms in fashion during the closing decade

[1] *Dialogues of the Dead*, p. 185.

of the seventeenth century. Incidentally, Prior himself essayed
every one of these verse forms in his own works. Among the
regular contributors to the *Journal* were Congreve, Sir Charles
Sedley, John Dennis and Prior. The second number of the *Journal*,
for February, 1691/2, contained "Stanzas by Mr. Prior" pref-
aced by the statement from Motteux, "While things like the
following stanzas by Mr. Prior shall be given or sent to me, you
may believe I shall be prouder of making them publick than my
own."

Well might Motteux hold up to the notice of his readers the
poem that had come to him by post from The Hague, for it
proved to be the best poem that he was ever to print in his
magazine. As published the following year in the third Dryden
Miscellany, it bore the title "Heraclitus," thus indicating that
Prior was at the time tinged by the mood of the "dark philosopher," but the poem is better known by its dedicatory title
mentioned above. Unlike the college verses it is no practice
piece but one which is characteristic of much of Prior's mature
work in that it strikes the note of disillusionment:

> Howe'er 'tis well, that while Mankind
> Thro' Fate's perverse *Maeander* errs,
> He can imagin'd Pleasures find,
> To combat against real Cares.
>
> Fancies and Notions he pursues,
> Which ne'er had Being but in Thought:
> Each, like the GRAECIAN Artist, woo's
> The Image He himself has wrought.
>
> Against Experience He believes:
> He argues against Demonstration,
> Pleas'd, when his Reason He deceives;
> And sets his Judgment by his Passion.

The fifth stanza contains the often quoted lines, in which Mr.
Doughty sees a "very modern touch":

> Our Hopes, like tow'ring Falcons, aim
>   At Objects in an airy height:
> The little Pleasure of the Game
>   Is from afar to view the Flight.

The sentiment of the ninth stanza may have furnished Gray with the thought of one of his best known lines:

> If We see right, We see our Woes:
>   Then what avails it to have Eyes?
> From Ignorance our Comfort flows:
>   The only Wretched are the Wise.

The young man's melancholy seems to have resulted from a disappointment in love, if we read the last stanza aright:

> We wearied should lie down in Death;
>   This Cheat of Life would take no more;
> If You thought Fame but empty Breath;
>   I, PHYLLIS but a perjur'd Whore.[2]

The above conjecture is borne out by two other poems, "A Song" and "An Ode," both having the subtitle "To his Mistress," which were also published in the *Gentleman's Journal* in 1692. These are but two of a group of love poems composed during this period. To distinguish them from the "Cloe" poems of later date, we call them the "Celia" poems, since they apostrophize a disdainful lady of that name. They are in plaintive mood and are reminiscent of an affair of the heart which the poet took seriously. The song, a short poem in two quatrains, is in the style of the conventional complaint of the ardent lover to the cruel fair one:

> Whilst I am scorch'd with hot Desire,
>   In vain, cold friendship you return;
> Your Drops of Pity on my Fire,
>   Alas! but make it fiercer burn.

---

[2] "To the Honorable Charles Montague, Esq.," *Poems on Several Occasions*, p. 20.

Ah! wou'd you have the Flame supprest
That kills the Heart it heals too fast,
Take half my Passion to your Breast,
The rest in Mine shall ever last.[3]

The *carpe diem* theme is employed in the ode, a less spontaneous piece than that just quoted and one which reminds us of Dr. Johnson's remark that Prior tried to be "amorous by dint of study":

I

While blooming Youth, and gay Delight
Sit on thy rosey Cheeks confest;
Thou hast, my Dear, undoubted Right
To triumph o'er this destin'd Breast.
My Reason bends to what thy Eyes ordain;
For I was born to Love, and Thou to Reign.

II

But would You meanly thus rely
On Power, You know I must Obey?
Exert a Legal Tyranny,
And do an Ill; because You may?
Still must I Thee, as Atheists Heav'n adore;
Not see thy Mercy, and yet dread thy Power?[4]

III

Take Heed, my Dear: Youth flies apace:
As well as CUPID, TIME is blind:
Soon must those Glories of thy Face
The Fate of vulgar Beauty find:
The Thousand LOVES, that arm thy potent Eye,
Must drop their Quivers, flag their Wings, and die.

The next five stanzas only expand the idea of the last one quoted above, depicting the fate of the lady upon the decay of her

---

[3] "Song to his Mistress," *Dialogues of the Dead*, p. 36.
[4] Cf. lines 7 and 8, canto II, *The Rape of the Lock:*
　　"On her white breast a sparkling cross she wore,
　　Which Jews might kiss and Infidels adore."

beauty and advising her that constancy in love mitigates the
sorrows of age:

IX

So shall I court thy dearest Truth;
  When Beauty ceases to engage:
So thinking on thy charming Youth,
  I'll love it o'er again in Age:
So TIME it self our Raptures shall improve;
While still We wake to Joy, and live to LOVE.[5]

Of all the "Celia" poems, the song beginning "In vain You
tell your parting Lover" is the finest; it is less derivative, and
is marked by finished workmanship and delicacy of feeling:

In vain You tell your parting Lover,
You wish fair Winds may waft Him over.
Alas! what Winds can happy prove,
That bear Me far from what I love?
Alas! what Dangers on the Main
Can equal those that I sustain,
From slighted Vows, and cold Disdain?

  Be gentle, and in Pity choose
To wish the wildest Tempests loose:
That thrown again upon the Coast,
Where first my Shipwrackt Heart was lost,
I may once more repeat my Pain;
Once more in dying Notes complain
Of slighted Vows, and cold Disdain.[6]

We know nothing of the circumstances under which these
poems were written. Little private correspondence has survived
to give us a picture of Prior's personal life during his sojourn at
The Hague. Stepney is responsible for the statement that Prior
always had "a tender heart equally divided betwixt his Mistress
and his Muse." Who was the lady who could wring such plaintive notes from Prior's Muse? A passage from a letter to Stepney
promises to be enlightening:

[5] "An Ode," *Poems on Several Occasions*, p. 8.
[6] "A Song," *ibid.*, p. 19.

Ollinda is miraculously recovered from folly and (if one may believe her scrawl) resolves to be *resnabel*. I am perfectly friends with her: how easily we pardon those we love![7]

But nowhere is there to be found a clue to Ollinda's identity.

Confidential letters went often during these years from The Hague to Dresden, where Stepney was envoy to the Elector of Saxony, but unfortunately the only one of Prior's which remains is the one from which we have just quoted. From Stepney's answers, however, we may speculate about Matt's flirtations and his professions of belief in Platonic love. We learn that Prior had arranged a corresponding acquaintance between Stepney and a young London widow, Mrs. Frances Holmes,[8] into which "Catt" entered only half-heartedly, being at the moment deep in an intrigue with a married lady in Dresden, which he dramatically declared involved "danger, expense and adultery."[9]

A rather amazing letter of Stepney's to this Mrs. Holmes, whom he had never seen, throws light on Prior's sentiments concerning love at that time and shows them to be infinitely more chaste than those voiced in the "Cloe" poems in later years. Stepney told the lady that he was himself "disposed to embrace Prior's opinion by beginning with the speculative part of love," since distance precluded physical demonstration. Furthermore, he attributed Matt's cold Platonic philosophy— of preferring the soul to the body and reason to passion—to the same obstacle of distance. The hint that Prior might desire more than mere friendship with the widow can only be interpreted as a bit of fiction on Stepney's part. There follow some racy remarks on the wisdom of Prior's point of view. They indicate that Matt still held a naïve and romantic attitude toward the fair sex which contrasts sharply with Stepney's coarseness:

[7] *Longleat Papers*, III, 38, Prior to Stepney, Hague, Dec. 11/21, 1694.

[8] Presumably the Mrs. Frances Holmes to whom Lawrence Prior, in his will proved in 1690, left his gold watch and diamond ring.

[9] P. R. O., *Stepney Papers*, 105/60, Stepney to Prior, Dresden, Nov. 24/Dec. 4, 1693.

But if he [Prior] pretend to establish these Maxims as constant truths, I fear his reputation will suffer in point of Manhood and I leave the women to punish him for so dangerous a doctrine. . . . Since to make love perfectly, methinks Body is as necessary an Ingredient as Brandy is in Punch. Your Witt and friendship are very good sugar and nutmeg, but there must go something more to make the Dose compleat.[10]

Our secretary at The Hague had far to go before reaching the devil-take-her mood of middle age.

The fair one who was sharing Prior's heart with his Muse just now was a Mrs. Danvers. She is constantly mentioned in his correspondence with Lord and Lady Lexington, of whom she was perhaps a cousin. In writing to them of the death of Queen Mary, Prior declared that the sad event had left "a Platonic void" in his heart that could not be filled unless Mrs. Danvers should effect a cure by taking his pleas more seriously. That he was now possessed of a coach and two hundred pounds ready money was a perquisite that a young woman ought not to dismiss lightly.[11]

The next chapter in their story deals with a lovers' quarrel, the cause of which the scanty records do not reveal. Prior blamed himself for it, admitting that he had called Mrs. Danvers "names." Almost simultaneously with the quarrel a passport matter bobbed up, which by no means soothed the feelings of Mr. Prior. There came to his office to apply for passage to Vienna a Mr. Sutton, a young chaplain who was a kinsman of Lord Lexington's. For some reason, obscure, unless it was the irrationality of jealous love, Prior regarded the handsome clergyman as a rival and his appearance on the scene as inauspicious, inasmuch as he himself was out of favor with the lady. However, Prior supplied Sutton with plenty of passports and dispatched him on his journey. This he did for the sake of Mrs. Danvers' soul, so he averred, but "as for her body, let them look after it that are able to fortune it, and my neglect of it

---

[10] *Ibid.*, Stepney to Mrs. Holmes, Dresden, Dec. 7/18, 1693.
[11] Lexington MSS, Prior to Lord Lexington, Hague, Feb. 25/Mar. 8, 1695.

may proceed from my despair of possessing it."[12] Mrs. Danvers, however, was not to be so summarily dismissed from his thoughts. Two months later he was still dreaming of her at night and cursing his impecuniosity, which made winning her impossible.[13] Three years later she was still Mrs. Danvers, and we assume that Prior's jealousy was unfounded.[14]

The third disturber of Matt's private peace is a less shadowy lady. While on a holiday in London, Prior became acquainted with Elizabeth Singer, a young poetess of some note. She was a celebrated beauty. Her fan, decorated with an exquisite painting of Venus in her chariot drawn by sparrows, is said to have set many a susceptible heart aflutter. An animated and dainty creature, with fine auburn hair, sparkling blue eyes, fair complexion, no wonder she became the toast of the day. Among her many admirers were two such different men as Isaac Watts and Matthew Prior.

One of Miss Singer's early poems is a graceful pastoral dialogue called "Love and Friendship."[15] In it two shepherdesses, Amaryllis and Silvia, in the seclusion of their Virgilian grove are debating the respective merits of love and friendship. Amaryllis, true daughter of Venus, sighs for the lovely youth Alexis, while Silvia prays to the "chaste goddess of the groves" to restore to her the fair nymph Aminta. It seems that the poet herself was torn, at the moment, by conflicting emotions. That Prior may have been partly a cause of her unrest is revealed in a poem he wrote to her, entitled "To the Author of the Foregoing Pastoral."[16] In all editions of his works it is preceded by a copy of Miss Singer's "Love and Friendship."[17] Since his piece is an

[12] *Ibid.*, Prior to Lexington, Hague, April 30/May 10, 1695. See also letter of May 19/29.

[13] *Ibid.*, Prior to Lexington, Hague, July 12/22, 1695.

[14] *Ibid.*, Prior to Lexington, Paris, April 1/11, 1698.

[15] *Poems on Several Occasions*, p. 26.

[16] *Ibid.*, p. 29.

[17] In the Preface (p. xxiii) to the first authorized edition of his *Poems on Several Occasions* (1709), Prior wrote: "I must likewise own myself obliged to Mrs. Singer, who has given

answer to hers, it seems certain that he aspires to play Alexis to her Amaryllis. He gallantly swears, however, that if friendship be the extent of her vows, then he too will sing its praises. But if, as he fears, he is right in suspecting that the poem implies the presence of a rival, he prays:

> May'st thou, howe'er I grieve, forever find
> The Flame propitious, and the Lover kind,

and that perhaps some time she may have pity for

> the mournful Swain
> Who loving much, who not belov'd again,
> Feels an ill-fated Passion's last Excess;
> And dies in Woe, that Thou may'st live in Peace.

The poetical argument—really a subtle wooing—was prolonged. An early editor has said that Prior was so fascinated by Miss Singer's charms that "he continued to pour out his passion in divers vehicles."[18] How long the exchange of noble sentiments endured, we do not know. We infer that Miss Singer retreated, leaving Prior in the field. This belief is supported by the delightful little poem "To a Lady: She Refusing to Continue a Dispute with Me":

> II.
> In the Dispute whate'er I said,
>   My Heart was by my Tongue bely'd;
> And in my Looks You might have read,
>   How much I argu'd on your side.

> V.
> Alas! not hoping to subdue,
>   I only to the Fight aspir'd:
> To keep the beauteous Foe in view
>   Was all the Glory I desir'd.

---

me leave to Print a Pastoral of Her Writing; I wish she might be prevailed with to publish some other Pieces of that kind, in which the Softness of her Sex, and the Fineness of her Genius, conspire to give Her a very distinguishing character."

[18] See "Life of Matthew Prior" in Prior, *Poetical Works*, Edinburgh, 1869, p. vii.

VII.

Deeper to wound, She shuns the Fight:
  She drops her Arms, to gain the Field:
Secures her Conquest by her Flight;
  And triumphs, when She seems to yield.[19]

An early marriage might have been expected for a woman of such charm and spirit, but the poetess was by no means a social butterfly. Elizabeth Singer's father was a Nonconformist minister who gave his daughter a pious upbringing. As a child she studied French and Italian, practiced her music faithfully, and wrote verses. In 1694 and 1695, when she was only twenty, she was the chief contributor of verse to the *Athenian Mercury*, that curious *Notes and Queries* of the decade. The fifteenth volume of the magazine was dedicated to the "Ingenious Pindarick Lady of the West," as the editor called her. In 1706, still a spinster, she addressed a poem to Isaac Watts on his *Poems Sacred to Devotion*, reëchoing the theme of "Love and Friendship":

III.

No gay *Alexis* in the grove
  Shall be my future theme;
I burn with an immortal love,
  And sing a purer flame.

IV.

Seraphic heights I seem to gain
  And sacred transports feel;
While, WATTS, to thy celestial strain
  Surpriz'd I listen still.[20]

Watts was eager to meet the poetess who had thus complimented him. Perhaps he could light the flame which she had forsworn. In due time he proposed marriage to her, but she declined him sweetly, as the story goes, saying, "Mr. Watts, I

[19] *Poems on Several Occasions*, p. 29.
[20] Rowe, *Miscellaneous Works*, I, 70.

only wish I could say that I admire the casket as much as I admire the jewel."[21] Does not this rebuff suggest that Prior may have lost Philomela's favor because he, too, possessed an unhandsome countenance? Finally at thirty-five Miss Singer married Thomas Rowe, a handsome, serious youth of twenty-two, who died five years later of tuberculosis.[22]

Mrs. Rowe devoted the remaining years of her life to works of charity and to writing poems of devotion. She lionized every poet whom she met, even gushing over the great Mr. Pope as the "darling of her heart."[23] Prior, too, shared in her praise, and she addressed a poem to him on his "Solomon," which she admired because of its solemnity:

> A Muse devoted to celestial things
> Again for thee profanes th' immortal strings.[24]

Surely the earlier poem which the "again" implies was "Love and Friendship." One is inclined to think that it was most fortunate that this friendship remained Platonic. It is impossible to imagine the Prior of

> 'Tis the mistress, the friend, and the bottle, old boy![25]

as the husband of the pious Elizabeth Rowe.

Holidays in England furnished Prior with themes other than love. While visiting Lord Dorset at Knole in June, 1694, he spent much time among the paintings as he had at Burleigh five years before. In a portrait which showed the Earl's young son holding a large cat upon his lap, Prior saw an opportunity to point a moral. Playfully he transformed the cat into a "blush-

---

[21] Thomas Wright, *Isaac Watts and Contemporary Hymn-Writers*, p. 76.

[22] In an account of the life of Mrs. Rowe prefixed to her *Miscellaneous Works* (Vol. I, p. viii), Theophilus Rowe, Thomas's brother, has this to say: "Amongst others, 'tis said, the famous Mr. Prior would have been glad to share the pleasures and cares of life with her. . . . But Mr. Thomas Rowe was the person reserved by Heaven to be the happy man, both to be made and to make happy."

[23] Helen Sard Hughes, "More Popeana," *P.M.L.A.*, XLIV, 1090.

[24] Rowe, *Miscellaneous Works*, I, 166.

[25] The line is from "A Two Part Song," *Dialogues of the Dead*, p. 158.

ing maid," foretold the pleasures of the soft embrace, and warned the youth of the jealousies of the Queen of Love.[26]

The prologue was another popular medium of poetry at which Prior tried his hand. He furnished one for the young Mrs. Manley's play, *The Royal Mischief*,[27] in which he begged indulgence for her years. Another, he composed for little Lord Buckhurst to speak at Westminster School. The lines,

> To learn our parts we left our midnight bed,
> Most of you snored whilst Cleomenes read:[28]

are most likely reminiscent of Matt's own days at Westminster.

Prior's poems were appearing in the miscellanies of the time—Gildon's, Tonson's, and others. The poet knew that if used with caution his Muse might be a valuable aid in securing for himself a place in the world of affairs. One pitfall he must avoid if he hoped to cultivate the friendship of the great and thereby improve his fortunes. Although he might with impunity attack Louis XIV and other enemies of England, he had already seen changes enough in the ministry at home to make him realize that it was unsafe to attack men in high office. Consequently he substituted for political satire the safer but duller panegyric. One of these panegyrics is the "Hymn to the Sun," written to be sung on New Year's Day 1693/4 before Their Majesties. The music fortunately was composed by the great Purcell. Like most of Prior's other political pieces it shows how dull a truly witty poet could be even if he brought to his task a genuine enthusiasm for his king.

» 2 «

When news reached The Hague early in January, 1694/5, of the death of Queen Mary from the dreaded scourge of smallpox, the grief of the people was heartfelt. The Queen had come to Holland seventeen years earlier as a young bride of sixteen,

---

[26] *Poems on Several Occasions*, p. 17.
[27] *Dialogues of the Dead*, p. 134.   [28] *Ibid.*, p. 95.

lovely and gay, and she was genuinely admired by the people. Gloom settled upon every one, and Prior heard nothing but the "dismal sound of bells and the more dismal chime of many bad poems on too good a subject."[29] The Queen's death was naturally the occasion for much elegiac verse, Dutch as well as English. Of course a contribution was expected from Prior. Congreve, Steele, Stepney, Walsh, Dennis, and many others sang their dirges. Tonson solicited a poem from Prior, who was so upset with grief that he was "thrown into a colic"; certainly he was in no mood for writing. That his emotion may have been compounded of a strange mingling of self-interest and grief, he himself recognized. In reading between the lines of a letter to Lord Lexington we detect his attempt to justify his silence with an exaggerated expression of sorrow:

Since the horrid loss of Her Majesty, at naming of which my Lord will sigh and my Lady will cry, I protest I have written nothing but nonsense, which is a present I humbly offer to some of my correspondents, but it is not so very proper for you. Upon this occasion I have lost my senses and £100 a year, which is something for a philosopher of my circumstances; . . . I have given notice of this cruel change to the States and Ministers here, in a long trailing cloak and a huge band, the one quite dirty with this thaw, the other really slubbered with my tears. I am so much in earnest in this sad affair that people think I am something very considerable in England, that have such a regard to the public, and it mades me cry afresh when they ask me in what county my lands are. Whether this proceeds from loyalty or interest God knows, but I have truly cried a basin full. *Je ne puis plus*; 'tis impossible for me to tell you the sorrow that reigns universally in Holland: these people, who never had any passions before, are now touched, and marble weeps. . .[30]

Elegies poured in to the booksellers in London from all quarters. Not among the worst was one from Stepney, who sent

[29] *Longleat Papers*, III, 46, Prior to Shrewsbury, Hague, Jan. 4/14, 1694/5.

[30] *Lexington Papers*, 46, Prior to Lexington, Hague, Jan. 14/24, 1694/5. Prior's fears about his pension from the Queen were unrealized, for it was later added to his extraordinaries.

his poem to Tonson, asking him to show it to Montague and Congreve and to forward a copy to Prior, "who perhaps may send some amendments."[31] Still Prior had not contributed his "mite." To Lord and Lady Lexington he sought to excuse himself by saying: "I am as yet so afflicted for the death of our dear Mistress, that I cannot express it in bad verse, as all the world here does; all that I have done was to-day on Scheveling sands, with the point of my sword:—

> Number the sands extended here;
> So many Mary's virtues were;
> Number the drops that yonder roll;
> So many griefs press William's soul.[32]

Although Prior designed a commemorative medal, the powers in London still clamored for a poem from him. "If you think this will acquit you . . ." wrote Vernon, "you will be mistaken, for they say you are not to come off with a posey and a shred from Horace. . . ."[33] We learn from a letter of Stepney's to his sisters that Prior had already bestirred himself: "As soon as the King gets to Holland, you will have one, a poem of Prior's making. I have just received a copy of it. The style is not heroic but very good of its sort."[34] This was evidently a hasty judgment, for a few days later Stepney tore the poem to pieces. Prior's criticism of Stepney's poem on the same subject had been likewise unsparing. Stepney's letter containing the criticism is very long; we quote only the best part:

I have carefully perused thy Ode and must honestly confess it is in my mind the worst piece I ever saw of yours. Do not think I speak this out of envy for your poetry, or in revenge for your severe reflexions you made on mine, but upon mature and impartial considerations.

[31] *Baker Papers*, (Royal Hist. MSS. Com. Report II, 71) Stepney to Tonson, Lipstadt, Feb. 14/24, 1695.

[32] *Lexington Papers*, 62, Prior to Lord and Lady Lexington, Hague, March 1, N. S., 1695.

[33] *Longleat Papers*, III, 50, Vernon to Prior, Whitehall, Apr. 19/29, 1695.

[34] P. R. O., *Stepney Papers*, 105/55, George Stepney to Frances and Dorothy Stepney, Dresden, Mar. 19/29, 1694/5.

After giving a general comment on the poem, Stepney made a specific examination of stanza after stanza, which he found full of absurd metaphors, unnatural rhymes, and incomprehensible passages. If too much haste had ruined his own poem, he thought, then too long dreaming had spoiled Prior's. He considered the motto—taken from Horace's ode on Virgil's grief for the unexpected death of Quintilius—the best part of the piece and suggested that it be printed alone.[35]

Much of "Catt's" criticism was beside the point. What he failed to notice was that Prior was using a conventional form that was unsuited to his genius. The poem was neither bombastic nor unduly flattering. The structure was simple and regular, and each stanza, in ballad meter, expressed a concise thought in clear and vigorous language. As the poem was not written until three months after Mary's death, there was more about William in it than about Mary: it sought to comfort the King by reminding him of his duties to the nation.[36] Prior held to his original intention to present the forty-one stanzas to the King, who was expected at The Hague in April. It was agreed that Tonson was to print them later. For the printer, Prior had no love; he even hoped the poem would remain unsold, he said, and thus contribute to the breaking of the "cur."[37] The King, he doubtless knew, would never read the tribute.

The recapture of Namur by the English and their allies later in the same year afforded Prior an opportunity to redeem himself from the failure of the poem on the Queen's death. Aptly appropriating for his motto the Horatian text, *dulce est desipere in loco*, he returned to the light bantering tone of his epistles to Fleetwood Sheppard and burlesqued Boileau's ode on the taking

[35] *Ibid.*, Stepney to Prior, Dresden, April 2/12, 1695. The motto to which Stepney referred is the opening stanza from Book I, Ode 24.

[36] "An Ode, Presented to the King, on His Majesty's Arrival in Holland, After the Queen's Death, 1695," *Poems on Several Occasions*, p. 35.

[37] *Trumbull Papers*, I, 465, Prior to Trumbull, Hague, April 16/26, 1695.

of Namur by the French three years previously. In this,[38] certainly one of his most successful poems, Prior turned each one of the pompous verses of Boileau against him. The French poet had taken great pains with his poem and considered it one of his best,[39] an opinion in which modern criticism, pronouncing it an "unfortunate bit of Pindarism," has not concurred. Prior wished to bring out his parody anonymously and enjoined Tonson to silence. "A secretary at thirty is hardly allowed the privilege of burlesque," he told his printer. To Tonson, Prior also gave minute instructions for the printing and for the distribution of his poem to all the politically important persons in London:

If you think this trifle worth your printing, 'tis at your service, and I recommend it to your care. I would have you therefore show it immediately to Mr. Montague . . . possibly he may alter a line or two in it, as he has either humour or leisure, to make it any way intelligible. You must print the French on one side, and with so much room between the stanzas as that the English may answer it, which you see is usually 12 lines, that is 3 alternate stanzas in English to one of 10 lines in French, tho sometimes it is but 8, and once but 4; I do not pretend it is an exact answer, nor do I care; 'tis only sense to those who understand the original, and probably may lye the lumber of your shop with some of my former works; but this is more immediately your business to consider. I will positively have no name set to it. . . . You may see what Sir Fleetwood says to it before you print it: maybe he may find some conceit better for a title than that I have given it, or another motto. Do all that as you will, but once more no name. Lose no time in this great affair and send a dozen over to me directed in a cover, à Monsieur Cardonnel, Secretaire de Monsieur Blathwayt, Secretaire de Guerre de sa Majesté, à la Hague: and then you must give 2 dozen to Mr. Chancellor of the Exchequer, which I have begged him to dispose of; in doing all this you may lose by publishing a bad piece, and will oblige, Sir, your most humble servant, M. Prior. Besides those I speak of for Mr. Montague, pray give one to everybody

[38] "An English Ballad, on the Taking of Namur, by the King of Great Britain, 1695," *Poems on Several Occasions*, p. 47.
[39] Boileau-Despréaux, *Œuvres*, p. 569, Boileau to Racine, June 4, 1693.

you did last time, except the Lords Justices and Lords of the Treasury, for Mr. Chancellor will do that himself.[40]

Secretary Trumbull did not agree with Prior in his insistence upon anonymity for the poem; he considered that the battering of Boileau's poem was as much to England's honor as was the bombarding of the castle and the taking of Namur.[41] With Trumbull's verdict, the Wits of the London coffeehouses readily agreed. With genuine relief they turned from the superabundance of dirges with their deep black borders and vapid verses to the new folio that had just issued from Tonson's bookshop, in which the French ode and the English ballad were printed side by side, declaring that "in wit as in arms England had been victorious."[42] The lively ballad meter, the gay trifling with Boileau's high-flown similes, the witty take-offs on the French generals, Boufflers and Villeroy, and the patriotic enthusiasm for King William—

> 'Tis Little WILL, the scourge of *France*;
> No Godhead, but the first of Men—

make the poem even today, in spite of its many allusions to forgotten events, the most readable of all the political poems of the decade.

When Prior reissued the poem, he carefully revised the text and improved many of the stanzas. Thus the first stanza in the 1695 version of the poem

> Was you not drunk, and did not know it,
> When you thought *Phoebus* gave you law?
> Or was it not, good Brother Poet,
> The chaste Nymph *Maintenon* you saw?
> She charm'd you sure, or what's the matter
> That Oaks must come from *Thrace* to dance?
> If Stocks must needs be taught to flatter
> You'll find enough of them in *France*[43]

---

[40] *Gentleman's Magazine*, N. S., II, 464, Prior to Tonson, Hague, Sept. 13/23, 1695.
[41] *Longleat Papers*, III, 64, Trumbull to Prior, Whitehall, Sept. 17/27, 1695.
[42] See Macaulay, *History of England*, V, 55.   [43] *Poems on Several Occasions*, p. 348.

became in all later editions

> Some Folks are drunk, yet do not know it:
> So might not BACCHUS give you Law?
> Was it a Muse, O lofty Poet,
> Or Virgin of St. CYR, you saw?
> Why all this Fury? What's the matter,
> That Oaks must come from *Thrace* to dance?
> Must stupid Stocks be taught to flatter?
> And is there no such wood in *France*?
> Why must the Winds all hold their Tongue?
> If they a little breath should raise;
> Would that have spoil'd the Poet's song;
> Or puff'd away the Monarch's praise?[44]

The discovery of the plot against the life of William in 1696 moved Prior to write another poem in praise of the King.[45] Prior's admiration for William was equaled only by his indignation at Louis, whom he imagined to be the instigator of the plot. Like the poems of his contemporaries on the same theme it is a poor effort and from first to last contains no lines that can compare with any in the poem on the taking of Namur.

» 3 «

To the year 1696 belongs a poem which Prior neglected to publish during his lifetime but which deserves to be ranked with the ode to Charles Montague, the song beginning "In vain you tell . . .," and the "English Ballad on the Taking of Namur," if it is not indeed superior to all of them. The manuscript title of the poem is "Written at The Hague in 1696," whereas the title by which it is generally known, "The Secretary," was not used until 1766, forty-five years after the poet's death.[46]

In "The Secretary" the poet described with happy phrasing

[44] *Ibid.*, p. 47.
[45] "Presented to the King, At His Arrival in Holland After The Discovery of the Conspiracy, 1696," *ibid.*, p. 53.   [46] *Poems on Several Occasions*, London, 1766, II, 65.

his sallying forth on a weekend in a little Dutch chaise, his
Horace in his left hand and a nymph at his right, to a retreat
where he might enjoy the delights of love undisturbed by dull
official duties and cares:

> While with labour assid'ous due pleasure I mix,
> And in one day atone for the bus'ness of six,
> In a little Dutch-chaise on a Saturday night,
> On my left hand my HORACE, a NYMPH on my right.
> No Memoire to compose, and no Post-Boy to move,
> That on Sunday may hinder the softness of love;
> For her, neither visits, nor parties of tea,
> Nor the long-winded cant of a dull refugée.
> This night and the next shall be her's, shall be mine,
> To good or ill fortune the third we resign:
> Thus scorning the world, and superior to fate,
> I drive on my car in processional state;
> So with PHIA thro' Athens PYSISTRATUS rode,
> Men thought her MINERVA, and him a new GOD.
> But why should I stories of Athens rehearse,
> Where people knew love, and were partial to verse,
> Since none can with justice my pleasures oppose,
> In Holland half drowned in in'trest and prose:
> By Greece and past ages, what need I be try'd,
> When the Hague and the present, are both on my side,
> And is it enough, for the joys of the day:
> To think what ANACREON, or SAPPHO would say.
> When good VANDERGOES, and his provident VROUGH,
> As they gaze on my triumph, do freely allow,
> That search all the province, you'd find no man there is
> So bless'd as the *Englishen Heer* SECRETARIS.[47]

Here is a jolly poem; the plaintive mood and the disappointments in love seem forgotten. The "nymph" was doubtless
"Flanders Jane," no cold, disdainful fair one but a woman who

> Eat and drank, Play'd & Work't, laught & Cry'd, lov'd & hated,
> As answer'd the end of her being Created—

so the poet said of her in a later piece.

[47] *Dialogues of the Dead*, p. 96.

Some editions of Prior's works offer the following variation of the last two lines of the poem with what Leigh Hunt called "its touch of yawning dialect":

> That, search all the province, you'll find no man *dar is*
> So bless'd as the *Englishen Heer Secretaris*.

But this version is not in any of the manuscripts at Longleat or Welbeck, nor in the *editio princeps* (*Miscellaneous Works*, 1740), nor in any edition of Prior's poems until that of 1766.

Thackeray was the first to comment that Prior wrote "The Secretary" "in a strain and with a grace not unworthy of his Epicurean master." In its gay and nimble anapaests the poem foreshadows the Cloe poems and other light pieces written in the author's happiest moods. Without doubt Horace and Cloe proved for Prior his luckiest inspirations.

CHAPTER V

"Fluttering about Paris"

» 1 «

AFTER King William had affixed his seal to the Treaty of Ryswick, he and his party set sail from The Hague in the middle of November, 1698. Long and noisy had been the demonstration that celebrated the peace; magnificent had been the ball in honor of the King's birthday. The triumphal progress of the party was eagerly followed in London, where further celebration had been planned. Upon the royal arrival, bells pealed forth the joy of the people that the long war was at an end. St. Paul's, the great unfinished church of Sir Christopher Wren's, opened its doors for the first time on December 2 to honor the signing of the treaty, and it was a day of wholehearted thanksgiving for the entire country.

Prior, too, was happy. After the long term of exile in Holland, where at times the uncertainty over his office and his insufficient remuneration had caused him much anxiety, he was overjoyed to be back in London. George Stepney had recently been appointed to a position on the Board of Trade and Plantations. He and Matt together called upon old friends in Channel Row. May we not forgive Matt if he felt the natural pride of the returning hero and basked in the warmth of his friends' approbation?

Changes in office, Prior learned, had been many. Charles Montague was now First Lord of the Treasury. Vernon had succeeded Trumbull as one of the two principal Secretaries of

State, and the powerful Whig Junto had driven Sunderland from his office.

Prior expected to be off to Ireland before Christmas to take up his duties as secretary to the Lords Justices,[1] but no sooner had he arrived in London than a sudden change was made in his plans. On November 29, Shrewsbury notified the Lords Lieutenant of Ireland that other duties would delay Prior's arrival in Dublin.[2]

The King was planning to reopen diplomatic relations with his former enemy, Louis XIV, by sending Lord Portland to Versailles as Ambassador Extraordinary. Prior, much to his surprise, was appointed secretary of the Embassy. So he did not go to Dublin after all, although he held the position there *in absentia* for about two and a half years. The new appointment was one that might well plant envy in the heart of every young diplomat in His Majesty's service, even though it was generally thought that the mission in Paris would be short-lived. Ten years of conflict had kept loyal Englishmen away from France. Here was an opportunity to see for oneself the glories of the Sun King, to gaze upon the wonders of Versailles. Little did Prior foresee that the most important years of his diplomatic career were to be spent in the French capital.

On December 11, the *Postman* announced his appointment.[3] A month later, January 11/21, the same news sheet reported that Lord Portland and his party had departed for Paris on the previous day.[4] King William spared no expense in making the Embassy magnificent so that his devoted minister might do him credit at the most splendid court of Europe. Eighty servants

---

[1] P. R. O. *Calendar of State Papers, Domestic*, 1697, p. 487. Richard Yard to Sir J. Williamson, Nov. 26, 1697: "Lord Jersey thinks of going for Ireland as one of the Lords Justices of that Kingdom soon after Christmas. Mr. Prior will go away sooner."

[2] *Ibid.*, p. 492, Shrewsbury to Lords Justices of Ireland, Nov. 29, 1697.

[3] The *Postman*, Dec. 9–11, 1697. "We hear that Matthew Prior, Esq. is appointed Secretary of the Embassy to France."

[4] *Ibid.*, Jan. 8–11, 1697/8: "Yesterday the Earl of Portland set forward for France, with the character of His Majesty's Ambassador Extraordinary."

and ninety carriages and saddle horses comprised Portland's equipage. Rapin, the historian, went along as tutor to the Earl's young son, Lord Woodstock; Jean de Robethon, as secretary for French affairs; and Dr. Martin Lister, as physician. Special secretaries had been ordered to Paris a month ahead to prepare for the coming of the Ambassador. Twelve young gentlemen of "honorable birth and ample fortune," among whom were Lord Raby, Colonel Stanhope, Spencer Compton, Christopher Codrington, and Charles Boyle, accompanied the Ambassador at their own expense. If the array of names is not so imposing as that of the company which the Duke of Buckingham took with him to Paris on a memorable errand for Charles II in 1670, when Dorset, Sedley, Dr. Sprat, and Samuel Butler were of the party, it was nevertheless representative of the young men of rank who were to become active in affairs in the duller, more prosaic days of Queen Anne and the first George. We cannot criticize William if more prominent men were lacking in Portland's train. The King had asked the great John Locke to go, but he declined the honor on account of ill health.[5]

The journey to Paris in the bitter cold weather took eleven days, the party finally reaching there late in the afternoon of January 31. The Ambassador was lodged in the Hôtel d'Auvergne in the Rue de la Planche, which the owner generously placed at his disposal. The gentlemen of his train found lodgings in the neighborhood. All met at mealtime in a dining hall hurriedly erected for the Ambassador in the gardens of the Hôtel, where any English traveler of character in Paris was welcome to dine.

Portland sent Prior to Versailles on the day after their arrival to present the Ambassador's compliments to Monsieur de Torcy, Secretary of State for Foreign Affairs. Prior gave Torcy a copy of Portland's credentials and one of his own commission. Torcy received Prior "with all the civility imaginable" and graciously signified his high esteem of Portland. Prior explained

[5] Bowen, *Luctor and Emergo*, pp. 29, 30.

that their public entry and audience would have to be post-poned because contrary winds and heavy ice on the Seine near Havre de Grâce held fast their boat, laden with the many carriages. He asked therefore, in Portland's name, for a private audience with Louis XIV, and an audience was arranged for February 4 at nine o'clock in the morning.[6]

The Ambassador and his party were then kept busy by a succession of diplomatic calls and formal social affairs. On the night before the audience they were entertained by Antoine, Duc de Grammont, at a fete at which the principal noblemen of the Court were introduced to the English visitors. The next morning Portland, Prior, and several other members of the group arose at dawn, donned their best raiment, and set out under Boufflers's escort on the fourteen mile drive to Versailles, where they had their audience with Louis XIV. Many more audiences with the members of the royal family followed—with "Monseigneur" (the Dauphin) and his three sons, the Duc de Bourgogne, the Duc d'Anjou and the Duc de Berry; with "Monsieur" (the King's brother and Duc d'Orléans) and "Madame" his wife. At one o'clock, there were other introductions, notably to Marie Adelaide, the charming but spoiled child wife of the Duc de Bourgogne. Dinner was served in Torcy's apartments for the English guests. Grammont, Tallard (the newly appointed Ambassador to England), and the Archbishop of Rheims were also present. Towards evening the visitors returned to Paris after what must have been an impressive day for Prior.

Within a few days Lord Portland and his party were special guests at a grand levee of the King's, a brilliant affair, typical of the splendor and lavishness of the Court of Versailles. The gay program of social activities was too strenuous for Prior, and he fell ill with a violent cold. He may have contracted it in the galleries of Versailles, a cold and drafty place in winter, where even the wine froze in the glasses at the King's table.

[6] *Journal de l'ambassade extraordinaire*, p. 4.

After he had regained his health and found time, he wrote to his friends and apologized for not having sent them as he had promised, his first impressions of Paris. Lord Dorset was genuinely concerned over Prior's illness: "I could almost wish you out of all public affairs that I might enjoy your good company oftener, and share with you in that ease and lazy quiet which I propose to myself in this later part of my life, either at home or in some warmer climate."[7] Matt joked about his illness with Montague and Jersey, telling them that he had been dying, but as matters stood with him at present he thought he could hold out some years longer; at least he was trying how far "patience and posset drink would help."[8] He had really been at death's door, but not liking the prospect he had made all imaginable haste to return.[9]

While confined to his room Prior turned to French history for reading. On the flyleaf of Mézeray's history of France[10] he wrote some Horatian verses reflecting the despondency of a man just recovering from a serious illness, yet wearily clinging to life:

> Whate'er thy Countrymen have done
> By Law and Wit, by Sword and Gun,
> In Thee is faithfully recited:
> And all the Living World, that view
> Thy Work, give Thee the Praises due,
> At once Instructed and Delighted.
>
> Yet for the Fame of all these Deeds,
> What Beggar in the *Invalides*,
> With Lameness broke, with Blindness smitten
> Wished ever decently to die,
> To have been either MEZERAY,
> Or any Monarch He has written?
>
> It strange, dear Author, yet it true is,
> That down from PHARAMOND to LOÜIS,

---

[7] *Longleat Papers*, III, 199, Dorset to Prior, London, March 6/16, 1698.
[8] *Ibid.*, 192, Prior to Montague, Paris, Feb. 8/18, 1698.
[9] *Ibid.*, 189, Prior to Jersey, Paris, Feb. 4/14, 1698.
[10] François Eudes de Mézeray, *Histoire de France*, 3 Vols., 1643–1651.

All covet Life, yet call it Pain:
All feel the Ill, yet shun the Cure:
Can Sense this Paradox endure?
Resolve me, CAMBRAY, or FONTAINE.

The Man in graver Tragic known
(Tho' his best Part long since was done)
Still on the Stage desires to tarry:
And He who play'd the *Harlequin,*
After the Jest still loads the Scene,
Unwilling to retire, tho' Weary.[11]

As Kerr remarks, "The *Invalides* here is an essential touch." One must see, he continues, "the veteran against Mansard's stately dome, the individual against the stately pageant of history."[12] We like to recall the affection which Scott, that later painter of "the stately pageant of history," had for the poem. Reminded of it towards the close of his life while traveling with Lockhart, he repeated the poem "without break or hesitation," and his son-in-law, who told the story, realized that Scott had been applying the lines to himself.[13]

The large number of secretaries employed in Lord Portland's service made it unnecessary for Matt to exert himself too greatly after his illness. "I have little more to do," he wrote, "than to make a leg thrice a day for my chocolate, my dinner and my supper, and run about the rest of my time as fast as two lean nags can carry me like Bartholomew Coates to gape or to buy, and pay my respects to rare company, monks, poets, tailors, academicians, nuns, seamstresses, booksellers and players."[14] His idleness, however, did not last. Portland set him to work copying his long epistles to King William.[15] On March 1, he

[11] "Written in the Beginning of Mezeray's History of France," *Poems on Several Occasions,* p. 99; *Longleat Papers,* III, 202, Prior to Dr. Aglionby, March 14/24, 1698.
[12] Kerr, *Restoration Verse,* p. 415.
[13] Quoted by Dobson in *Selected Poems of Matthew Prior,* p. lxix. Dobson observes that Scott seems to have known Prior by heart, for the lines from Mézeray came at the end of a long string of quotations from "Alma" and "Solomon."
[14] *Longleat Papers,* III, 190, Prior to Jersey, Feb. 4/14, 1698.
[15] For Portland's letters to William III in Prior's hand, see *Correspondendentie van Willem III en van Hans Willem Bentinck,* I, 234, *et seqq.*

was sent to Marly to invite the Princes and Princesses of the Blood to appear in the processional at Portland's grand public entry.[16] Matters of precedence proved difficult, as was usual on such occasions. Portland's coach, according to the plans of the *Introducteur des ambassadeurs*, was to follow that of the Duchesse de Verneuil, widow of a natural son of Henri IV. This arrangement did not satisfy Portland. He protested immediately and sent Prior back to the *Introducteur*, who finally arranged the order of carriages to the Ambassador's wishes.

When the much delayed ceremonial day came at last, it was one that did great credit to King William and to the crown he wore. William, rarely ostentatious, well knew the benefit to England of making a great display before the French. His Ambassador rode through Paris in a magnificent carriage, decorated with fluttering orange ribbons and drawn by eight Neapolitan grays in velvet trappings. The streets and balconies were lined with cheering throngs. No foreign minister had ever made such a superb entry. Behind him in the carriage of "Monsieur" rode Prior, accompanied by Lord Woodstock, Lord Raby, and the *escuyer* of "Monsieur." Prior kept an official record of the order of events for the use of future ambassadors but asked his correspondents to excuse him from giving them personal accounts, knowing that they were not without details of the ceremony, as it had been described fully in the *Gazette de France*.

Doubtless he was relieved that the long anticipated occasion was over and was glad to take up his work and resume correspondence with his friends. Montague, Jersey, Vernon, and Albemarle were the men at King William's Court most favored with Prior's letters about diplomatic affairs. We have looked almost in vain for any literary gossip from the poet-secretary. It appears, however, that he was not on intimate terms at this time with the Wits who frequented Will's Coffee House. Most

---

[16] *Journal de l'ambassade extraordinaire*, p. 15.

interesting for the general reader are those parts of his letters which record impressions of the French people.

» 2 «

Prior did not care for the French during this first visit to Paris. Later, in the days of the Tory ministry, he, like Bolingbroke and Swift, found the flattery of Louis and the French court gratifying. His prejudice against the French had probably originated during the war when he had heard at The Hague only the worst reports about the enemy. While Lord Portland's party was outwardly treated with great civility, Prior doubted the genuineness of the welcome accorded them. "These people," he wrote to Montague, "are all the same, civil in appearance and hating us to hell at the bottom of their hearts."[17] Even at the end of nine months he held the same opinion: "The generality of the nation are empty, superficial, ill people, just fit to be oppressed and misused as they are." He felt that the *lex talionis* was the only law to be applied in dealing with them.

Since the peace had been made from necessity alone, Prior was inclined to be distrustful of Louis and to watch his every move. At first he thought that Louis was reluctant to renew the struggle, at least until after the death of the Spanish King, Charles II. For this, Prior gave less credit to Louis than to Madame de Maintenon, who through her "incredible power ruled him [Louis] as absolutely as Roxalana did Solyman," and who kept him from war not because of friendliness toward England but because she feared that war was detrimental to his health. All business "went through her hands, and Diana at Ephesus made a much less figure than she did." Furthermore, she encouraged Louis in all his schemes of self-glorification. He lived "at Marly like an Eastern monarch, making waterworks and planting melons" and leaving "his bashas to ruin the land," provided they were constant in bringing in their tribute.[18]

[17] *Longleat Papers*, III, 204, Prior to Charles Montague, Paris, March 31/April 10, 1698.
[18] *Ibid.*, 207, Prior to Dorset, Paris, April 14/24, 1698.

The poverty and wretchedness of the people everywhere, the poet found heart-rending. The whole kingdom was poor, and all the wealth of it in the hands of *partisans* and *fermiers*, who had drained the people and were in turn to be squeezed by the government. Yet, in spite of the poverty on all sides, the common people displayed a strange veneration for their King. He might have their last sou "as well by their own inclination as his power *pour la gloire*." On the other hand, the people of quality hated him for his ruthless squandering of the resources of the country. There was nothing so extravagant as their expressions of resentment in an *auberge* at night, although they might as well be hanged as neglect to rise at five next morning to be at Versailles by eight.[19]

The beauty of the royal palaces and gardens made direct appeal to Portland, who frequently dwelt upon their loveliness in his letters to King William. Yet Prior visualized only a display of extravagance and royal vanity. Indeed, the vanity of the Sun King furnished him with some of his most telling witticisms, such as his characterization of Louis in his letter to Keppel, lately honored by William with the title of Earl of Albemarle: "Le Roy a beaucoup de santé pour un homme de soixante ans et plus de vanité qu'une fille de seize."[20]

A letter to Montague reveals less elegant thoughts on the King's personal vanity:

The monarch as to his health is lusty enough, his upper teeth are out, so he speaks a little like old Maynard,[21] and picks and shows his under teeth with a good deal of affectation, being the vainest creature alive even as to the least things. His house at Versailles is something the foolishest in the world; he is strutting in every panel and galloping over one's head in every ceiling, and if he turns to spit he must see himself in person or his Vicegerent the Sun with *sufficit orbi*, or *nec*

19 *Ibid.*, 192, Prior to Montague, Paris, Feb. 8/18, 1698.
20 *Ibid.*, 195, Prior to Albemarle, Paris, Mar. 1, 1697/8, N. S.
21 Sir John Maynard, famous lawyer.

pluribus impar. I verily believe that there are of him statues, busts, bas-reliefs and pictures above two hundred in the house and gardens.[22]

Such vanity could not be imputed to King William. One is here reminded of the old anecdote without which no account of Prior would be complete. While looking at the famous battle pieces by Le Brun in the galleries at Versailles, he was asked if King William's palace at Kensington had any decorations to match them. "The monuments of my master's actions," he is said to have replied proudly, "are to be seen everywhere but in his own house."[23]

In his Commonplace Book,[24] however, he has left more sober reflections, free from the malicious wit which he indulged in for the entertainment of his friends:

I was melancholy at Versailles and Marly to see such magnificence in the house and gardens, and such poverty and beggary around. His statues indeed are as if they were alive, and if it did not look too much like a turn, I would say his subjects look like statues.[25]

Louis Bertrand, modern French royalist, denounces criticism of Louis XIV for his wanton extravagance as vulgar democratic sentimentality. "There will always be peasants who through fault of their own or someone else's are hungry and homeless," he exclaims, "but there is only one Versailles and one Marly; and only one man could have built them."[26] Other critics have accused Louis XIV himself of committing a more grievous democratic fault, that of confusing size with grandeur. Prior was no sentimental democrat even though the thought of the blood and tears spilt in the building of Versailles made him melancholy; nor would he have seen how vulgar and bourgeois was Louis's

[22] *Longleat Papers*, III, 192, Prior to Charles Montague, Paris, 8/18, 1697/8.
[23] *History of His Own Time*, p. 30.
[24] Welbeck Abbey, Prior MSS, *Miscellanys in Prose and Verse by Matthew Prior, Esq.*, a quarto volume in vellum with title page in the handwriting of Prior's secretary, Adrian Drift.
[25] *Ibid.*, "Commonplace Book with Notes and Sketches in Prose and Verse by Matthew Prior."
[26] Louis Bertrand, *Louis XIV*, p. 208.

taste for mere bigness, since such terms were unknown in his day. Yet his sturdy British common sense was shocked both by the sufferings of the people and by the inordinate vanity which plunged Louis into delusions of grandeur.

» 3 «

Prior next turned to gossip about members of the royal family, using his pen freely and somewhat viciously. The Dauphin, whom he saw at the lovely palace of Meudon, he thought a little like Prince George of Denmark in his dullness and apathy—perhaps not so sober, however, for, while Princess Anne's consort kissed no one except her, "Monseigneur" kissed "toutes les filles de l'opera sans distinction." He aptly described the beribboned, berouged "Monsieur" (Philip of Orleans, brother of the King) as a *"petite marionette* with a cracked voice, who chatters much and says nothing."[27] "Madame," the blunt, honest Elizabeth Charlotte, was, unlike the feather-brained "Monsieur," no target for satire and thus escaped the malice of Prior's pen. German born and bred, she had long been in France, but was not of it. Throughout her life she remained wholly German. She delighted in chatting with Portland about her friends and kinsmen in Germany, including her aunt, the Electress Sophia of Hanover. Years earlier she had vainly cast her eyes on King William with matrimonial intent. Soon after Queen Mary's death she even broached the topic of marriage between William and her daughter, the young Duchesse de Chartres. When this plan failed, she declared, "I have come to the conclusion that religion spoils many things in this world."[28] Despite these rebuffs and the influence of the Court of France, she remained William's well-wisher for many years. Yet she

[27] *Longleat Papers*, III, 195, Prior to Albemarle, Paris, Feb. 19, March 1, 1697/8.

[28] *The Correspondence of Elizabeth Charlotte of Bavaria, Princess Palatine, Duchess of Orleans, called Madame at the Court of Louis XIV*, ed. by Gertrude Stevenson, I, 145. The Princess Palatine to the Duchess of Hanover, Nov. 11, 1696.

freely spoke her mind. "Un roi n'est pas un ange,"[29] she once wrote to Portland, and she took his side in the final break between him and William.

Prior seldom mentions Madame de Maintenon except, as we have seen, as the strict *gouvernante* of the King. Apparently he did not even guess at her actual position at the Court as the morganatic wife of Louis. The announcement that her niece was to marry the eldest son of the Duc de Noailles amazed him. In writing of the reception which Madame de Maintenon held for the princesses and ladies of the Court on this occasion, Prior delighted in malicious talebearing:

She was in her bed; the Duchess of Burgundy came into her chamber, had a chair set for her, but did not sit; all of which mummery was concerted beforehand; and consequently the other ladies could not sit whilst the Duchess stood. Thus, my Lord, this woman is a *je ne sçay quoy*, which everybody reasons of as he thinks good, and of whom nobody can determine what character she really has.[30]

What has seemed like obtuseness on his part is easily accounted for: Portland and his company never had an audience with Madame de Maintenon. Patroness of the royal exiles at Saint-Germain, she declined to see the English Ambassador or any of his train. Was not Portland the official representative of the heretic king who had usurped the throne of the good and pious James, martyr to the holy Roman religion? Although granddaughter of Agrippa d'Aubigné, Huguenot poet and fighter, she became the greatest foe of heresy, more bigoted than any cleric.

With Torcy, Louis's experienced and able Minister of Foreign Affairs, Prior was to have many contacts. After their first few interviews he all too hastily came to the conclusion that Torcy was utterly lacking in ability and that he held his position only

[29] *Correspondentie van Willem III en van Hans Willem Bentinck*, II, 324, The Princess Palatine to Portland, Fontainebleau, October 1, 1699.

[30] *Longleat Papers*. III, 202, Prior to the Earl of Manchester, Paris, March 25/April 4, 1697/8.

because he had been born a Colbert and had married the daughter of Pomponne. Later Prior very sensibly changed his opinion.

The royal exiles at Saint-Germain occupied a great deal of his attention. Louis's hospitality towards them and their vain hopes of returning to England amused and annoyed Prior in turn. He sent every scrap of gossip which came to him by divers channels to the secretaries in London. Often the news he received from spies or malcontents was not worth the trouble of sending, and he learned at Paris, as Vernon did in London, that mere impostors were offering up their spurious tales of Jacobite plots for gold. He was deeply troubled that Louis could receive King William's Ambassador and entertain James and Mary on the very same day. It seemed to him a proof of duplicity on the part of the French King, a sign that he did not intend to keep the peace.

The members of the Embassy were constantly exasperated to encounter in the Paris taverns and in the antechambers at Versailles men who had, two years earlier, plotted William's assassination. Prior considered it a disgrace that such "outlaws and cutthroats" were harbored at Saint-Germain. The most precarious commission entrusted to Portland was to induce Louis to remove James from France, or at least as far from England as Avignon. The rumor that Louis was planning to live at Saint-Germain because it was "his native air and more proper to him than Versailles"[31] led Portland to believe that his task would not be a difficult one. As time passed, however, Prior became convinced that such hopes were vain. No diplomatic urging would be of any avail so long as Madame de Maintenon befriended the exiled monarchs. The Duc de Lauzun, James's French adviser, attempted to insinuate himself into Prior's good graces with the object, so Prior believed, of finding out when Queen Mary's pension of 50,000 pounds, promised at Ryswick, would be paid. King William was withholding pay-

[31] *Ibid.*, 194, Prior to Vernon, Feb. 18/28, 1697/8.

ment of this sum until he should be satisfied with the behavior of the Court at Saint-Germain. Their conduct, Prior explained to Lauzun, could not be satisfactory so long as they daily received people from England and sent thither others forbidden by the laws, and at the same time concealed and underhandedly encouraged men suspected or convicted of the "most horrid parricide and assassination that ever was intended."[32]

In spite of assurances to Lauzun that the English government pitied James rather than feared him, Prior was apprehensive about the "nest of rogues" at Saint-Germain. He was constantly on the alert for signs of any new villainy that might be hatching. The Jacobites themselves received with savage oaths the news that Portland was striving to have them removed from Saint-Germain. "The Duke of Berwick and his myrmidons threaten us with fire and sword," Prior wrote to Vernon. He took a malicious delight in forwarding whatever news would discredit the royal exiles in the eyes of his superiors in London. The rival factors at the shabby Court—the Middletonians and the Melfordians, whom he whimsically called the Whigs and Tories, were always fighting among themselves:

Three or four fellows have been killed last week at Saint Germains by their countrymen and comrades . . . thus disorders and murders reign where this unhappy man lives, and his domestic affairs are governed just as his three kingdoms would have been.[33]

All these disturbances induced Prior to maintain a sizable army of spies; to engage in considerable spying, himself, among the Paris coffeehouses; to become acquainted, as he said, with half the starving English and Irish about Paris.

It was inevitable that Prior should sometime or other meet King James and his party at the French Court. Portland, who remained in France less than five months, studiously avoided

---

[32] *Ibid.*, 252, Prior to Portland, Paris, Aug. 12/22, 1698.
[33] *Ibid.*, 233, Prior to Portland, Paris, July 5/15, 1698.

them, always absenting himself from Court functions whenever he expected James to be present. This pleased James so much that he declared that "the rebels dare not look him in the face, and that he never saw above one or two of Bentinck's crew." Jersey, who succeeded Portland, was equally successful, although he escaped meeting James at Versailles by only a quarter of an hour on the day that he had his private audience with Louis XIV.[34]

Prior was not so cautious as his superiors. One afternoon King Louis with his Court and the ministers from all the foreign courts went to Saint-Cloud to be present at the christening of the infant child of the Duc de Chartres. Prior decided to attend the ceremony out of courtesy to the child's grandparents, "Monsieur and Madame," who, being less under Madame de Maintenon's sway, were more friendly than any of the others to "Bentinck's crew." He afterwards sent to Vernon the following account of the occasion:

I saw King James and his Queen (pray do not hang me for so doing), and there was nothing so odd as to see the Duke of Berwick and Lord Middleton traversing the gallery on one side, and I [*sic*] and Lord Reay, of the good Mackay brood, on the other side, each looking on the other with an air of civility mixed with contempt. The gentlemen belonging to the Duke d'Orléans and Chartres were embarrassed enough to call him one moment *le roy d'Angleterre* to them, and speak to me the next of *le Roy Jacques*: it was, as most human things are, a farce ridiculous enough . . .[35]

On the same subject, he wrote to Montague:

I faced old James and all his Court the other day at Saint Cloud, *Vive Guillaume!* You never saw such a strange figure as the old bully is, lean, worn, and rivel'd; not unlike Neal the Projector; the Queen looks very melancholy, but otherwise well enough; their equipages are all very ragged and contemptible.[36]

[34] *Buccleuch Papers*, II, 624, Jersey to Shrewsbury, Paris, Sept. 21/Oct. 1, 1698.
[35] *Longleat Papers*, III, 257, Prior to Vernon, Aug. 17/27, 1698.
[36] *Ibid.*, 259, Prior to Montague, Aug. 20/30, 1698.

Prior's curiosity about the royal household was not satisfied until he saw still another member of the ill-fated family, the mysterious young Stuart Prince, now a child of ten, whom some doubting Thomases still believed to be a supposititious child. Few Englishmen, except James's loyal adherents, had seen the child since the bleak stormy night when Lauzun had guided the infant and mother safely out of London and escorted them to France to place them under the protection of Louis XIV. One afternoon, as the Prince passed through the great apartments at Versailles, accompanied by Lord Perth and Lord Melford, Prior saw for the first time the child whom they called the "Prince of Wales." These two Jacobite ministers, somewhat astonished to encounter an Englishman who did not pay his respects to their royal charge, stared at Prior and then whispered something to the young Prince. The child looked back at Prior, but, receiving no gesture of homage, passed on down the long corridor, stopping to say his prayers and to cross himself before the altar. Prior told Portland and Vernon that the boy, while not handsome, was very lively, and a true papist. The child was being brought up with all the abhorrence imaginable to heresy, Prior said, and no Protestant servant of any condition whatsoever was permitted to come near him. This chance meeting gratified Prior's curiosity, and we hear no more of encounters with the exiles at Saint-Germain.

» 4 «

By the end of April, Portland was planning to return to England. The government had spent fifty thousand pounds on his Embassy, and the young men in his train had used their own money lavishly. Prior's paltry three hundred pounds advance money was gone, and he was obliged to call upon Montague for funds from the Treasury. Ill in health and idle—Portland was oversupplied with secretaries—Prior was likewise anxious to be recalled. Paris was expensive. His duties were unimportant. He dreaded a repetition of the unhappy experiences he had suffered in Holland. Moreover, the royal exiles at Saint-Germain cramped his sociable nature. Although Versailles would be more gay now that the melancholy and sober observance of Lent was over, he could attend no social affairs at Versailles to which King James and Queen Mary were invited.

In spite of Prior's eagerness to return to England, the ministry had other plans for him. He was ordered to remain in charge of the Embassy until Portland's successor should come to Paris. Disappointed at such a turn in his affairs, Prior blamed Portland for his ill-fortune and turned to the Ambassador's rival for sympathy. Portland had promised Prior to write to William concerning an increase in his salary. Impatiently Prior poured fourth his grievances to Albemarle in a letter inexcusably ungenerous and disloyal:

Il me promet même d'en écrire au Roy, d'en parler, de la faire, et tout ce qu'on voudra, mais on oublie quelque fois les choses où on n'est pas visiblement intéressé?[37]

It seems incredible that Prior should have put so much trust in the self-indulgent Albemarle. Portland's rival was, however, Jersey's intimate friend; besides, his influence with the King was in the ascendancy. Although Portland had written promptly as he had promised, Albemarle might understand better than he the plight of a secretary *ad interim* in Paris with too meager funds to cut a figure in the diplomatic circles of the French Court when he would no longer have recourse to the Ambassador's table, but would have to take his meals in an *auberge*, would have to go on foot to the French ministers, and would have to maintain a secretariat with two servants, whereas the Embassy had had eighty lackeys.

News that Jersey had been appointed to succeed Portland cheered the despondent Matt, even though he expected that he would be kept in Paris so long as Jersey remained there. He was

---

[37] *Ibid.*, 211–212, Prior to Albermarle, Paris, Apr. 23/May 3, 1698.

still worried over the meagerness of his salary. "Dear Horace! I have a sentence of him upon most occasions," he wrote to Montague, "but I find nothing applicable to staying in Paris upon 40s. a day where one's coach costs one *louis* and one's lodgings another, before I or mine have eat or drank."[38]

Portland did not at once leave for England but remained in Paris incognito until June 18. Prior's movements during these weeks are not accounted for, owing to a break in his correspondence. Perhaps he accompanied Portland to Fountainebleau, whose natural beauty Portland greatly admired, or perhaps he assisted the Ambassador on wearisome shopping expeditions when furniture must be selected, especially beds and brocatelles, to suit the royal Master's taste. Prior's resentment toward Portland seems to have cooled. "Let them jumble up my fortune as they please," he wrote to Montague, "there is a fate in things which overcomes all human forecast, and Providence may turn up for us what we never thought of for ourselves."[39] He must have considered it an especial favor when he was asked to accompany Portland on his homeward journey as far as Chantilly, there to be the guest for three days of the Prince de Condé.[40] In the mornings they rode out to see the beauties of the place; in the afternoons they hunted wild boar; in the evenings they were entertained with music and dancing.

"Monsieur le Prince" was no great military leader like his illustrious father, the great Condé, but took infinite pains with Chantilly, constantly striving to improve its beauty. Much of the conversation over the meat and the wine—the best Prior had tasted in France—concerned future plans for the Prince's estate. Portland later sent to Condé, through Prior, a plan of the labyrinth at Sorgvliet, which they had discussed during this visit.

[38] *Ibid.*, 216, Prior to Montague, Paris, May 11/21, 1698.
[39] *Ibid.*, 215, Prior to Montague, Paris, May 11/21, 1698.
[40] Henri Jules de Bourbon, son of the great Condé.

Upon his return from Chantilly, Prior discovered that Lord Clare,[41] one of King James's "gang," had moved into his lodging house during his absence. Fearing that Lord Clare's servants might steal his papers and money, Prior had his valuables removed to safer keeping and forbade his servants to have anything to do with Lord Clare's.[42] This was not the first time that Jacobites had encamped near him. Suspicious of their designs, he decided to take a house of his own, where he might be unmolested by these rogues.[43]

It was now early summer and there was little official business. The Court went the round of the royal palaces and finally attended the military review at Compiègne. Louis took a rest from what he called "le métier de Roi," and forbade anyone to interfere with his pleasure. Prior remained in Paris, busying himself with routine secretarial affairs and attending to errands for Portland. He must keep an eye upon the Jacobites and report to the Secretaries in London the names of all the English who visited the royal exiles. Samuel Pepys's nephew came over to Paris, and Vernon was sure that Uncle Samuel had "sent no underhand compliments to his old master, having professed to the contrary," but, "since young men and ladies might sometimes be libertines and forget good advice," he wanted Prior to look after the young Pepys. These fears proved groundless. Prior was able to assure Vernon that the young man had conducted himself innocently enough and that he had not gone near Saint-Germain. Of somewhat greater diplomatic importance were the memorials the secretary submitted to Torcy for the reclamation of merchant ships taken during the war and for the freeing of Protestants from the French galleys. Portland knew that Prior was not busy and thus expected him to relay every bit of gossip about their friends and the Court. The errands he left for Prior to attend to were various. He had to

---

[41] Brother-in-law to the Duke of Berwick.
[42] Strong, *Letters . . . at Welbeck*, p. 251.
[43] *Longleat Papers*, III, 242, Prior to Portland, Paris, July 14/24, 1698.

prod Rigaud to complete the ex-Ambassador's portrait, to remind Lenôtre to send plans for the gardens at Windsor, and to procure from Mansard drawings for the King's houses in Holland.

Paris itself was dull in the summer. During the season the English gentlemen had been delighted with the light rollicking comedies of Regnard, Dancourt, and Dufresny, the contemporary dramatists, as well as with the more brilliant works of Racine, Molière, and Corneille. Now the *Comédie Française* was closed, and Prior was disappointed at finding only one opera to attend. "Everybody goes four times a week to the opera," he told Montague, "to see Bellerophon kill the Chimera"—quite tiresome for the "dog days," he thought.[44]

Earlier in the season he had heard an opera called *L'Europe Galante*[45] at the *Palais Royal*, which portrayed how the French, Spanish, Italians, and Turks made love. The French, who visited the opera so often that they acquired the habit of following the singer, were actors almost as much as those employed upon the stage. At the opera Prior sat next to a man who was enthusiastically accompanying the singer with his own voice. Prior began to rail at the performer on the stage, using all the terms of reproach at his command, until the Frenchman, ceasing from song, expostulated with Prior for such harsh censure of one who was confessedly the ornament of the stage. "I know all that," said Prior, "but he sings so loud that I cannot hear you."[46]

His observations of the French theater influenced his reaction to the violent controversy provoked in England at the moment by Jeremy Collier's indictment of the profaneness and immorality of the English stage. In his Commonplace Book he set

---

[44] Bodleian Library, SC. 25427, *MS Montague*, d. 1, fo. 99, Prior to Montague, Paris, July 30/Aug. 9, 1698. The opera was Lully's *Bellérophon*, a *tragédie lyrique* in 5 acts and a prologue.

[45] By André Campra. An opera ballet in 4 acts and a prologue.

[46] Dr. Johnson's "Life of Prior" in *Lives of the Poets*, ed. George Birkbeck Hill, II, 199.

down his opinion that Collier was not much in the wrong; that English plays were too licentious, and that dramatists affronted the people when they declared that they "wrote baudy" because nothing else would take. The French would not tolerate such license, he commented, not because they were squeamish, for they were as bad as the English, but because their sense of decorum forbade them to violate the rules of good taste. He agreed that the clergy should not be defamed in drama; on the other hand, he felt that Collier was too touchy about the abuse of the worthies of the cloth. Furthermore, the eulogies upon the parsons amounted to so many panegyrics upon Collier himself.[47]

We should like to find other comment on the current literary topics and figures of the day. However, we may remind ourselves that the sun of French classicism had already set. Paris was no longer the Paris of the four great masters of classical poetry who had brought so much luster to the earlier half of Louis's reign. Gone were the days when, at the *Mouton Blanc* or at the *Croix de Lorraine*, Boileau, Molière, Racine, and La Fontaine gathered to discuss the principles and practice of their art. Racine and Boileau were still living and still great friends, but all too soon Boileau would be left to live on at his villa in Auteuil, a solitary figure, a relic of a golden day. Prior wrote without comment to John Ellis of Racine's death in April 1699.[48] It was not until the summer of that year that Prior became acquainted with Boileau. A very plausible reason for his not having enjoyed earlier the acquaintance of the *Beaux Esprits* is found in the letter to Montague from which we have already quoted:

There is some tolerable satisfaction in the company of some of their men of Learning, but those who expect most preferment from Court are a little shy of being much with me.

Amusing comment on other subjects is to be found in the

---

[47] Welbeck Abbey, Prior MSS.
[48] Brit. Mus., *Add. MSS*, 28,928, fo. 112, Prior to John Ellis, Paris, April 12/22, 1699.

correspondence of some English visitors to Paris at the turn of the century. The callow young Addison, starting out on his tour of the continent in August, 1699, was amazed at the lack of modesty among the froward French hussies and wrote to Montague that he had scarcely seen a blush since he left Calais.[49] Interestingly enough, Prior had communicated similar but infinitely more worldly observations to Montague a year earlier:

The women here are all practiced jades, *unam cogneras omnes noras*; they are all painted and instructed so that they look like one another. They have nothing of nature nor passion. The men neglect them and make love to each other to a degree that is incredible, for you can pick your boy at the Tuileries or at the play.[50]

The palace gardens were a favorite promenade for the English gentlemen who had come over with Portland. Even the good Dr. Lister found the middle walk in the Tuileries betwixt eight and nine of an evening in June the most agreeable place in the world.[51] Most probably he did not notice the girls on patrol duty there, whose charms furnished Prior with many an idle story for his friends in London.

« 5 »

Prior was growing tired of his "imaginary honours" and was eager to turn them over to Lord Jersey, whose arrival in Paris was delayed by illness. He continued to nag Portland about an increase of salary. This came in due time, and as he had wished, it dated from his departure from London, but was in the form of bounty money, lest it should establish a precedent.[52] While waiting for his increase, he dunned Montague for the five hundred pounds due him as arrears. He described himself as cutting a

[49] *Ibid.*, 7121, Addison to Montague, Paris, Aug. 1699.
[50] Bodleian Library, SC. 25,427, *MS Montague*, d. 1., fo. 99, Prior to Charles Montague, Paris, Aug. 9, N.S., 1698.
[51] Lister, *An Account of Paris at the close of the Seventeenth Century.*
[52] *Correspondentie van Willem III en van Hans Willem Bentinck*, II, 95, Portland to Vernon, Sept. 5, 1698. See also Vernon's reply, *ibid.*, 98.

comical figure, "fluttering about Paris in a gilt chariot with three footmen in gay coats" while the "galoonman, the taylor, the harness-maker, the coachman" hovered about his back door and grew troublesome.[53]

While Jersey was recovering from his illness, Prior rented and furnished a house for him. Like his own *maisonnette*, as he called it, it was in the Marais, "dans le plus mauvais endroit de la ville," none being available elsewhere. To justify his choice he did all he could to make the apartments charming, and to divert (so he told Albemarle) "la petite colère de Madame." For this cause, he had been "vitrier, blanchisseur, menuisier," in turn. He had again sent to England for "Flanders Jane" and had installed her as housekeeper in his own little house, as he had done in Holland. To Montague he confided that "a certain distemper that was very epidemical" made this change in his domestic life desirable. Rumor spread among the young secretaries in London that a Miss Cross with whom he had a *liaison* was also one of his domestics, but it was doubted that he could keep a pair in his house who could live amicably together.[54] Like the "palace" in Duke Street in later days, the house in the Marais was a place where his friends might appease their hearty English appetites with boiled mutton and custards.

The arrival of Lord and Lady Jersey in September revived for Prior something of the social gaiety of the last years at The Hague. Although Jersey's Embassy was not so lavish or so expensive as Portland's, Lord and Lady Jersey were friendly and hospitable. Unlike the sober Calvinist Portland, they liked the French and found them good people to live with. A Roman Catholic, Lady Jersey adapted herself more successfully to French society than Portland had. The Embassy became the link between English and French society. As time passed, more English men and women found their way to Paris. Lady Jersey

[53] Bodleian Library, SC. 25,427, *MS Montague*, d. 1., fo. 99, Prior to Montague, Paris, Aug. 9, N. S., 1698.

[54] *Longleat Papers*, III, 321, Richard Powys to Prior, Whitehall, March 2/12, 1698/9.

was joined by other fine ladies from England, such as Lady Falkland, Lady Sandwich, Lady Salisbury, some of whom secretly paid their respects to the exiles at Saint-Germain. She became dissatisfied with the quarters in the Marais, and demanded a more fashionable house in the exclusive Faubourg Saint-Germain. Jersey's public entry and reception were very ordinary compared with Portland's. Few of the many civilities heaped upon the brother-in-law were shown to Jersey. Tallard had written to Louis XIV that Jersey was an agreeable man but one of very limited understanding, adding that Lady Jersey was the cleverer of the two.

For Jersey's entry Prior had purchased new clothes, new equipages. The occasion was so devoid of splendor that the new finery hung unused in his closet, and he looked about for other ceremonials which his trappings might adorn. He begged Portland to secure for him the special envoyship to Nancy. The Duc de Lorraine had recently married the Duchesse de Chartres, daughter of "Monsieur" and "Madame." Prior thought that his qualifications were strong. Nancy was in his province, he was "known to the Duchess in person," he might gain some knowledge of the constitution and inclination of the Court at Nancy which might be of value to a secretary at the French Court.[55] To his keen disappointment, however, he was passed over in favor of Richard Hill and had to be satisfied with witnessing in Paris the marriage of the young lady, "virtuous and well educated, not handsome but very agreeable," to the Duke, of whom he did not hear great praise.

All during October Jersey remained away from Court at Fontainebleau for fear of meeting Louis's guests from Saint-Germain. Finally, Prior, who was impatiently idling his time away in Paris while all the other ministers were at Fontainebleau, thought he saw early in November what would mean the resumption of diplomatic activities. Directions came from

[55] *Ibid.*, 299, Prior to Portland, Nov. 28/Dec. 8, 1698.

King William in Holland for Jersey to go to Fontainebleau, where he and Prior arrived late one evening. Prior sought out Torcy immediately to tell him that Jersey desired an audience with the King that very night. Torcy replied at first that it would be impossible for the King to grant an interview; already he was being prepared for his devotions on the morrow, which was All Saints' Day. Jersey acquainted Torcy with the reason for his sudden appearance, whereupon a private audience was arranged for ten o'clock that night. On the following morning Jersey and Prior returned to Paris, and Jersey immediately took post for Loo, conveying to King William the French King's resolutions to keep the peace.[56]

What was the exact reason for Jersey's sudden departure for Holland? The correspondence of Prior does not enlighten us. In a letter to Winchester, he hinted at two purposes but, fearful that the French might open his letter, pleaded forgiveness for not writing more explicitly. He intimated that the journey had something to do with the plans of William and Louis for avoiding a war on the death of the King of Spain, or that it concerned instructions for Jersey's conduct toward King James.[57] Tallard attributed the real cause of Jersey's summons to Loo to a new turn in the relations between William and his two Dutch favorites; and Tallard was invariably right.[58]

This turn was precipitated by Portland's request that d'Allone (formerly Queen Mary's secretary and later one of Portland's in Paris) be made Secretary of Dutch Affairs, an office which Albemarle regarded as his own private property; thereupon the spoiled favorite withdrew from court and sulked in the country. The appointment was regarded in some quarters as a sign of Portland's return to royal favor. Prior wrote d'Allone a lively letter of congratulation, saying "now at least I know if a man

---

[56] *Ibid.*, 282, Prior to Portland, Paris, Oct. 24/Nov. 3, 1698.

[57] *Ibid.*, 288, Prior to the Marquis of Winchester, Paris, Nov. 4/14, 1698.

[58] Grimblot, *Letters of William III and Louis XIV*, II, 182, Tallard to Louis XIV, November 3, 1698.

has extraordinary virtue and merit when the King in the face of all the world does me the justice to confirm my opinion."[59] Tallard, who reported to Louis XIV all the gossip of the English Court, informed his master that Jersey, as the most intimate friend of Albemarle, had been summoned to effect a reconciliation between William and his former favorite. D'Allone was, accordingly, to take his orders from Albemarle, instead of directly from the King. Tallard pictured endless disputes resulting from such an arrangement, for he foresaw that d'Allone's devotion to the Earl of Portland was so great that it would be out of the question for him to take his orders from Lord Albemarle.

In spite of the fact that Jersey's peregrination in behalf of Albemarle was interpreted as having grave diplomatic importance, negotiations concerning the Spanish succession were all the time being conducted between William III and Louis XIV through the medium of Tallard, the astute and wise French Ambassador. These negotiations were begun, even before Tallard went to London, through the efforts of Portland, whose mission to Paris had been no mere complimentary one but had involved the serious question of the peace of Europe after the death of the imbecile King of Spain, Charles II.

About these negotiations Prior knew very little, although ever since he had arrived in Paris he had kept a vigilant eye on the affairs in Spain and had frequently filled his letters to Montague with comments upon the health of Charles II, which he considered a barometer watched by all the politicians to determine whether peace or war was in the offing. Unless some agreement should be reached before the death of the Spanish King, war was inevitable; hence the interest in the bulletins from the King's bedside.

The question of the Spanish succession was complicated. In view of the fact that not only the Electress of Bavaria but also

[59] *Longleat Papers*, III, 288, Prior to Abel d'Allone, Paris, Nov. 4/14, 1698.

the Dauphin of France and the Archduke of Austria were rival claimants to the throne, William hoped that some agreement would be reached before the demise of the King. According to his first will, Charles II had ceded his vast possessions in Spain, Italy, the Netherlands, and America to Joseph Ferdinand, the young Bavarian Prince. Towards the middle of July, Tallard brought to William proposals from Louis which furnished the basis of the treaty as it was signed by Portland and Sir Joseph Williamson at The Hague in October. By this treaty, afterwards known as the First Partition Treaty, the main part of the Spanish inheritance—Spain, the Netherlands, and the possessions in America—was to go to the Electoral Prince Joseph Ferdinand of Bavaria, but important consolation prizes were assigned to France and Austria. Milan was to go to the Austrian claimant, while Naples and Sicily were to be added to the French crown.

The news of the death of the eight-year-old Joseph Ferdinand in February upset all the plans William had carefully laid. Rumors came to Prior that certain French factions were for setting Louis's grandson, the Duc de Berry, upon the Spanish throne "without any doubts or difficulty." He was therefore alarmed by the latest word from England that Parliament was disbanding the army, for he feared that England would be unable to hold longer the balance of power. Lest his correspondents should make light of his apprehensions, he justified them on the ground that English diplomats abroad did not see things as did those at Westminster.

Paris was alive with comment on the reduction of King William's troops, and at Saint-Germain crowds of noisy Jacobites in *café* and *auberge* drank publicly the healths of the parliamentary leaders.[60] All such demonstrations of satisfaction vexed the patriotic Matt, whose peace of mind was further disturbed when Villeroy began to ply him with questions as to how the English could look for respect or make alliances while they

[60] *Longleat Papers*, III, 314, Prior to Montague, Paris, Feb. 1/11, 1698/9.

could not possibly come to their neighbor's assistance with a single man or how they could hold the balance of power in Europe while there was possibility of invasion any day.[61]

Ever since Portland's departure Villeroy had been manifesting a curiosity about English political affairs extraordinary in a Frenchman. He was aware that King William was at the moment at odds with his Parliament. The death of Queen Mary had cut the only tie that had held a large number of his subjects, particularly the Tories. Parliament had reduced his army to a meager seven thousand men, had compelled him to reduce his Dutch Guards, and to cancel Irish land grants to his favorites. The *Maréchal* did not fail to gloat over the breaking of William's troops. Prior countered by discoursing on the nature of the English government and on the action of preceding Parliaments and convinced Villeroy for a time, at least, that the move of the present Parliament was not to be interpreted as favoring "the people at Saint Germans." Prior was certain that Villeroy hated the English heartily, and he knew that his answers did not satisfy the General for long.[62]

Prior was viewing English political affairs in a new light. His Whiggism, hitherto uncritically accepted, was being weakened by Villeroy's persistent catechizing. Jersey's High Tory opinions, too, doubtless influenced Prior. The French monarchy offered an example of a strong, stable government which ruled without party faction. Why might not so strong a government be established in England under the beneficent rule of William, "the greatest man and kindest master in the world"? As a result of these reflections, Prior was emboldened to write a long letter to Portland, who, as a Dutchman, had no party ties and who, as a close friend of William's, would be sympathetic to any suggestions for strengthening his royal master's hands. In the letter Prior told Portland that the King's interests suffered

[61] *Ibid.*, 313, Prior to Portland, Paris, Feb. 1/11, 1698/9.
[62] *Ibid.*, 329, Prior to Portland, Paris, April 1, 1699.

because some of his ministers were more loyal to their party interests than to their monarch. Prior not only advocated a strong monarchy but attacked the Latitudinarian divines (mentioning Bishop Burnet by name) and expressed distrust of popular will. Could there be any difference, he asked, if the "nation were hurt by bad subjects or by a bad king"? And had not the nation suffered as much from popular rage in 1645 as from arbitrary power in 1688? Furthermore, Prior declared that the speech of the King on his accession, in which he promised to sustain the greatness of the monarchy, was more pleasing to his subjects than any made since. The mass of the English people, Prior said, loved the glory of the monarchy and, if rightly handled, would uphold the King.[63]

Such opinions, Prior knew, were heretical for a young Whig secretary, and he urged Portland not to share them with the other ministers. Certainly such deep-dyed Whigs as Montague and Vernon must not know of these essays into philosophical Toryism. Yet Prior probably hoped that the letter might come to the attention of the King. At any rate, it is oddly like one from Sir John Suckling to Henry Jermyn, designed for the eyes of Charles I.[64]

A week later Prior wrote more strongly to Portland, arguing that the King should direct his Council firmly rather than be guided by their advice. The Whigs, Prior said, had given the King "good words" and had done their best in Parliament for his interests, yet the Country Party, which was obstructing the King's policies, was composed of men who were, and had always been, Whigs. On the other hand, the Tories, who from principle ought to support the King, were peevish; they voted against the King's policies simply because they were not in favor at Court. The remedy for these evils, Prior said, was for the King, by his goodness and kindness, to win to his side men

---

[63] *Ibid.*, 318-321, Prior to Portland, Paris, March 1/11, 1698/9.
[64] Sir John Suckling, *Works, 1910*, p. 322.

from all parties and to visit with displeasure the recalcitrant. Such, said Prior, were the tactics used by King Henry VII, King Henry VIII, and Queen Elizabeth, who "were our best princes and ruled us best."[65]

Portland expressed satisfaction with Prior's letters and intimated that he had shown them to King William.[66] The King, perhaps, did not take such gratuitous advice unkindly, because, as Mr. Bickley has pointed out, he had been confronted, since his accession, with two problems: prosecuting the war with France, and enlisting the support of his ministers for the war.[67] At first he had tried to govern through a ministry composed of both Whigs and Tories. But when the Tories opposed the war policies, he found that he must depend wholly upon the Whigs. Soon he discovered that the Whigs stood for a limitation of the powers of the Crown, and that the more advanced among them even leaned towards republicanism. William, ever jealous of his kingly powers, may have given Prior's opinions serious consideration. Mr. Rigg thinks that they did have influence on royal counsels.[68]

Prior enjoyed the turn that his zeal for the King's interests had taken. His loyalty to William never wavered. He resented any gloating by French political leaders over William's difficulties with Parliament and relayed to his friends in England the French soldiers' praise of King William—"Le premier homme de son métier! Le plus beau prince du monde."

Prior wrote to Portland no further dissertations on kingcraft, but many long gossipy letters about the Court and the *beau monde*. The balls and masques given in the great apartments at Versailles by the King were often the topics of Matt's letters. Sometimes more informal entertainments were held in the private suite of Madame de Maintenon or in the apartments of the

[65] *Longleat Papers*, III, 328, Prior to Portland, Paris, March 1/11, 1698/9.
[66] *Ibid.*, 326, Portland to Prior, Kensington, March 16/26, 1698/9.
[67] Bickley, *Life of Matthew Prior*, p. 136.
[68] *Longleat Papers*, III, xii, Introduction by J. M. Rigg.

Dauphin. Supper would be served at nine. The ball would begin at ten. The guests would be elegantly attired in fancy costumes. At eleven masques would arrive. A monstrously tall gentleman, disguised as a lady and enveloped in an enormous cloak, would appear at the door, walk to the center of the room, and, making a deep bow, let the cloak fall to the floor. Out would spring figures from Italian comedy—Harlequin, Scaramouche, Polichinello—all of whom would dance exceedingly well to the strumming of many guitars. "All the world was masqued," Prior wrote after one of these affairs which lasted until dawn. "This and the devotion and ashes we are in today is all at present."

At a dinner at the Comte de Marsan's, the guests quizzed Prior about developments in England. Why had the Duke of Ormonde quitted his post in the Guards? And why had Portland refused to go to meet the King at Newmarket? Prior apologized to Portland for writing of the topic; of course the conjectures of the French were wrong, and he hoped that there was nothing to their surmises and guesses.[69] Portland's prompt reply suggested that the break with the King was beyond remedy. He was keenly aware of the fact that men loved to gossip everywhere, particularly in Paris. He expressed sincere friendship for Prior, although he realized its future uselessness.

Many of the French, deeply interested in their recent guest, who had been a favorite with them, were stirred by all these rumors concerning Portland's retirement from Court. Prior found himself cornered and catechized about Portland's retreat—"by all the world from 'Monsieur le Prince' down to Caillières."[70] Portland's friends were loyal and sympathized with him. "Madame," as we have observed, took his side. Her friend, Christina de Meyercrone,[71] could not say enough in his defense. When she questioned Prior about the matter, he replied in writing that it had been Portland's desire to leave and that his

[69] *Ibid.*, 341, Portland to Prior, Windsor, May 1/11, 1699.
[70] *Ibid.*, 347, Prior to Jersey, Paris, May 17/27, 1699.
[71] Wife of the Danish Ambassador in Paris.

friends had been unable to persuade him to change his mind. Prior suggested that Madame de Meyercrone should "try everything," for he was in despair.

Madame de Meyercrone may have doubted Prior's sincerity. At any rate, she immediately forwarded his letter to Portland, expressing the hope that Prior's sentiments were as sincere as her own.[72] His own letter to Portland of the same date, if not sincere, was, as Marion Grew (Portland's biographer and none too friendly to Prior) says, an excellent example of all that was proper under the circumstances, and a very good imitation of sincerity.[73] Prior spoke of his extreme despondency, which scarcely permitted him to write, and concluded by hoping that it would not be long before he would see his "protector and patron at Court."[74]

Portland sent Prior a kind and courteous reply, and there the regular correspondence between them ceased, a circumstance which has led Prior's critics to assume that he had no further use for Portland after his retirement from Court. Macaulay's undocumented report of a conversation between Prior and one of Portland's friends, who was attempting to win Matthew back to his former patron, perhaps best represents the secretary's attitude on his present necessity:

"Excuse me," said Prior, "if I follow your example and my lord's. My Lord is a model to us all, and you have imitated him to good purpose. He retires with half a million. You have large grants, a lucrative employment in Holland, a fine house. I have nothing of the kind. A court is like those fashionable churches into which we have looked at Paris. Those who have received the benediction are instantly away to the Opera House or the wood of Boulogne. Those who have not received the benediction are pressing and elbowing each other to get near the altar. You and my Lord have got your blessing, and are quite right to

---

[72] *Correspondentie van Willem III en van Hans Willem Bentinck*, II, 317, Prior to Madame de Meyercrone, May 19, 1699. *Ibid.*, 316, Madame de Meyercrone to Portland, May 20, 1699.
[73] See Grew, *Willem Bentinck and William III*, p. 367.
[74] *Longleat Papers*, III, 343, Prior to Portland, Paris, May 10/20, 1699.

take yourselves off with it. I have not been blest, and must fight my
way up as well as I can."[75]

» 6 «

Portland's place as "protector and patron at court" was now
taken by the more amiable, less reserved Jersey. Some time before November, 1698, a rumor had been circulated that the Duke
of Shrewsbury would at last resign his seals and that Jersey
would succeed him, but Jersey retained his post in Paris for
several months, although absent in England much of the time,
and the faithful Vernon acted as Secretary for both the Northern
and Southern Departments.

In April Jersey's appointment was definitely announced, and
the Earl of Manchester (Montague's cousin and son-in-law) was
named to succeed him in Paris. Prior realized that he must make
haste if he were to get back to England; otherwise he might be
expected to remain abroad indefinitely. He was weary of being
away from home; he felt that he had come to the end of all that
his present employment could give him, and that he was now
fitted for more important posts. He was ordered, however, to
remain in Paris until Manchester should arrive. From previous
experience, he feared that this meant another long delay before
he could return to England. Lord Jersey obligingly promised to
take him to London to be his under-secretary, a prospect not so
dazzling as the role he was playing in France.

Montague regretted Prior's decision to take the minor position in the office in London, believing that Matt ought not to
be so impatient for advancement. He believed that he and his
kinsman Manchester would be able to do as well by Prior as
Jersey would. Furthermore, he told one of Stepney's sisters
that he felt that Prior was falling into an inferior post, for it
paid but five hundred pounds a year. It is evident that Prior's
friends were concerned about his haste to leave Paris. Miss

[75] Macaulay, *History of England*, chap. XXIV.

Stepney asked Montague to acquaint Powys with his opinion, knowing that it would be relayed to Prior;[76] later when she was writing to George she expressed pity for Prior's foolhardiness. The shrewd George wondered why Prior should want to leave Paris and advised him to stay. Matt resented the officiousness of his old friends. Their commiseration smacked too much of loyalty to the Montague interests. They even belittled Jersey and questioned his right to be both Secretary of State and a Lord Regent. This was the world and made one laugh.[77] Stepney was well situated. He had a thousand pounds a year from the Board of Trade and idled away his time playing one-and-thirty-bone-ace with his "adorable Electress" at Berlin.[78] How angry Prior was with all the family! They knew nothing of how he had had to "flutter away the Devil and all in this monkey country, · where the air was infected with vanity, and extravagance was as epidemical as the itch in Scotland."[79] He would ask Jersey to get him a place on Stepney's Board of Trade. Then the Puggies (the Stepney spinsters) need waste no more pity on him.[80]

Prior would heed no one's advice; he was determined not to remain in Paris unless His Majesty should command him to do so. Montague, although greatly annoyed by Prior's decision, sent him the bounty money for which he had asked.

When writing to thank Montague, Prior revealed a bit of gossip about himself. It was rumored that he had been married to Lady Falkland, widow of the Lord Falkland who had been appointed to succeed Dursley at The Hague in 1694 but who had died before assuming office. The gossip had gathered such momentum that the London *Post Boy* carried an announcement of the marriage, declaring that the lady was said to be worth 50,000 pounds sterling, but Prior disposed of the story thus:

[76] *Longleat Papers*, III, 334, Richard Powys to Prior, Whitehall, April 10/20, 1699.
[77] *Ibid.*, 351, Prior to Jersey, May 27/June 3, 1699.
[78] Sophia Charlotte, wife of Frederick of Prussia.
[79] *Longleat Papers*, III, 327, Prior to Montague, March 22/April 1, 1699.
[80] *Ibid.*, 348, Prior to Jersey, Paris, May 20/30, 1699.

I remember I jested with you once on that subject, but in truth never thought of it more than as a thing utterly impracticable. She is an old Troy that will not be taken in ten years, and though fifty strong fellows should get in to her by stratagem, they might e'en march out again at a large breach without being able to set her on fire, but one single sentinel as I am with a thin carcase and weak lungs might lie before her walls till I eat horse-hides and shoe-leather, unless you kindly sent me some refreshments from the Treasury.[81]

Lady Falkland was no more pleased with this matrimonial announcement than was Prior. "My widow was scandalized at her being married to me by all the Gazettes in Europe," he told Jersey. "She is gone for England rude as a bear, and mad as hot weather can make her."[82] There, according to Jersey, "she ventured her pretty person in the dust of London," but not in the best of humor. Attired in the very latest creation of Paris, she disdainfully criticized Lady Jersey's wardrobe, telling her that neither her "manteau, petticoat, commode nor anything was in fashion."[83]

The attachment to Jersey provoked the warmest feelings of friendship that Prior was ever to experience. As the friendships dating from the earliest days of boyhood cooled, his devotion to Jersey became more ardent. The contrary advice of others, who doubted his wisdom in wanting to leave the diplomatic post at the first court in Europe for a minor post at Whitehall, drew Matt closer to the generous courtier, to whom he felt the deepest sense of obligation and gratitude. Surely, loyalty could go no further than this pledge:

I will live with you, my lord, with a desk, or without one. I lived with you at The Hague, I returned with you into England, I was to have gone with you into Ireland, I stayed for you in France, I long to come to you in England, and I will never go from thence till you send me. My obligations to you are unspeakable, and so is my zeal for your

---

[81] *Ibid.*, 342, Prior to Montague, Paris, May 10/20, 1699.
[82] *Ibid.*, 348, Prior to Jersey, May 20/30, 1699.
[83] *Ibid.*, 358, Jersey to Prior, Whitehall, June 12/22, 1699.

service. What would people have? This is my case, I will print it, and shew it to mankind, and I will be happy in receiving your commands, whether they will or no.[84]

The last few months that Prior spent in Paris were notable for his acquaintance with the French literary men, and we find him going to dine one evening with Boileau, Fontenelle, Abbé Régnier, and Monsieur Dacier[85] at some fine home in Charonne,[86] and perhaps the next "with Boileau and the *beaux Esprits* at Auteuil."[87] With pardonable pride he cherished a compliment which Boileau made upon him: "Patience, I live amongst my savants, and Boileau says I have more genius than all the Academy."[88] As for that, Jersey warned, "If you don't come quickly away, Boileau and that flattering country will spoil you."[89] It is probable that Boileau never knew that Prior had treated the "Ode sur la prise de Namur" with levity, and one is reasonably sure that Prior never informed him thereof. Boileau, no doubt, shared "mutton and custard" with Prior at his little house in the Marais, and must have been introduced by him to the Earl of Manchester, at whose home he was later a frequent guest.[90] When Addison visited Paris shortly after Prior left for London, he met the famous Boileau at Manchester's.

To the last, Villeroy kept up his catechizing of Prior, whom he would invite to dinner when he was curious about news from England. Both Portland and Jersey had warned Prior to be on his guard, but Prior seems to have suspected Villeroy's motive from the beginning:

[84] *Ibid.*, 356, Prior to Jersey, Paris, June 10/20, 1699.

[85] André Dacier, minister and editor of texts and husband of Mme. Dacier, the Greek scholar and opponent of Lamotte de Houdard in the *Querelle des anciens et des madernes.*

[86] See Wickham Legg, *Matthew Prior*, App. B, p. 293, Prior to Jersey, Paris, June 7/17, 1699. (Middleton Park Papers).

[87] *Ibid.*, App. B, p. 295, Prior to Jersey, Paris, June 21/July 1, 1699. (Middleton Park Papers).

[88] *Ibid.*, 300, Prior to Jersey, July 8/18, 1699.

[89] *Longleat Papers*, III, 372, Jersey to Prior, Whitehall, July 13/23, 1699.

[90] Oldmixon, *Life and Posthumous Works of Arthur Maynwaring*, p. 17.

My Governor is always with Louis XIV, and I dare swear pumps me to tell half an hour after the effect of his questions; he is an excellent courtier, but if they had no abler heads than he, we might sleep in quiet.

When "Beau" Stanyan arrived in July, Prior felt that his exile was nearly over. With ill-concealed egotism, he boasted that Stanyan would not outrival him in popularity with the French:

I have shown my successor twice at Versailles, they say he is *bien fait, bel homme, ma foy, mais Monsieur Prior a-t-il de l'esprit?* always follows. The man is well enough truly, but he has a quiet lazy genius that will not *brille* enough at Versailles, nor be feared enough at the Coffeehouse amongst the bullies of St. Germans.[91]

Finally, in August, Manchester reached Paris. Prior remained a while to be of service in getting Manchester, who was stopping at his house, settled. The new Ambassador did not make a favorable impression on "Flanders Jane."

Jane complains that his Excellence blows his nose in the napkins, spits in the middle of the room, and laughs so loud and like an ordinary body that she does not think him fit for an ambassador.

Whatever Manchester lacked in social grace was abundantly compensated for by Lady Manchester's beauty and charm.[92] Prior's critical attitude toward Manchester was but temporary. On better acquaintance a friendly relation was established between them. By the end of August the Manchesters were settled, and Prior was anxious to be off.

There yet remained the final audience with Louis XIV, at which Prior made his farewells. The King was very civil to him, voicing the hope that he was going home to some honorable employment, since everyone at Court had said that he deserved it. Moreover, he hoped to see Prior in Paris again in some

---

91 Wickham Legg, *Matthew Prior*, App. B, p. 300, Prior to Jersey, July 8/18, 1699.
92 *Ibid.*, p. 308, Prior to Jersey, July 29/Aug. 8, 1699.

higher character. Prior then thanked the King for all the favors he had received while in France, and after a further exchange of compliments, the ceremonious adieux were made.[93] Armed with a letter from Torcy containing a most flattering testimonial[94] to his wise conduct and his ability and voicing regret at his departure, Prior was ready to leave. On August 26 he sent this spirited message to Jersey:

I have wound up my bottom, I have liquored my boots, and my foot is in the stirrup: that is I leave Paris tomorrow.[95]

---

[93] Strong, *Letters . . . at Welbeck*, p. 251.

[94] Paris, Archives . . . , *Correspondance Politique, d'Angleterre*, 204, Torcy to Jersey, Aug. 18, 1699.

[95] Wickham Legg, *Matthew Prior*, p. 104, Prior to Jersey, Paris, Aug. 16/26, 1699.

CHAPTER VI

The Roving Diplomatic Agent

» 1 «

SHORTLY before setting out from Paris, Prior learned that King William was at Loo shaping the articles for a new treaty. The death of the Prince Elector of Bavaria had invalidated the First Partition Treaty; the question of the Spanish Succession must be reopened. King William was troubled: in failing health, beset by an unruly Parliament which attacked his land grants to Dutch and Huguenot favorites and reduced his army to a mere handful of men, he undertook, almost singlehanded, the difficult problem of making a treaty with Louis which would secure the peace of Europe to the advantage of England and Holland and would also satisfy the Emperor of Austria.

Prior obtained permission to return to England by way of Holland, for he had several ideas brewing in his mind and was eager to see the King. One problem that he wished to lay before His Majesty was that of the Irish secretaryship, to which he had been appointed some two years and three months earlier (May 17, 1697). Prior's superior officers in Ireland, the Earl of Galway in particular, were growing impatient over his prolonged holding of the position *in absentia*. Moreover, Matthew had his eye upon a position on the Board of Trade—he had no scruples concerning pluralism. Should there be no vacancy on the Board at that time, he declared that he would ask the King's leave to "serve as an honorary in that commission till an advantage fell." Perhaps he was also shrewd enough to anticipate some employment in making the treaty if he were on hand at the opportune moment.

The journey to Holland, as Prior recorded it in his Diary, was not uneventful. He stayed the first night at Peronne, dined the following day at Cambrai and spent the second night at Valenciennes at the home of the governor of the province. From Valenciennes, Prior passed through Brussels and Antwerp to Rotterdam, arriving there between two and three o'clock in the morning. After much difficulty at this inopportune hour, he procured a boat to ferry him across the Maas, but he got no farther than midstream before a sudden storm arose, accompanied by terrific thunder and lightning. The boat almost capsized, and Prior nearly lost his life. Finally the storm passed, and he reached the opposite shore in safety.[1] Exactly one week after bidding "Adieu Paris et les beaux yeux," he was strolling among the trim gardens at Loo, waiting for Albemarle to present him to the King.

Of all the matters in Prior's mind, the dispute with Lord Galway over the Irish secretaryship was uppermost. The Earl of Galway was now the dominant member of the Board of Lords Justices that governed Ireland. Despite his Irish title, he was a Huguenot, formerly the Marquis de Ruvigny, who had sought refuge in England after the Revocation of the Edict of Nantes. He served King William long and faithfully as a soldier in Ireland, became one of his favorites, and was rewarded with an enormous land grant and the Lord Justiceship.

When first appointed to the post in Ireland, Prior was at The Hague, as has been noted, but, it was thought that he would soon be free to go to Dublin. According to custom he employed a deputy, Henry May, to serve in his stead. This step proved unwise, or so Prior learned when, having finished his duties at The Hague, he was sent not to Ireland but to Paris, and his absence was unduly prolonged. With characteristic lack of

[1] Strong, *Letters . . . at Welbeck*, App. V, p. 258.

foresight, he had failed to arrange with May the share of the profits each should derive from the office. At first May sent Prior the lion's share of the fees, but, after performing the duties of the office for months, he began to claim all the profits. Angered because May was "taking advantage of him," Prior asked John Tucker, who had originally recommended May, to arbitrate the dispute.

From this time—September, 1698 until September, 1699—a voluminous triangular correspondence ensued. Prior protested vigorously to Tucker about May's conduct and threatened to draw up a *factum* from their letters to present at Whitehall as evidence of the justice of his contention. Before doing this, however, he demanded of May an exact statement of the fees for the fifteen months.[2] May, somewhat subdued by Prior's peremptoriness, agreed to remit for the time past whatever amount Tucker might name but more boldly refused to make any pledge for the future.[3] Ill with gout and vexed at being drawn into the dispute, Tucker regretted that his two friends had not determined the *quantum* at the beginning.[4]

To aid in the arbitration, Tucker called in John Ellis. They felt that they had been deceived in May, who seemed both unreasonable and unfair.[5] One third of the fees, they said, was ample compensation for the deputy. Disregarding the ruling of the arbiters, May sent Prior a full account of the receipts—1385£, 19 s.—for the preceding seventeen months but deposited with the Treasury only half the amount.[6] Naturally, May was dissatisfied with the meagerness of his share. "No clerk in the kingdom earned his money so hard,"[7] he thought; and we are inclined to agree with him. When, in the following September, Prior asked for the yearly statement of accounts, May sent one

[2] *Longleat Papers*, III, 266, Prior to May, Paris, Sept. 7/17, 1698.
[3] *Ibid.*, 280, May to John Tucker, Dublin, Oct. 15/25, 1698.
[4] *Ibid.*, 283, John Tucker to Prior, Whitehall, Oct. 27, Nov. 6, 1698.
[5] *Ibid.*, 296, John Ellis to Prior, Whitehall, Nov. 17/27, 1698.
[6] *Ibid.*, 299, May to Prior, Dublin, Nov. 26/Dec. 6, 1698.
[7] *Ibid.*, 300, May to Tucker, Dublin, Dec. 3/13, 1689.

for the first eight months only, asserting that he had been appointed first secretary by Lord Galway and the Duke of Bolton in April. To the Treasury, therefore, he remitted only two-thirds of the fees, holding out the full amount for the four summer months.[8]

Although May was justified in feeling that he was unfairly treated, Prior was technically in the right. Vernon had given May to understand distinctly that he was accountable to Prior for all the profits.[9] Nor was Prior more greedy in the matter of fees than other secretaries in similar positions. Addison, while secretary to Lord Wharton (Lord Lieutenant of Ireland), was equally demanding, although his salary was much larger than Prior's.[10]

The trouble Prior had with his deputy was nothing compared to his later difficulties with Galway. So long as Jersey was serving as an absentee Lord Justice, Galway raised no objection to Prior's remaining in Paris. He congratulated Prior on his appointment, hoped that his stay in Paris would be brief, and asked him to write of himself and of affairs in France. He considerately explained his reasons for reducing the fees of the secretary. Prior, for his part, attended to errands for Galway and complied with his request to write.

The situation took a new turn, however, when Jersey resigned from the Irish Justiceship upon becoming Secretary of State. The Duke of Bolton continued in his position but preferred to remain in England. Jersey was succeeded by the Earl of Berkeley—the former Lord Dursley—Prior's first employer at The Hague. Berkeley was an amiable man; certainly he was not one to oppose the strong-minded Galway. With Jersey gone, Prior rightly felt uncertain about his own tenure in Ireland. Galway wanted a secretary at hand; he was averse to keeping

[8] *Ibid.*, 376, May to Prior, Dublin, Sept. 12/22, 1699.
[9] *Ibid.*, 121, Vernon to Prior, Whitehall, May 21/31, 1697.
[10] See Robert H. Murray's article, "Addison in Ireland, some unpublished Letters," in *Nineteenth Century and After*, May-June, 1914, LXXV, 1067–84, and 1257–74.

the place open for Prior longer; he disapproved heartily of pluralism and would not encourage it in his own bailiwick. At once he notified Prior, as yet in Paris, that, since the Justices could no longer hope for his coming, they would give the post to Mr. May.[11]

Prior knew that the stern and uncompromising Galway was no man to be cajoled into changing his mind. He angrily endorsed the communication as "Galway's sentencing letter" and forwarded a copy to Jersey, of whose help he was confident. "I thank God," he wrote, "I can hate and love, and the objects of my different passions are the Earls of Galway and Jersey. I wish I may vex the one as heartily as I shall always endeavour to obey the other."[12]

But the quarrel had hardly begun. Prior was growing more and more restive in Paris; since he could not be at home to plead his cause, he felt it necessary to enlist his friends' assistance. Jersey promised to take the matter to the King by way of Albemarle, whom Prior considered an ally. Prior himself laid the case before the other Lords Justices, Bolton and Berkeley. He even renewed correspondence with Portland—to the extent of one letter—in the hope that his former chief might intercede for him with the King. Galway was using him "hardly" Prior said; other secretaries were excused when their duties overlapped, but he was being sacrificed in order that Mr. May might become first secretary and that a countryman of Galway's might become second secretary. Furthermore, Galway had waited to attack Prior's position until Portland resigned—"so when the pillar is removed the ivy that depended upon it falls."[13]

A curt ultimatum from Galway reached Prior just as he was preparing to leave Paris. Briefly it was this: the Lords Justices had never said that Mr. May was Prior's deputy—the office had never been held by a deputy—from its very nature it could not

---

[11] *Longleat Papers*, III, 358, Galway to Prior, Dublin, June 13/23, 1699.
[12] *Ibid.*, 369, Prior to Jersey, Paris, July 5/15, 1699.
[13] *Ibid.*, 366, Prior to Portland, Paris, July 13, 1699.

be so held, the Board had long awaited Mr. Prior's arrival. Furthermore, the Earl quoted a statement from Albemarle (dated April 29, 1699) to the effect that by accepting the recent appointment in Lord Jersey's office Prior had automatically vacated the Irish secretaryship.[14] Prior was astonished by this revelation. Apparently he had been ousted from the office three months previously. He vented his ill-humor on Jersey: "King" Galway was a "fanatic prince," more absolute than King Louis; and as for Ireland, it was a "boggy country."[15] Jersey consoled him by predicting that Galway would stir up such a row that, for the sake of peace, William would make a place for Prior in England. In this event would not Prior thank Galway for meddling?[16]

Soon, however, it was Galway's turn to draw in his horns. Prior's appeal to those in higher authority having been successful, the Lords Justices were notified to continue him as secretary. Upon receipt of this word, Galway wrote direct to the King reasserting his position but acknowledging his duty to obey His Majesty's commands. Meanwhile Prior had had a private audience at Loo with King William. Feeling quite puffed up, he presumptuously wrote to "King Crop," saying that precedents for the employment of deputies might be found in the "annals of the kingdom of which his Excellency was one of the governors."[17] The impertinence of this flat contradiction aroused Galway's Gallic fury. He forwarded the letter to the King, intimating that it would be a particular affront to him if he were ordered to reinstate Prior as secretary.[18] A mean retaliation certainly—even the mild Berkeley commented that

<hr />

[14] *Ibid.*, 371, Galway to Prior, Dublin, July 11/21, 1699.

[15] Wickham Legg, *Matthew Prior*, p. 111, Prior to Galway, Loo, Aug. 28/Sept. 8, 1699. (Middleton Park Papers).

[16] *Longleat Papers*, III, 375, Jersey to Prior, Whitehall, Aug. 22/Sept. 1, 1699.

[17] Wickham Legg, *Matthew Prior*, p. 111, Prior to Galway, Loo, Aug. 28/Sept. 8, 1699. (Middleton Park Papers.)

[18] *Ibid.*, p. 113, Galway to William III, Dublin, Sept. 12/22, 1699. (Middleton Park Papers.)

it was a cruel thing to endeavor to "cut a man's throat with his own pen."[19] Nevertheless, if Galway had been unreasonably implacable, Prior had been insolently determined.

The King was by this time inclined to sympathize with Galway. But Albemarle and Blathwayt pleaded Prior's cause so earnestly that William agreed to have him reinstated.[20] It was admitted that a point had been shaved, if not strained, in restoring his *status quo*. The victory, then, went to Prior. The Lords Justices must swallow their pride and obey the order from Court. Berkeley and Bolton accepted His Majesty's commands dutifully, but Galway was not so amenable. As a final protest, he sent in his resignation,[21] which, needless to say, was not accepted. Prior never went to Ireland, and Mr. May retained the secretaryship. The King conveniently had other plans for Prior. He provided him with an additional allowance of 600 pounds per annum until a new place should be found for him in London.[22] Thus the dispute terminated as Jersey had predicted.

» 2 «

During the private audience, which lasted for an hour and a half, the King questioned Prior about the events of the past nineteen months in France, and, satisfied with his report, commended him for his conscientious service and congratulated him on his wisdom in avoiding a blind loyalty to Portland. Prior explained tactfully that he had been His Majesty's secretary; he had respected Portland as His Majesty's Ambassador, but in Portland's personal affairs he had not taken either side. As to the future, the King assured Prior that he would "take care of him" and ordered him to The Hague, which he had not visited for two years. There he divided his time between the Dutch

---

[19] *Longleat Papers*, III, 378, John Ellis to Prior, Whitehall, Sept. 22/Oct. 2, 1699.
[20] *Ibid.*, 377, Blathwayt to Prior, Loo, Sept. 19/29, 1699.
[21] *Buccleuch Papers*, II, 628, Galway to Shrewsbury, Dublin, Nov. 11/22, 1699.
[22] Strong, *Letters . . . at Welbeck*, App. V, pp. 260, 262. (Prior's Diary.)

"Heers" and the "French Excellencies." Tallard and Bonrepos[23] were very cordial, but the gaiety of Paris had spoiled him for the dull life in Holland. He slipped easily into the Tory disdain for the mercantile and Calvinistic republic—an attitude prevailingly popular, ten years later, during the administration of Harley and St. John. Frankly he was bored. "Je m'ennuye ici comme un chien," he wrote Jersey, "after the noise and bustle of Paris, one had as good live in a tomb as here."[24] In contrast to Prior's own mood Portland's seemed strangely gay, quite that of the philosopher in retirement.

Prior's boredom vanished when Jersey arrived. His duties as under-secretary began at once, and, since Jersey was Secretary of State for the Southern Department with the Paris embassy in his jurisdiction, Prior's correspondence was mainly with Manchester. Perhaps Matt was unexpectedly glad to take up the threads of his Paris life which he had so eagerly broken off two weeks before.

The negotiations for the Second Partition Treaty moved slowly. The Austrian emperor, as usual, was in no hurry to sign. Annoyed by the delays, King Louis began to grow suspicious of King William and recalled Tallard to France. King William realized that he must act at once to restore Louis's good humor. He therefore returned immediately to England, whence he expected to make his next move.

Jersey and Prior accompanied the King to London. On board the royal yacht, Prior was let into the secrets of the treaty, which he knew but "imperfectly." Jersey outlined Prior's immediate task. As soon as Prior should reach London, he must read the treaty through with Portland; he must then return immediately to France, confer with Manchester, attend his lordship at his first audience with Louis XIV, and carry back to

---

[23] Bonrepos was the French envoy at The Hague.

[24] Wickham Legg, *Matthew Prior*, p. 316, Prior to Jersey, Hague, Sept. 5/15, 1699. (Middleton Park Papers.)

King William an account of this audience.[25] After a crowded day in London, spent in conferring with the King in the forenoon and with Portland in the afternoon, Prior left for Dover the next morning. A rough crossing in the packet boat and a hasty journey overland brought him to Paris and to Lord Manchester. The two channel crossings within three or four days had taxed Prior's strength; he looked leaner than ever—even a good crossing in those days required ten hours. Time was valuable and he was impatient to accomplish his errand.

It was early November, and the French Court was tarrying at Marly. Although Manchester requested a private audience, Louis refused to break his rule of never transacting business at Marly. Prior and Manchester must wait, then, until King Louis returned to Versailles.

The secrecy of Prior's errand necessitated his remaining close to the Embassy in the Faubourg Saint-Germain. As an excuse for not going out to see his friends, he pleaded illness. His enforced idleness confined him to the company of Lord and Lady Manchester and Stanyan, for all of whom he quickly developed a warm friendship. In spite of Prior's efforts to remain in secret, the Jacobites discovered his presence in Paris, and it was said that King James hoped that Prior would displace Manchester,[26] who as a Whig was more suspicious of the French Court and Saint-Germain than Jersey had been. Was Prior not the friend of the Jerseys, the one an opportunist in religion, the other a Catholic, neither of whom was unsympathetic to the Jacobite cause? And had not Prior's animosity towards the exiles at Saint-Germain softened under his friends' influence? Jersey, we may note, was an avowed Jacobite in the next reign. When Prior's Whig enemies were out for his scalp in 1715, it was remembered against him that he and Jersey had urged William to covenant with France for the succession of the young "Prince of

[25] Strong, *Letters . . . at Welbeck*, App. V, p. 255. (Prior's Diary.)
[26] Cole, *Memoirs of Affairs of State*, p. 82, Manchester to Charles Montague, Dec. 8, 1699.

Wales"—later James III—upon the death of Queen Anne.[27]

After a delay of nearly ten days word came from Torcy that Louis would see Prior and Manchester. On the night of November 14, they drove to Versailles in a "Berlyn" to be ready for their audience the following morning. The King received them at the conclusion of the regular Sunday morning levee. Torcy had already acquainted him with Prior's mission; otherwise Louis must have wondered at the unexpected return. Louis expressed surprise that William had not signed the treaty before leaving Holland. It was Prior's commission to assure "His Most Christian Majesty" that William was keeping his word and that the treaty would be signed.

Prior immediately left Paris for London, where his return was anxiously awaited. King William was well pleased with the success of the errand.[28] The peace, as Prior said, was "on foot again." Moreover, the King had at last found Englishmen who could negotiate diplomatic business as creditably as did Louis's trusted envoys. Both Prior and Manchester were gratified to have an important part in the negotiations and to know that Tallard was no longer the all indispensable agent in the treaty. Prior also rejoiced in Tallard's real or imagined chagrin.

The return journey to London made Prior ill. "I contracted a Cold in the Voyage, and wisely increased it by running about these two Days. I am blooded and keep my Chamber to-day,"[29] he dictated in the letter which carried to Manchester word of his safe arrival. For almost two months he could attend to little public business. When he grew stronger, he was employed in adjusting some articles of the treaty and in arranging with Lord Somers to have the broad seal put upon it.[30] William had per-

---

[27] Addison, *Works*, VI, 665, Addison to Charles Delafaye, London, June 9/20, 1715.

[28] See his letters to Portland, dated Nov. 8, 10, 12, 1699, in *Correspondentie van Willem III en van Hans Willem Bentinck*, I, 348, 349.

[29] Cole, *Memoirs of Affairs of State*, p. 76, Prior to Manchester, Nov. 3/13, [*Sic*] 1699. The Manchester Correspondence may also be found in Prior's *History of His Own Time*. In both works the above letter is misdated. The probable date for it is Nov. 13/23, 1699.

[30] Strong, *Letters . . . at Welbeck*, App. V, p. 261. (Prior's Diary.)

suaded Louis to agree that the Austrian candidate, Archduke Charles, should become King of Spain and of the Spanish possessions in America upon the death of Charles II. This agreement was the basis of the Second Partition Treaty. As a compensation for giving up her aspirant's claim, France was to receive Naples and Sicily (as in the First Partition Treaty), as well as Milan, which she was to exchange with the Duc de Lorraine for his province, now in French possession. It was this proposal, the giving of the two Sicilies to France, which aroused a mighty storm in England as soon as the news of the treaty transpired. Tory squires in the country and Whig merchants in the city joined in denouncing an article which might result in Louis's closing the Mediterranean to English merchant ships engaged in the Turkish and Levantine trade.

In his diary Prior mentions proposals on foot between William and Louis at the time the treaty was signed which would have forestalled any hazard to English trade with the Levant. He specifies one provision to which the French seemed agreeable, namely, that the Duke of Savoy should be awarded the two Sicilies, and that the French in exchange should take Savoy and Piedmont. This scheme Prior thought "an admirable proposal and a great instance of the King's wisdom."[31] Unfortunately these anticipatory measures came too late to be incorporated in the treaty. Time was short. The death of the King of Spain was expected hourly. On February 21/March 3, 1699/1700, the treaty was signed in London by Portland and Jersey, Tallard and Briord. Its subsequent fate at the hands of a frenzied parliament we leave for the moment.

» 3 «

Prior was now back in the thick of the political and literary world of London for which he had long been hankering. His

[31] Strong, *Letters . . . at Welbeck*, App. V, p. 264. (Prior's Diary.)

Matthew Prior, c. 1700

From painting by Kneller

diplomatic apprenticeship had been marked with notable success. William had recognized his ability and had entrusted him with important business. He could look forward to positions of greater responsibility in England. He had returned with an added sense of loyalty to his King and to his country. "I had rather be thought a good Englishman, than the best poet or greatest scholar that ever wrote," was one of his sayings. Eager to settle down immediately, he purchased a residence and garden in Duke Street, Westminster, adjoining St. James's Park. "Matthew's Palace," as his house was later called, became famous in the literary-political annals of the first two decades of the eighteenth century. Here he wrote much of his best verse, entertained his friends with "sack and *Solomon*," recounted his adventures, political and amorous, in Holland and France, and hatched schemes for the good of the Kingdom. The Earl of Dorset, now in declining years, was frequently an honored guest at Matt's dinners of "Bacon-Ham and Mutton-chine," at which George Stepney and the Montague brothers, "Lord Dorset's boys," were often present. It was good to be home again with friends of Channel Row days even though time and circumstances had led them into different convictions and different loyalties. Domestic comfort was pleasant in contrast to the itinerant life of the last nine years. That Prior was wearied of foreign travel is evident in a little poem which he had scribbled on the flyleaf of Robbe's Geography while on his recent errand in Paris.[32] The poem voices that popular ideal of the age, a cultivated life in rustic retirement. Prior, however, was not ready for retirement to the country—Down Hall with its Virgilian and Horatian delights came twenty years later. Although he followed a poetical convention derived from Cowley, Horace, and Martial, the following lines suggest a distinctly personal longing. Especially do they seem autobiographical when we recall Prior's recent ad-

[32] *Méthode pour apprendre facilement la géographie* by Jacques Robbe, *ingénieur et Géographe du Roi*, 2 vols., Paris, 1678.

ventures on his triangular course from Paris to Holland, thence
to London, and back again to Paris:

> Of All that WILLIAM Rules, or ROBE
> Describes, Great RHEA, of Thy Globe;
> When or on Post-Horse, or in Chaise,
> With much Expence, and little Ease,
> My destin'd Miles I shall have gone,
> By THAMES or MAESE, by Po or RHONE,
> And found no Foot of Earth my own;
> GREAT MOTHER, let Me Once be able
> To have a Garden, House, and Stable;
> That I may Read, and Ride, and Plant,
> Superior to Desire, or Want;
> And as Health fails, and Years increase,
> Sit down, and think, and die in Peace.[33]

The New Year found him ready to print a new poem, the
Carmen Seculare, his last and most elaborate praise of King
William.[34] If the forty-two tedious stanzas lack the true poetic
fire, we may recall that they were written while the poet was
recovering from a severe illness. The steady stream of tribute to
William is interrupted only by brief praise of Ormonde, Dorset,
and Jersey, while mention of Montague is conspicuous by its
absence.

Prior was now improved in health, well enough at least to be
cross with Stanyan because of the size of his account for extraordinaries. He himself had so often been reproved on the same
score that perhaps he relished issuing the rebuke. He was also
annoyed with himself because he had necessarily been neglecting
Manchester's business, but he promised to attend to it as soon as
his health would permit him to "tumble more freely" among his
papers. To divert Prior from his melancholy mood, Stanyan sent
him copies of some recent French verse. Prior thought the poems
rather inferior, but asked his friend nevertheless to keep him informed about all new dramatic poetry.

[33] *Poems on Several Occasions*, p. 98.   [34] *Ibid.*, pp. 104, 120.

His illness did not wholly interfere with his social life, or so we judge from this letter:

To-morrow night Batterton [*sic*] acts Falstaff, and to encourage that poor house the Kit Katters have taken one side-box, and the Knights of the Toast have taken the other. We have made up a Prologue for Sir John in favour of eating and drinking, and to rally your toasts, and I have upon this occasion four lines upon Jacob. We will send you the whole Prologue when we have it together.

N. B.—My Lord Dorset is at the head of us, and Lord Carbury is general of the enemy's forces, and that we dine at my Lord Dorset's, and go from thence in a body. How my health will answer to this, if you should ask, since I came from the Gravelpits but on Saturday, I answer that I only sit down to table when the dessert comes, eat nothing but roasted apples, and drink sack and water.[35]

Here is the earliest reference we know of to the Kit-Cats, that great gathering of the Whig Lords and their literary protégés. It is Prior's only mention, save a reference to his expulsion ten years later, of this tribunal "where wit and beauty" were "decided by a plurality of voices." The Club held a weekly rendez-vous at the Cat and the Fiddle, where Jacob Tonson, founder and presiding genius, pronounced the mutton pies exceeding good. Prior and his convivial companions would dine well and then, heated with good port, fall to discussing politics and petticoats, drinking toasts to the fair ones, and damning Tory treason. Just as in later days, Harley, St. John, and Swift were to gather into the Tory Brothers Club the promising writers of the moment, so did Tonson, Dorset, and Montague assemble in a Whig fraternity such literary figures as Congreve, Rowe, Addison, Steele, Vanbrugh, Stepney, and Maynwaring. What were Prior's four lines to Jacob, written no doubt in a moment of gratitude for the honor that the first of all booksellers had bestowed upon him? We shall probably never know, since they must have been too amiable to survive the party animosity of

[35] *Longleat Papers*, III, 394, Prior to Stanyan, Whitehall, Jan. 8/19, 1699/1700.

1710 which declared Matt no longer a poet, pronounced him a turncoat, and ousted him from the Club. Prior, on his part, retaliated by declaring that Tonson was a blockhead like all members of his fraternity from the time of Chaucer's scrivener. We should like to know more of Prior's relations with the Kit-Cats. Even from his earliest membership in the Club rabid Whigs like Maynwaring looked upon him as an outsider and made his secession to the Tories inevitable.

The "Prologue for Sir John," we identify with a poem published in *Poems on Affairs of State*. It is a long poem of thirty-nine vigorous though unpolished lines. It proclaimed that good old English comedy was as superior to French importations as English beef and beer were to "meagre soup and sour champagne," and it called upon the audience to

> Shew your Disdain those nauseous Scenes to taste,
> Where French Buffoon like leanest Switzer drest,
> Turns all good Politics to Farce and Jest.
> Banish such Apes, and save the sinking stage;
> Let Mimes and squeaking Eunochs fill your Rage;
> On such let your descending Curse be try'd,
> Preserve plump Jack, and banish all beside.[36]

In spite of a hearty preference for English comedy, Prior was still eager for news of the latest successes on the French stage, one of which was Antoine de la Fosse's much talked of play, *Thésée*. Stanyan repeated a message from one of the leading contemporary poets of Paris, Jean Baptiste Rousseau, "who says he is very much your servant, and desires me to tell you so."[37] Rousseau belonged to a group of *salon* poets, chief among whom were the Marquis de la Fare and the Abbé de Chaulieu, composers of *petit vers sur des sujets légers*, usually addressed to friends of exalted rank. Although his sojourn in France brought Prior acquaintance with this group, his own society verse strikes a

---

[36] *Poems on Affairs of State*, II, 218, 219.
[37] *Longleat Papers*, III, 395, Stanyan to Prior, Paris, January 10/20, 1699/1700.

deeper note than does that of any of these writers of poetic trifles.

Unlike the correspondence with Stanyan, which ran much to small talk about literary acquaintances in Paris, the dispatches to Manchester bristled with comment on political events in England, as well as on routine diplomatic affairs in France. Since Manchester was Charles Montague's cousin and stepson, there are numerous references to Charles, whom Prior saw frequently between letters.

Montague was at present under attack from the Tory opposition in Parliament. A leading Tory journalist, Charles Davenant,[38] was preparing for publication a satirical treatise on ministerial abuses, especially the land-grant evil. This question was often discussed hotly by the circle of young Tory leaders to which Davenant belonged and with whom Prior occasionally dined. From them Prior learned that Davenant would use in his satire political figures of the reign of Edward II, one of them being John de Mointagu, Minister of Finance. The other two characters were Flambard and Gaveston, easily recognized as Somers and Portland. The similarity of the names Mointagu and Montague was, of course, no mere coincidence, and Davenant made a bold attack upon King William's minister in the figure of Mointagu, who was also ''a kind of *Surintendant des Finances* . . . a little insolent fellow, who, from a low degree and without any great merit of his own, and only by the King's favor, was got into great employments when giving offence by his Pride and Arrogance, the great ones at last fell upon him.''[39]

Prior's comments on this indictment of his friend and of the Whig ministry are strangely inconsistent and indicate that the ardor of his admiration for his friend was cooling. To Manchester, he wrote that the book was a ''scandalous Libel against the Government''[40] and that it was considered ''very scurrilous

[38] The eldest son of Sir William D'Avenant, author of *Gondibert*.
[39] Charles Davenant, *A Discourse of Grants and Resumptions*, p. 384.
[40] Cole, *Memoirs of Affairs of State*, p. 91, Prior to Manchester, Whitehall, Dec. 7/17, 1699.

against my Lord Chancellor, and our dear Friend Charles."[41]
To Stanyan, he wrote more frankly, "Davenant's book is highly
saucy, but I think it has done no real mischief to our friend in
particular [Montague], though in general it was and is but a
hint to show everybody where they should be angry."[42]

Montague must have become quite accustomed by this time to
abusive attacks on his character, his personal appearance, his
position. That he was vain, avaricious, and arrogant is undoubtedly true. But the charge that he lacked great merit was
unfounded. No other man of his time was responsible for so
many projects for improving governmental services. His skill
as a brilliant parliamentarian and his financial genius in establishing the Bank of England cannot be denied. He was the
first person to propose a public library for London and to initiate
plans for the proper keeping of the public records. Having
trusted to his pen for political advancement, he in turn aided
most of the struggling young writers of the age. Steele paid him
a just compliment: "Your patronage has produced those arts,
which before shunned the commerce of the world, into the service of life; and it is to You we owe, that the man of wit has
turned himself to be a man of business."[43]

Prior's attitude toward the friend of his schooldays was becoming increasingly objective and independent—similar, in
fact, to his present attitude toward Portland. No longer could
Prior say to Montague:

Here, Master, *amicitiae aeternae* with all my soul! I protest to you I
take part in everything that happens to your affairs. . . . If people have
affections after death. . . . I shall doubtless love you longer than I am
aware of.[44]

Since returning to London he had made friends with many of
Montague's political enemies. Furthermore, he had his own way

[41] *Ibid.*, p. 76, Prior to Manchester, London, Nov. 3/13, 1699.
[42] *Longleat Papers*, III, 393, Prior to Stanyan, Whitehall, Jan. 8/19, 1699/1700.
[43] Dedication to the *Tatler*, Vol. IV, April 7, 1711.
[44] *Longleat Papers*, III, 250, Prior to Montague, Aug. 5/15, 1698.

to make and would not allow old friendships to hinder him. That Matt and Charles still maintained cordial relations, if not warm ones, we infer, however, from the fact that Prior drew up for Montague in December, 1700, the preamble to his patent as Baron of Halifax.[45]

» 4 «

The years spent abroad brought changes not only in Prior's friendships but in his political loyalties. While in France, he had evolved a theory of statecraft, we may remember, which called for a strong and beneficent monarchy free from the ills of party factions. Hitherto all his public associations had been conducive to Whig loyalty. He had been a Whig as a matter of course, since his friends and patrons were Whigs, although he had thought little about Whig principles. The Whigs, moreover, had generally furthered King William's policies; the Tories had in the main hindered them. In Paris, Prior's observations of government, where party factions were unknown, and his close relations with his High Tory friend, Jersey, exposed him to theories of government more Tory than Whig. He resented the conditions whereby a party clique had grown rich and corrupt from the spoils of office. Was he turning Tory? Not yet, for his theory of government excluded the idea of party adherence; furthermore, the Tories in the present Parliament were unorthodox in refusing to support King William.

Now that he was in London Prior had no fair opportunity of seeing his theories put into practice. Indeed, his viewpoint was out of harmony with the times, although, as Rigg has pointed out, it was substantially the same as that later developed by Bolingbroke in his *Idea of a Patriot King* and adopted by George III in the early part of his reign "with no very happy results."[46] Prior, we have noted, looked back to the reigns of

[45] Montague, *Works and Life*, p. 61.
[46] *Longleat Papers*, III, xii, Introduction by J. M. Rigg.

Henry VIII and Queen Elizabeth for his models of government without party. Professor Oliver Elton has declared the idea of a single party to be "foreign to the English temper" and to the "English political structure,"[47] and Sir Adolphus W. Ward has termed Bolingbroke's *Patriot King*, which may have derived something from its author's friendship with Prior, as a "fabric of sand" that became a "heritage of the winds."[48]

Prior was in a quandary. He might cut himself free from old Whig loyalties, but he could not ally himself with the Tory combination in Parliament which was savagely attacking the King's policies and making the last years of his reign miserable. Again and again he expressed his sympathy for the Whig ministers under Tory fire. Of Somers, he wrote to Manchester:

I must congratulate your happiness that you are out of this noise and tumult, where we are tearing and destroying every man his neighbor. To-morrow is the great day when we expect that my Lord Chancellor will be fallen upon; though God knows what crime he is guilty of, but that of being a very great man and a wise and upright judge. Lord *Bellamont*, you will read in the votes, was fallen upon to-day; thus every day a minister, till we reach the King. By next post, I shall, I presume, be able to write you what relates to matters on your side. I am heartily tired with them on our side.[49]

The above letter, with its avowed admiration and sympathy for Somers, strengthens the belief that Prior wrote the verses on Lord Somers, ascribed to him in a manuscript copy of the poem in the Bodleian Library although there is no copy among the Prior papers either at Longleat or at Welbeck.

I.

When Envy does at Athens rise,
And fills the town with murmurs loud,
Not Aristides great and wise,
Can 'scape the busy factious crowd.

[47] *A Survey of English Literature 1730–1780*, II, 236.
[48] *Cambridge History of English Literature*, IX, 258.
[49] Cole, *Memoirs of Affairs of State*, p. 103, Prior to Manchester, Whitehall, Feb. 12/23, 1700.

II.

Each common vote augments the cry,
Nor he that holds the fatal shell,
Can see a cause or reason why
But being great and doing well.[50]

Throughout the spring, Prior watched with growing disgust the attacks of the Tory Parliament upon the Whig ministers. The simple way to remedy the awkward political situation did not occur to him any more than it did to King William or to any one else. The idea, as developed in modern parliamentary government, that the ministry must be of the same party as the parliamentary majority was not then recognized. But after Portland and Albemarle had both been threatened with attainder under the accusation of obtaining exorbitant grants and after the motion had been made that no foreigners except Prince George should be admitted to the King's Council, William prorogued Parliament. Jersey then advised him to dismiss his Whig ministers and form a Tory ministry. The King, consulting Tory leaders, pledged himself to a Tory council if they would guarantee a stable ministry. The inevitable had come. The days of the Whig Junto were over. Somers gave up the seals of his office, Shrewsbury resigned his position as Lord Chamberlain, and Jersey succeeded him.

This last change left Prior stranded, his brief term as an Under-Secretary of State at an end. Within a very few days, however, the King found other employment for him. Although there was no vacancy on the Board of Trade at the moment, King William ordered Prior's name to be added to the commission, so that whenever one should occur, it might be announced that the place was already supplied. Toward the end of June, John Locke, pleading ill health, sent in his resignation. When

[50] Bodleian Library, SC 29,558, fo. 27. Here the poem is entitled "On the Report of My Lord Somers's having to be remov'd from his office of Ld. High Chancellor. By Mr. Prior." It was published in *Poems on Affairs of State*, II, 247, where it bears the title "On Some Votes against Lord S-rs. Written about the year 1701."

Prior succeeded him, there was considerable talk. The Whigs attacked the appointment. They felt that it should have gone to a loyal Whig. The talk had not subsided when, at Hampton Court on June 28, 1700, Prior "kissed the King's hand for his appointment." To avoid unpleasantness, he waited to see the King in the Drawing Room, which was under the supervision of Jersey, rather than be presented by one of the "Whig Gentlemen of the Bed Chamber" in the King's private rooms, where such ceremonies usually took place.[51] The pettiness of party differences long rankled in Prior's mind, and years later in his essay on Opinion he voiced his scorn of this kind of tyranny:

A Party Man indeed, and such most of Us are, or must be, is an Animal that no Commentator upon Human Nature can sufficiently explain. He has not his Opinion, how sorry a World so ever it may be, in his own keeping. *Quo ad hoc* he is Mad, must speak without believing what he understands, without enquiring he Acts as implicitly according to the word of Command given out by the heads of his Faction as a Carthusian or a Jesuit does to the Will of his Superior. The Lye of the Day is the Rule of his life, and as his Judgment depends upon that of other Men, he must justify every thing that his Party Acts with the greatest Injustice, till from the Degrees of Warm and Violent, he comes up to Furious and Wicked. *Foenum habet in cornu*, and every body is obliged to yield or run from him.[52]

The Board of Trade and Plantations, to which the King had appointed Prior in the teeth of party opposition, had a wide range of authority. It supervised the government of all the American colonies, West Indian as well as continental; it regulated the great trading companies; it controlled the commerce of England with other nations. The business that came before the Board was so extensive and varied that finally a daily program was worked out. It ran something like this: Mondays were set aside for the reading of letters, memorials, and petitions; Tuesdays and Wednesdays for the conduct of plantation

[51] Strong, *Letters . . . at Welbeck*, App. V, p. 262.
[52] *Dialogues of the Dead*, p. 201.

business; Thursdays for the regulation of foreign trade; Fridays for the consideration of laws passed in the plantations.

All chief officers of state from the Bishop of London to the First Lord of the Admiralty were *ex officio* members of the Board, but were excused from attendance at ordinary meetings. In addition, there were eight members upon whom the duties generally devolved, and who were paid a salary of one thousand pounds per annum. When Prior became one of this number, his colleagues were John Pollexfen, Sir Philip Meadows, Abraham Hill, William Blathwayt, George Stepney, Lord Lexington, and the Earl of Stamford, the presiding officer.[53] From three to five of these "paid" members made a quorum. Prior's devoted friend, Adrian Drift, was deputy clerk of the Board. Though the reports of the Board bear the signature, "Matt: Prior," in faded ink, along with those of the other members in regular attendance, we cannot discover what Prior's individual attitude on any colonial question may have been, for the records contain only the final decisions and no account of the preliminary discussions. Certainly this position gave Prior a broader scope for his talents than was offered by the petty sinecures held by some of his friends. He should have held it for life, but he lost it when it became a political plum during Queen Anne's reign. It brought him into touch with Colonial leaders like William Penn and Peter Schuyler, and his name was known to the Colonists themselves. Samuel Sewall was acquainted with one of Matt's brief verse epitaphs even before it was published in England.[54]

The King left for Holland on July 4. In August Jersey followed

---

[53] *Documents relative to the Colonial History of the State of New York,* III, xv.

[54] Samuel Sewall, *Diary;* Letter Book II, 142, Jan. 15, 1721/2. "Inclosed Mr. Prior's Epitaph [which Govr. Saltonstall had not seen before]:

> Monarchs and Heraulds, by your leave
> Here ly the bones of Matthew Prior;
> The Son of Adam and of Eve,
> Can Bourbon, or Nassau, go higher?"

The epitaph with slight variations was first published in a *New Collection of Poems on Several Occasions by Mr. Prior and Others, 1725.*

William, leaving his new estate, the manor of Squeries in Kent, in Prior's charge. By the end of the summer Prior was asking permission to go to Holland. Jersey obtained the King's consent for him, impressing upon him the necessity of arranging his work so that the business of the Board of Trade would not be neglected.[55] Just why Prior was so eager to make this journey is not entirely clear. Before he could leave, Jersey got wind of the rumors that were being circulated about the trip and wrote Prior that the King was still willing for him to come, but failed to see any reason for his coming.[56] Perhaps King William was not anxious to have around him a young man like Matt with such a keen nose for news. At any rate, Jersey sent this word: "I hope this will come in time enough to prevent your coming hither . . . though I must own that it is very hard that one must comply with a prating malicious world."[57] Gossip had spoiled Prior's plans.

The only surviving child of the Princess Anne, the nine-year-old Duke of Gloucester, died on July 30. Soon after this sad event Lord Manchester warned King William that Anne was corresponding with James, her father.[58] If James would consent to her accepting the crown on William's death for the rest of her lifetime, she would agree to use her influence to pass the succession on to her brother. While in Holland, King William made a point of conferring with the Electress of Hanover, and shortly afterwards she consented to the agreement whereby she and her heirs would succeed to the throne of England after the Princess Anne. The Electress, now a sprightly old lady of seventy, had already been approached on the subject of the succession by Stepney, who reviewed the whole English situation in a letter remarkable for its wise statesmanship and tact.[59] Per-

[55] *Longleat Papers*, III, 415, Jersey to Prior, Breda, Aug. 29/Sept. 9, 1700.
[56] *Ibid.*, 416, Jersey to Prior, Loo, Sept. 6/17, 1700.
[57] *Ibid.*, 419, Jersey to Prior, Dieren, Sept. 19/30, 1700.
[58] Lamberty, *Mémoires pour servir a L'histoire du XVIIIme siècle*, I, 121.
[59] Onno Klopp, *Correspondance de Leibnitz avec l'électrice Sophie de Brunswick Lunebourg*, II, 208, George Stepney to the Electress Sophia, London, Sept. 11/21, 1700.

haps it was after the King's return to England that Prior and Jersey advised William to enter into an agreement with Louis to guarantee the succession of James III. William replied that he could never agree to betray his people. Jersey was intimate with Henry Hyde, Earl of Rochester, Anne's Jacobite uncle, and gossip had connected Prior's projected visit to Holland with his carrying a message from Rochester to Jersey. If Prior and Jersey at this time favored the succession of Anne's half brother at her death, they were doomed to disappointment. The King had used Stepney rather than Prior in laying plans for the succession.

"Mad and Knave" the world might be, as Jersey said it was, but Prior was restless to be in the thick of things and chafed at being left behind in London. Though he had often complained of the dullness of life abroad, he probably found this summer in London as dull as others elsewhere had been. He turned to a variety of tasks to occupy his time—attending the meetings of the Board of Trade, revising *Carmen Seculare* for a new edition, and making frequent trips to Squeries. The Earl of Jersey had left the plans for remodeling the house at Squeries in Prior's care. Along with a packet of plans for alterations in the new estate, Prior sent Jersey a sample of the handwriting of Lady Mary Villiers, the Earl's little daughter, saying, "Lady Mary, you see, writes well, and is a very good child."[60] Jersey thanked him with fatherly pride: "I find you know my weakness, or else you would never have sent Miss Mary's writing, though I own it very pretty for her age." It may have been at this time that Prior wrote the charming poem, "To a Child of Quality Five Years Old, the Author Forty, Written in 1704,"[61] which Dobson

---

[60] *Longleat Papers*, III, 422, Prior to Jersey, London, Oct. 3/14, 1700.

[61] *Dialogues of the Dead*, p. 85. This long title is first found in *Miscellaneous Works*, p. 25, and is repeated in all later editions of Prior's Works. There is an evident discrepancy in dates here. Certainly Lady Mary, who was married in 1710 to Henry Thynne, heir to Longleat, widowed and remarried in 1711 to Landsowne, was more than five years of age in 1704. Lansdowne's niece, Mrs. Mary Delany (in her *Autobiography and Correspondence*, Boston, 1882, I, 16) speaks of Lady Lansdowne as having been about thirty-seven years

has called "the crown of Prior's achievement," and Swinburne, "the most adorable of nursery idylls that ever was or will be in our language":

I.

Lords, knights and squires, the num'rous band,
That wear the fair Miss Mary's fetters,
Were summon'd by her high command,
To show their passions by their letters.

II.

My pen amongst the rest I took,
Lest those bright eyes that cannot read
Shou'd dart their kindling fires, and look,
The power they have to be obey'd.

III.

Nor quality, nor reputation,
Forbid me yet my flame to tell,
Dear five years old befriends my passion,
And I may write till she can spell.

IV.

For while she makes her silk-worms beds,
With all the tender things I swear,
Whilst all the house my passion reads,
In papers round her baby's hair.

V.

She may receive and own my flame,
For tho' the strictest prudes shou'd know it,
She'll pass for a most virtuous dame,
And I for an unhappy poet.

VI.

Then too alas! when she shall tear
The lines some younger rival sends,
She'll give me leave to write I fear,
And we shall still continue friends.

---

of age in 1717. According to Mrs. Delany's reckoning, Lady Mary must have been born about 1690. A passport to Paris in 1698 includes her along with her parents. It seems more likely that the year when Prior wrote the poem was 1700, when she was ten and he, thirty-six.

VII.

> For as our diff'rent ages move,
> 'Tis so ordain'd, wou'd fate but mend it,
> That I shall be past making love
> When she begins to comprehend it.

The poem calls to mind some verses of Marvell, Waller, Etherege, and Sedley on a similar theme, yet Prior's poem is more than a conventional exercise. The winsome Lady Mary with her flaming hair done up in curl papers—the poet's *billet-doux* serve the purpose—takes shape before our eyes, and we can easily imagine the "unhappy poet" a willing victim to her wiles. But Matthew's prophecy

> That I shall be past making love
> When she begins to comprehend it

was false. In 1711, Lady Mary—still very young, although a widow—was married to George Granville, Lord Lansdowne, who was only two years Prior's junior. For complicity in the Jacobite plot of 1715, Lord Lansdowne spent almost two years of confinement in the Tower. Lady Lansdowne shared his punishment with him. Soon after her release, she asked permission to have a copy made of the original Kneller portrait of her that Prior owned. For some reason, he refused the request.[62] She is said to have been very handsome, very gay, and very fond of masculine admiration. But she did not "pass for a most virtuous dame"; Lansdowne's niece, Mrs. Delany, wrote of Lady Mary that she was extravagant, given to dissipation and libertine manners, acquired in France.[63]

» 5 «

On November 1, 1700, the King of Spain, whose life had been hanging by a thread for months, rallied feebly and then died.

---

[62] *Longleat Papers*, III, 458, Mary, Lady Lansdowne of Biddeford to Prior, Sept. 4/15, 1718.

[63] Mrs. Mary Delany (Mrs. Pendarves), *Autobiography and Correspondence*, ed. by Lady Llanover, London, 1861–1862, I, 81–82.

King William, who had just returned from Holland, was now doubly disappointed that the obstinate Austrian Emperor had not signed the Partition Treaty. He sent for Prior, intending to intrust him with another secret errand, this time to Brussels. His commission was to tell the Elector of Bavaria that the King of England desired to keep affairs in the *status quo* until the Austrian Emperor should declare his intentions and that meanwhile the Elector should continue to act as Governor of the Spanish Netherlands. William's plan was frustrated. Before Prior started for Brussels a special dispatch arrived from Lord Manchester saying that Louis, rather than abide by the treaty, had decided to accept the Spanish King's will, which provided that Philip of Anjou should be set upon the throne of Spain.[64] In the words of the impetuous Spanish Ambassador, the Pyrenees had ceased to exist. Louis had rashly upset William's carefully laid plans and had touched off the spark that was to plunge Europe into a decade of war.

At first William was determined that Louis should be forced to keep his word. He would send Prior once more to Paris, with an order to Manchester to demand publicly the execution of the treaty. By the time that his wrath had cooled, he had disclosed his plans to Rochester and Godolphin, his new Tory ministers, who advised him not to insist on the treaty, for public sentiment favored the will rather than the treaty.[65] With prevailing opinion in England against him, there was nothing for William to do but hide his disappointment over the failure of his treaty, recognize the grandson of his enemy as Philip V of Spain, and wait patiently for an opportunity to get even with Louis.

As a consequence of the failure of William's plans, Prior did not go to Paris, nor did he again visit the Court of Louis XIV until a compliant Tory ministry sent him there on a secret errand for peace eleven years later. His journey now canceled,

[64] Strong, *Letters . . . at Welbeck*, App. V, pp. 263–64. (Prior's Diary.)
[65] Paris, Archives . . . , *Correspondance Politique, d'Angleterre*, 190, fo. 24, Tallard to Louis XIV, Dec. 10/20, 1700.

he sent to Manchester an account of the political situation in England. Parliamentary elections were under way, the campaign being marked by unprecedented corruption and bribery. Prior had decided to stand for Parliament as representative from Cambridge and asked Manchester to write a letter in his behalf to the university. In accordance with his aversion to party government, he scorned both the Whigs and Tories, preferring to appear as a "Moderate," or as he expressed it, "we take it to be our play to be for those who will support the Crown rather than oblige either party." He conveniently changed his views on the Partition Treaty—Prior was not a man to cling to an unpopular issue. He now thought it fortunate for King William that Louis had preferred the will to the treaty at a time when everybody was "peevish against the Court (though with reason God knows) about the treaty."[66]

The idea of representing his university in Parliament was not new, it having been in his mind ever since the days of his Paris secretaryship when some of his friends had suggested that he seek that honor. At that time he had sought to obtain for Cambridge a set of Greek types from the royal presses in Paris by which the famous Louvre edition of the classics was published. Much correspondence was carried on with the French authorities, but Prior left Paris before the matter was settled. The French at first made stipulations which the university authorities could not accept. Upon the title page of every book, they insisted, must be inserted the words, *Cantabrigiae Typis Academicis Caracteribus Graecis Regis Christianissimi*. Furthermore, the payment for the type must be made in books from England, and the formula for the ink used in the recent publications of Horace and Virgil must be given to the French Royal Press. The Earl of Manchester continued Prior's bargainings. The long inscription was finally shortened to *Typographei Regis*, and a "kind of com-

---

[66] Cole, *Memoirs of Affairs of State*, p. 269, Prior to Manchester, London, Dec. 10/20, 1700.

munication" *propter bonum accommodum reipublicae literae* was
established between the university and the French Royal Library. Perhaps it was in recognition of these efforts that the
university in the spring of 1700 awarded Prior the degree of
Master of Arts. His visit to Cambridge for the conferring of the
degree, as well as his frequent communications with the university, where he still held a fellowship, had other consequences.
The suggestion that he represent his university in Parliament
appealed to his vanity. Since it was too early, however, to an-
nounce his candidacy, he merely expressed a desire to serve the
university on any or all occasions.

By October he was astonished to learn that his friends thought
he had given up his parliamentary ambitions. Though he declared that he had more freedom and leisure than he had enjoyed
in ten years, he would not bestir himself except to address a
letter to James Talbot, Fellow of Trinity College, Cambridge,
setting forth his qualifications, his political principles, and his
conduct as candidate. On the subject of his qualifications he
was most eloquent:

I presume they[Prior's friends at Cambridge] had an eye to my having
been from the age of sixteen and to my continuing till that of thirty-
four a member of that community, not a pensioner or a fellow-com-
moner, but scholar of the house and fellow of a college, my name constantly in the books and my correspondence with my friends kept up,
as well as my having acted abroad in several stations so as to capacitate
me in all probability to represent so illustrious a body.

About his political principles, he spoke vaguely, stating in
general terms his ideal of government without party:

To this I add that I understand they would have some person whose
principle it was to represent, as occasion might require, their steadiness
to support the true rights of the English monarchy and the real preser-
vation of theirs and the nation's liberty.

Nor would he make an active campaign although Talbot advised him to come to Cambridge and appoint a "professed

agent" in St. John's, where Hammond, the present incumbent, a High Tory, was the "idol of that society:"

I would no more plead my merit to be a Parliament man than Coriolanus would shew his wounds to be a Consul, and my proceeding in and desisting from my first intention will be wholly governed by the encouragement or coldness which I may receive from the University.[67]

Anthony Hammond, Prior's opponent, had no scruples against appearing publicly as a candidate. To impress the electors, while on visits to Cambridge, he wore his gown, kept chapel and hall, and bowed to all he met. Friends urged Prior to manifest an industry similar to that of his opponent. At last Prior did discuss his candidacy with Gower only to learn that he was already pledged to Hammond. The Master of St. John's assured Prior of his respect and admiration but advised him not to appear without a fair prospect of success, believing that defeat would only lessen his chances another time.[68] Such advice could only increase Matt's fear of humiliation should he display too great an interest and then fail of election. Lacking the support of the Master of his own college, Prior decided to withdraw from the race.[69] Hammond won the election from his Whig opponent, Henry Boyle, only to be defeated the following year by a greater man, Sir Isaac Newton, when a Whig reaction returned many of that party to office. It was not until years later that Prior again sought the place, with as little success, it might be said in passing, as before. He was destined never to represent his university in Parliament.

Having failed to win the support of his university, he turned for encouragement to the Earl of Dorset, who gave him the pocket borough of East Grinstead in Sussex as a consolation. Prior's career in Parliament was indeed brief, undistinguished, and, from a personal point of view, unfortunate. When the

[67] *Longleat Papers*, III, 422, Prior to J. Talbot, London, Oct. 4/15, 1700.
[68] *Ibid.*, 430, Dr. Humphrey Gower to Prior, Ely, Dec. 11/22, 1700.
[69] Brit. Mus., *Stowe MSS*, 755, fo. 39, Prior to J. Talbot, Dec. 19/30, 1700.

House of Commons met in February, the Tories, who had prevailed in the election, decided to profit by the unpopularity of the Partition Treaty and bring the former Whig ministers to punishment. The impeachment of Somers, Orford, Portland, and Halifax was therefore ordered, although three of them had known nothing of the treaty until after it was signed and had disapproved of it as soon as they learned its import. At first, Portland and Jersey alone had been in the secret. Nevertheless the King decided to let his former ministers bear the brunt of the failure of the treaty. On April 1, Portland was impeached, and on April 12, Prior and fifty-five other members formed a commission to translate the correspondence between Vernon and Portland relating to the treaty.[70] Two days later, the three other lords were also declared guilty of high crime and misdemeanor. Not a word was said about Jersey's connection with the treaty, although Jersey had been privy to it and his name, along with Portland's, was attached to it when it was signed. The Tories had no intention of embarrassing one of their own number. The votes stood ten against Somers, forty-five against Orford, and fifty against Halifax. Prior voted in favor of all the impeachments and was at once accused of treachery to Halifax and Portland. That, as he later wrote,

> Matthew, who knew the whole Intrigue
> Ne'er much approv'd That Mystic League

signifies little, for in the same poem[71] he spoke disparagingly of the Treaty of Utrecht. He could have disapproved of the Partition Treaty and yet voted against the impeachments. Only one of the six articles preferred against Halifax in the impeachment charges referred to the treaty; the others attacked his acceptance of grants. Sir James Montague generously explained Prior's vote for the impeachment of his brother:

[70] House of Commons, Journal, 1701, 130, William III, 487.
[71] "The Conversation, A Tale," *Dialogues of the Dead*, p. 77.

Mr. Prior has often owned that he was more embarrassed, and less knew what to do than in any transaction that happened to concern him either before or afterwards . . . he found himself driven to this difficulty, either to desert his Master William, by owning that the lords accused were not consulted with by His Majesty in the carrying on of that treaty, or to fall in with the majority of the House of Commons in voting them the advisers, which was at that time thought the easiest expedient to free the King from the clamour of taking measures so contrary to the interest of England.[72]

Such was Prior's own explanation. Although then it may have satisfied the Chief Baron of the Exchequer, today it sounds somewhat disingenuous and unconvincing. The fact that Jersey approved of the impeachment influenced Prior considerably; furthermore he wanted to stand well with the majority in Parliament, and at the same time to shield the King.

As a consequence of this unfortunate vote, a friendship which had begun when Matt and Charles were children was broken. Halifax was shocked by Matt's disloyalty and for several years would have no correspondence with him. But he never sought revenge and even spoke of Prior in kindly terms. Prior eventually begged Halifax to renew the friendship, saying that it "ought to be continued to our graves." However, Matt's conduct in the affair was inexplicably ill-humored as an entry in his diary reveals:

5th Jan: 170⅘. Mr. James Montagu went to see Mr. Prior, but was denied.[73]

Perhaps James had called in the hope of receiving some explanation of the whole matter. In spite of Matt's sulkiness, he behaved amiably and declared that the friendship between himself and Matt "never ceased till death parted them."[74]

Stepney thoroughly disapproved of Matt's disloyalty. From him there came a cold but polite letter. He regretted that false

[72] Sir James Montague's "Memorandums," in Prior, *Selected Poems*, ed. Dobson, p. 217.
[73] Strong, *Letters . . . at Welbeck*, App. V, p. 266.
[74] Sir James Montague's "Memorandums," in Prior, *Selected Poems*, ed. Dobson, p. 219.

constructions had been placed on a conversation which he had held with Prior before departing from London; he had let Prior's last two letters go unanswered, being unable to distinguish, from Vienna, between friend and foe; furthermore, he feared that his letters "though never so innocent," might be falsely construed as his discourse had been.[75]

To Halifax, Stepney expressed frankly his opinion of Prior. While he did not mince matters, there is a wistful remembrance of the days when the two boys had been Matt and Catt in Channel Row:

Mr. Prior had declared himself so far before I left you that I am not surprised at what has happened since, though I cannot but be concerned for one I have known so long, and the rather because I am now too old to contract new friendships. If this Parliament should be broke . . . I hope my Lord Dorset's good intention will not be so far imposed upon as to set him [Prior] up again as Representative. He has been nibbling towards drawing me into a correspondence with him, but I waived it in as cold a manner as I could.[76]

In September an act of Louis XIV furnished William with the necessary motive for overruling his Tory ministers and dismissing the insurgent Parliament. King James having died at Saint-Germain on September 13, Louis, according to his promise, promptly recognized James's son as James III, King of England. The Treaty of Ryswick was, as Stepney said, "torn to tatters."

Prior was not a member of the new Parliament which met the following winter. Probably Dorset, a fast friend to all the lords impeached, refused him the pocket borough. In the paper warfare carried on between the parties in the December election, the Whigs published a "Black List" of one hundred and sixty-seven particularly obnoxious Tories. Prior's name is to be found on this list in company with those of such High Tories as Hammond, Davenant, and St. John.[77]

---

[75] P. R. O., *Stepney Papers*, 105/63, Stepney to Prior, Vienna, June 29/July 9, 1701.
[76] *Ibid.*, Stepney to Halifax, Vienna, August 13/24, 1701.
[77] *Somers Tracts*, IV, Part 3, pp. 34–37.

Prior's desertion of his friends did not go unnoticed by the pamphleteers; several attacks on him were published in *Poems on Affairs of State*. Two of them indicate Dorset's displeasure and Prior's pains to make amends. Of one, "England's Late Jury," five lines suffice to show the trend of the satire:

> The times are likely sure to mend,
> When P—r rules the State;
> P—r the Noble *Dorset's* friend
> (For whom the Learned World contend)
> Justly deserves his Hate.[78]

In the other, "A Reformation of Manners," Daniel Defoe resorted to scurrilous remarks about Prior's early career in his uncle's tavern, a means of vilification to which Prior's political enemies often stooped:

> And with the nauseous Rabble that retire,
> Turn out that Bawdy Saucy Poet P—r,
> A Vintner's Boy the Wretch was first preferr'd,
> To wait at Vice's Gates and Pimp for Bread.
> To hold the Candle, and sometimes the Door,
> Let in the Drunkard, and let out the Whore,
> But as to Villains it has often chanc'd,
> Was for his Wit and Wickedness advanc'd,
> Let no Man think his new Behavior strange,
> No metamorphosis can Nature change;
> *Effects are chain'd to Causes*, generally
> The Rascal born will like a Rascal die.

The author of "The True-Born Englishman" had written a popular poem that had done William more service than Prior's dull *Carmen Seculare*. He had discovered what he considered a satire of Prior's on King William, and so the "Reformation of Manners" continues the charge:

> His Prince's Favours follow'd him in vain,
> They chang'd the Circumstance, but not the Man.

_____

[78] *Poems on Affairs of State*, III, 369.

> While out of Pocket, and his Spirits low,
> He'd beg, write Panegyricks, cringe and bow;
> But when good Pensions had his Labours crown'd,
> His Panegyricks into Satyrs turn'd,
> And with a true Mechanick Spirit curst,
> Abus'd his Royal Benefactor first.
> O what assiduous Pains does P—r take,
> To let great D—— see he could mistake!
> Dissembling Nature false Description gave,
> Shew'd him the Poet, and conceal'd the Knave.[79]

The only poem of Prior's which might have been taken as a satire on King William is a little verse fable, facetious and in poor taste, that is more an attack upon parties than upon King William. As published in *Poems on Affairs of State* it was ascribed to a Lord J——s, but there is a copy of the poem with slight variations among the Prior papers at Longleat:

> *A Fable.*
>
> In *Aesop's* Tales an honest Wretch we find,
> Whose Years and Comforts equally declin'd;
> He in two Wives had two domestick Ills,
> For different Age they had, and different Wills;
> One pluckt his black Hairs out, and one his Grey,
> The Man for Quietness did both obey,
> Till all his Parish saw his Head quite bare,
> And thought he wanted Brains as well as Hair.
>
> *The Moral*
>
> The Parties, hen-peckt W——m, are thy Wives,
> The Hairs they pluck are thy Prerogatives;
> Tories thy Person hate, the Whigs thy Power,
> Tho much thou yieldest, still they tug for more,
> Till this poor Man and thou alike are shown,
> He without Hair, and thou without a Crown.[80]

---

[79] *Ibid.*, II, 356.

[80] *Dialogues of the Dead*, p. 316. A copy of the poem is also to be found in *Hanoverian State Papers*, British Museum, *Stowe MSS.*, 222, fo. 124, with the following endorsement by M. Robethon, private secretary to William III and afterwards to the Elector of Hanover: "Esops-Tale, 1701 par le Sr. Prior."

It is gratifying to know that Stepney's resentment against Matt did not last forever. In December, 1702, he wrote in a warmer mood. He was even in no hurry for Prior to pay him the "forty-nine pieces as the Spanish Friar has it"—an allusion to a small debt that Prior owed him. But a new Whig poet had taken Prior's place in the friendships of Stepney and Halifax; he was Joseph Addison. While Addison was in Vienna, Stepney had found him good company. Stepney praised the "Essay on Medals" as an "ingenious" piece and sent Prior for "present use" a manuscript copy of Addison's "Letter from Italy," inscribed to Halifax.[81] Furthermore, to please Halifax, Stepney gave Addison a handsome letter of introduction to the Electress. Thus we may see Addison's favor with the Whigs rising as Prior's declined.[82]

On February 21, 1702, while King William was hunting near Hampton Court, his horse stumbled, throwing him so violently to the ground that his collarbone was broken. The injury was such a shock to his health that he never recovered from it; after a few weeks of severe suffering, he succumbed to death, which he had so often faced valiantly upon the fields of Flanders. What Prior's thoughts on the death of the gallant fighter may have been are unrecorded; he left no panegyric such as he had written when he was "making his bows and soliciting an embassy."

A last act of King William's which concerns us here was his formation of the Grand Alliance between England, Holland, and Austria to carry on the struggle against Louis XIV. Into partnership with him he took John Churchill, then Earl of Marlborough. Two years after King William's death Prior hailed the rising Marlborough in a poem of praise. It contained an oblique and tardy lament for the "First of Men, and Best of Kings":

[81] P. R. O., *Stepney Papers*, 105/66, Stepney to Prior, Vienna, Dec. 16/27, 1702.
[82] *Ibid.*, Stepney to Halifax, Vienna, Dec. 16/27, 1702.

BELGIA receives Him [Marlborough] welcome to her Shores;
And WILLIAM's Death with Lessen'd Grief deplores.
His Presence only must retrieve That Loss:
MARLBRÔ to Her must be what WILLIAM was.
So when great ATLAS, from these low Aboads
Recall'd, was gather'd to his Kindred-Gods,
ALCIDES, respited by prudent Fate,
Sustain'd the Ball, nor dropp'd beneath the Weight.[83]

---

[83] *Poems on Several Occasions*, p. 130.

CHAPTER VII

Middle Years in London

» 1 «

ON ST. GEORGE'S day, April 23, 1702, Princess Anne was crowned Queen at the age of thirty-seven. Unlike her chatterbox sister Mary, Anne was silent, moody, dull. Her consort, Prince George, honest Danish soldier that he was, contributed nothing to the English Court but a ponderous dullness and a wistful blindness to the shortcomings of the dowdy and corpulent Anne, whose hearty appetite continually demanded food. Anne's gastronomical indulgences resulted in attacks of gout, in swathings and bandages, so that at her coronation she had to be wheeled to Westminster Hall in a sedan and carried across Broad Sanctuary to the ceremonies.

When the new reign opened, Prior was thirty-seven years old —just the age of his queen. His loyal and intelligent service under King William should have augured well for him. His commission on the Board of Trade and Plantations was renewed promptly, but to a man of Prior's ambition this was a relatively unimportant position. During the last few months before William's death he had sought, without success,[1] to obtain the keepership of the records in the place of Sir Joseph Williamson. His vote on the impeachment, he suspected, was the cause of his failure. But all was changed with the coronation of Anne. The Tories felt that now they had a sovereign who was their very own and were eagerly awaiting the distribution of royal favors. By his vote on the impeachment Prior had bid for a seat in the

[1] Luttrell, *Brief Historical Relation*, V, 98, Oct. 9, 1701.

Tory bandwagon. The four impeached lords were soon to be replaced; there would be two new Secretaries of State; hence an appointment as under-secretary was not unlikely for Prior. Already he had one friend in the new ministerial household—Jersey, who was continued as Lord Chamberlain.

All signs pointed to a period of domestic quiet. The Whigs were subdued; the good Queen's Tory supporters filled the offices. There was nothing to disturb the serenity so long as the ministers should acquiesce in Marlborough's plans. Marlborough, soon after Anne's accession, departed for the Continent, and the War of the Spanish Succession began its long course, sustained by the inexhaustible wealth of England and Holland and by the undiminishable armies of the Austrian Empire. French mothers, who had prematurely expressed their joy at the death of William, believing that it meant the end of war, were now beginning to hush their children with the national lullaby, "Malbrook s'en va-t-en guerre." In England, the Duke had left his friend Godolphin, as Lord Treasurer, to rule the national purse strings, and his wife, the Duchess, to rule the Queen. The reign of the Marlboroughs had in reality begun, as Jersey and his friends, especially Prior, were soon to learn to their sorrow.

In London, life was uneventful enough—as quiet as the last years of the reign were stormy. So it was with Prior. From his house in Duke Street, he sauntered to the meetings of the Board of Trade at the Cockpit or joined his High Tory friends at the Smyrna Tavern. In spite of all his expectations, he was not so happy in London as he had hoped to be. He was too restless, too discontented, to settle down to the dull existence so shrewdly described in his lines on "Sauntering Jack and Idle Joan," who

> led—a kind of—as it were;
> Nor wish'd, nor car'd, nor laugh'd, nor cry'd;
> And so they liv'd; and so they dy'd.[2]

---

[2] *Poems on Several Occasions*, p. 183.

Records of his activities during the opening years of the reign of Queen Anne are scarce. When his under-secretaryship of state terminated in the summer of 1700, the long flow of diplomatic correspondence of ten years ceased. His position on the Board of Trade did not entail official letters, and since he was not fond of letter-writing unless that duty were a part of his business,[3] there are no letters for the years 1701 to 1703 to aid the biographer. His correspondence was scant also during the years immediately following. Moreover, he is mentioned so rarely by his literary contemporaries during these years that one might almost think he had been exiled to an American plantation. Perhaps, since all loyal Whigs after the impeachment trial regarded him as a renegade and an ingrate, he was merely being ignored. The chief source of information concerning Matt at this time is certain personal reflections, jotted down in his diary with neither method nor regularity, but revealing his disappointment and discouragement at repeated drubbings of fortune.

His life, however, had brighter aspects. He could so successfully lay aside the cares of business to don the jester's cap at the Smyrna Tavern that he became noted as a Wit—Sichel even calls him the Pierrot of English literature.[4] Prior himself has commented on the two sides of his nature:

> In public employments industrious and grave,
> And alone with his friends, Lord, how merry was he.[5]

Furthermore, the reassuring note of the *carpe diem* philosopher is sounded often in Prior's verse, notably in these lines:

> The Moments past, if Thou art wise, retrieve
> With pleasant Mem'ry of the Bliss they gave.
> The present Hours in present Mirth imploy;
> And bribe the Future with the Hopes of Joy.[6]

---

[3] *History of His Own Time*, p. 181.
[4] Sichel, *Bolingbroke and his Times*, I, 284.
[5] *Dialogues of the Dead*, p. 129.
[6] *Poems on Several Occasions*, p. 195.

A Whig official of the period records that Prior was "very factious in conversation"—a comment, no doubt, on his sharp tongue and ready repartee.[7] Even persons who smarted from his witticisms had to admit his cleverness. Defoe, though disgruntled with all High Tories and perhaps personally angry with Matt, made grudging reference in *The Consolidator*[8] to the poet's wit. Swift, too, thought him a "good companion" though not a "fair one," for he "left no elbow room for others."[9] Certainly Prior's wit was the subject of much contemporary comment, and Dr. Freind, who wrote Prior's epitaph, leaves unsettled the question as to whether Prior was "in his writings the more elegant poet or in his conversation the more facetious companion."[10]

Prior expressed himself freely about the nature of wit in the "Essay upon Learning," where he named the Earl of Dorset as the perfect Wit. Wide reading, Prior thought, should form the background of raillery; one should never be as witty as one could; wit should never be used as a sword but rather as a shield. In all these respects Dorset excelled, he said, and in addition Dorset always tempered his severest satire with compliment. The Earl's companions, the Duke of Buckingham and Fleetwood Sheppard, had been acknowledged Wits, but Prior thought the one too much inclined to burlesque—witness *The Rehearsal*—and the other to romance and improbability.[11] Prior followed his own criteria well and was accorded high place as a Wit by the Queen Anne men.

As an "elegant poet," to borrow Dr. Freind's phrase, Prior was achieving distinction. His verse was praised by Congreve:

> If Addison, or Rowe, or Prior write,
> We study 'em with Profit and Delight.[12]

[7] Macky, *Characters of the Court of Great Britain*, p. 135.   [8] *The Consolidator*, p. 27.
[9] Patrick Delany, *Observations upon Lord Orrery's Remarks*, London. 1754, p. 202.
[10] Translation by Samuel Humphreys, in his edition of Prior's *Poems on Several Occasions*, III, 54.   [11] *Dialogues of the Dead*, p. 186.
[12] "Of Pleasing; an Epistle to Sir Richard Temple."

The good Dr. Garth paid him compliment with a far-fetched conceit:

> When Stepney paints the godlike act of Kings,
> Or what Apollo dictates Prior sings,
> The Banks of Rhine a pleas'd attention show,
> And silver Sequana forgets to flow.[13]

But perhaps Prior himself was more pleased with the soft words of Anne Finch, later Countess of Winchilsea:

> Thy melting Numbers and polite address,
> In ev'ry Fair raise passion to excess
> To cultivate the heart, or charm the mind.[14]

There follows the conventional simile of the bird who mimics his "teacher's note"—such an imitation, says the poetess, is her verse.

Lady Winchilsea frequently mentioned Prior in her poems.[15] Since her husband, Heneage Finch, was a member of the same High Tory family as Daniel Finch, Earl of Nottingham, the leader of the faction to which Prior and Jersey belonged, we assume that it was through Nottingham that Prior became acquainted with her.[16]

His poems continued to appear in the many miscellanies of the time. The Fifth Part of Tonson's *Miscellanies*, published during the winter of 1703/4—perhaps the choicest collection of verse of the early years of the reign of Queen Anne—contained no less than eighteen poems of Prior's, in addition to selections from Dorset, Addison, Congreve, Lansdowne, Mrs. Singer, and other poets of the hour. There was considerable variety among Prior's verses in the volume. Fontainesque tales like "Hans Carvel"

[13] *The Dispensary*, Canto IV. [14] Prior, *Miscellaneous Works*, p. xx.
[15] Wellesley College Library, Lady Winchilsea MSS, pp. 61, 83. See also "A Tale of the Miser and the Poet," *Poems of Anne Countess of Winchilsea*, p. 191.
[16] Another female writer who sang Prior's praises was the learned Elizabeth Elstob, who in the preface to her *Rudiments of Grammar* (London, 1715, p. xxvi), referred to "that darling of the Muses, Prior, with whom all the poets of ancient and modern times, of all nations, or of our own, might seem to have entrusted the chief secrets and greatest treasures of their art."

and "The Ladle" appeared in the company of such solemn pieces as the "Dying Hadrian to his Soul" and the paraphrase of the thirteenth chapter of First Corinthians. Although most of the selections included by Tonson had been published elsewhere, the charming "To a Child of Quality" made its first appearance here, as well as several light amorous odes and songs in that rococo style which pointed directly to the *Rape of the Lock*. Tonson's heavy drawing upon Prior's poetical stock indicates that Prior was the leading poet during these years—the Wasp of Twickenham was still but a "bright eyed urchin."[17]

Prior, now a "thin hollow-looked" man just turned forty, cultivated his gift for gay trifling verse and produced many other fabliaux, epigrams, odes, and songs, a really representative selection of which was not published until circumstances forced him to bring out an authorized volume in 1709. But he was not duly impressed by the reputation his poetry had brought him. Increasingly frequent were his reiterations that he was only a poet by accident and that it was high time for him to quit Parnassus. None of the literary-political men of the period could afford to devote all his time to writing. Not until the tremendous success of Pope's *Homer* do we find a poet whose works proved so lucrative that he could be independent of patronage. Furthermore, the fashionable attitude towards letters was that dictated by Boileau in his *L'Art poétique* and translated by Dryden thus:

> Let not your only bus'ness be to write;
> Be virtuous, just, and in your friends delight:
> 'Tis not enough your poems be admir'd;
> But strive your conversation be desir'd.[18]

But one could not enjoy the reputation of poet or Wit in Augustan society unless he were rewarded by an income larger

[17] In 1703 John Walsh, London music publisher, printed Prior's "A Song" (*Poems on Several Occasions*, p. 63) with music by John Eccles in *The Monthly Mask of Vocal Music*, p. 29, and in 1704 reprinted the poem with Eccles's music in *A Collection of Songs for One, Two and Three Voices . . .* , p. 59.

[18] Dryden, *Poetical Works*, App. I, p. 916.

and more regular than that derived from a commission on the
Board of Trade, especially if one were as prodigal or as epicurean in his tastes as Prior. With the clean sweep of the Whigs
on the coming of Anne to the throne, there were plenty of offices
to be had and there were no objections, legal or social, to
pluralism. One need look back no further than to the previous
reign for illustrations of party patronage. Had not Halifax,
starting out as the poor son of a younger brother to an earl,
battened on the spoils of office, and was he not now comfortably
settled in a fat sinecure from which even the Tories could not
dislodge him? Prior's chief handicap was his lack of family influence. The Montagues and George Stepney, while they may
have been as poor as Prior when they were all at college, did not
lack that *sine qua non* which was more indispensable in the time
of Anne than in that of William.

No doubt Prior looked longingly back to the more liberal
days of King William, when the antecedents of a political
servant were less important than his trustworthiness. Queen
Anne, less approachable than William and hemmed in by social
prejudices, was not inclined to promote to high office a person
of "mean extraction"—thus she once referred to Prior. Of the
same mind were the High Tory leaders—Nottingham, Seymour,
and Rochester, who in spite of Jersey's pleading, snubbed Prior.
With the passing of the Whigs, Prior's old friends, Vernon and
Manchester, were succeeded as Secretaries of State by Nottingham and Hedges. It seems ironical that Prior should have expected so much from these Tories whose party was traditionally
disdainful of the self-made man. He held now only his commission on the Board of Trade. Despite all his bright hopes of the
new reign, he was unable to wheedle an additional appointment from the ministers. Only four months after the coronation
of Anne, Prior made an entry in his diary pouring out disappointment and bitter resentment at the ingratitude of his fellow
men:

August 20, 1702.
I have met with such Ingratitude and found so ill returns in the World
that makes me have so vile an opinion of mankind in general that in
some humours I persuade myself that my friendship with my Ld
Jersey will one day break and I prepare my Self as it were for it; tho'
I have no reason for any such thought from any action of my Lord to
me; and tho' in Justice I ought to be blamed for the Wildness of this
Imagination. I have cried twenty times upon forming the imagination
of my Ld Jersey dead, while he was yet in good health.[19]

Here there is not only a Swiftian misanthropy but also a deep
melancholy, which Mr. Doughty explains as but the reflex of
Prior's passion for life. From one who was outwardly a representative of the age of common sense, this romantic sensibility
comes as a surprise, but it may account for those minor notes
that we often find even in the lighter poems of Prior.

Ten months elapsed before another entry was made in the
diary. For the date June 24, 1703, there are two entries in the
same morbid vein as the one quoted above:

Midsummer day happened the greatest private affliction to me that I
ever was sensible of, tho' I did not know it till 4 days after: and the
next day I had an affliction of the same kind (more domestic) which
both made me so Melancholy that Life was a burthen to me for a long
time.

Reflecting about this time on my own life I concluded that however I
had mistaken the path of life proper for me I was not born for a Courtier
being in my temper too passionate and too open in my conversation.[20]

What the two "private afflictions" were—the one, the greatest he had ever experienced, the other, the "more domestic"—
we are not told. Disappointment at the hands of men whom he
had trusted for preferment, foreboding that he would be robbed
of his most valued friendship, disillusionment about his own
proper career in life—all befell him in quick succession during
a brief space of time.

Prior's alliance with the High Tories resulted, unfortunately,

---

[19] Strong, *Letters . . . at Welbeck*, App. V, p. 265.   [20] *Ibid.*, p. 265.

in his becoming the pawn of the two factions of the Tory party. High Tories and Moderates disagreed about the national war policies. Nottingham and Godolphin engaged in a little duel in which Prior, as Nottingham's man, for the first time incurred the disfavor of the powerful Lord Treasurer. In the summer of 1703, Godolphin, overruling an objection from Nottingham, sent Richard Hill as trusted envoy to Turin. Hill, though a Tory was not a High Tory; he had no Jacobite sympaties and was heartily in favor of England's pursuing the war against Louis on all frontiers. His mission in Turin was to persuade the Duke of Savoy to enter the war on the side of the Allies. Since Nottingham had been balked in this appointment, he sought to maintain his influence by proposing that Prior take a post at Venice. Godolphin firmly rejected this proposal, explaining that Hill could attend to any necessary diplomatic business in Venice on his way to Turin.[21] Hill's errand was a success, and he remained in Turin for several years as Godolphin's trusted agent, while it was Prior's fate to court the favor of the implacable Lord Treasurer patiently, unsuccessfully.

In the autumn of this same unhappy year, Colonel George Villiers, the husband of Matthew's cousin Katherine, was drowned in Italy. Prior mourned the death of his friend in a poem, an imitation of Horace—the 28th Ode of Book One.[22] It is one of the best of his serious poems, having a smoothness and inevitability of phrasing such as he admired in his model. The theme of the poem—man's powerlessness in the face of destiny—reflects the mood of gloom which had beset Prior temporarily and which was always nearer the surface than is generally supposed.

With a letter to Richard Hill, both a friend and rival, Prior enclosed a copy of the poem, suggesting that it might bear com-

[21] Brit. Mus., *Add MSS*, 29,589, fo. 153, Godolphin to Nottingham, Sept. 9/20, 1703. See also Hugh Elliott, *Life of Sidney, Earl of Godolphin*, p. 273.

[22] *Poems on Several Occasions*, p. 121.

parison with Horace. Since the letter, which has not been published elsewhere, contains much tart comment, we quote it here:

Your rebuke, my Dear Mr. Hill, is so justly founded and so gently worded that it leaves room for no manner of answer on my side. I own I ought to have written to the man to whom I owe a thousand obligations, and I once more promise you that I will write to the friend who can so kindly forgive my neglect: but what the devil to write? ay, that is the question; why was my Lord Jersey put out and my Lord Kent put in? Why do you chase a partridge and so not harm a cuckoo? Why has S'ms got 50 thousand pound by gaming, yet I threw out 2 hands last night and lost my crown, *sic voluit fortuna jocari*; for I seriously believe nobody can give you or me a reason, at least nobody attempts so doing it: I will send you no news, that is Mr. Ellis's province: a new parliament or no new parliament is now the great doubt: which, I think, Harley, who, under my Lord Treasurer, is the minister; can only determine. My Lord Treasurer had the garter yesterday. Everybody is in good humour for the news from Germany, King Galway is going to Portugal, Rook railed at for not doing impossibilities. We of the laboring Board of Trade are half a year in arrears, Cecil is sick. We do not know if he can live or no. Bl[athway]t has as much fire and liveliness as ever, and everything is *comme chez nous*: apropos, is there any hope of my coming to Venice, and if there is, pray give me, as Sir Joseph used to phrase it, a dash of your pen. Adieu, my dear Mr. Hill, keep yourself from being knocked on the head, and believe me from my soul, nobody loves you with more truth and zeal than,

Yours ever,
Mat Prior.

I send you a melancholy paper of Verses which I made upon poor Villiers' death, if you have your Horace by you, compare 'em. I have made your compliments to Lord and Lady Jersey. You are in the right of it in thinking I will always stand by him as firm as any Roman *libertus* did by his Master. Once more, my dear Mr. Hill, adieu.[23]

So Prior was again in financial difficulties: his pay on the Board of Trade was half a year in arrears, and the Venice post

[23] Pierpont Morgan Library, Prior MSS, Prior to Richard Hill, Westminster, July 7/18, 1704.

was but a forlorn hope. His ignorance as to why Jersey had been dropped two months earlier (May, 1704) from the position as Lord Chamberlain must have been a mere pretense. Certainly there was no secret about the political changes that had taken place.

Jersey, as well as Seymour and Nottingham, had opposed Marlborough from the very beginning of the new reign in which they had been oddly brought together by the Queen's friendship for the Marlboroughs and by her High Tory preferences. But the ill feeling between the two families had long existed. In the early days of the reign of William and Mary, when Edward Villiers was Queen Mary's Master of the Horse, Sarah had slighted Elizabeth Villiers, his sister. From that moment Jersey hated the Marlboroughs cordially and fostered in Queen Mary a distrust of them.[24] Since the beginning of the war, Jersey and his friends had tried to undermine Marlborough's influence. They objected to England's fighting in Flanders and Germany and declared that England should confine her participation in the war of the Spanish Succession to the sea. They fought against the land tax, opposed a regular army, and flouted an alliance with the Dutch, whom they detested on principle. The Queen grew increasingly impatient with these arrogant and dictatorial High Tories. Upon the urgent prevailings of Sarah and Godolphin, she dismissed both Seymour and Jersey, and forced Nottingham to resign. With the appointment of Kent, a mild Whig, as successor to Jersey, we note the beginning of a gradual change—largely the result of Sarah's proselyting—which finally brought Godolphin and Marlborough over to Whig sympathies, and made possible the coalition ministry of 1705.

Since Prior was known as a "creature of Lord Jersey's," his prospects were now less bright. His one friend at Court was in disgrace; yet he would stand by Jersey "as firm as any Roman

[24] Viscount Garnet Joseph Wolseley, *The Life of John Churchill, Duke of Marlborough*, II, 260.

libertus did by his Master." His salary was in arrears. He was was making frantic efforts to get back into a diplomatic secretaryship. Worse still, as we shall see, he had got himself into the bad graces of the powerful Sarah. *Sic voluit fortuna jocari.*

» 2 «

Because of her outspoken Whig sympathies, her fiery temper, her utter domination of the Queen, her greedy acceptance of favors of office and money, Sarah was an easy target for Tory satire. Even by 1704 attacks upon her had become quite frequent. Well might she have ignored the abuse of her enemies, but it seems to have rankled. When writing *Characters of Her Contemporaries,* many years later, she took revenge on those whose libels against herself and her family she could neither forget nor forgive. A brief quotation from one of these libels will indicate the trend of the satire which she justly resented:

> I'll mount to Honour's Stage;
> My easy Minor ne'er shall be of Age.
> Her crown shall be the foot-stool to my Name,
> Her Sceptre but my Hobby-horse to Fame.
> Nor shall she dare, at my directing Nod,
> To own her Kindred, Friends, her Church, or God.
> And, while my Hero does her Foes subdue,
> My Moderation shall her Friends pursue.
> Thus I the Height of Glory will attain,
> And A[nne] shall wear the crown, but S[arah] reign.
> Ch[urchil]l shall rise on easy St[uar]t's Fall
> And Blenheim's Tower shall triumph o'er Whitehall.[25]

At a moment when anonymous lampoons were being showered upon the mighty Duchess, it was well nigh inevitable that a poet—both a mischievous Wit and a friend of her husband's enemies—should be under suspicion. The particular lampoon

[25] "Upon a great lady's visiting the Tomb of Duke Humphrey the good, duke of Gloucester, at St. Albans, 1704."

which so aroused her fury and which she accused Prior of writing, we do not know. Certainly it was an evil hour for Matt. To have cast his lot with the High Tories, now in disfavor, was bad enough, but to incur the wrath of the "Torpedo in Petticoats," was political suicide.

Prior felt it imperative to see the Duke, but Marlborough was, at the moment, making a flying trip to The Hague to reassure the Dutch that, in spite of High Tory opposition, the campaign of 1704 would be vigorously pursued. With alacrity, Prior went to Godolphin to clear himself—or in the words of his diary: "I applyed myself to my Lord Treasurer, and alledged my innocence (as I very safely and conscientiously might)." Godolphin seemed convinced of Prior's innocence and promised to report the conversation in such a way that the Duchess would be mollified. As soon as the Duke returned, Prior hastened to exonerate himself. Marlborough assured Prior that he did not believe him to be the author of the libel, saying that his own willingness to discuss the matter "in so free and open a manner" was proof of his confidence.[26]

From now on, Prior was diligent in letting no victory of Marlborough's, no matter how slight, pass unnoticed by congratulatory letter. In Marlborough's secretary, Adam Cardonnel, he found an ally; they had been friends since early days at The Hague, and Cardonnel frequently sighed to chat with Prior at his "headquarters in Duke Street over a bottle." Unfortunately, Prior had no such friendly intercessor with the Duchess. In fact, her confidential secretary, Arthur Maynwaring, an inflexible Whig, detested Prior, who, he declared, had been "raised by the Whigs from a very mean beginning," had "deserted the party that had preferred him," and had "fallen in with those men" who had opposed King William's foreign policy.[27]

Maynwaring was no stranger to Prior; he had been one of the

[26] Strong, *Letters . . . at Welbeck*, p. 108. (Prior's Diary. "Entry: about Jan: 1704.")
[27] Oldmixon, *Life and Posthumous Works of Arthur Maynwaring*, p. 157.

elegant young gentlemen in Lord Portland's embassy to France.
Once a loyal follower of James, he became one of the most ardent
of William's admirers. Through Halifax's patronage he fell into
the fat position of Auditor of Imprests. Anne Oldfield, the celebrated actress, was his mistress. His influence over the Duchess
was remarkable. He had the knack of keeping on good terms
with her even during all her tantrums, and was the only person
who could make adverse criticisms to which she would listen.
When he lay dying at the Marlborough estate near St. Albans,
in 1712, the Duchess wept, realizing that she was losing a true
friend. For Prior to assert his innocence to the Duchess directly
was impossible; to hope that Maynwaring would intercede
for him was futile. He therefore continued to court the Duke
himself, enlisting the aid of the friendly Cardonnel. A congratulatory letter upon the victory at Schellenberg brought a
kindly acknowledgment from the Duke.[28] Though, unlike
Congreve and other solicitors for Court favors, Prior neglected
to lament the death of the young Marquis of Blandford, the
only son of the Marlboroughs', he did not fail to celebrate in
verse the battle of Blenheim. He sent two copies of his poem
with a "very civil letter" to the Duchess, asking her to present
one of the copies to the Queen. Admiral Churchill, the Duke's
brother, delivered Prior's peace offering to the Duchess. Some
days later, the Admiral returned Prior's pacquet unopened with
word from the Duchess that she "would not receive anything
of his writing," for "she was persuaded that he could not mean
well by her or her family."[29]

The Duke's reception of the poem was quite different. Obliged
to be early on horseback the morning after the poem reached
him, he asked Cardonnel to forward to Prior his thanks and re-
assurance of friendship upon all occasions. Cardonnel tried to
recall the Duke's exact words, and the cordiality of the letter

[28] Marlborough, *Letters and Dispatches*, I, 384, Marlborough to Prior, Aug. 3, 1704.
[29] Strong, *Letters . . . at Welbeck*, p. 109.

must have somewhat offset the obstinate ill-humor of the Duchess.[30]

The poem,[31] entitled "A Letter to Monsieur Boileau Despreaux," recalls to mind the "Ballad on the Taking of Namur." In the Blenheim poem Prior attempted to recapture the bantering tone of the earlier piece by twitting Boileau on his awkward use of certain place names of a previous campaign. That the present campaign offered no such difficulty, the poet proves in the succeeding ten or fifteen lines, which are fairly embroidered with "harmonious names." Mockery is abandoned for panegyric in the conclusion, and the poet covets a genius equal to that of Boileau—his "old friend, old foe"—to render adequate praise to the great Marlborough and to the Queen, "a new Elisa":

> But We must change the Style.—Just now I said,
> I ne'er was Master of the tuneful Trade.
> Or the small Genius which my Youth could boast,
> In Prose and Business lies extinct and lost:
> Bless'd, if I may some younger Muse excite;
> Point out the Game, and animate the Flight:
> That from *Marseilles* to *Calais* FRANCE may know,
> As We have Conqu'rors, We have Poets too;
> And either Laurel does in BRITAIN grow:
> That, tho' amongst our selves, with too much Heat,
> We sometimes wrangle, when We should debate;
> (A consequential Ill which Freedom draws;
> A bad Effect, but from a Noble Cause:)
> We can with universal Zeal advance,
> To curb the faithless Arrogance of FRANCE.
> Nor ever shall BRITANNIA's Sons refuse
> To answer to thy Master, or thy Muse;
> Nor want just Subject for victorious Strains,
> While MARLBRÔ's Arm Eternal Laurel gains;
> And where old SPENCER sung, a new ELISA reigns.

Though Prior's poem was far above the fustian which had

[30] *Longleat Papers*, III, 433, Cardonnel to Prior, Camp at Treves, Oct. 20/31, 1704.
[31] *Poems on Several Occasions*, p. 125.

appeared, it did not satisfy the ministry. There was no catchy simile to suit the exacting ear of Godolphin, patron of jockeys rather than of poets. Consequently it remained for Halifax to groom Addison, his new protégé, for the task. *The Campaign* duly appeared, with its apt figure of the Duke riding in the whirl-wind and directing the storm. Addison was at once rewarded with the position of under-secretary of state, an office Prior had sought to obtain from the High Tory faction through Jersey's influence.

The year 1705 passed without any change in Prior's fortunes. He grew uneasy about his tenuous hold upon his position on the Board of Trade, however, as the Whigs became clamorous for appointments in return for supporting Marlborough's increas-ingly expensive campaigns. Did he ever regret the vote on im-peachment and his subsequent attachment to the extreme Tory faction, whose party views were as much at variance with his own as those of the extreme Whigs? Ever since his vote on impeachment, his political fortunes had been linked, for good or ill, with those of Jersey, his closest friend. Since Jersey could no longer help him, Prior was currying favor with Marlborough. This is not to be regarded as a desertion of Jersey, who was him-self endeavoring to placate Marlborough and Godolphin. Nor was Prior sacrificing his avowed political principles, for the Duke, like Godolphin and the rapidly rising Robert Harley, was a Moderate, who disapproved of the dominance of either Whigs or Tories. In following the Duke's fortunes, however, Prior would eventually have to seek favors from the Whigs, but that is looking ahead. He assiduously congratulated the Duke upon all his victories and received from him cordial acknowledgments. The Duchess was still unrelenting, and Matt was decidedly troubled. When the Duke returned to England in November Prior besought him to dispel the Duchess's ill-feeling. The Duke treated the matter lightly, remarking that women have their "humours"—a weakness which Mr. Prior, though not a married man, must surely understand. The present "humour" of the Duchess, he said, was not to be taken too seriously.

While yet uncertain of his new patron's attitude toward him Prior learned of the serious illness of his old patron and benefactor, the Earl of Dorset. The sole surviving member of the Wits of the merrier days of King Charles II, Dorset was now hopelessly old, a semi-imbecile, dying. In 1703 he had married Anne Roche, a woman of very obscure position.[32] Intent on keeping him well guarded from his family in hopes of securing a large portion of his fortune for herself, she would permit few persons to see the Earl. His family, considering the necessity of appointing guardians, sent Prior down to Bath to ascertain whether Lord Dorset were still of sound mind. Having obtained access to the Earl, Prior reported to the family: "Lord Dorset is greatly declined in his understanding, but he drivels so much better sense even now than any other man can talk, that you must not call me into court as a witness to prove him an idiot."[33] On January 29, 1705/6 the Earl died, and though Prior penned no memorial poem, the dedication to the collected edition of his poems in 1709 gave him wider scope for tribute than any poem would have done.

» 3 «

Bonfires flared and guns boomed almost constantly while London celebrated Marlborough's many victories in the year 1706. Prior, as we know, never failed to send a congratulatory letter on such occasions. Despite the fact that his panegyric pen was growing stale, the great victory of Ramillies in May, 1706, demanded a poem. He dutifully wrote the verses but made apology in the preface:

[32] "Lord Dorset, after a thousand actions that plainly showed me he had entirely lost his senses, has completed all by marrying Joanny Roche," Stepney learned from his cousin, Erasmus Lewis. (Lewis to Stepney, Whitehall, Oct. 17, 1704; in John M. Kemble, *Papers and Correspondence Illustrative of the Social and Political State of Europe from the Revolution to the Accession of the House of Hanover*, London, 1857, p. 434.)

[33] Wraxall, *Historical Memoirs of My Own Time*, ed. H. B. Wheatley, 1884, III, 137.

I only beg Leave to add, That it is long since I have (or at least ought to have) quitted Parnassus, and all the flow'ry Roads on that Side of the Country; tho' I thought myself indispensably obliged, upon the present Occasion, to take a little Journey into Those Parts.

The Queen, who read little besides books of piety and official documents and petitions, took the poem "very kindly." The Tories "cryed up the poem too much"; the Whigs, determined to find fault, pronounced it an "imitation of an obsolete form of verse," declared "its style a little hard," and even doubted that so good a poet as Prior had written it.[34] The ode on "The Glorious Success of Her Majesty's Arms," on the whole, is tedious; yet single stanzas have an easy flowing style:

> Me all too mean for such a Task I weet:
> Yet if the Sovereign Lady deigns to Smile,
> I'll follow HORACE with impetuous Heat,
> And cloath the Verse in SPENSER's Native Style.
> By these Examples rightly taught to sing,
> And Smit with Pleasure of my Country's Praise,
> Stretching the Plumes of an uncommon Wing,
> High as OLYMPUS I my Flight will raise:
> And latest Times shall in my Numbers read
> ANNA's Immortal Fame, and MARLBRÔ's hardy Deed.[35]

The Whig criticism of the poem is not far wrong. A real admiration for Spenser could not break through the stiff Augustan manner, and, in spite of the generous sprinkling of archaisms and historical allusions borrowed from the *Faerie Queene*, the result is no more satisfactory than the rococo version of the "Nut Brown Maid" of approximately the same date. Furthermore, the experiment with the Spenserian stanza failed the author's purpose—"to make the number more harmonious."[36]

That Prior was a genuine lover of Spenser may best be shown by the following lines from a later poem, "Colin's Mistakes":

[34] Strong, *Letters . . . at Welbeck*, p. 109. (Prior's Diary.)
[35] *Poems on Several Occasions*, p. 163.
[36] See the preface to the Ode, *Poems on Several Occasions*, p. 160.

And much he lov'd, and much by heart he said
What Father *Spenser* sung in *British* Verse.
Who reads that Bard desires like Him to write,
Still fearful of Success, still tempted by Delight.[37]

That he fully realized the difficulties of attempting to imitate Spenser, an unfinished poem of his indicates. Herein he declares that when he is bidden to imitate Spenser, he might just as well sally forth with King Arthur's shield or King Edward's sword.[38] But, after all, perhaps Spenser as a model was only an afterthought. As in the other formal panegyrics, Horace was his pattern from the beginning.

Pride of authorship led Prior to send copies of "The Glorious Success of Her Majesty's Arms" far and wide. Dr. Humphrey Gower and Sir Thomas Hanmer were among those favored. The copy for Hanmer was accompanied by a letter which marks the beginning of a correspondence of more than usual interest. Hanmer, a member of Parliament and a moderate Tory, was a country gentleman who affected a contempt for party politics and a zeal for polite learning. After he retired from politics he published a pretentious edition of Shakespeare, which won a place in the *Dunciad* because Pope thought it pompous.[39] In contrast to the flattering and importunate epistles to Marlborough, the letters to Hanmer are delightful examples of the familiar style:

If you can bear with the worst poetry in the world because the author is more than any man your servant, my present will be very acceptable. I wrote you no news, for that is only proper for the *Postboy* and the

[37] *Dialogues of the Dead*, p. 80.
[38] In the Welbeck Abbey, Prior MSS the lines run as follows:

> Bid me climb the Highest Hill and fetch the Eagle's Nest
> Bid me Dive into the Sea and bring the Coral
> The Mountain should not seem high nor the Sea deep
> Bid me go into the etc.
> No dangers daunt the Heart wch Venus has inspir'd
> But when Thou bidst me Imitate Spenser I drop my pen
> As well I might go out with Arthur's Shield or Edward's Sword.

[39] Book IV, l. 115.

Gazette, and remarks upon news I leave to the *Observator* and the *Review*. Prose, you see, Sir, is below me, I have left method for rage, and common sense for enthusiasm. As soon as I recover from this distemper, and can think my mare a better beast than Pegasus, you will be troubled with me.[40]

Sir Thomas promptly acknowledged the poem and invited Prior to his home at Euston:[41]

But now your journey to Parnassus is over, pray change horses and come into thicker air. Since your Pegasus has carried you so well, you need not doubt your mare, for you keep one as idle in the stable as the other; and if a fond muse will follow you on foot hither, perhaps we may show you as proper shades for you to converse in as any other place.

The invitation reached London while Prior was away. Weeks passed before he replied, continuing the analogy:

All *fourberie* apart I will certainly mount my terrestrial steed, and you shall see a gentle squire come pricking o'er the plain. A fortnight hence.[42]

To explain the postponement of the visit, he had only "frivolous and scandalous" excuses to offer. His absence from London may have been due to his appointment, already mentioned, as Linacre Lecturer at St. John's—certainly no frivolous business. This academic matter disposed of, Prior renewed his job-hunting activities in London.

Party leadership was fast becoming unstable. Marlborough and Godolphin had striven to keep the Coalition balance, but it was the Whigs who were supporting the war policy. In return for this support they demanded a greater share of the spoils of power. One of their signal successes was in forcing upon Queen Anne as her Secretary of State, Sunderland, a man whose very name she hated. Yet Godolphin and Sarah together wore down

---

[40] Hanmer, *Correspondence*, p. 100, Prior to Hanmer, Westminster, July 9/19, 1706.
[41] *Longleat Papers*, III, 434, Hanmer to Prior, Euston, July 18/29, 1706.
[42] Hanmer, *Correspondence*, p. 101, Prior to Hanmer, Westminster, Aug. 8/19, 1706.

the Queen's opposition to Sunderland so that he obtained the office which he had long coveted. Other changes in the ministry were to follow.

It is not surprising then that Prior, who had an eye to the future, realized that he must turn to the Whigs for assistance. Of the alienation of most of his earlier friends, we have spoken; that he was in a dilemma is obvious. In desperation he decided to seek out the Montague brothers again. Sir James, always kindly disposed, was forgiving; but it was the more influential Charles, whom he besought to intercede with the Duchess of Marlborough. So long as the Duchess was angry with him he would receive no employment—of that he was certain.

While waiting in almost a fever of anxiety to hear from Lord Halifax, Prior was sent to Godolphin to deliver a message from Lord Jersey. The moment was inopportune: neither the Lord Treasurer nor Marlborough was disposed to lend a willing ear to any of Jersey's political pleas. Godolphin therefore received Prior coldly. So distraught was Prior, that his usual good judgment deserted him, and he had the temerity to lay his own troubles before Godolphin. The Lord Treasurer responded icily and promised vaguely to protect him "if he could."[43] It was plain that Matt would get no help from that quarter.

Prior felt himself slipping. No word coming from Lord Halifax, Prior rather desperately decided to write him a letter, the first since their estrangement six years earlier. The letter, which has not been published elsewhere, is of interest in that it indicates that Prior's feeling of insecurity had driven him to seek favors even from Sunderland:

It is too late to recapitulate the differences that have happened between us, or to dispute the reasons that occasioned them. It is proposed at present to thank you for your generosity and assistance whenever you saw any danger threaten the man whom you once honored with the title of your friend. I know a great many ill people have endeavored

---

[43] Strong, *Letters . . . at Welbeck*, p. 110. (Prior's Diary.)   •

to calumniate me to your Lordship and to some of your friends, but I hope you know me well enough not to believe them and tho' I may suffer the misfortune, I desire you to think I will not, (as I have not hitherto) any way deserved the blame. I am very much obliged to Sir James Montague for his kind concern in my poor affairs and take this occasion of assuring your Lordship that my respects to you and your family are inviolate, and I appeal to him if in all my discourses and actions I have not on all occasions justified the truth of what I now write. I know no otherwise than [by] the rumour of this town and a half intimation from a great man who has protected my small interest if I am to be continued in my present station or commanded elsewhere. In either case I have reason to hope my fortunes may not be diminished. The favour I would therefore desire of your Lordship is to mention me to my Lord Sunderland, with whom in every station (whilst I have the honour to continue in the service) I must have affairs, that his Lordship would receive me as a man who had obligations to my late Lord, his father, and who by my diligence and duty in His Majesty's service would deserve his favour and protection.

I must detain your Lordship one moment longer; amongst many prose afflictions, I have one that is poetical. Some rogue of a bookseller has made a very imperfect collection of what he calls my writings. The whole is mutilated, names printed at length and things written near twenty years since, mingled with some written the other day; in such a manner as may do me harm, part of the Mouse is likewise inscribed, which I had little to say to otherwise than as I held the pen to what Mr. Montague dictated. I mention this, my Lord, desiring your Lordship to believe this book was printed without my knowledge or consent; and I add to it that since I had the unhappiness of being separated from your Lordship's company I never have written anything that could possibly merit yours or any of your friend's displeasure. I am ashamed to be your debtor so long as to pecuniary matters, as to others, my Lord, Your Lordship sees in what manner I desire to continue my obligations to you.[44]

The collection of verse to which Prior referred was a slim volume containing seventeen of his poems published at the end of January, 1707, by the "unspeakable" Curll. Some passages from the "City-Mouse and the Country-Mouse" were included;

[44] Brit. Mus., *Add. MSS*, 7121, fo. 49, Prior to Halifax, Feb. 4/15, 1707.

also the two satires dating from university days and, quite inopportunely, the "Epistle to Sir Fleetwood Sheppard,"[45] which contained the little pleasantry leveled at Halifax. This odd assortment was not representative of the body of Prior's poems, which had been accumulating in Jacob Tonson's bookshop. But the statement in his own edition, which appeared two years later,

. . . a Collection of Poems has lately appeared under my Name, tho' without my Knowledge, in which the Publisher has given Me the Honor of some Things that did not belong to Me; and has Transcribed others so imperfectly, that I hardly knew them to be Mine,

is not wholly true, as Mr. Waller has shown.[46] The one good result of the pirated edition was that it prompted Prior to bring out what he called an "indifferent collection of Poems, for fear of being thought the author of a Worse."[47]

» 4 «

In March, 1707, Prior's affairs neared a climax. Godolphin told him that there would be a change in the membership of the Board of Trade and Plantations. Prior tactfully remarked that he had heard the news from common talk, but he had not imagined that he would be concerned. He was relying, he said, upon the Lord Treasurer's protection, and, even if the Queen should see fit to remove him, he hoped that he might depend upon his Lordship's goodness to find something else for him. To this, Godolphin answered coldly that Prior might be among those dismissed; the Queen had a great many others to provide for.

[45] The title of this poem in Curll's edition is "A Second Epistle to Sir Fleetwood Sheppard."

[46] *Poems on Several Occasions*, p. vii; *Dialogues of the Dead*, p. vii.

[47] Prior's diplomatic disclaimer of authorship of certain poems in Curll's edition was preceded by an announcement by Tonson in the *Daily Courant*, January 24, 1707. "Whereas it is Reported that there is now Printing a Collection of Poems which the Publishers intend to call Mr. Prior's, This is therefore to inform the World, that all the Genuine Copys of what Mr. Prior has hitherto written, do of right belong and are now in the hands of Jacob Tonson, who intends very speedily to publish a correct Edition of them."

Prior, summoning a bit of philosophy from St. Paul and Epictetus, responded with dignity that he must be satisfied with what his superiors thought proper for him. Godolphin closed the interview by promising in a vague way that he would be taken care of. Marlborough counseled patience and said that he would intercede with the Queen and Godolphin.

In spite of these promises, the blow fell on April 22, 1707. While Prior was attending a meeting of the Board on that day, he learned that there was a warrant for a new commission on which his name and the names of three of his associates were missing. Godolphin gave little comfort: Prior was in Her Majesty's favor, and something would be done for him; but he must have patience and discretion; as for the place on the Board of Trade, it was no longer his. Prior never forgave Godolphin's shabby treatment of him. Years later he recalled with bitterness that the words of the "wise Lord Godolphin" had been "Things change, and times change, and men change," when, as Prior put it, "he turned me out for having served him."[48]

Rumor naturally followed Prior's removal from office. Addison—now Sunderland's under-secretary—wrote Stepney that Prior would try to procure the headship of Eton college if the present master should be appointed elsewhere.[49] Prior was not appointed to this collegiate post, but he did become involved, for a few days at least, in another position for which orders would have been as essential as for Eton. Hastily he accepted an offer to become secretary to the jovial Sir Jonathan Trelawney, recently consecrated Bishop of Winchester, under the misapprehension that it was to be a kind of sinecure and that he would be able to keep "entire liberty of life." Upon the publication of this news, tongues were set wagging, much to Prior's chagrin. In spite of his discomfiture, there is something amusing in his account of the episode.

[48] P. R. O., *State Papers, France*, 78/158, Prior to Bolingbroke, Paris, March 6/17, 1713/4.

[49] Addison, *Works*, V, 363, Addison to Stepney, Sept. 27/Oct. 8, 1707.

In a few days the good nature of the town, at least that part of it which wished me no good, carried a glorious story, that I had a provision of six hundred pounds a year settled on me, was to live at Farnham with the Bishop, had abandoned all thoughts of ever serving or depending on the Court, had turned my thoughts wholly towards orders, was to have all the ecclesiastical preferment the prelate could heap upon me, and in the meantime, was to set up High Church, and cut down all the bishop's woods into fagotts to burn dissenters: this civil turn might on one hand very easily have ruined me at Court, from whence I had every good reason to expect some present favour, and might have hindered my return into business hereafter: and, on the other hand, upon a nearer view of the thing I found it not considerable, and such as neither could or ought to be managed by deputation; it comprehended the business of a whole diocese, and was to be managed by some person who should wholly apply himself to it; and, however great my Lord Bishop's intended kindness and complaisance might be to me, it was pretty reasonable his secretary should always be near him: upon these views and reflexions I declined the offer, which (to tell the truth) I had too suddenly embraced. . . .[50]

Prior wished to withdraw from the appointment immediately, gracefully. In order to retain the bishop's good will, however, he had to perform several secretarial errands, and it was no doubt incongruous to see the ungodly Matthew dogging the bishop's steps when the ecclesiastic paid his homage at Windsor or when he was initiated into the Order of the Garter.

In August Prior heard that Stepney was ill. We regret to say that he immediately began to angle for his friend's post. Catt had proved to be a shrewder politician than Matt. "Near is my shirt, but nearer my skin" was a favorite proverb of Stepney's, of which the Secret Committee in 1715 chose to remind Prior. Always a wise diplomat, Stepney enjoyed the confidence of both Marlborough and Godolphin. He had not only retained his position on the Board of Trade when Prior was dropped but had also circumvented Harley's efforts to remove him from his Viennese post in favor of Henry St. John. While Harley was

[50] Hanmer, *Correspondence*, p. 108, Prior to Hanmer, Westminster, June 24/July 5, 1707.

absent from London visiting kinsfolk in Wales, Stepney had maneuvered to have his status at Vienna raised to that of Plenipotentiary with additional allowance.[51] Unfortunately he did not live long to enjoy his successes. As soon as news of his illness reached London, candidates applied for his offices. Sir Philip Meadows wanted his place on the Board of Trade.[52] Prior, as well as others, sought his diplomatic post. To all applicants, Marlborough sent the same reply; there would be no thoughts of supplying Stepney's place while there was hope of his recovery.[53] To Prior, Marlborough committed himself thus far, "If it should please God to dispose of him otherwise, you will have the earliest notice of it."[54] In confidence the Duke told Godolphin, "Whilst there are any hopes of his life, I beg nobody may be spoken to. If I knew anybody proper for this station I would take the liberty of naming him."[55] Stepney did not improve but died at his home in Chelsea in September and was given an imposing funeral in Westminster Abbey with dukes, earls, and viscounts among his pallbearers. In his will he left Prior fifty pounds in cancellation of the old debt of many years standing.[56] Whether Prior made further application for the post is uncertain. At any rate, he did not succeed Stepney.

Undaunted by the fact that all his efforts at a reconciliation were ignored, Prior pursued Halifax with the persistence of the desperate, finally going to him, ostensibly, to make a New Year's call. Halifax was aloof and unforgiving; the conversation, one-sided. Matt made bold to inquire if his Lordship had ever tried to set him right with the Duchess of Marlborough. The question vexed Halifax, who replied evasively that it had

[51] P. R. O., *Stepney Papers*, 105/75, Stepney to George Montague, Vienna, July 18/29, 1705.
[52] Marlborough, *Letters and Dispatches*, III, 690, Marlborough to Sir Philip Meadows, Oct. 2, 1707.
[53] *Ibid.*, 609, Marlborough to Lord Raby; to Sir Philip Meadows, Oct. 2, 1707.
[54] *Ibid.*, 530, Marlborough to Prior, Aug. 25, 1707.
[55] *Ibid.*, 547, Marlborough to Godolphin, Sept. 1, 1707.
[56] There is a copy of Stepney's will in Somerset House.

not been convenient for him to do so. Then turning the talk to his own troubles, he suggested retiring to Bushey Park and taking Matt with him. Something rather cryptic also was said about Halifax's hope that Prior would be restored to the Board of Trade. Prior came away from his interview with a sense of futility. Was Halifax a great man, anyway?[57] Prior's reflections might have been less gloomy had he known that his one-time master had likewise incurred Sarah's displeasure—but that is not our story.

Halifax not proving helpful, Prior turned to Marlborough with more abject servility than ever. Surely his desperate plight atones for his fawning appeals to the Duke: he was in poor health, heavily in debt, and out of employment, with only a small pension to live on. The pension came from Marlborough's "private purse," or so Sarah claimed, but Prior referred to it as "Her Majesty's bounty by which I exist."[58] In view of Marlborough's lack of generosity, the Queen's bounty seems the more likely source of the pension. From May until October, 1708, he kept his cause constantly before the Duke, but to no avail.[59]

During these months Prior was occupied with a venture of a different nature—the publication of his poems, which he mentioned casually to Hanmer, who was then renewing his invitation to Euston:

. . . I am tyed by the legg here by a business so frivolous to anybody but myself, that I am ashamed to mention it . . . by the next return of the carryer my friend Mr. Drift and I will pack up the very little of this summer's product worth sending you.[60]

---

[57] Strong, *Letters . . . at Welbeck*, App. V, p. 266. The entry is dated "The 2d or 3d of Jan^ry 1709."

[58] *Reference Catalogue of British and Foreign Autographs and Manuscripts*, ed. by Thomas J. Wise, London, 1893, Prior to Godolphin, Westminster, July 28, 1709.

[59] On May 28 he asked the Duke to induce Godolphin to restore him. On Oct. 19, he congratulated the Duke on the taking of Lille. See Hist. MSS. Com., Eighth Report (Marlborough Papers), 36a.

[60] Hanmer, *Correspondence*, p. 116, Prior to Hanmer, Westminster, Sept. 9, 1708.

Thus we are introduced to *Poems on Several Occasions*. Appropriately Prior dedicated the volume, "a garland of goodwill," to Lionel, Earl of Dorset, son of his first patron. If any verses of his, he said, "should appear in print under another name and patronage than that of an Earl of Dorset, people might suspect them not to be genuine." The dedication proved to be a biographical sketch of the young earl's father, and though fulsome in its praise, it is an admirable example of Queen Anne prose, lucid and delightful to read.

In quick succession Prior applied to Marlborough for aid in securing the place on the Board of Trade, made vacant by the death of Lord Herbert of Cherbury,[61] and for a post at Florence.[62] The Duke did not heed the appeals, and Prior reverted to the idea that the displeasure of the Duchess was still the cause of his failure.

What was his next move in seeking reinstatement? It proved to be the dispatching of copies of *Poems on Several Occasions* to both the Duke and the Duchess, with the shameless declaration that the only valuable pieces in the collection were those which were tributes to the "great Duke." The Duchess must have relented for the time being, or, at least, Prior thought so. He wrote the Duke, who was on the Continent, that she had received the *Poems* "kindly" and that she had said that he had not deserved her ill will.[63] Several months passed, and Prior received no tangible evidence of her Grace's favor—his reinstatement must have been the result of his wishful imaginings. In a remarkable letter, probably the last which Matt ever wrote to the Duke, there is proof that he was again the great Sarah's suppliant:

. . . I assure myself that I continue in your Grace's favour, and in that assurance I place the welfare of my life; but one of those things which

---

[61] Duchess of Marlborough, *Private Correspondence*, II, 389, Prior to Marlborough, Westminster, Jan. 28/Feb. 8, 1708/9.

[62] *Ibid.*, 386, Prior to Marlborough, Westminster, Nov. 16/27, 1709.

[63] *Ibid.*, II, 390, Prior to Marlborough, 1709.

would make life much easier to me than it is at present, is my being released from the fear of lying under my Lady Duchess's displeasure. . . . But if in my own person I may say what I most desire, it is, that I may have the liberty of laying myself at my Lady Duchess's feet, and of begging her to hear me demonstrate my innocence as to anything that might have offended her, and to accept my service in whatever may hereafter oblige her: in one word, my Lord, to shew her Grace the contents of this letter. I have lost my employment after sixteen years' service; fare it well. I still subsist, God Almighty bless your goodness and bounty for it. I desire no more of my Lady Duchess than that she would not think me a villain and a libeller. I beg no other *éclaircissement* of what is past than that she would forget it; and with the most solemn protestation I aver, that I have ever esteemed her as one of the best of women, and would justify that esteem with my life, which, at present, is no great compliment, for in truth I grow pretty weary of it. Your Grace will be pleased to indulge this request of the most unhappy, but the most faithful of your servants.[64]

Notwithstanding all Prior's submissions and protestations, the Duchess never forgave him. In later years, when she accorded him a place in her character sketches she declared that he was the author of a vile libel against her and that he had had a share in the abuse of her and her husband in the articles in the *Examiner*. He had been educated in a tavern, she continued, and had a soul as low as his education, incapable of anything truly great or honorable.[65]

Prior's courting of the Marlboroughs—the panegyric poetry, the cajolery, and the flattery—all failed. The Duke never directly turned him off, but, more exasperating, he kept him waiting, hoping.

» 5 «

From the recital of these importunities to Marlborough, it is a relief to turn to the volume of poems which Prior published in 1709, as well as to poems of similar themes in later volumes. Twenty years had elapsed since his verse had begun to appear in

[64] *Ibid.*, 386–88, Prior to Marlborough, Westminster, Nov. 16, 1709.   [65] *Ibid.*, 138–40.

Miscellanies, yet, like Dorset, he had been in no hurry to prepare a collected edition. Curll, that "rogue of a bookseller," had furnished a motive for publication, and the poet's "unhappy leisure" the opportunity to assemble his works. Had political appointments continued to come to Prior, his poems might have remained in the *escritoire* of his Duke Street home or in Tonson's bookshop, only to be edited by his executors after his death.

Prior was modest about his writings. Elsewhere we have noted his references to his "indifferent verse" and to his intention of quitting the "flowery roads" on Parnassus. Any "poetic genius" that might have been ascribed to him in his youth, he felt, had been extinguished by his preoccupation with prose and business. Prose and business—they manifested the real spirit of the first decade of the eighteenth century. Poetry might be pursued by statesmen in their idle hours; even Godolphin and Harley scribbled verses, but no Wit could devote himself entirely to the Muse. It is not surprising then that *Poems on Several Occasions* was the only new collection of verse by an eminent poet to appear during the reign of Queen Anne.[66] The poems fall into four groups if we follow the author's cue in the preface: they are "Public Panegyrics," "Amorous Odes," "Serious Reflections," and "Idle Tales."

The "Public Panegyrics" are arranged chronologically and occupy a third of the volume. These we have already considered, since they bear a direct relation to Prior's public career and either reflect certain events or glorify certain persons of the years 1690 to 1706. "The Ode on the Glorious Success of Her Majesty's Arms," discussed above, is the last of a long train of sycophantic verse, part of which is, fortunately for the reader, omitted from the 1709 volume.

The "Serious Reflections" range from the solemnly dull college

---

[66] I am not forgetting Pope, whose first volume of collected poems did not appear until 1717.

exercise on Exodus to the hauntingly sad "Lines Written in Mezeray," and form the smallest part of the collection. They are in distinct contrast with the bawdy tales and epigrams. In the dedication, Prior promised to lay at his Lordship's feet, hereafter, the product of his "severer" studies when he should have bound up his "fuller sheaf." One of these severer studies must have been "Solomon," which, like Addison's *Cato*, was circulated among admiring friends many years before it was finally published. Certainly no one of his contemporaries had so good a right to spin out a poem on the text that "the pleasures of life do not compensate the miseries." But before "Solomon" was begun, poems on equally grave themes appeared. The line, "And life an ill whose only cure is Death," comes, curiously enough, not from "Solomon," as might be expected, but from a poem published as early as 1693.[67] Prior was, says Mr. Bickley, oppressed by a sense of the infinite and the unknowable, of man's impotence in the face of his destiny.[68] Consequently, such poems as the ode addressed to the memory of Colonel Villiers, the imitation of Hadrian's lines to his soul, the translation of the famous chorus from Seneca's *Troas*[69] were sincere expressions of his troubled heart. Prior had read widely in the philosophers, but finding in them no satisfactory refutation of his doubts he turned to Montaigne, a spirit more congenial. Both Prior and Montaigne "lay on a pillow of doubt," says Professor Barrett.[70] Both men, we might add, were inconsistent in their skepticism. Neither was an unbeliever so far as his church was concerned. Prior was as loyal a Church of England man as he was a patriotic Englishman. For the natural religion of many of his contemporaries or for irreligion, he had neither patience nor understanding.

[67] To Dr. Sherlock, on his Practical Discourse Concerning Death," *Poems on Several Occasions*, p. 102.
[68] Bickley, *The Shorter Poems of Matthew Prior*, p. xxiv.
[69] "Seneca, Troas. Act 2d. The Chorus Translated," *Dialogues of the Dead*, p. 321.
[70] W. P. Barrett, "Matthew Prior's Alma," *Mod. Lang. Rev.*, XXVII (1932), 456.

Who e'er forsakes Old Mother Church
And of new Doctrines makes profession
Will find himself soon left i[n] th[e] Lurch
Or cited to the Quarter Session.

I learn to think no precept strange
That Convocation can propose
Nor ever wish nor seek for change
Except in Mistresses & Cloaths.[71]

Although Prior thought highly of his serious poems, it is to the "Amorous Odes," the "Idle Tales," and other examples of his *vers de société* that we now turn for his best work. Social verse is his genre and of it he is a master. One detects a critical blindness in his omitting from the volume of 1709, as well as from the volume of 1718, such gems as "The Secretary," "To a Child of Quality," "The Dialogue between Daphne and Apollo," and the "Twenty-four Songs set to Music by Several Eminent Masters." In spite of the fact that Prior regarded "Solomon" as his masterpiece, who is there today who would not prefer "The Merchant to Secure His Treasure," "To a Child of Quality," or "A Better Answer" to all the lines in "Solomon"? It is in light verse that Prior excels, and these and a half dozen other poems are his finest pieces. To quote Professor Trent, they are "in all probability the unapproachable masterpieces of English familiar verse."[72]

Society verse we have been taught to regard disdainfully. Such poetry lacks high seriousness, or, to borrow another of Arnold's critical *dicta*, it is conceived and composed in wit, whereas genuine poetry is conceived and composed in the soul. From those who demand always the wine of poetry, it is perhaps vain to expect a more catholic taste. Rather must one who enjoys the lighter Muse be a "connoisseur of the tea of poetry," as Professor Elton has said, "but he must insist with Oriental punctilio on the elegance and the perfection of the service."[73]

[71] *Dialogues of the Dead*, p. 356.   [72] Trent, *Longfellow And Other Essays*, p. 181.
[73] Oliver Elton, *A Survey of English Literature, 1730–1780*, I, 30.

Society verse as Prior and the Restoration Court Poets wrote it is a product of Cavalier culture and reflects a world of fashion long since vanished from this earth. Much of it was tossed off in leisure moments by earls and baronets, by parliamentarians and diplomats—by men of the world with the worldly man's view of life. In it we do not look for greatness but for perfection. It must be brief, graceful, sparkling. It must be of faultless workmanship and unobtrusive polish. It must be written in the easy, familiar style with rhymes never forced but seeming absolutely inevitable.

Austin Dobson once declared that Praed was the supreme writer of society verse,[74] but there is a universality, an elegance, a sophistication, a fragility in Prior's verse that is lacking in Praed's. Frenchmen could appreciate Prior—and many did, as the great number of translations and imitations in *Le Mercure de France* and elsewhere during the eighteenth century testify.[75] Most society verse of the nineteenth century, whether it is Praed's, Oliver Wendell Holmes's or Austin Dobson's—to mention the work of three of the best craftsmen of the age—is local, ephemeral, attenuated, and above all, sentimental.

Readers who favored Praed, Professor Trent once declared, "were generally inclined to sacrifice a little art if they could thereby gain a little sentiment."[76] Moreover, they preferred the Victorian "milady" to Prior's Cloes and averred that Prior had not the proper respect for women. He was, they said, too cynical, too coarse, too jaunty. They did not doubt that he was a past-master of graceful gaiety and debonair raillery, but they de-

---

[74] Quoted by Frederick Locker-Lampson in *Lyra Elegantiarum*, p. xviii.

[75] It is not true, as has been stated, that the French poets during the eighteenth century ignored Prior when they began to borrow from the English poets. Soon after Abbé Yart introduced the poetry of Prior to the French reading public in his *Idée de la poésie angloise*, the first two volumes of which appeared in 1749, French poets began to translate and imitate Prior. At least eight of Prior's poems appeared in translation in the *Mercure de France* between 1759 and 1774, in addition to Yart's translations. The poems preferred were the light amorous pieces, one of which, *Cupid Disarmed*, was imitated twice and praised highly for its delicacy.

[76] Trent, *Longfellow and Other Essays*, p. 181.

clared that he lacked true feeling and tenderness. They did not deny that these qualities could be found in his poems to children, but they wished that he had always written thus. They preferred sentiment to light-heartedness in love and shuddered at the worldly point of view they found in his lines to Phillis:

I

Phillis, since we have both been kind,
And of each other had our fill;
Tell me what pleasure you can find,
In forcing nature 'gainst her will.

II

'Tis true, you may with art and pain
Keep-in some glowings of desire;
But still those glowings which remain
Are only ashes of the fire.

III

Then let us free each other's soul,
And laugh at the dull constant fool,
Who would Love's liberty controul
And teach us how to whine by rule.

IV

Let us no impositions set,
Or clogs upon each other's heart;
But, as for pleasure first we met,
So now for pleasure let us part.

V

We both have spent our stock of love,
So consequently should be free;
Thyrsis expects you in yon' grove;
And pretty Chloris stays for me.[77]

If the twentieth-century writer of light amorous verse has freed himself from the namby-pambyness of his Victorian prede-

[77] "To Phillis. Set by Mr. Smith," *Dialogues of the Dead*, p. 155.

cessors, he still is inclined to be sentimental, to indulge in self pity. Moreover, if he seems sometimes to approach Prior and the Restoration poets in frankness and lightheartedness, he does not match them; for what they achieved with ease and naturalness, he can only obtain with grim determination.

Several forces united to produce in Prior a perfection unmatched in his time or in ours. Very early in life he became devoted to Horace, that greatest master of light verse of antiquity, whom he imitated consciously and successfully. Then he was introduced by Dorset to the courtly Wits—Sedley, Rochester and Etherege, who, like Suckling and Carew maintained the traditions of the Sons of Ben—and he proved so apt a disciple that he may be called the last of the courtly poets. His sojourns in France brought acquaintance with the *petits poètes sur les sujets légerès*, from whom he acquired a French accent or quality for his verse. From Horace he learned grace, polish, elegance; from Dorset a command of the natural, easy tripping meter, as well as a disposition to temper wit with tenderness; from the French, the inevitability of phrasing that gave his verse the fragility of Sèvres china, the delicacy of the *fêtes galantes* of Watteau.

If we define a fragile poem[78] as one that is so delicately rhythmed, so inevitably phrased that not a word or a rhyme could be altered without shattering the beauty of the whole, what more fragile poem could be found than the ode beginning with the line, "The Merchant, to secure his Treasure," and entitled by Cowper in his Latin translation, *Cloe and Euphelia*?

> The Merchant, to secure his Treasure,
> Conveys it in a borrow'd Name:
> EUPHELIA serves to grace my Measure;
> But CLOE is my real Flame.

---

[78] The definition is taken from "Matthew Prior, His Relation to English Vers de Société," by Harvey W. Thayer, *Sewanee Rev.*, X, 180–98, April, 1902.

My softest Verse, my darling Lyre
Upon EUPHELIA's Toylet lay;
When CLOE noted her Desire,
That I should sing, that I should play.

My Lyre I tune, my Voice I raise;
But with my Numbers mix my Sighs:
And whilst I sing EUPHELIA's Praise,
I fix my Soul on CLOE's Eyes.

Fair CLOE blush'd: EUPHELIA frown'd:
I sung and gaz'd: I play'd and trembl'd:
And VENUS to the LOVES around
Remark'd, how ill We all dissembl'd.[79]

To comment further on such inimitable stanzas would be superfluous. Like the ode "To a Lady" this poem is the *chef-d'oeuvre*
of tact. Equally neat and pat are "The Question," "Lisetta's
Reply," and "Her Right Name."

"The Merchant, to secure his Treasure" begins a series of
poems about Cloe—dainty pieces which Austin Dobson calls
"wax-flowers to verse." In one of the series,[80] Cloe goes ahunt-
ing only to lose her way and be mistaken by Apollo for Cynthia,
much to the delight of an impudent Cupid, who laughs to see
the god in error. In another,[81] Cupid himself, misled by a likeness, shoots Venus, whom he mistakes for Cloe. Again[82] there is
the *motif* of mistaken identity, when Venus upon seeing How-
ard's portrait of Cloe bathing, takes it for her own image and is
vexed with the painter for his daring. Still other poems follow
Cloe through numerous playful adventures with Cupid, whom
she finally disarms completely. These are Prior's contributions
to the graceful, conventional, unimpassioned love verse then in
fashion. The mythological fictions, considered despicable by
Dr. Johnson, are pure decoration—a mere vehicle for Prior's
whimsies about his mistress.

[79] *Poems on Several Occasions*, p. 42.
[81] "Cupid Mistaken," *ibid.*, p. 62.
[80] "Cloe Hunting, "*ibid.*, p. 59.
[82] "Venus Mistaken," *ibid.*, p. 63.

In a second group of poems centering on Cloe, the scene is shifted from imaginary woodlands of an unpredicated time to substantial London of Queen Anne's day. Instead of mythological characters, there are real persons engaging in brilliant repartee. To Cloe, to her fickle lover, and to Lisetta, a rival, the poet propounds riddles and questions provocative of witty answers on the perennial themes of love and beauty. A little poem, "The Question," indicates that Cloe's place is not unchallenged:

> What Nymph shou'd I admire, or trust,
> But CLOE Beauteous, CLOE Just?

To this query, Lisetta replies self-confidently:

> Sure CLOE Just, and CLOE Fair
> Deserves to be Your only Care:
> But when You and She to Day
> Far into the Wood did stray,
> And I happen'd to pass by;
> Which way did You cast your Eye?[83]

In more serious vein is "The Garland,"[84] a fragrant poem which pictures Cloe in pensive mood:

> Ah Me! the blooming Pride of May,
> And That of Beauty are but One:
> At Morn Both flourish bright and gay,
> Both fade at Evening, pale, and gone.

It is a vexed Cloe who speaks in "Cloe Jealous,[85] chiding her lover for his riddles and epigrams, trifles though they be:

> For mind I what You late have writ,
> Your subtle Questions, and Replies:
> Emblems, to teach a Female Wit
> The Ways, where changing Cupid flies.

---

[83] "The Question, to Lisetta," and "Lisetta's Reply," *Poems on Several Occasions*, p. 72.
[84] *Poems on Several Occasions*, p. 73.
[85] *Ibid.*, p. 75.

Cloe affects, for the most part, a light-hearted acceptance of her lover's philanderings and of the decay of her own beauty, but abandons pretense in these haunting lines:

> Yet car'd I not, what might presage
> Or withering Wreath, or fleeting Youth:
> Love I esteem'd more strong than Age,
> And Time less permanent than Truth.

"A Better Answer" concludes the dispute between the poet and Cloe. Here Prior manifests a skill in setting himself right with capricious mistresses, which was more than poetic. He looks into her "blubbered" pretty face and says:

> To be vext at a Trifle or two that I writ,
> Your Judgment at once, and my Passion You wrong:
> You take that for Fact, which will scarce be found Wit:
> Od's Life! must One swear to the Truth of a Song?

And the next stanza is calculated to soothe:

> What I speak, my fair CLOE, and what I write, shews
> The Diff'rence there is betwixt Nature and Art:
> I court others in Verse; but I love Thee in Prose:
> And They have my Whimsies; but Thou hast my Heart.

A sentiment befitting the straying male in any age is then offered as the crowning bit of strategy:

> So when I am weary'd with wand'ring all Day;
> To Thee my Delight in the Evening I come;
> No Matter what Beauties I saw in my Way:
> They were but my Visits; but Thou art my Home.

The tears are surely dried by now, and Cloe must laugh with Matt at these droll solecisms:

> Then finish, Dear CLOE, this Pastoral War;
> And let us like HORACE and LYDIA agree:
> For Thou art a Girl as much brighter than Her,
> As He was a Poet sublimer than Me.[86]

---

[86] *Ibid.*, p. 78.

To turn from the exquisite daintiness of the Cloe poems to their prototype in real life is to discover that Prior's nymphs were no ladies of high degree. Their social anonymity is proof of their obscurity. Pope has told us that Cloe was a "poor mean creature," and Dr. Johnson, that she was a "despicable drab"; but they both had one of Prior's later mistresses in mind. The "black-eyed gipsy" who looked after Matt's domestic affairs for nearly twenty-five years, both at home and abroad, masquerades as Cloe, Flanders Jane, and Jinny the Just:

> At the Hague in her Slippers and hair as the Mode is
> At Paris all Falbalow'd fine as a Goddess
> And at censuring London in smock sleeves and Bodice
>
> She ordered Affairs that few People cou'd tell
> In what part about her that mixture did dwell
> Of Vrough or Mistress, or Medemoiselle. [87]

That Cloe's real name was Jane is a safe surmise. Probably she was the Jane Ansley to whom Prior left a bequest of a year's wages, mourning and fifty pounds. That she was a widow and cook-maid seems certain. "'Tis known a cook-maid roasted Prior" [88] comes from Pope, who, envious perhaps of the more robust pleasures denied himself opined that Prior was "not a right good man." Jane—or Cloe—was a country girl, kind and merciful and pious:

> CLOE Beauty has and wit,
> And an air that is not common;
> Every charm does in her meet,
> Fit to make a handsome woman.
>
> But we do not only find
> Here a lovely face or feature;
> For she's merciful and kind,
> Beauty's answer'd by good-nature.

---

[87] *Dialogues of the Dead*, p. 360.

[88] Pope, *Works*, ed. Elwin and Courthope, VI, 64, Pope to Henry Cromwell, July 12, 1707.

> She is always doing good,
> Of her favours never sparing,
> And, as all good Christians should,
> Keeps poor mortals from despairing.[89]

Lest the last line should seem extravagant or only due to the exigencies of rhyme, there is Prior's prose statement to support the poetical compliment: "One of her scrawls fortifies my mind against affliction more than all Epictetus."[90]

Cloe makes her final bow in "Jinny the Just," an epitaphic poem which combines happily the light touch with sincere feeling:

> Retire from this Sepulchre all the Prophane
> You that love for Debauch or that marry for gain
> Retire least Ye trouble the Manes of J——
>
> But Thou that know'st Love above Intrest or lust
> Strew the Myrtle and Rose on this once belov'd Dust
> And shed one pious tear upon Jinny the Just
>
> Tread soft on her Grave, and do right to her honor
> Let neither rude hand nor ill Tongue light upon her
> Do all the small Favors that now can be done her[91]

Our grief over the beloved's demise is tempered, however, when we realize that Jane outlived Prior and married a cobbler.[92]

Although Cloe long remained with Prior as housekeeper— "her place being *quam diu bene se gesserit*"[93]—she had to share the affections of the poet with the aforementioned Bessy or Elizabeth Cox, the Lisetta of several poems. Lisetta admitted that

---

[89] *Dialogues of the Dead*, p. 167.

[90] Hanmer, *Correspondence*, p. 120, Prior to Hanmer, Aug. 4, 1709.

[91] *Dialogues of the Dead*, p. 363. Canceled verses, *ibid.*, p. 403, indicate that Jane was still living when the poem was written.

[92] Shenstone seems to have had authentic information about Cloe. On a blank page in his own copy of Prior's *Poems*, he wrote: "Prior's Cloe was a chearful gay facetious old woman, that used to laugh with a profusion of good humour until she was almost ready to die, at the conceit of her being a Poet's Flame. And Prior, we may be sure, was equally delighted with ye Excellence of her understanding." See Marjorie Williams, *William Shenstone*, pp. 119, 120.

[93] Hanmer, *Correspondence*, p. 170, Prior to Hanmer, Paris, Jan. 3, 1714/5.

Jane was Cloe, but claimed that she herself was "Emma of *The Nut Brown Maid.*" This statement, which is quoted by Dr. Arbuthnot, seems significant since it corroborates what we now know of the two rivals.[94] Elizabeth Cox may not have been more beautiful than Jane, but she was undoubtedly younger, and we may be sure that it was not without bitterness that Jane saw herself superseded—the fate of many mistresses from time immemorial.

Another nymph, Nannette or Nancy, comes tripping in on sprightly verse. In real life she was Anne Durham, whom Prior set up in business—probably an ale house—and likewise remembered in his will. The jolly little poem "Her Right Name" indicates that Nancy knew her betters, for she puts as a final query,

> And which am I most like, she said,
> Your CLOE, or Your *Nut-brown Maid?*[95]

The fourth and last group of poems, the "Idle Tales," includes the inimitable "An English Padlock," "The Dove," and the three Fontainesque tales, "Hans Carvel," "Paulo Purganti," and "The Ladle." In ease, gayety and wit, knowledge of human nature, and command of the familiar style they have not since been surpassed. Although they are, as Saintsbury says, out of fashion today, since "they are too naughty for the old fashioned and not nasty enough for the Modernists,"[96] they were immensely popular in the eighteenth century. It is interesting to note the attention paid to them by critics from Pope to Hazlitt. Pope thought that Prior had happily caught La Fontaine's manner, and French critics of the day called Prior an English La Fontaine. Years later, upon Boswell's recalling that Lord Hailes censured Prior as a writer of impure tales, Dr. Johnson came to the rescue of the poet whom he was later to treat un-

---

[94] *The European Magazine,* XIII, 8, Arbuthnot to Henry Watkins, London, Oct. 10, 1721.
[95] *Poems on Several Occasions,* p. 173.
[96] George Saintsbury, *The Peace of the Augustans,* p. 53.

fairly in *Lives of the Poets*. "There is nothing in Prior," he said, "that will excite to lewdness. If Lord Hailes thinks there is, he is more combustible than other people."[97] Scott, of conventional mold, thought Prior "the most indecent of tale tellers" and noted how often he saw his works in female hands, but conceded that "it was not passages of ludicrous indelicacy that corrupt the manners of people."[98] Hazlitt, a more discriminating critic, liked "The Dove" best of all the tales. "No one," he said, "could insinuate such a knavish plot, a tender point, a loose moral, with such unconscious archness and careless raillery" as Prior. Further, he compared Prior's muse to a wanton flirt, an adept at blindman's buff, who told what she should not but knew more than she told.[99]

Successful as Prior might be with amorous songs no more ethereal than those of Horace or with idle tales as earthy as La Fontaine's, he failed utterly in his effort to retell for an Augustan audience the "Nut Brown Maid." As Courthope has said, Prior's *Henry and Emma* is "a futile effort to apply the external classical style to what is in essence romantic."[100] Guthkelch thought something might be said for Prior's poem, but it seems to be the supreme example of that eighteenth-century penchant for turning the charmingly simple and direct speech of an earlier age into the elaborately stilted rhetoric dear to the Augustan heart. Although the original had recently been published in the *Muses Mercury*, January, 1707, Prior republished it in his collected edition in order that readers might compare the medieval poem with its rococo improvement. Prior adhered to the theme of the original, but elaborated the setting, added a wholly superfluous plot, introduced mythological fictions, and changed the spirited dialogue for long-winded declamations in

[97] Boswell, *Life of Johnson*, Oxford Edition, II, 147.
[98] Lockhart, *Life of Sir Walter Scott*, Edinburgh, 1839, II, 283.
[99] William Hazlitt, Lectures on the English Poets, *Works*, V, 106.
[100] W. J. Courthope, *History of English Poetry*, V, 117.

rhymed couplets.[101] Prior's version was popular throughout the eighteenth century. It was translated into French[102] and German.[103] It was set to music by Dr. Arne and used as an interlude.[104] Cowper was "bewitched" by *Henry and Emma* and took issue with Dr. Johnson's "fusty rusty" remarks on an "enchanting piece." Modern criticism, unmoved by Dr. Johnson's moral condemnation, is closer to that of Lamb, who called it a "vapid paraphrase of a fine old ballad."

Besides *Henry and Emma*, many of Prior's other poems were set to music during the century. The *Twenty-four Songs set to Music by Several Eminent Masters*,[105] light airy songs in the Restoration manner, we have already mentioned. Eleven other pieces, chiefly epigrams, were published as canzonets, the music being furnished by John Travers, organist of His Majesty's Chapel Royal.[106] No other poet between Dryden and Burns was honored by having so many of his poems set to music.

[101] The most penetrating criticism of *Henry and Emma* is found in Walter Raleigh's *Six Essays on Johnson*, London, 1910, pp. 145ff.

[102] *Mélanges de poësie angloise contenant . . . Henry et Emma, imité de la belle brune de Chaucer*, par Matthieu Prior, Paris, 1764.

[103] *Heinrich und Emma, Ein gedicht aus dem Englischen des Herrn Prior*, Leipzig, 1753.

[104] *Henry and Emma, a new Poetical Interlude.*

[105] *Lyric Poems; Being Twenty-four Songs Never before Printed by the Late Matthew Prior, Esq. Set to Music by Several Eminent Masters*, London, 1741.

[106] *Eighteen Canzonets for Two and Three Voices. . . Set to Music by John Travers*, London [1745?]

CHAPTER VIII

The Journey to Paris

» 1 «

THE YEAR 1710 marked both the downfall of the Godolphin ministry and the end of the Marlboroughs' influence over the Queen. Indeed, Prior had begged favor of Godolphin and the Duchess long after their power had begun to wane. Into their places had stealthily insinuated themselves two of the slyest of political intriguers—a kitchen maid, Abigail Masham (née Hill), and her cousin, Robert Harley, known to his enemies as "Harlequin" or "Robin the Trickster." As early as the summer of 1707, shortly after Prior's dismissal from the Board of Trade, the Duchess suddenly discovered that the poor relation to whom she, out of the goodness of her heart, had given a place in the Queen's bedchamber, was becoming a most dangerous rival. To be sure, the Duke and the Duchess could hardly reproach each other for their lot. The Duchess had repeatedly warned the Duke not to have dealings with Harley, whom she called a "sneaking fellow," or with his political crony, St. John, neither of whom she trusted. She was delighted when the Spanish revelations, following closely upon the confessions of treason on the part of Gregg, an underling in Harley's employ, forced Harley to resign from the ministry in 1708. Yet Harley out of office proved more dangerous to the Duchess and the Whigs than Harley in office. Smuggled by Abigail into the Queen's presence through a backstairs entrance from a garden at Windsor, he soothed the ears of the poor, pious Queen, who had been cowed by the stormy bursts of temper of the Duchess and harassed by her eternal demands for offices for her friends—those troublesome Low Church Whigs.

Meanwhile the Whigs blundered. The Queen's secret advisers urged her to assert herself. The trial of Sacheverell reacted as a boomerang against the Whigs, and when they demanded for Somers a place in the Cabinet, Anne replied that it was a question of whether she should submit to the five tyrannizing lords or they to her.

A colorful event of the early months of 1710 was the arrival from Boston, under the charge of Colonel Peter Schuyler, of four Iroquois chiefs. Fearing that the native costume would shock London and, more especially, offend the Queen's modesty, the Colonel decked his protégés out in "black underclothes with scarlet ingrain cloth mantle." They attended a performance of *Macbeth* at the Haymarket, were dined by William Penn at the *Taverne du Diable* in Charing Cross, and were received by the Queen at Windsor. She was so impressed by the dignity of her strange subjects that she promised to send more missionaries to their people, lest French priests win the Five Nations over to Louis XIV. The sachems in return gave her belts of wampum, avowing their readiness to take up the hatchet and aid her in the reduction of Canada. Perhaps it was at this time that the young Alexander Pope, whose pastorals, published the previous year in Tonson's *Miscellanies*, had brought much applause from the critics, conceived the idea of writing some "American Pastorals."

The visit of the Indians was not without its political significance. The Indian chiefs had been presented to the Queen by the new Lord Chamberlain, the Duke of Shrewsbury, who, after a ten year rest from political activities, spent partly in exile on the continent in search of health and partly in seclusion at his estate in Oxfordshire, had returned to Court as an ally of Harley and the Tories, much to the displeasure of his former Whig associates. To Prior, the appearance of these American wards of the Board of Trade under the chaperonage of an old friend and patron—destined from this time on to play a curiously important role in the confidence of the Queen—could only bring the hope that he might now regain his position on the Board of Trade.

Political changes followed rapidly after Shrewsbury's appointment. Sunderland and Godolphin both fell. Harley became Chancellor of the Exchequer; Dartmouth and St. John, Secretaries of State; Harcourt displaced Sir James Montague as Attorney-General. The new ministry under Harley's guidance in 1710 was composed of Moderates—High Tories and extreme Whigs were left out in the cold. Jersey repeatedly solicited Shrewsbury, Dartmouth, and Harley for a place in the cabinet. They could not or would not break down the opposition of the Queen, who was as firmly opposed to Jersey as Marlborough and Godolphin had been.[1] As a consequence, Prior was again without a loyal friend to plead his cause at Court. By July there were rumors—the daily press even published the news—that Prior had been restored to the Board of Trade, and his friends wrote to congratulate him. Since he had not received official appointment, the situation was embarrassing. In September St. John temporarily relieved Prior's anxiety with this message: "The Queen has been spoke to in your affair. She is inclined to show you her favour and is indifferent which commission she places you in."[2] Yet in the following month the vacancy on the Board of Trade was filled by another man.[3] Perhaps Prior decided to take his case directly to the Queen. At any rate, we learn from a memorandum of the Duchess of Marlborough's that he read his correspondence—presumably that between the Marlboroughs and himself—to the Queen, hoping to enlist her sympathy.[4]

Pope never wrote his American Pastorals, and Prior never

---

[1] *Dartmouth Papers*, V, 298, Jersey to Dartmouth, Sept. 26, 1710; *Longleat Papers*, I, 200, Shrewsbury to Harley, July 13, 1710. *Portland Papers*, V, 49, Jersey to Harley, July 13, 1711.

[2] *Longleat Papers*, III, 441, St. John to Prior, Sept. 11/22, 1710.

[3] Arthur Moore.

[4] Hist. MSS Com., Eighth Report, App. I, 15a. The entry is dated December 3, 1710.

regained his place on the Board of Trade. Another winter came before Prior was given an appointment, this time on the Board of Customs. Meanwhile he was employed in various capacities by the new ministry. It may be assumed that he continued to draw his pension from the Queen's bounty, which may have been increased now that Godolphin no longer held the purse strings.

» 2 «

An excursion into journalism occupied Prior during the summer of 1710. The new ministry, feeling the need of a party organ, employed some of the keenest Tory minds and pens to launch such a paper. On Thursday, August 3, 1710, the *Examiner* appeared for the first time, its editor announcing that his design was to examine a "great variety of papers, neither so correct, so moral, nor so loyal" as they should be and "to set the people right in their opinions." Every day, so he declared, he saw the town "imposed upon by false wit, false learning, false politics and false divinity." His chief business, he continued, would be "to instruct his country-men": perhaps he might "endeavor now and then to divert them." The first twelve numbers—less diverting than instructive—were written by a syndicate of Tory Wits, including Atterbury, Dr. Freind, Dr. William King, and Prior. Possessing neither distinction of style nor force of argument, these papers have rarely tempted the biographers of the Wits into the perilous game of ascription. The sixth paper, the liveliest of the lot, is patently Prior's—but it is literary satire, not political. The third is concluded with a short satirical fable of his, evidently aimed at Godolphin. The tenth has been ascribed to St. John;[5] the eleventh to Dr. King.[6] Who were responsible for the other nine numbers?

If we turn to the opinions of the Whig rivals, who launched the *Whig Examiner* and the *Medley* in opposition to the *Examiner*,

[5] T. MacKnight, *The Life of Henry St. John, Viscount Bolingbroke*, London, 1863, pp. 158–89.
[6] George A. Aitken, *The Life of Richard Steele*, London, 1889, 2 vols., I, 292.

we shall find that Prior was accused of writing the greater number of the early papers. Maynwaring thought that Prior had the largest share in the early issues of the *Examiner*, or so said Maynwaring's friend and biographer, Oldmixon.[7] The Duchess of Marlborough wrote that she was "credibly informed" that Mr. Prior was the author of the *Examiner* and that Mr. St. John or Mr. Harley saw it before it was printed.[8] As we shall learn, Addison took Prior to be the author of the eleventh number, really Dr. King's. If Prior was the author of only one paper and of a brief satirical poem in another, he unjustly bore the brunt of the Whigs' attack. There is a likelihood that he was either in general charge of the paper or wrote more papers than have been proved his.

From the first, the *Examiner* clashed with the *Tatler*. In July Steele had printed in the *Tatler* a covert attack upon Harley.[9] On August 22, he published a paper on the two sorts of men, the Rigid and the Supple. The Rigid were men of principle who were loyal to their friends when their party was in disgrace. The Supple were as ready to change their principles as their clothes. Steele obviously pointed the satire at Prior, slyly using the fable against Godolphin in the third *Examiner* as evidence of Matt's suppleness. "It has been known," said Steele, "that a panegyric has been half printed off, when the poet, upon the removal of the Minister, has been forced to alter it into a satire."[10]

The Tory Wits set out to punish Steele for meddling in politics. The second *Examiner* sarcastically alluded to the "Letters to Louis XIV" in the *Tatler*. The fifth number devoted its whole space to a comparison of the political pabulum in the *Tatler* of August 12 with that in the *Gazette* of the same date and warned

[7] John Oldmixon, *The Life and Posthumous Works of Arthur Maynwaring*, p. 157.
[8] Duchess of Marlborough, *Letters . . . now first published from the Original Manuscripts at Madresfield Court*, London, 1875, p. 19.
[9] The letter from "J. Downs, the Prompter," *Tatler*, No. 193, July 4, 1710.
[10] The *Tatler*, No. 214, August 22, 1710.

"Isaac" not to indulge further in party warfare. The eleventh number was given over to personal abuse of Steele. Before glancing at it, we shall, however, turn to the one paper, the sixth *Examiner*, which Prior is known to have written.

Publication of a poem by Dr. Garth in praise of Godolphin gave Prior an opportunity to take a fling at the Whigs for his recent expulsion from the Kit-Cat Club and for their disparagement of him as a poet now that he had gone over to their enemies:

The Collective Body of the Whigs have already engrossed our Riches; and their Representatives, the *Kit-Cat*, have pretended to make a Monopoly of our Sense. Thus it happens, that Mr. P——r, by being expelled the Club, ceases to be a Poet; and Sir *Harry* F——e becomes one, by being admitted into it. 'Tis here that Wit and Beauty are decided by Plurality of Voices: The Child's Judgment shall make H——y pass for a Fool; And *Jacob's* Indulgence shall preserve Lady H——t from the Tallow-Candle.

It is the Misfortune of our *Athens*, like that of antient *Greece*, to be governed by a Set Number of Tyrants: The Works of Learned Men are weighed here by the unerring Ballance of Party, and he is sure to be most ingenious in his Writings, who is, in their Phrase, most thorough-paced in his Politics. *Treelooby* kept the general Applause for a whole Winter; while poor *Phaedra* could scarce get into the Theatre; 'till she had thrown herself at the Feet of one of these *Reguli*. It was in this Mint that a curious Piece of Poetical Workmanship was lately wrought, and, by the Masters of the Company, allowed as current and authentic Coin. Notwithstanding which Stamp of Authority, a Critic, unknown to me, has presumed to make some Observations about this Performance; both which, I hope Dr. *Bentley* will excuse me for publishing, since this is such Poetry as he has never found among the *Greek* or *Latin* Writers.

Prior then published Dr. Garth's poem along with a captious comment on the poem and its author, making now and then a thrust at Steele. The paper ended with a short riddle in verse, indirectly attacking Godolphin.[11]

[11] The *Examiner*, September 7, 1710.

Addison now leaped into this pen and ink quarrel, aiming, he said in the first number of the *Whig Examiner*,[12] "to give a rehearing to all persons who had suffered any unjust sentence of the *Examiner*—more an Executioner than an Examiner." Turning his guns on Prior, he continued:

I allow he has a happy talent at doggerel when he writes upon a known subject. When he tells us in plain intelligent language how Corsica's Ladle was lost in one hole, and Hans Carvel's finger in another, he is very jocular and diverting; but when he wraps a lampoon in a riddle, he must consider that his jest is lost to everyone but the few merry wags that are in the secret. This is making darker satires than ever Perseus made.

As for Prior's attack upon Dr. Garth's poem, Addison thought it wholly groundless and unjust. Furthermore, the thrust at Steele "was introduced for no other reason but to mention Mr. Bickerstaff, whom the author everywhere endeavors to imitate and abuse."

Thus we see that Addison answered Prior with surprising boldness. "Willing to wound" and daring on this occasion, at least, to strike as well, he struck with venom. Prior's attack upon Dr. Garth had been harmless ridicule. Addison reduced all Prior's poetry to mere doggerel and, casting aside for once his prudishness, he was himself as coarse as the maligned author of the "Idle Tales." Never could there have been any love lost between these two poet-wits, whose paths frequently crossed. Sitting opposite one another at Kit-Cat dinners, the heedless Bohemian and the cautious prig must have eyed each other with suspicion. Nor did their relations improve upon further association.

The *Whig Examiner* expired after five issues, only to be immediately followed by the *Medley* under the patronage of the Duchess of Marlborough and edited by Maynwaring. The Whigs tried to win over Dr. Garth to share in the responsibilities of

[12] The *Whig Examiner*, September 14, 1710.

editorship, but he wisely declined; and Addison, knowing that Swift was soon to take charge of the *Examiner*, also withdrew. The *Medley*, written mostly by Maynwaring, with occasional contributions from Oldmixon and a single paper from Steele, proved a feeble antagonist for the *Examiner*.

Although Addison referred no more to Prior in the *Whig Examiner*, he again took up the cudgels in the *Tatler*, No. 239,[13] a reply to the eleventh *Examiner*,[14] which, as we have said, is now attributed to Dr. King. The substance of the attacks and counterattacks need not detain us. A writer on one side frequently berated a writer on the other for a paper written by one of his colleagues. Thus the eleventh *Examiner* charged Steele with a paper (the *Tatler*, No. 229) that Addison had written, in which he had spoken of "the numberless vermin that feed upon this paper; . . . the small wits and scribblers, that every day turn a penny by nibbling at my lucubrations." By way of retaliation the eleventh *Examiner* insinuated that the mention of vermin implied that the "Tatler" himself had recently been sleeping in a sponging house—a hint very close to the truth. There were many other veiled allusions to Steele's straitened circumstances. Addison, in the *Tatler*, No. 239, accused the author of the obnoxious *Examiner* paper of "stealing from himself" and of writing criticism that would "make a man of sense sick, and a fool merry." In order that his readers might know that he regarded Prior as the author of the offensive paper, Addison quoted the following lines from Ovid's *Metamorphoses:*

> Quae nec reticere loquenti,
> Nec prior ipsa loqui didicit.

So far the *Examiner* had made little progress as a party organ. It had merely engaged in squabbles, ungenerous and unjust, with its Whig opponents. What the paper needed, Harley told Swift, was "some good pen" to keep up the spirits of the party.

[13] October 19, 1710.   [14] October 12, 1710.

This criticism was rather uncomplimentary to Prior and his confederates, who had thus far kept the *Examiner* going, but it was substantially correct. The journal had lacked a unified policy. Swift brought to it a firm, vigorous hand, a bold and positive party program.

Swift, on November 2, began his drive against the war and the fallen Whig ministry. His attack culminated in the famous letter to Crassus in which Marlborough was accused of avarice.[15] The war, said Swift, had been created by the Whig Junto and prolonged in the interest of the stockjobbers and the moneyed men of the city. The welfare of the nation had been subjected to the interest of the Dutch. The Queen and the constitution had been flouted by Republicans and Grandees. The landed interests, he continued, had long been hoodwinked by profiteers, and the Church had been humiliated by an unholy alliance between Presbyterians and Atheists.

The *Examiner*, now having a purposeful tone, was read regularly by the country clergy to their parishioners. The Whigs, in spite of the journal's change of hands, still believed that Prior was a contributor and ascribed to him several savage attacks on Marlborough. He was actually in danger of being insulted in the streets.[16] His reputation as a wit and a poet was suffering. "His poems," said Swift, had "contracted a stupidity many years after they were printed."[17] Following Addison's example, the Whig writers harped on Prior's "doggerel" and bawdy tales to the exclusion of the more chaste verse:

> Could I tell, to make you marvel,
> Such a tale as conjur'd Carvel,
> Cou'd I fly my fancy higher
> And out-tell the tell-tale Prior;
> Cou'd I on Apollo's anvil
> Beat out Rhimes like gentle Gr——,

---

[15] The *Examiner*, February 8, 1710/11.
[16] *Journal to Stella*, February 9, 1710/11.
[17] The *Examiner*, March 8, 1710/11.

> How might I employ my Talent
> And be politick and gallant?
> Robin should be my Pomponius
> And friend Harry my Petronius.

Thus Oldmixon jingled in the *Medley*.[18]

In order to call off the pack of angry Whigs, Swift decided to let it be known in the twenty-sixth number of the *Examiner* that Prior was no longer the author of the paper. They had, Swift declared, "openly taxed a most ingenious person as author of it; one who is in great and very deserved reputation with the world, both on account of his poetical works, and his talents for public business"; further, he was a person who was entirely innocent and whose greatest fault was "too much gentleness towards a party, from whose leaders he had received quite contrary treatment."

» 3 «

Swift's *Journal to Stella*, begun in September 1710, gives us many glimpses of Prior's activities, social and political, during the next year or so. Prior and Swift frequently dined together or joined "the cluster of wise heads at the Smyrna." After dinner they would sit through the long winter evenings complimenting each other on their mutual wit and poetry, or when the days began to lengthen they would walk briskly around St. James's Park. "Mr. Prior," Swift told Stella, "walks to make himself fat, and I to bring myself down; he has generally a cough, which he calls only a cold; we often walk around the Park together."[19]

A "strange remedy," Swift called the exercise; but if they did not share equally in the benefits to their health, they shared equally in the congeniality of their minds. Both disappointed courtier and frustrate poet found much to hate in a cruel and stupid world, yet both in their lighter moments could join in the cry *vive la bagatelle*. To compensate for his frustration, Swift always sought the company of poets and, as he had formerly

[18] The *Medley*, October 16, 1710.   [19] *Journal to Stella*, February 21, 1710/11.

cultivated Addison and was later to cultivate Pope, he now enjoyed the companionship of Prior, whose career in certain respects paralleled his own. Both had been associated with Lord Berkeley; both had deserted the ungrateful Whigs for the Tories, now rich with promises. There is little to compare in their writing. Prior's prose was the more charming; Swift's the more vigorous. The friendship proved more profitable to Swift than to Prior,[20] for under Prior's influence, Swift wrote some of his easiest and most graceful verse and several political lampoons. One of the latter, anonymously read one evening over heavy potations of wine at Harley's, provoked the two friends to rally each other as the author of it. The other Wits joined in the fun, and the whole group was soon uproariously merry.

The Tory Wits formed the habit of meeting at Harley's once a week to exchange verses and gossip, to initiate new schemes for the discomfiture of the Whigs, and to further plans for strengthening their own party. Swift and Prior were leaders in the group, which included the best Tory brains of the day. Among them was the genial but gossipy Dr. Arbuthnot, the Queen's physician, whom Dr. Johnson declared "the first man among them . . . the most universal genius, being an excellent physician, a man of deep learning and a man of much humour." St. John, the brilliant schemer, was always expounding Tory doctrines and proclaiming the right of the Tories to party spoils. Another member, who figures prominently in the anecdotes of the period, was Peterborough, the knight-errant, the hero (in his own eyes) of countless adventures in love and war—in brief the best-known Englishman from Spain to Austria, from England to Italy. Presiding over the circle was the host, the torpid but kindly Harley, who made no pretensions to learning and had no special political philosophy but who was withal a rare handler of men and situations.

[20] For Prior's influence on Swift's verse, see F. Elrington Ball, *Swift's Verse*, chaps. v and vi, pp. 102–47.

The record of these Tory gatherings, largely written in the *Journal to Stella*, reveals that the Wits indulged in shameless punning, Swift and Prior being among the worst offenders. "Lord Carteret set down Prior t'other day in his chariot," Swift related, "and Prior thanked him for his charity."[21] Prior persisted in punning until the end of his days, and he once proudly declared that he had made a hundred puns in forty-eight hours. Swift was the author of what Prior swore was the worst pun he had ever heard. Since Swift relayed it to Stella, he evidently thought better of it himself: "At dinner at Lord Harcourt's," Swift explains, "we had coarse doily napkins fringed at each end, upon the table to drink with. My Lord Keeper spread one between himself and Prior," and Swift remarked that he was glad to see there was "such fringeship" between Prior and his Lordship.[22]

The Tory Wits had so enjoyed each other's company at those informal meetings that St. John decided to organize them into a club to be known as the Brothers. There was, he resolved, to be "none of the extravagance of the Kit-Cat, none of the drunkenness of the Beef-Steak." His aim, so he said, was "to advance conversation and friendship and to reward deserving persons." In spite of St. John's opposition to extravagance, the expenses of the meetings, which were held first at some tavern or coffeehouse, became so great that Harley was provoked, and it was decided that in the future the members should entertain the group in their own homes.

When it was Prior's turn to entertain the Brothers, he sent Harley an invitation in verse:

> Our Weekly Friends To-morrow meet
> At MATTHEW's Palace, in *Duke Street*;
> To try for once, if They can Dine
> On Bacon-Ham, and Mutton-Chine:
> If weary'd with the great Affairs

---

[21] *Journal to Stella*, January 4, 1710/11.   [22] *Ibid.*, April 23, 1711.

Which Britain trusts to Harley's Cares
Thou, humble Statesman, mays't descend,
Thy Mind one Moment to unbend;
To see Thy Servant from his Soul
Crown with Thy Health the sprightly Bowl:
Among the Guests, which e'er my House
Receiv'd it never can produce
Of Honor a more glorious Proof—
Tho' Dorset us'd to bless the Roof.[23]

Frequently the Brothers would put their heads together and produce a satire. Collaboration was the easiest way of insuring the anonymity which they desired. Marlborough was often the target of these satires, which Prior, more often than not, was blamed for writing. Swift's comment on one of the joint compositions is evasive: "I was in the City today and dined with my printer, and gave him a ballad made by several hands, I know not whom. I believe Lord Treasurer had a hand in it; I added three stanzas; I suppose Dr. Arbuthnot had the greatest share."[24] Sir Charles Firth thinks that the "ballad made by several hands" is the nine-stanza satire on Marlborough, "A Widow and her Cat," often ascribed to Prior. Another poem, "When the Cat's Away the Mice may Play," written about the same time, has likewise been attributed to Prior. Such ascription, Firth points out, is absurd; the poem was plainly directed against Harley and Mrs. Masham.[25]

There is no evidence that Prior wrote any satires on Marlborough during these years. It would have been a rashly imprudent thing for him to do: Maynwaring was constantly on his trail. In the *Medley* he was quick to point out to Swift that a friend of the Examiner's had once paid high compliments to the Duke, and by way of illustration he maliciously quoted lines from Prior's ode "On the Glorious Success of Her Majesty's Arms."[26] That is not to say that Prior may not have furnished

[23] *Poems on Several Occasions*, p. 188.
[25] *Review of English Studies*, I (1925), 456.
[24] *Journal to Stella*, January 4, 1711/12.
[26] The tenth *Medley*, December 4, 1710.

his brother Wits with material for their lampoons on the Duke and for their derogatory papers in the *Examiner*—it was not his wont to practice such restraint.

Prior valued the friendships with the Brothers, and, when diplomatic duties took him abroad, he recalled sentimentally the enjoyment of their company. Yet tradition has it that often, after spending an evening with the Brothers, he would feel constrained by such "celestial colloquy" and would seek relief by smoking a pipe and drinking a bottle of ale with a common soldier and his wife in Long Acre before going to bed. The soldier, Mr. Dobson imagines, "may have carried a halbert under my Uncle Toby!" The wife was doubtless the captivating Betty Cox. Such tales led Dr. Johnson to remark about Prior that "in his private relaxations he revived the tavern." What if he did? After all, "Down-Hall," "Daphne and Apollo," "Jinny the Just," and many another poem testify that Prior had a keen eye for character. Under the glittering make-believe of Queen Anne society, life was real, colorful, crude; and Matt, a more normal person than most of his contemporaries, one who craved life in all its variety, knew where to find it. If his zest for living demanded robust expression and Falstaffian experience, it also furnished an escape from unhappy thought. The idea suggests further resemblance between Prior and Montaigne. As Mr. Barrett has observed, both Prior and Montaigne "sought relief in *la science de l'oubli* . . . and gave themselves willingly to small folk."[27]

» 4 «

A strange trick of fortune had put two widely different men, Harley and St. John, at the head of the ministry. Yet for years a warm attachment had existed between them, and St. John had looked up to Harley, whom he called "The Master," in somewhat the same way that Prior had once looked up to Halifax.

[27] W. P. Barrett, *Mod. Lang. Rev.*, XXVII (1932), 458.

Harley, despite such deference, was a small, insignificant man of pious background, who always favored moderation, since moderation suited his secret, cautious, devious ways. His ruling passion was his family, to whom he was devoted and for whom he labored to establish a fortune. His greatest diversion was his famous library, and he would neglect an important business engagement to purchase a new manuscript for his collection. St. John, seventeen years his junior and only thirty-one when he became Secretary of State, was handsome, brilliant, reckless. By the standards which Pope applied to Prior, St. John was not a "right good man." He acquired mistresses as Harley acquired manuscripts, and Voltaire is responsible for the story that when the *demi-mondaines* of London learned that St. John had become Secretary they knowingly said to each other "eight thousand guineas of income, my sisters, and all for us."[28] With these two men Prior was to be constantly associated for the next four years and dependent upon their fortunes. Harley, Prior was to find solid and steadfast, although secretive and dilatory; St. John, a merry wag, who mixed business with pleasure. The Secret Committee, it is said, found St. John and Prior "unseasonably witty during the most important and solemn negotiations";[29] the town was set tittering when the Committee published a letter from St. John to Prior in which the Secretary informed the Plenipotentiary in Paris that he was writing his letter "upon the finest desk in the Universe; Black Betty's Black Ace."[30] In the crisis of 1715, St. John lost his nerve and fled, blaming Prior for his difficulties; whereas Harley remained to face the music.

Although questions of policy and personal jealousies arose that ultimately split Harley and St. John asunder, there was one question upon which they were agreed, and that was peace with France. With the actual peace negotiations, Prior was soon to be connected. His knowledge of the French language, his popu-

[28] Voltaire, *Works*, LXV, 430, Voltaire to Comte de la Touraille, Ferney, April 24, 1776.
[29] Prior, *Poetical Works*, ed. Gilfillan, p. xi.
[30] Bolingbroke, *Authentic Memoirs*, p. 31.

larity at the French Court, his mastery of commercial affairs, as well as of diplomatic procedure, all fitted him for such service.

But before passing to Prior's secret journey to France, let us glance at the preliminary steps in the negotiations which led up to it. A dark and mysterious course was pursued, such as was consistent with the character of Harley and as was dictated to a great extent by the exigencies of the situation. In order to open negotiations for peace with the enemy, the ministry had to work in secret. They must get rid of the popular idol, Marlborough; they must hoodwink their rivals, the Whigs; they must steal a march on their allies, the Dutch. While such unscrupulous tactics are condemned by the modern historian, the fault, it should be remembered, lay as much with the diplomacy then in vogue as with the ministers themselves.

A channel for carrying on secret communications with France was close at hand, only to be had for the asking. Jersey, seeking to ingratiate himself with the ministry, introduced to Harley a fat, genial French priest, François Gaultier, who, as chaplain to the Austrian Ambassador, had resided in London during the entire period of the war, and had sent secretly to the French Court such news of affairs as Torcy might wish. Entertaining sidelights upon English statesmen, Tory and Whig, are these messages of Gaultier's, in which few events, political, social, or literary, are left unrecorded. Especially revealing is the picture of Jersey, ever ready to serve the cause of peace, as well as that of the Pretender, even though his eagerness led him to express hopes for French victories and to accept a bribe of three thousand pounds from Louis XIV.[31]

In December, 1710, Harley directed Gaultier to dispatch a communication to Torcy stating that the ministry were determined upon peace and that they would give up their demands

---

[31] For important parts of the correspondence in 1710–1711 between Gaultier and Torcy in Paris Archives . . . , *Correspondance Politique, d'Angleterre*, Vols. 230–32, see G. M. Trevelyan's "The Jersey Period of the Negotiations leading to the Peace of Utrecht," *Eng. Hist. Rev.*, XLIX, 100–105.

for the Spanish Succession provided security was assured to English trade.[32] Shortly afterwards Gaultier went to France to deliver in person to Torcy messages from Harley, Shrewsbury, and Jersey, all of whom were absolutely resolved to end the war, but were convinced that for reasons of state and for their own protection the treaty could not be begun in England.[33] Torcy was greatly surprised at this sudden prospect for peace, but when Gaultier returned to England he carried assurance of Torcy's desire to coöperate with the English ministers.

All during the winter of 1711 negotiations were continued, although for a time they were delayed by Harley's procrastinations. In April the transactions were speeded up when St. John took charge while Harley was recovering from wounds inflicted by a would-be assassin, the French *émigré*, Guiscard. St. John, against Harley's wishes, was now necessarily admitted to the entire secret of the negotiations.

Under St. John's orders, then, Gaultier again crossed to France with a verbal report of the peace conditions acceptable to the English. He was instructed to put these suggestions into the mouths of the French statesmen but to make it appear that the suggestions were originating spontaneously. The proposals were these:

1. A security for British trade in the Mediterranean, in Spain, and in the West Indies.
2. A barrier for the Dutch, sufficient for them and satisfactory to the English.
3. Satisfaction to the Allies.
4. A settlement of the Spanish Succession that would be agreeable to the English. This, Gaultier was to say, was in favor of Philip, although at the Conferences England would at first press the right of Charles.[34]

---

[32] Paris, Archives . . . , *Correspondance Politique, d'Angleterre*, 230, fo. 238, Gaultier to Torcy, Dec. 23, 1710.
[33] *Ibid.*, 232, fo. 81, Mémoire in Gaultier's own handwriting.
[34] Cobbett's *Parliamentary History*, Vol. VII, App. I, p. ciii.

On April 11/22 Torcy signed a paper embodying the English proposals, which Gaultier promptly took over to England. For a time, however, the negotiations were at a standstill. Harley was busy after his recovery from his wounds, obtaining his new honors—the staff of Lord Treasurer and the title of Earl of Oxford. An event suddenly occurred, however, which favored expediting the negotiations. During the month the Emperor Joseph of Austria died, leaving as his heir his brother, the Archduke Charles, who, as we know, had been recognized as King of Spain by England and the Allies rather than Philip of Anjou. The prospect of a union of the crowns of Austria and Spain proved as alarming to the English ministry as had the former prospect of a union of the crowns of Spain and France under Philip, the original *casus belli*. Consequently Harley, or Oxford, as he shall be designated hereafter, and his ministers were ready to make one concession to the French: they would acknowledge the right of Philip to the Spanish throne. Towards the end of June they advised the Queen to send Gaultier back to France and to send Prior along with him.

So, with a passport describing him as one Jeremy Matthews and under the pretext of taking a little trip into Suffolk to visit Sir Thomas Hanmer, Prior left London on July 1/12, 1711, accompanied by his "fellow traveler," the abbé. On their way they stopped at Squeries with Lord Jersey, who gave Gaultier messages for Torcy.[35] They crossed the channel in a fishing boat unnoticed by anyone except John Macky, officer in charge of the channel packet boats, who promptly notified St. John that an English gentleman had taken passage for France. St. John ordered Macky to keep his discovery a secret but to watch for the man's return.[36] About nine days after their departure from London, Prior and Gaultier arrived at Fontainebleau, which Prior had first visited thirteen years before as a young secretary.

[35] Paris, Archives . . . , *Correspondance Politique, d'Angleterre*, 233, fo. 43.
[36] *Political State of Great Britain*, II, 203; IX, 313.

For a long time the only available account of Prior's errand was to be found in Swift's pamphlet *A Journey to Paris*. Torcy's *Memoirs*, published in 1752, gave a brief version of the French side of the story, but no English record was published until Prior's own account from his private journal was printed by the Historical Manuscripts Commission from the *Portland Papers* at Welbeck Abbey.[37] Another source, now in the *Archives des Affaires Étrangères*, is Torcy's memorandum for Louis XIV. These two documents supplement each other: Torcy's being ampler at the beginning of the conference and including Gaultier's report; Prior's a more thorough summary of the conference after it had got under way.

Upon arrival at Fontainebleau, Gaultier related to Torcy the happenings in England since his last journey, and, after making his report, he presented Prior, whom Torcy welcomed as an old friend. Having exchanged compliments, Gaultier withdrew, and Prior showed Torcy his credentials, his powers being stated in three lines under the Queen's sign manual, but neither dated nor countersigned by any minister.[38]

Prior's powers were limited. He had no authority to negotiate. He might, however, discuss the proposals with Torcy, so long as Torcy did not get the better of the argument. If he did, Prior was to retreat behind the letter of his instructions and protest that he had no power. The latter plan, Torcy, of course, did not know, but he was surprised at the meagerness of Prior's powers, having inferred from Gaultier's report that the English Plenipotentiary would have full power to negotiate. Before showing the proposals to Torcy, Prior learned from him that Louis XIV was empowered to treat for Philip. The proposals submitted by Prior on July 10/21 in behalf of England were briefly these:

[37] Endorsed, "Journal of my Journey to Paris to be looked over and digested." It covers the ten days from July 12/23 to July 23/Aug. 3.

[38] Anne R.

Le Sieur Prior est pleinement instruit et authorisé de communiquer à la France nos demandes Préliminaires et de nous en rapporter la reponse. A. R.

1. Great Britain would make no peace but that which would be to the satisfaction of her allies. The Dutch, the Emperor, and the Duke of Savoy should have barriers. The trade of Holland must be secured. Great Britain must have positive assurance that the crowns of France and Spain should never be united.

2. For herself, Great Britain demanded the monopoly of the *Assiento* and equal opportunities with France in Spanish America; Newfoundland must be ceded to Great Britain; the trade of Hudson's Bay must continue as it then was; all lands in America must remain in the possession of those they should be found to be in at the conclusion of the peace; Louis must recognize the Protestant Succession, must demolish Dunkirk, and agree to let Gibraltar and Port Mahon (Minorca) remain in the hands of Great Britain.

Torcy was amazed at the great advantage—as he saw it— that England demanded. Furthermore, he was annoyed; he had counted on his own diplomatic skill to reduce demands, if necessary, but Prior's authority was so limited as to make strategy useless. He decided, therefore, to postpone further discussion until the proposals could be shown to King Louis. During the following day, July 11/22, Torcy advised with Louis XIV, and in the evening he again met Prior. After a preliminary skirmish of wits, they settled down to a careful reading of the proposals. Prior interrupted to point out the importance of the concession the English were making in permitting Philip, Louis's grandson, to remain on the throne of Spain. Torcy retorted that since the successes at Brihuega and Villa Viciosa Philip was quite secure on his throne, from which the Allies had been unable to dislodge him; moreover, the Dutch, as well as the English, were offering to let Philip reign in Spain and to treat for peace on that condition. Secretly rejoicing at the easy terms of the English ministers, he further protested that they must not ask too much and warned Prior that they had rivals in the field.[39] Then he sprang a surprise: he produced three letters from Pettkum, the Holstein resident at The Hague. One of the letters, he said, had arrived that very afternoon. Would M. Prior care to hear them?

The import of the letters was that the Dutch desired the French to renew negotiations with them; that they would offer better terms than England; that England was planning to deceive the French; that the Whigs were in sympathy with Holland, whereas the Tories were in league with the Allies and were resolved to continue the war. The most recent missive from Pettkum offered to give the French whatever terms they might name. Torcy recorded that Prior was irritated by these letters,[40] but Prior, in his account, declared:

I could not forbear laughing, and said that if M. Pettkum were no better apprized of the inclination of the States towards a peace than he was of the desires of the English towards the prolonging the war, I thought his advice would not weigh much with M. de Torcy.[41]

"I show you these letters," replied Torcy, triumphantly, "that you may see the plainness and openness with which His Majesty will treat with England if the propositions you bring leave any possibility of it." With mock seriousness he asked if Prior had any other memoir with whose proposals France might comply. Prior responded blandly that M. de Torcy must be rallying him—he had been quite honest in asserting that he had only the one memoir, and that he was powerless to recede one iota from any point in it. "La Paix ne se fera pas donc, Monsieur," protested Torcy, "lisez vous même vos demandes préliminaires."

Putting all raillery aside, Prior and Torcy now took up the proposals in order. The demands of the English for Gibraltar, Port Mahon, and four towns in the West Indies so staggered Torcy that he challenged Prior: "Vous avez été dans la commerce,

[39] Paris, Archives . . . , *Correspondance Politique, d'Angelterre*, 233, fo. 49.
[40] *Ibid.*, 233, fo. 50.   [41] *Portland Papers*, V, 34.

réfléchissez un peu sur ce mémoire." What was it, he expostulated, that Great Britain wanted but to be master of the Mediterranean and of Spain, to possess all the Indies, and to take away from France all that appertained to that crown in America! Unshaken by Torcy's explosiveness, Prior protested that the English must have a genuine security for their commerce in the Mediterranean and the places in America as shelters from pirates. Torcy objected that if the English demanded such advantages, so would the Dutch, and if so, why not the French? In that event, how could the Spanish King call himself Lord of the Indies? The English, he argued, needed no such favors, since their advantages at the hands of Philip would be infinitely greater than at the hands of the Archduke, whom they had vainly endeavored to seat upon the throne.

Prior stubbornly maintained that the claims of the Dutch need not prove embarrassing, as the article ceding the places in the West Indies would be incorporated in a secret document. England, he continued, would not oppose any desire of France for places in America. Furthermore, the Archduke had already promised England such advantages, and England alone. Naturally enough, Torcy laughed out of court the agreements that the Archduke had made over lands which did not belong to him. When Prior countered that the English proposals were honestly made and that even the Spaniards would thank the English for protecting them from the English and Dunkirk pirates, the former of which were the worst of the lot, Torcy rejoined: "You will never make Spain believe that it is to their advantage to take away their country."

The discussion growing hot, Prior rather adroitly reminded Torcy that he had no power to discuss—all that had gone before to the contrary. When the next article, known as the *Assiento*, which provided England a monopoly, formerly enjoyed by France, of supplying slaves to Spanish America, was read, Torcy shouted, "*Impossible, impossible!*" and Prior, knowing what store the ministry set on this privilege, was sick at heart. Still he was firm in asserting that peace could be made on no other basis.

Torcy also objected to the next article, which concerned colonial possessions in North America, for it demanded that not only Newfoundland but also Hudson's Bay and Acadia should be turned over to the English. "Voici encore une autre impossibilité," he declared. Prior then put forward the following historical arguments: all Hudson's Bay was originally English—the very name bespoke it; Hudson in the year 1610 sailed through and possessed himself of the bay; the names of all the banks and towns even in the French maps had always been and were still English; and as to Newfoundland, the words *terre neuve* were but the interpretation of the English name; and even before that name was given to the place, it was discovered by Sebastian Cabot, claimed by the English in the time of Henry the Eighth, and known by the name of Avalon.[42]

To such irrefutable arguments Torcy had no answer, although he did again refer to the subject feelingly: "You ask in America all that which [with] our sweat and our blood we have been endeavouring for a hundred years past to acquire."[43] Thus began the struggle between the English and the French for possession of America, which was to culminate in the Treaty of Paris in 1763, when France lost all.

The Dutch Barrier, next in point of order, was more amicably discussed, Torcy acquiescing completely, since on this question the English demands were more favorable to the French than to the Dutch. Torcy sighed and wished that he might satisfy the rest of the English demands as easily. Once more he tried to make Prior tell him just what would satisfy the English ministry, but Prior was on his guard and refused to be ensnared. The meeting adjourned upon Torcy's announcing that Louis would not agree to all the proposals but would consider them again on the following day.

[42] *Ibid.*, V, 36, 37.   [43] *Ibid.*, V, 37.

Louis would not send Prior back with an absolute refusal. He therefore ordered his Council to consider the proposals and report their opinion. To the Council he added two experts on mercantile affairs, Nicholas Mesnager and La Laude Magon.[44] Several days would elapse before the two men would arrive. When Torcy met Prior (July 13/24) he asked if Prior would mind waiting. Prior consented to the delay, and Torcy returned to the discussion of the English demands in the Mediterranean and in Spanish America. After considerable debate, in which he revealed his ability to defend his nation's interest against the most astute diplomat of the time, Prior said with finality: "We are a trading nation and as such must secure our traffic; Her Majesty and her ministry judge it absolutely necessary that this branch of our trade be secured."

On a Sunday evening, two days later, the third meeting was held in the Gardens of Fontainebleau. "It was dark enough," Prior records, "to conceal who we were."[45] This time the discussion chiefly concerned the South Sea Company, which Torcy regarded as a menace to French trade; Prior maintained that it would cause a more equal distribution of traffic and a freer circulation of commerce in the whole of Europe. Again Torcy tried to combat the English demand for the four places in Spanish America. Again Prior repeated his arguments maintaining that this "was the only basis and foundation of a negotiation."

Three days later, in the evening at the usual hour of nine, but at Torcy's lodgings, the final conference was held. Since the last meeting, the King's Council had studied the English proposals, but the more they pondered them the less they liked them. What, after all, asked Torcy, did the English intend? Did they not aim at a monopoly of trade? And if the nations of Europe partitioned America, would not the Spaniards lose it entirely?

Increasingly irked by Prior's limited powers, Torcy flaunted new messages from the Dutch. He said that King Louis would

[44] Paris, Archives . . . , *Correspondance Politique, d'Angelterre*, 233, fo. 55.
[45] *Portland Papers*, V. 39, 40.

not listen to them but would send over by Prior a plan of his own, as reasonable and as extensive as he could make. This announcement surprised Prior; he asked Torcy what it meant. Torcy explained that when Prior should return to England Mesnager should accompany him, bearing the King's proposals. Prior promised that the envoy would receive as warm a welcome as he himself had received in France. He had not the power to make any countersuggestions.

At last the King's plan was ready. To Prior's amazement, it contained only an answer to the articles relating to the Allies in general and not a word about England's demands in particular. When Prior pointed this out, Torcy replied that Mesnager would have full power to negotiate. The main obstacles, he explained, to an immediate agreement were the articles of commerce, but he was hoping that they could be adjusted.'[46]

The day before Prior left Fontainebleau, he was granted an audience with Louis XIV. We may imagine that he felt somewhat elated as he set out for the King's chambers, where he was due at six o'clock in the evening. The King was walking up and down his apartment when Prior was admitted. Upon Prior's first obeisance, the King bowed, leaned back against a table, and said, "A ça, Monsieur. Je suis bien aise de vous voir, vous parlez Français je sçay." Prior, with his customary graciousness and wit replied: "Sire, pour pouvoir exprimer la joie que je sens de revoir votre Majesté dans une santé si parfaite, je devrais mieux parler Français qu'aucun de vos sujets." Then followed an exchange of mutual assurances that both nations desired the peace and that both would do all in their power to bring it about. They agreed that no time should be lost, because, said Louis, both nations were "descendues du même sang, et qui ne sont pas ennemies que par necessité."[47]

"Taking my leave," Prior writes, "I said that I wished His Majesty long life and prosperity; that wherever my duty called

---

[46] On July 21/Aug. 1.   [47] *Portland Papers*, V, 41, 42.

me I should always retain a great veneration for his person and acknowledgment of his favors I had received in France."

» 5 «

Accompanied by Mesnager and Gaultier, Prior embarked for England as secretly as he had left. He might well congratulate himself upon successfully carrying out the instructions of the ministry. He had got the better of Torcy in every argument. He spied out the weakness of France without revealing any of the weaknesses of his own nation. Should the ministry have any compunctions about stealing a march upon the Dutch, he could tell them of Pettkum's letters.

All went well on the return voyage until the travelers reached Deal. The meddlesome Macky had, it seems, followed instructions better than St. John had intended. Overzealously he had employed all his men between the forelands to watch for the return of the mysterious English gentleman who had stealthily gone over to France. Macky at once seized the trio and, recognizing Prior by his lank figure in spite of an elaborate disguise, remonstrated with him for using an alias. Prior produced his pass, but Macky refused to accept it and lodged him in jail while awaiting orders. Macky promptly notified Marlborough and Sunderland of this action. At once the news of Prior's journey was out. Sunderland informed the Dutch and Austrian ministers that peace negotiations were on foot. The Austrian minister had to be quieted by the promise that England would make no peace terms without satisfaction to the Allies.[48]

Fast post horses carried orders from Whitehall for Prior's release. St. John threatened to hang Macky for his officiousness. The customs official escaped this dire fate by fleeing to Antwerp, where he remained in disgrace until after the accession of George I.[49] After this delay, Prior and his companions reached London

[48] James MacPherson, *History of Great Britain from the Restoration to the Accession of the House of Hanover*, II, 494.
[49] *Portland Papers*, V, 303, John Macky to Oxford, July 1, 1713.

on August 7/18, and Prior immediately reported to his Queen. The disclosure of his secret mission vexed him exceedingly. The Whigs promptly made what capital they could out of it. Maynwaring published "An Excellent New Song, Called Matt's Peace, or the Downfall of Trade," in which he prophesied that "Poor Matt in the pillory" soon would be seen:

> The news from abroad does a secret reveal
> Which has been confirm'd both at Dover and Deal
> That one Mr. Matthews once called plain Matt
> Has been doing at Paris the Lord knows what,
> But surely what they talk of his Negotiation
> Is only intended to banter the Nation
> For why have we spent so much treasure in vain,
> If now at the last we must give up Spain.

But Prior's errand to France inspired more lasting literature. The *Journal to Stella*, under date of August 31, carried this entry:

I have told you that it is now well known that Mr. Prior has been lately in France. I will make a printer of mine sit by me one day, and I will dictate to him a formal relation of Prior's journey, with several particulars, all pure invention.

Swift's account pretends to be a translation from the French of a story by Monsieur de Baudrier, who called himself secretary to his Excellency, a Monsieur Matthews, but who is only a valet in Swift's eyes. It describes Prior's arrival at Boulogne, an interview there with Torcy, and one with Madame de Maintenon and Louis XIV at Versailles, inspiring in the reader a confidence in the high character of the English Plenipotentiary and a feeling that the national welfare was in safe hands. Scraps of conversation overheard by the valet, such as M. Matthews's lamenting the death of his friend Boileau, furnish *vraisemblance* to the story which could not have been better had Prior given Swift a detailed account of the journey. Although Swift spoke of his little fiction as "mere pleasantry," it was aimed to stop the clamor of the Whigs who were disgruntled with the peace plans so far.

Certainly it gave the public something to talk about and proved to be a better seller than Maynwaring's ballad. By September 24 (thirteen days after publication) it was still selling. Curiously enough among the *Correspondance Politique, d'Angleterre*, in the *Archives des Affaires Étrangères* in Paris there are a few excerpts from Swift's pamphlet, translated into French by the hand of Pecquet, Torcy's secretary. It is safe to surmise that a copy of Monsieur de Baudrier's story was sent to Torcy by Gaultier.[50]

Prior himself was quite annoyed over the pamphlet. On the day it was published, St. John and Swift dined with him in Duke Street. Prior showed the pamphlet to Swift, exclaiming angrily, "Here is our English liberty." Beginning to read aloud, Swift said he liked the story mightily and envied the rogue the thought. Had it come into his head, he continued, he would have written it himself. Prior, who should have guessed its author, had to stand a good deal of chaffing from his friends. Oxford would call him by no other name than Monsieur Baudrier.[51]

But to return to the peace negotiations. Conferences were started in London as soon as Mesnager had rested from his journey, and the Queen had been made conversant with details of Prior's errand. Mesnager was secretly lodged at Prior's home in Duke Street, which became for some time the unofficial headquarters for mysterious and important business. The first official meeting was attended by Mesnager, Oxford, Shrewsbury, Dartmouth, St. John, and Jersey. The recent victory of Marlborough at Bouchain stiffened the stand of the English, who were not in a conciliatory mood. The French expected that England would be able to pledge her allies in the same manner in which France was acting for Spain, but as soon as Mesnager mentioned the compensation that his King desired from the Al-

---

[50] Paris, Archives . . . , *Correspondance Politique, d'Angleterre*, 235, Supplement.
[51] *Journal to Stella*, Oct. 9, 1711.

lies for his concessions to Great Britain, St. John ruled that the discussions be confined to the points relating to the English only.

On August 24/September 4 another conference was held, at which Oxford, St. John, Dartmouth, and Prior were present. Since Dartmouth, in whose province negotiations with France belonged, was, like Oxford, unsure of his French, St. John, fluent in French and dominant in personality, presided over the meetings. On this day the much discussed Dunkirk question came up. St. John demanded the complete demolition of the town. Tentatively agreeing to this proposal, Mesnager argued that restitution to the French must be made of Lille and Tournai —according to his account the suggestion was not at the time rejected.

Throughout the month of September the conferences dragged on. Mesnager was told repeatedly that he might as well go back to France because the negotiations were at a standstill. Again and again he was reminded that the continuance of the war was the only alternative. The deadlock was broken when Gaultier volunteered to go to Versailles and inform Louis of the *impasse*.

These meetings were only preliminaries, we must remember. The final word would be said at the Peace Congress, soon to be held in Holland. It was generally conceded that the Earl of Jersey would be the first Plenipotentiary from England to the Congress in recognition of his instrumentality in bringing about the preliminary negotiations. Popular rumor branded Jersey as a Jacobite; and it must be admitted that he had been variously entangled. During the late summer of 1711 he wrote to Oxford explaining that the accusations of Jacobitism were utterly false and were attributable to nothing save the malice of his enemies; further he craved the opportunity to justify himself to the Queen. Oxford, apparently satisfied, inscribed on the back of the letter "vindicated from Jacobitism."[52] With the appointment as Plenipotentiary in the offing and in view of a rumor that he

[52] *Portland Papers*, V, 69, Jersey to Harley, Aug. 4, 1711.

would be made Lord Privy Seal, Jersey realized that he was at last to be reinstated and was happier than he had been for years. But most unexpectedly he died from a stroke of apoplexy on August 26/September 6.

It is necessary here to digress from the business of the peace to discuss the effect of Jersey's death on Prior. To no one could it have been a greater blow. Prior had remained loyal to Jersey through adversity as well as prosperity. To the deep affection which he bore his friend, the following letter testifies:

> Westminster. Aug. 28, 1711.
>
> Dear Sir Thomas Hanmer,
>
> If ever you knew the tenderness of a true friendship you will pity my present condition, when I tell you that my dear Lord Jersey went seemingly well to bed on Saturday night, and at five on Sunday morning died—be his spirit forever happy and his memory respected. The only moment of ease which I have found since this cruel blow is just now while I complain and write to you. Time and necessity I know cure all our sorrows; but as yet I feel a load upon my spirits which I conceal from the world, and which must be too hard for human nature if it lasts. I know you loved my Lord Jersey, and I hope I trouble you while I give you an account of his death: The Queen, the nation, mankind has lost a pattern of honor, integrity, and good manners; you, Sir, have lost a man who understood your merit, and courted your friendship; after you have wept for him, Sir, as I beg you to do, I will wish in recompense that those years which he might reasonably have expected, may be added to yours; in the meantime I desire you to believe that till I lie extended on the bier as I saw my poor Lord this morning, I remain most sincerely and inviolably,
>
> Your obedient and humble servant
> Mat. Prior.[53]

The death of Lord Jersey brought an adjournment to the conferences, which were not resumed until Gaultier returned to London. From then on the meetings were held at Prior's house. The English were relieved to learn that France was willing to concede to their demands, Louis merely insisting upon an

---

[53] Hanmer, *Correspondence*, p. 129, Aug. 28, 1711.

equivalent for Dunkirk to be determined at a future congress—
a solution which seemed simple enough at the time. Flushed
with their success, the English ministers made further efforts to
extort terms from France.

But it was not ordained that things move so smoothly. St.
John startled the conference by reporting that Parliament would
consider it a misdemeanor for any loyal Englishman to treat
with a prince who harbored the Pretender. Mesnager op-
portunely reminded the group that they were concerned with
preliminaries, not with a treaty, thus providing a loophole that
satisfied even the most timid negotiators. A misunderstanding
about fishing rights in Newfoundland next arose. No final settlement of the rights could be made until the Peace Congress should
meet, but the French, who made a lucrative business of cod-
fishing and drying, were told that they might continue this
privilege for the time. A few days after this agreement was
reached, Prior again upset their plans by telling Mesnager that
the London merchants were objecting to the article on fisheries.
Prior should have been more positive in dealing with the problem—long a troublesome one. Really he seems to have been
playing for time while awaiting the news of St. John's St.
Lawrence expedition, which if successful, would exclude the
French from Newfoundland entirely, even from their fishing
rights. Mesnager was adamant, however, saying that his King
would rather continue the war than yield this point. Temporarily, the matter was disposed of when the English decided not
to contest the question further.

The news that the Dutch envoy was on his way to England in
spite of the Queen's protest hastened the conclusion of this preliminary negotiating. On September 27/October 8 three documents representing the final agreements of the two nations were
signed. One was a preliminary treaty between France and
England; another was a general treaty for the Allies; and the
third was a secret article about Savoy. Although the Queen

designated eight ministers as Plenipotentiaries to sign these articles with Mesnager and, of more significance to us, empowered "our trusty and well-beloved Matthew Prior, Esquire,"[54] to sign also, the documents finally bore the signature of only two of those named.

Prior was a valued member of these conferences, as the Queen's naming of him along with the ministers would indicate. Furthermore there is St. John's recommendation of him to the Queen: "He is the best versed in matters of trade of all your Majesty's servants who have been trusted in this secret; if you should think fit to employ him in the future treaty of commerce, it will be of consequence that he has been a party concerned in concluding that convention which must be the rule of this treaty."[55]

Thus Prior's secret trip to France, the nocturnal conferences in the gardens of Fontainebleau, the bargainings of the London meetings culminated in what has gone down in history as "Matt's Peace"—a term first used derisively by the Whigs. The Queen was in a good humor over this preliminary treaty. The cession of Gibraltar and Port Mahon was a safeguard to the nation's commerce; and the concessions in America were of far-reaching importance in the future trade with the colonies, an advantage which Prior, perhaps, was the only one to foresee. The Whigs, it is true, when they made an investigation of the preliminaries in 1715, seized upon the fact that no demand for the removal of the Pretender had been made and that Anne was not to be acknowledged as Queen until after the treaty proper had been signed. This was a weakness, but, on the whole, the Queen was eminently satisfied with the work of her ministers. In an audience with Mesnager just before he returned to Paris, she sent compliments to King Louis, saying that she was eager to accelerate the peace.

[54] House of Commons, *Report from the Committee of Secrecy*, App., p. 5.
[55] Cobbett's *Parliamentary History*, Vol. VII, App. 3, p. cxi.

CHAPTER IX

"His Excellency, Matthieu"

» 1 «

THROUGHOUT the autumn of 1711 Prior enjoyed the dubious pleasure of being the most talked-of man in London. It was expected that he would be employed in new diplomatic duties of greater dignity and importance, for his knowledge of trade and his previous connection with King William's treaties made him the most valuable man for further employment in promoting peace with France. His qualifications fitted him certainly for the position of what is now known as a specialist in diplomatic affairs. St. John had already mentioned him to the Queen for the commercial treaty with France; and Prior had been told that he would be one of the three English plenipotentiaries to the Peace Congress which would meet at Utrecht at the beginning of the new year. Swift hailed the news of his friend's good fortune with delight, and said that he would have someone write an account of Prior's coming journey.[1]

After all that had happened in the interval between the conferences with Torcy at Fontainebleau and the signing of the preliminaries in London, a lull had come in the peace plans. The ministry had its hands full. The Whigs were in a rage over the preliminaries and flooded the town with pamphlets and lampoons attacking the terms. In the *Post Boy*, Maynwaring published a mock report of the peace, purported to have been written by Mesnager and Prior, and since Mesnager was a Knight of the order of St. Michael, Prior was dubbed a Knight

---

[1] *Journal to Stella*, September 25, 1711.

of St. Germans.[2] Indeed, the Whigs spread an alarm at Prior's connection with the peace, hinting Jacobitism in view of his close association with the late Lord Jersey.[3] Prior was nettled by all this notoriety. "If you have not heard from me," he wrote to Hanmer, "I take it that you have heard of me: and I am the man of the world that need least give an account of himself since every *Post Boy* can do it twice a week for me."

News of the failure of St. John's Canadian expedition reached London and gave Prior an opportunity to expatiate on the rascality of the Whigs, not only in England, but in New England: "We are a little disheartened at the disappointment we have mett at Canada, which is all owing to the avarice or treachery of the godly at New England: the same party are doing all the mischief they can in Old England, they are really such a race that the Palatins are more our countrymen than they."[4] Prior was of course wrong in attributing the failure of the expedition to the colonists. Walker and Hill (Abigail's brother) lost their nerve and abandoned their plan of attacking Quebec after they had reached the St. Lawrence, leaving Nicholson, the leader of the Colonial auxiliaries, to shift for himself. Seeking to justify themselves, the two leaders unfairly blamed the defeat upon the New Englanders.[5]

Although St. John silenced the seditious libels against the ministry by having fourteen of the most troublesome printers hailed before the Court of the Queen's Bench and prosecuted,— Maynwaring's printer among them—[6] the ministry had other opposition to face, not so easy to quell. Buys, the Dutch envoy, came to London and noisily proclaimed his opposition to the peace proceedings. Count de Gallas, the Imperial minister in

---

[2] *The Post Boy*, September 11, 1711. According to Oldmixon, *Life . . . of Maynwaring*, p. 339, Maynwaring published the postscript but did not write it.

[3] *Polwarth Papers*, I, 2, George Baillie of Jerviswood to Lord Polwarth, Nov. 13, 1711.

[4] Hanmer, *Correspondence*, p. 131, Prior to Hanmer, Westminster, Oct. 9/20, 1711.

[5] W. T. Morgan, *Queen Anne's Canadian Expedition of 1711*, The Jackson Press, Kingston, Ontario, Canada, 1928, p. 29.

[6] Boyer, *History of the Reign of Queen Anne*, X, 264.

London, after one glance at a copy of the preliminaries, voiced his anger with the Queen and her ministers, and made public the peace terms in the Whig *Daily Courant*. Opposition came from quarters closer home. Nottingham, incensed at his neglect by the new administration, joined the Whigs, denounced the peace proposals, and carried in the House of Lords his motion that no peace could be safe or honorable to Great Britain or Europe if Spain and the West Indies should be allotted to any branch of the House of Bourbon.

On December 15 Prior gave up all hopes for the ministry and told Swift that he feared they would all resign their places the next week.[7] Oxford, however, was not so discouraged and counseled patience. By the end of the month the whole situation had changed. On the twenty-ninth, came the *Gazette* creating twelve new Tory peers, and on the last day of the month Marlborough was turned out of all his offices. Oxford had saved the ministry and the cause of peace.

In a few days when Prior received his appointment as Commissioner of Customs,[8] hopes of going to the Peace Congress vanished. For a time it had seemed certain that he would be one of the three Plenipotentiaries, the others being Lord Raby, now Earl of Strafford, and Bishop Robinson. The Queen had reservations about sending abroad "people of mean extraction,"[9] but she had signed Prior's commission on Oxford's urging that Prior would be "useful."[10] St. John was ready to dispatch Prior,[11] and Swift, to congratulate "his Excellency on his noble advancement"[12] when opposition of the most contemptible sort came from one of the Plenipotentiaries. Strafford, proud of his descent from "Black Tom the Tyrant," refused to serve with a

[7] *Journal to Stella*, December 15, 1711.
[8] On January 25, 1711/12. Records of the Secretaries' Office, Custom House, London.
[9] Brit. Mus., *Lansdowne MSS*, 1236, fo. 253, Queen Anne to Oxford, Nov. 16, 1711.
[10] *Longleat Papers*, I, 217, Queen Anne to Oxford, Nov. 19, 1711.
[11] *Portland Papers*, V., 134, St. John to Oxford, Dec. 1711.
[12] *Journal to Stella*, Nov. 20, 1711.

man of as humble birth as Prior. Consequently, there was no third Plenipotentiary.

"I hear Prior is discontented and does not think the Court does well by him," wrote Strafford with feigned disinterestedness.[13] From Swift we have a more sympathetic report. Prior, he states, was ill and melancholy; he had suffered financial losses through the recent failure of his stock broker.[14] There was yet hope that he would be employed in the commercial treaty, but many points of the general treaty must be settled before the commercial disputes could be taken under consideration. A knowledge of customs regulations would be useful for such employment, but Prior was irked by the tedium of his daily routine. Prosaic work, he told Swift, "spoiled" his wit; and he dreamed of nothing but "cockets and dockets and drawbacks, and other jargon words of the customs house."

» 2 «

The cockets and dockets and drawbacks did not occupy all Prior's time. When the specific offers of Louis XIV were published in February, the ministry were dismayed to find that Louis, taking advantage of their temporary weakness, had raised his demands.[15] The Whigs rejoiced in their rivals' discomfiture, and Halifax characterized the French proposals before the House of Lords as "trifling, arrogant, and injurious to to her Majesty and her allies."[16] The situation called for one who could deal directly with Torcy. Therefore, Oxford ordered Prior, who was already handling a good deal of the Lord Treasurer's foreign correspondence, to resume his discussion by letter with Torcy. It was Prior's duty to press upon Torcy the necessity of abiding by the preliminaries.

[13] *Wentworth Papers*, 244, Strafford to Lady Strafford, London, Jan. 18, 1711/12.
[14] *Journal to Stella*, March 6, 1711/12.
[15] Felix Salomon, *Geschichte des letzten Ministeriums Koenigin Annas*, p. 141.
[16] Abel Boyer, *History of the Reign of Queen Anne*, X, 356.

All during the spring of 1712, the French looked upon Prior as their hope, even calling him their man and referring to him in their correspondence as Monsieur Rolland, the cant name by which they had formerly designated the Earl of Jersey.[17] Indeed, while it was still expected that he would be one of the Plenipotentiaries at Utrecht, they had laid rather crafty plans to win him to their side. He was to be offered a pension, fixed by Torcy at 500 pounds, an amount Gaultier recommended raising to 705 *per annum* to offset Prior's remuneration at home.[18] Nothing further is recorded of the proposed bribe except a vague reference to an offer to "our ally, M. Rolland" (Prior) as soon as he should be appointed.[19]

To Torcy's anxious inquiry as to why Prior was not sent to Utrecht, Gaultier replied that Oxford preferred employing him in the secret negotiations.[20] Torcy refused to accept this explanation. Time and again he expressed his impatience to see Prior, who, he expected, would stop in Paris on his way to Utrecht. Even King Louis, notwithstanding his refusal to recognize Anne as queen until after the treaty should be signed, was persuaded to write her a letter of good will in the hope that Prior might be the bearer of the reply. Torcy was annoyed at the dawdling of the negotiations at Utrecht:

One can see from the letters of the plenipotentiaries that the Bishop of Bristol and Lord Strafford act as if they doubted the intentions or the real temper of their Court. Since these may not be cleared up until M. Rolland goes to Holland, I have much impatience to learn of his departure, and I hope to have again the opportunity to see him here with you, as you continue to make me hope. I am always persuaded that during a sojourn of a few days he would advance the affair much more than many conferences at Utrecht could do.[21]

---

[17] Paris, Archives . . . , *Correspondance Politique, d'Angleterre*, 241, fo. 64, Gaultier to Polignac, London, Feb. 16, 1711/12.

[18] *Ibid.*, 234, fo. 82, Gaultier to Torcy, London, Oct. 14, 1711.

[19] *Ibid.*, Nov. 3, 1711.

[20] *Ibid.*, 237, fo. 17, Gaultier to Torcy, Jan. 27, 1712.

[21] *Ibid.*, fo. 45, Torcy to Gaultier, Feb. 8, 1712.

With the above letter to Gaultier, Torcy enclosed one to Prior, congratulating him on his appointment to the Customs but making it plain that he regarded the position only as a stepping-stone to something greater.[22]

Frequently Gaultier tried to soothe Torcy by sending word that Prior would soon be crossing the channel. Well might Torcy be impatient with the English Plenipotentiaries at Utrecht: they were not fully instructed as to the intentions of the government, and the discussions were often at a standstill while the negotiations progressed between the English ministers and himself.[23] The final business would be done publicly by the Peace Congress, but the secret work of Prior and Gaultier was prerequisite to any progress at Utrecht. Just at the moment when Prior began renewing his relations with Torcy, a series of calamities befell the French royal household, which, for a time threatened to upset all peace negotiations. An epidemic of measles of extreme malignancy was raging in Paris, and on February 12, Marie Adelaide, the young Duchess of Burgundy, succumbed. Nine days later her husband, then heir to the French throne, died of the same disease. Since the Dauphin, his father, had died of smallpox only ten months previously, the two sons of the Duke and Duchess were next in succession to the French throne. These children, only five and two years old, respectively, soon contracted measles, and the elder one died on the eighth of March, leaving the sickly infant, the Duke of Anjou, (afterwards Louis XV) heir apparent. Thus had three dauphins died within a year. According to the law of succession, this one frail child was the only barrier between Philip of Spain and the throne of France. Under these circumstances the English ministry demanded that Philip should renounce his succession to the throne of France. Torcy emphatically replied that the heir of

[22] *Ibid.*, 47, Torcy to Prior, Versailles, Feb. 8, 1712.
[23] There were, of course, other causes for the delays. The Dutch would not agree to Louis's proposals concerning their barrier, and the English and Dutch were at loggerheads over matters of trade.

France succeeded to the throne by virtue of the law of God, and that any attempt to set aside the succession would be null and void.[24] After conferring with Oxford and St. John, Prior sent Torcy a long, grave, and eloquent letter setting forth the dangers of such an uncompromising attitude. Affairs of such great consequence, he explained, recede when they cease to advance. Moreover, he warned that the two nations would be again plunged into war unless Parliament, the people, and the Allies were immediately assured that King Louis was not maneuvering for a union of the two crowns.[25]

For several weeks all negotiations were at a standstill, while Torcy sent[26] extracts of letters from Oxford, St. John, and Prior to the Princesse des Ursins, who, by her influence over the amiable young Queen,[27] dominated the dull-witted Philip, and was virtually the King of Spain. Torcy repeated Prior's warnings about renewal of war, stressing the inability of France to muster resources for further campaigning.

Much correspondence passed between London and Paris, Paris and Madrid. Torcy's first solution satisfied the English ministers in every detail but one. According to the plan, Philip must choose between the two crowns, but he could defer making his decision until such a time as he might become heir to the French throne.[28] St. John insisted that the choice must be made at once. Then there occurred to the devious mind of Oxford an alternative which would silence Whig opposition to Philip's remaining on the Spanish throne. He sent Gaultier to France with a fresh proposal, whereby Philip might exchange the throne of Spain with the Duke of Savoy for Sicily,[29] and await a

[24] Cobbett's *Parliamentary History*, VII, App. p. cxxxv.

[25] Paris, Archives . . . , *Correspondance Politique d'Angleterre*, 237, fo. 129, Prior to Torcy, London, 24th March/4th April, 1712.

[26] Duc de la Tremoille, *Madame des Ursins et la succession d'Espagne*, VI, 21, Torcy to the Princess, April 9, 1712.

[27] Marie-Louise-Gabrielle, of Savoy, younger sister of the Duchess of Burgundy.

[28] Paris, Archives . . . , *Correspondance Politique, d'Angleterre*, 237, Torcy to Oxford, Marly, April 8, 1712.

[29] In addition to Sicily, Philip would receive Naples, Piedmont, Savoy, and Montferrat.

possible succession to France.[30] Although this arrangement pleased both Queen Anne and King Louis, it appealed to neither Philip nor the Princesse des Ursins. Philip, openly contemptuous of the scheme, formally announced his decision to remain where he was and to renounce all claims to France.[31]

The settlement of the Spanish Succession brought England and France one step nearer a suspension of arms, and hence nearer Prior's commercial treaty. Yet Louis childishly refused to give up Dunkirk and wanted to take back Tournai. Prior begged Torcy to "finish the great points of the peace"; he offered as a special inducement that the treaty of commerce might then come *sur le tapis*, this being "the only way to raise your *douanier* to a *ministre*."[32] Torcy was only too willing to indulge Prior, but he had, after all, only limited prerogatives. Fervently Prior urged the evacuation of Dunkirk as the only measure to produce peace, prophesying that the approval of the act would be heard "depuis Utrecht jusques à Vienne."[33] He apologized for his lengthy "gasconnade anglaise" but reaffirmed his belief in the imperativeness of Louis's compliance.[34]

On July 11 the ministry instructed Ormonde to carry out the terms of the armistice, and one week later, Dunkirk was invested by British soldiers. As a consequence of Ormonde's withdrawing his army from Prince Eugene's, the French won at Denain on July 24 their first victory for years. The breach between England and her allies was now complete. "I make my compliments to you," wrote Torcy to Prior, "on the prompt chastisement that the Dutch have received almost as soon as you left them to the spirit of madness which possessed them. I am persuaded that you are not displeased to see them chastised. God grant that

---

[30] Oxford's plan, like King William's First Partition Treaty, would set aside the claims of both a Bourbon and a Hapsburg in favor of an outsider.

[31] Paris, Archives . . . , *Correspondance Politique, d'Angleterre*, 238, fo. 99, Torcy to St. John, Versailles, June 8, 1712.

[32] *Ibid.*, fo. 43, Prior to Torcy, May 12, 1712.

[33] *Ibid.*, fo. 208, Prior to Torcy, June 19, 1712.

[34] *Ibid.*, fo. 9, Prior to Torcy, June 29/July 8, 1712.

they may profit by it, and that the peace will be general."[35]
Fortunately for Prior, this letter did not fall into the hands of
the Secret Committee. It indicates a disregard on the part of the
English ministers for their former allies as well as a *rapprochement*
of the recent enemies. Further, it was outrageous for Torcy to
intimate that the English, or at least one of their trusted diplomats, might rejoice with the French over the defeat of the Dutch,
but he knew the way the wind blew in England, thanks to
Gaultier's unremitting dispatches.

The tone of this and all the other letters that passed between
Louis's prime minister—if we may so name Torcy—and the
humble Commissioner of Customs is intimate and friendly. Although Torcy thought Prior headstrong, he pleased him no end
by proposing soon after the armistice that they might then be
friends "publicly" as they had been "secretly."[36] Moreover, he
gave Matt unstinted praise: "Vous êtes du petit nombre de ceux
que sont bons à tous les emplois les plus difficiles et dont on ne
peut se passer dans les places où on les a mis."[37] He also recommended to Oxford that Prior be placed in charge of the delicate
negotiations in behalf of the Princesse des Ursins, whose sover-
eignty over certain territory in the Spanish Netherlands was
one of Philip's stipulations in his proposed renunciation to the
French throne.

Buried in the archives of the French foreign office in Paris is
a neglected chapter of Prior's life—his extremely fine letters
written during the strained months of 1712. They not only
testify to his dexterity in smoothing the path of the slow and
tedious negotiations leading to Utrecht, but they reveal him as
the gifted letter-writer, possessed of an elegant and fastidious
style and a rare fluency in French, which he employed to the
best advantage in delicate diplomacy as well as in the endless
compliments and acknowledgments demanded by eighteenth-

[35] *Ibid.*, fo. 58, Torcy to Prior, Fontainebleau, July 26, 1712.
[36] *Ibid.*, fo. 185, Torcy to Prior, Marly, June 10, 1712.
[37] *Ibid.*, 237, fo. 110, Torcy to Prior, Versailles, March 28, 1712.

century etiquette. No less a critic than Jusserand[38] has praised Prior's mastery of French, an uncommon achievement for Englishmen of the early eighteenth century. An apology to Torcy, "on se sert à la douane de Londres d'un tout autre langage qu'on n'ecrit à des premiers ministres de la France,"[39] would suggest that Matt was refreshingly humble about his epistolary style. Reassuringly, his correspondent replied:

Je ne serai point fâché quand je pourrai remarquer quelques traits du style de la douane de Londres. Je voudrais bien que celle de Paris sût écrire avec autant de force et découvrir par des raisonnements aussi pressants et aussi bien suivis l'injustice et la mauvaise foi de nos ennemis.[40]

» 3 «

When the Duke of Hamilton was delegated to go to France to take up personally some vexatious points in the negotiations, Prior was selected to accompany him. The prospect that Monsieur Prior's "gasconnades" would soon become "réalités"[41] pleased Torcy immensely, and he dispatched a welcome to Matt, saying, "You will see how much you are loved in France."[42]

Hamilton, however, was not destined to go to France, for St. John, disappointed and angry over having been created viscount rather than earl, was to be appeased only by being sent to the French Court in Hamilton's stead. This change did not affect Prior's plans. He accompanied St. John, the new Viscount Bolingbroke, who took along his secretary, Thomas Hare, and the Abbé Gaultier. The party reached Paris on August 6/17, and stopped with Torcy's mother, Madame Colbert de Croissy. Torcy came from Fontainebleau to join them, and for the first week of their stay they were overwhelmed with business on the one hand and social engagements on the other.

[38] Jusserand, *Shakespeare in France*, London, 1899, p. 181.

[39] Paris, Archives . . . , *Correspondance Politique, d'Angleterre*, 237, fo. 94, Prior to Torcy, London, March 24, 1712.

[40] *Ibid.*, fo. 139, Torcy to Prior, Marly, April 8, 1712.

[41] *Ibid.*, 239, fo. 92, Torcy to Prior, Fontainebleau, July 15/26, 1712.

[42] *Ibid.*, Torcy to Prior, Fontainebleau, July 28, 1712.

The business was handled with dispatch. Torcy found Prior more "opiniâtre" during the conferences than Bolingbroke, although he thought them both reasonable negotiators.[43] The four points to be settled before an armistice could be signed were the barrier of Savoy, the renunciation by Philip of the throne of France, new territories for the Elector of Bavaria, and the removal of the Chevalier (the Pretender) from France to Lorraine. In the midst of these discussions the committee learned that the Elector of Bavaria was visiting in the vicinity of Paris, and Torcy had some uneasy moments. All too lightly the question concerning the Elector was postponed, agreement was reached on all other points, and an armistice for four months was signed.

Early on a Sunday morning, four days after their arrival at Madame de Croissy's, the two English visitors were received in private audience by Louis XIV at the palace at Fontainebleau. First Bolingbroke, then Prior was conducted by Torcy into the presence of the Grand Monarch. Prior, the Marquis de Sourches records,[44] presented to the King from Queen Anne a letter tied with red silk, thought to have been his credentials, it being generally understood that he would remain in France after Bolingbroke's departure.[45] Sourches was in error about the contents of the letter, however, for Prior's commission did not arrive until the following month,[46] and the letter delivered to the King on this early morning in August must have been merely one of compliment. After a morning spent in admiring

[43] *Ibid.*, fo. 172, memorandum dated August 19, 1712.

[44] Marquis de Sourches, *Mémoires sur le reyne de Louis XIV*, XIII, 481.

[45] Oxford had written to Torcy on August 12: . . . "mon véritable ami, Monsieur Prior, qui scait toutes les démarches de cette négotiation, et qui en souhaite la réussite autant que personne, vous pourra témoigner les soins que j'ay pris de la mener du point ou elle se trouve, et le désir où je suis que vous y donniez la dernière main. Si cela fait, Monsieur Prior doit rester quelque tems a la cour de France, après la retour de my lord Bolingbroke." *Catalogue of Morrison MSS*, p. 148.

[46] Dated, Windsor, Sept. 13, 1712. Reine Anne au Roi très Chrétien accréditant M. Matthew Prior en qualité de Ministre Plénipotentiare. Paris, Archives . . . , *Correspondance Politique, d'Angleterre*, 239, fo. 274.

the gardens of Fontainebleau, Bolingbroke and Prior had dinner—a repast both "exquis et magnifique"—in Torcy's quarters.
There was choice music, much drinking of toasts and breaking
of glasses, Torcy proposing the health of Queen Anne, and
Bolingbroke that of Louis XIV.

Yet over all this festivity hung an ominous shadow. At this
very moment General Stanhope stopped in Paris on his way
back to England from the Spanish campaigns. Bolingbroke
offered to present him to Louis XIV, but Stanhope, loyal to the
memory of William III, refused to call at Fontainebleau and
returned to England to wage relentless war in Parliament for
his Whig principles. Two years later, when he replaced Bolingbroke as Secretary of State, he exercised his power to bring his
Tory predecessors to account for their truckling to France.

Bolingbroke, however, was not unduly disturbed by this
shadow of a future reckoning. He entered eagerly into the social
whirl of the French capital to which Torcy introduced him.
Prior was already acquainted in Paris—with both high life and
low. He and Bolingbroke were caught up in a round of dinners,
balls, theaters, and operas, where the easy French manner and
the fascinating women encouraged an abandonment to pleasure
not countenanced at the stiff formal functions at home. Bolingbroke's reputation as a wit and rake having preceded him, he
had nothing to lose. He flirted so openly and successfully with
the Comtesse de Parabère, a beautiful, dark, bronzed woman of
Spanish type, later a mistress of the Duc d'Orleans during his
regency, that all society was agog.[47] Nothing came of the affair,
however, save that upon his return to London Bolingbroke
wrote Torcy that he had left in Paris both his heart and his
health.[48]

---

[47] Marie-Madeleine de la Vieuville, born at Paris in 1693 and married in 1711 to Comte
de Parabère. For a brief account of her career, see M. Capefigue, *La Comtesse de Parabère et
le Palais Royal sous la Regence*, Paris, 1863.

[48] Bolingbroke, *Letters and Correspondence*, III, 44, Bolingbroke to Torcy, Whitehall,
September 10/21, 1712.

Prior and Bolingbroke were introduced into the Ferriol household in the Rue des Augustins, not far from the Rue Richelieu. The Pontchartrains, the Grammonts, the Contis, the Uxelles also lived in this fashionable neighborhood. The Ferriol family, as pictured in the memoirs of the time, was certainly an unsavory one, where liaisons, broken vows, and incest were the order of the day. Madame de Ferriol, unscrupulous in furthering her own interests and those of her brothers and sisters, capitalized her friendship with Bolingbroke and Prior to get for her rascally brother an abbey in the Duchy of Savoy. Probably the charms of a younger sister, Mlle. Claudine, who had just run away from the Convent of Montfleuri where she had taken the veil and who was in Paris seeking to have her vows annulled, were exerted in her brother's behalf. Still another member of the family was Mlle. Aïssé, the Circassian slave girl, who at the age of four had been brought from Constantinople by a brother-in-law of Madame de Ferriol to be entrusted to her care. An exotic and ravishing beauty, Aïssé was courted by many of the great nobles during the Regency. Of more interest to us is Lord Peterborough's infatuation for the fair young Circassian. When Peterborough stopped in Paris on a diplomatic errand to Savoy, Prior introduced him to the Ferriols, and the susceptible gentleman became so attracted to Aïssé that he forgot all diplomatic business and tarried in Paris an entire month. Jealously, however, Monsieur de Ferriol still regarded his ward as his special property. After his death she fell in love with the young Chevalier d'Aydie, but marriage being socially impossible, she gave herself up to a life of piety. She made a confidante of Madame Calandrini, wife of the Genevan Resident in Paris, with whom she exchanged scores of letters.[49] Madame Calandrini, as well as Aïssé, is often mentioned in the correspondence of Prior, since

---

[49] Aïssé's letters were first edited by Voltaire in 1758. For a charming essay on Aïssé, see Gosse, *French Profiles.*

he made repeated efforts to enlist the aid of the French ministry in an attempt to restore the family fortunes of the Calandrinis.[50]

Mlle. Claudine, who became the celebrated Madame de Tencin, was more daring than her sister and had a more spectacular career. There is a tale to the effect that Torcy intentionally brought Mlle. Claudine and the "inflammable" Secretary of State together so that the charmer might wheedle or steal from him certain valuable state papers.[51] The plan worked, and Bolingbroke is written down in history as having been "betrayed by his gallantries into a serious breach of official decorum which threatened gravely to compromise the Government."[52] It is said that by way of rebuke the Paris correspondence was taken out of his hands and given to Dartmouth. Credence is given to the story by the fact that later Madame de Tencin had an intrigue with the Minister of Police and acted as his spy.[53]

It is only with Madame de Tencin's early life that our narrative is concerned, but the list of her lovers, including as it does Fontenelle, the Scotch adventurer Law, the Chevalier Destouches, and Cardinal Dubois, is long and varied. By Destouches she had a child, which she abandoned on the steps of a Paris church. The infant was rescued, however, and grew up to be the encyclopedist d'Alembert. Finally, when a maddened lover shot himself to death in her presence, she suffered imprisonment in the Châtelet for several months. Upon her release, through with

[50] See Bolingbroke, *Letters and Correspondence*, III, 257, 300; IV, 73, 375, 414, 506.
[51] Cooke, *Memoirs of Lord Bolingbroke*, I, 217.
[52] Harrop, *Bolingbroke, a Political Study*, p. 139.
[53] The story has been accepted by most of Bolingbroke's biographers from Cooke to Petrie. On the other hand, Prior wrote to Bolingbroke about Madame de Tencin as if Bolingbroke had not met her. On August 24/September 4, 1712, he wrote: "Her [Madame de Ferriol's] sister is run away from a nunnery, and half protected, half bought off, is very handsome, very wild and half a heretique." Again, on August 29/September 9, 1712, he wrote: "She [Madame de Ferriol] has a sister that is run away from the nunnery and is now pleading the causes of her renunciation. I am glad you did not see her, she is very handsome and bucksome." *Hare Papers*. Was the intrigue, arranged by Torcy, so clandestine that it was kept from Prior?

amours and intrigues, she opened a *salon* which became the most brilliant in Paris.

One biographer[54] of Madame de Tencin declares that Prior was her first lover. Evidently she dazzled him, and Matthew was not averse to such pleasures. She is mentioned constantly in his and Bolingbroke's letters with a warmth of feeling that may be interpreted to mean much, or may be set down to the eighteenth-century penchant for extravagant compliment. Be that as it may, Prior's other women friends grew jealous of the wild, handsome heretic and made their little sallies at her expense. Prior, when distributing some gifts from Bolingbroke to the Ferriols, the Croissys and the Noailles, tried to perform the not easy duty like a "prudent and honest man." But the Duchesse de Noailles could not resist twitting him: "Matthieu est fripon naturellement; il en a bien la mine: Pardi! il a volé la moitié de mon eau-de-miel, il l'a donné à sa religieuse défroquée."[55]

Bolingbroke, Hare, and Gaultier left for London on the 24th of August. Prior parted from them with many pangs—more than was "proper or possible" to tell[56]—and waited for "something to do at court."

During these days of comparative freedom he dined every evening *en famille* with the Torcys in the Rue Vivienne. Loyally they would begin their meal by kissing their glasses to their respective sovereigns, King Louis and Queen Anne; then Madame de Torcy, who had both wit and humor and was Matt's apt pupil, would drink healths *à Harré et à Robin*, adding with a mischievous twinkle: "Mais je croy que Robin est trop sérieux pour nous."[57]

The Torcys furnish a marked contrast to the friends in the

[54] Masson, *Madame de Tencin.*
[55] Bolingbroke, *Letters and Correspondence*, IV, 372, Prior to Bolingbroke, Paris, October, 16/27, 1713.
[56] *Ibid.*, III, 52, Prior to Bolingbroke, August 24/September 4, 1712.
[57] Strong, *Letters . . . at Welbeck*, App. VI, p. 271, Prior to Oxford, Fontainebleau, Aug. 29/Sept. 9, 1712.

Rue des Augustins. Their family life was quite ideal. Even the hypercritical Saint Simon admitted that Monsieur de Torcy and his wife lived in complete harmony. Torcy has been pictured as the perfect type of an old French aristocrat, despite the fact that the Colberts were of bourgeois origin. He possessed the graces which we like to think of as being particularly French—punctiliousness, tact, charm. He was a shrewd statesman, moreover, and had no scruples against chicaning in the service of the Grand Monarch, whom he devoutly believed to be God's anointed. During his long term as minister of foreign affairs while a dozen English Secretaries of State came and went, he learned much of the English temperament.

Naturally we hear less of Madame than of her husband, yet Prior rarely neglected to send compliments to "mon adorable Madame de Torcy" even in diplomatic letters to Torcy. She ruled the household, which included a son and three daughters, wisely and well and presided graciously over their drawing-room gatherings. Jean Baptiste, a boy of ten at the time Prior frequented the Torcy home, later became the Marquis de Croissy and lived to the age of seventy-seven years. Françoise Félicité, the eldest child, was an attractive girl of fourteen at this time. Years later she began, in loving memory of her "excellent father," a biography of him, but her death in 1749 cut short its completion.[58] Had she lived to finish it, we might have caught glimpses from its pages of those intimate family parties in Paris during 1712–1715 when Prior was fully admitted as a member of the circle. The other children were Catherine Pauline,[59] a year younger than Françoise Félicité, and Constance, a baby of two years.[60]

Such a household as the Torcys' was a delight to Prior,

[58] In 1715, Françoise Félicité (1698–1749) married the Marquis d'Ancezune. Her unfinished biography of her father remained in manuscript until recently, when it was published in the *Revue d'histoire diplomatique*, 1932, 1933.

[59] Catherine Pauline (1699–1773) was married in 1718 to the Marquis du Plessis Chatillon.

[60] Constance (1710–1734).

possessed as he was of a tender love for children. We like to think that he wrote poems for them as he had done for the children of Dorset and Jersey, and as he later did for Oxford's granddaughter, "noble, lovely, little Peggy."

The Colberts were a clannish family. Consequently Prior was soon acquainted with all the relatives: the Duchesse de St. Pierre and the Marquise de Bouzols, Torcy's sisters; and the Duchesse de Beauvillier and the Duchesse de Chevreuse, cousins of Torcy's and wives of two of the most powerful gentlemen *en titre* at the French Court—men who had implicit faith in Torcy both as a man and as a statesman. So completely was Prior accepted as a member of the family that Torcy grew apprehensive:

Quant à Matthieu, il est plus maître chez moi que je ne le suis moi même, et si 'l n'en abuse pas, je lui en serai fort obligé.[61]

It may have been a pleasant family gathering at the Hôtel de Torcy which furnished one of the happiest anecdotes about Prior.[62] One evening after dinner, while everyone in the gay little company was singing in rotation the verses of a song with the refrain "Bannisons la Mélancholie," it came time for Prior to sing. Turning to the pretty demoiselle by his side—perhaps Françoise Félicité—he produced these extempore lines instead of following the words of the song:

> Mais cette voix et ces beaux yeux,
> Font Cupidon trop dangereux,
> Et je suis triste quand je crie
> Bannisons la Mélancholie.

The charming family dinners proved a welcome diversion for Prior now that his friends had left for London. When Bolingbroke had departed he had charged Matt with numerous per-

---

[61] Paris, Archives . . . , *Correspondance Politique, d'Angleterre*, 248, fo. 29, Torcy to Gaultier, Versailles, March 24, 1713.
[62] Dr. Johnson's "Life of Prior," in the Birkbeck Hill Edition of *Lives of the Poets*, II, 198.

sonal commissions to execute. Their first communications, therefore, are concerned with trivial but interesting details: Matt's purchase of an *escritoire* for his friend; a present of some truffles to her Majesty; the distribution of the aforementioned gifts. The truffles, delivered through Bolingbroke's kindness, pleased the Queen, who, having no inkling of their origin in the notorious Ferriol *ménage*, asked for more, which Prior, with an eye to business, eagerly dispatched.

One of these communications—a note from Matt to Harry—begins, "I need not tell you how well you are beloved here," and runs on to say that Madame de Ferriol was "taking on terribly" over his departure; that the runaway nun was foolishly talking of him all day long as if she had known him twenty years; and that the letter would never be finished if he continued to write of the "*folies* and the *je ne sçay quoys* of these people." But he did finish, and gracefully: "Adieu, my Lord. Pray write to me as a Secretary of State and as a friend."[63]

The purchase of the *escritoire* for "le cher Henri" assumed vast importance, involving the assembling on several occasions of the entire conclave of friends at Madame de Croissy's. Prior, Madame de Ferriol, M. d'Iberville, and Torcy's brother, the Bishop of Montpellier, all would be there. "Old Croissy" would preside like a martinet, but Madame de Ferriol was subtly influential in leading the group to her way of thinking. The proposed desk was discussed in detail and sometimes with heat. How much space would a quire of paper occupy?—the talkative d'Iberville was rapped over the fingers for presuming to know. What should be the relative positions of the bell, the ink-pot, and the sand-dish—the poor Bishop of Montpellier was hooted out of council for venturing an opinion. The deliberations called for action; inquiries must be made; the whole delegation

[63] *Hare Papers*, Prior to Bolingbroke, Paris, Aug. 24/Sept. 4, 1712. Omitted by Parke from his edition of Bolingbroke's *Correspondence* in 1798, with the following explanation in a footnote to page 153, Vol. III. "The Editor has been induced to omit many passages in the letters to and from Prior, which are either unimportant or of a private nature."

therefore rode forth in a great coach with prancing steeds to call upon three goldsmiths. As Prior related the story, the old lady would ask two hundred questions at each shop and receive a thousand compliments in return from the obsequious shop-keeper, who, though really wishing the whole party hanged, would accompany Madame to her coach and stand bareheaded in the driving rain only to be told to wait upon her further at the Hôtel de Croissy. "As well as I love you," Matt concludes this tale of a desk, "you shall never catch me bespeaking another."[64]

» 4 «

Running errands and distributing *billets-doux* for Bolingbroke might be diverting for a time, but Prior grew restive in Paris without official position. He had neither "power, commission, name, instruction, appointment, nor secretary"; he had to beg for audiences—the right of any recognized envoy; the French ministers did receive him, but he would be kept waiting for hours in antechambers while the envoys from even the pettiest states were given precedence.[65] It was all disagreeable and un-dignified, and Matt was ill besides. Cholera morbus was followed by dysentery—an especially evil combination, which the French physicians merely shrugged at, saying, "c'est l'usage." So severe was the illness that Matt had visions of death, of going perhaps to join Ulysses, Palimedes, and other celestials. A de-cided improvement, however, restoring his sense of humor, he made up his mind to reëmbrace life so that he might longer enjoy the company of Lord Bolingbroke and the Lord Treasurer, which was quite as good as that of the departed celebrities.[66]

While still almost too weak to hold a pen, he resumed his

[64] *Ibid.*, Prior to Bolingbroke, Paris, Oct. 10, N.S. 1712. Omitted by Parke, presumably, as being of too private a nature.

[65] Strong, *Letters . . . at Welbeck*, App. VI, 273, Prior Oxford, Fontainebleau, Sept. 1/12, 1712.

[66] Bolingbroke, *Letters and Correspondence*, III, 100, Prior to Bolingbroke, Paris, Sept. 9/20, 1712.

routine correspondence, often toiling with it far after midnight. There were dispatches to the deliberators at Utrecht, reports to Oxford and to Dartmouth—his "provincial"—to be sent regularly. Resumption of diplomatic relations also involved exchange of letters with the recently appointed Ambassador to Madrid, none other than Lord Lexington, whom Prior had known in his early days in the diplomatic service. It was not always business, however, that was written by the midnight taper. The official and technical correspondence with Bolingbroke is happily interspersed with jolly personal notes, marked private or secret, from "Matt to Harry," containing gossip about the fair ones, mistresses or what-you-wills that the gallant Secretary of State had left in Prior's care. Harry would write back in the same vein; hence the *affaires de coeur* of the two confidants are an open book for any who will trouble to piece the missives together. Bolingbroke was troubled. He had returned to London only to break off with a certain Jenny and to be annoyed by a perverse Peggy who would not "yield." Confiding this much to Matt, he jealously asked to be remembered to the nun, and maliciously reminded him that Nannette was well, thanks to information received from Dick Shelton.[67] Briefly but to the point, Matt replied:

As well as I love you, Dick Shelton is a rogue even in having named Nannette to you. Claudine is better the point. [*sic*] Jenny and you will reconcile—if Peggy does not yield.[68]

At the end of September, papers naming Prior as Minister Plenipotentiary arrived. They were delivered by Drift, who remained to serve as secretary. Prior was told the welcome news that his stay in France would not last much longer. He must settle the commercial treaty, and then he would be sent to Utrecht. Now that the armistice was in effect, it was fitting that England have an ambassador at Versailles, and Drift

[67] *Hare Papers*, Bolingbroke to Prior, Whitehall, Jan. 7/18, 1712/13.
[68] *Ibid.*, Prior to Bolingbroke, Paris, Jan. 12/23, 1712/13.

brought word that the Duke of Hamilton had once again been named to represent Her Majesty in Paris. One might wonder why Prior, who knew more about the peace negotiations than any man in England except Bolingbroke, was not rewarded for his services by being named Ambassador. But no man of such humble birth as Prior was fitted to be Ambassador, or so Queen Anne thought. Consequently Hamilton, vain, frivolous, and weak, was given the honor that rightly should have gone to the industrious Plenipotentiary.

A stupid blunder on Dartmouth's part concerning the recognition of Philip by Lord Lexington nearly precipitated a break in the peace plans. In short, Dartmouth had instructed Lexington not to acknowledge Philip as King of Spain until he had agreed to all the English demands. When Dartmouth wrote to Prior to learn the reaction of the French Court to these instructions, Prior was dumbfounded at such a misunderstanding of the "renunciation" clause in the treaty. Immediately and concisely, he replied to Dartmouth: "The Renunciation which Philip makes is to France, and as King of Spain, in which quality he must be supposed invested or the renunciation itself is not good."[69] Bolingbroke, likewise astonished, wrote with vigor:

For God's sake, dear Matt, hide the nakedness of thy country, and give the best turn thy fertile brain will furnish thee with, to the blunders of thy countrymen, who are not much better politicians than the French are poets.[70]

News of Dartmouth's *faux pas*, fortunately, went no farther than the French Court; Lexington duly acknowledged Philip, and the affair blew over.

Prior next turned to the problem of the disposition of Tournai. The Dutch maintained that it was a necessary part of their barrier, while the French demanded its restitution and expected

[69] P. R. O. *State Papers, France*, 78/154, Prior to Dartmouth, Fontainebleau, Sept. 1/12, 1712.
[70] Bolingbroke, *Letters and Correspondence*, III, 64, Bolingbroke to Prior, Whitehall, Sept. 10/21, 1712.

the English ministry to help them retrieve it. Since their recent defeat at the hands of the French through the withdrawal of the English troops, the Dutch were daily winning sympathy in England, not only from Whigs but from Tories, some of them good friends of the ministry. With considerable firmness, Prior argued that by holding out for Tournai the French were imperiling all hopes for peace. Solemnly he pictured to Torcy the dangers of delay—the power of Whig sentiment, the uncertainty of the Queen's health—but Torcy, unconvinced that Tournai was the only impediment to peace, brought up the Elector of Bavaria's claims, which, we may recall, Bolingbroke had left unsettled when he was in Paris. At last, after days of dispute, Torcy yielded.[71] As a sort of compromise, Prior was to deliver personally to Queen Anne a letter from King Louis, pressing the claims of the Elector. It is a wordy epistle expressing Louis's "particular regard" for Queen Anne, reiterating his earnest desire for the peace and stating that he would await with impatience the return of M. Prior, whose conduct he found "very agreeable."[72]

Had it been possible for Matt to sense the compliment in the above dispatch, he would very summarily have been cast down by Torcy's and Bolingbroke's pleasantries at his expense. On setting off for London in October, 1712, he was oppressed with the two-fold nature of his obligation. For the sake of the public good, the peace must be concluded; and, for the sake of his neck, the mission must not fail. Figuratively the shadow of the gallows lay across his path: "Though Matthieu be the most insufferable of human beings," Torcy jested to Bolingbroke, "I believe, my Lord, he is still honest enough to labor faithfully, and to do his best to finish our work. We have therefore agreed that he shall set off for England to assure you . . . of our real and

---

[71] See two letters, Torcy to Bolingbroke, Versailles, Oct. 15/26, 1712, Bolingbroke, *Letters and Correspondence*, III, 161, 166.

[72] Cobbett's *Parliamentary History*, VII, cxcviii. The letter is dated Versailles, October 28, 1712.

sincere desire to conclude with you: Finish the business, then my Lord, and send back Matthieu as soon as possible that I may have the pleasure of hanging him, according to agreement, if the peace is not concluded by his Majesty's giving up Tournay."[73]

Prior reached London by October 25/November 5. His arrival, signifying to the public mind that the negotiations were about to be concluded, was hailed by a rise in stocks and bonds. Bolingbroke was satisfied with the word Prior brought back of Louis's willingness to concede Tournai and notified Torcy that instructions for everything were being entrusted to "his Excellency Matthieu," who, in spite of his "unhappy physiognomy," ought not to be hanged as yet.[74]

Prior was detained, though, in London, in order that the Duke of Hamilton might travel with him to Paris. On November 15, the very eve of his departure, the Duke was killed by Lord Mohun in the duel made famous in *Esmond*. This unfortunate occurrence further postponed Prior's return to Paris. To Torcy's impatient inquiries about Matt's prolonged absence, Bolingbroke promised that "the wooden-faced gentleman" would soon be on his way. Torcy, picking up the expression, answered:

I shall find as many charms in the *visage de bois* as in Madam de Parabère, when I receive from him intelligence from you. I should not probably have ventured to use so honorable a phrase, did I not suppose him to be now on this side of the water, and consequently out of reach of my letter. I would not he should have to reproach me upon his arrival, for he would find method to be revenged.[75]

In the contest over Tournai we cannot fail to be impressed with the firmness which Prior displayed in debate. It is interesting to note that while he was pressing the acceptance of the Tournai clause, Gaultier was trying to prevail upon Bolingbroke

[73] Bolingbroke, *Letters and Correspondence*, III, 166, Torcy to Bolingbroke, Versailles, October 15/26, 1712.

[74] *Ibid.*, 169, Bolingbroke to Torcy, Whitehall, Nov. 11/22, 1712.

[75] *Ibid.*, 213, Torcy to Bolingbroke, Versailles, Dec. 10, N.S., 1712.

to renounce it. Prior proved to have the more persuasive tongue —the clause, as we have seen, was accepted. Gaultier was piqued:

Je voudrais de tout mon coeur que votre Excellence fît pendre Matthieu à son retour pour lui avoir persuadé qu'il était absolument nécessaire pour finir le grand ouvrage que le roi cédât la ville de Tournay aux Hollandais.[76]

After Hamilton's death the Duke of Shrewsbury was named Ambassador to France. Prior, without waiting for Shrewsbury's company left London for Paris on December 1/12. At Calais he was met by the Governor of the port, driven through the streets in a great coach with an escort of soldiers amid the beating of drums, and accorded a cannon salute. The acclaim was gratifying. On the whole, the journey was successful. Two troublesome matters, Tournai and the future of the Elector of Bavaria, were settled.

Prior fell to work with great industry as soon as he reached Paris, conferring late and early on matters pertaining to the commercial treaty—now *sur le tapis*—and dispatching almost daily enormous packets so filled with business and so utterly devoid of any chitchat that Bolingbroke became inquisitive about his friend's private life. At length he appealed to Sir Thomas Hanmer, then in Paris, for personal news of Matt, saying "we hear much of a certain eloped nun, who has supplanted the nut-brown maid."[77] Torcy from Versailles good-humoredly poked fun at Prior's pertinacity:

Under the outward semblance of Matthieu, you have sent us, my Lord, the legitimate son of M. Buys; nothing is wanting but for him to fill his glass like his father. He is otherwise as much a Dutchman, and I think more *opiniâtre*. We have been forced to yield and conform to his wishes; still he was not contented; but I hope you will be, and that all

---

[76] Paris, Archives . . . , *Correspondance Politique, d'Angleterre*, 240, fo. 137, Gaultier to Torcy, November 9, 1712.

[77] Bolingbroke, *Letters and Correspondence*, III, 275, n.d.

the obstacles that retarded the signing of the peace are about to be removed.[78]

Prior was busier than he had ever been before. He had reached the highest diplomatic rank of his entire career. He knew that his work was important and that he was indispensable in the making of a much desired peace. He was held in esteem by Queen Anne and King Louis, by Oxford and Torcy. He had Drift, a congenial friend of long standing, to relieve him of many burdensome details. His remittances were coming regularly from the Lord Treasurer, and he was happier than he had been for many years.

The appointment of Shrewsbury as Ambassador Extraordinary was a wise choice and gratified Prior. As Lord Chamberlain, he had been in touch with the negotiations since the very beginning, and during the preliminaries he had insisted upon fair terms for the Allies. True, he was ineffectual and would leave Prior to bear the burden of the details, with which he was necessarily unfamiliar. A hypochondriac, he was constantly pleading ill health and begging to be relieved of his offices, though no man of his time had ever been honored with so many positions. Whatever he lacked in industry, he made up for in dignity and presence. He was therefore a fit representative of the English crown at the magnificent French Court. Always gracious, kindly disposed, and considerate, he would be a more agreeable colleague than the arrogant Hamilton.

Shrewsbury took up his post at a very critical time in the making of the treaty of Utrecht. The two most disputed points were the commercial treaty and the article in the general treaty concerning North America. The French were now demanding Cape Breton as well as the fishing rights in Newfoundland. The English ministry flatly refused to accede to both demands, claiming that France had not abided by the "most-favored-nation" clause of the commercial treaty. A misunderstanding,

[78] *Ibid.*, III, 272, Versailles, Dec. 29, 1712.

for which Prior was responsible, had occurred. Believing that he was carrying out the desires of the ministry, he persuaded the French to consent to the *amicissima gens*. Craftily then, the French negotiators removed the phrase from its context, placed their own interpretation upon it, giving it "another color and turn," and sent word to Utrecht that an agreement concerning duties on imports had been reached. Prior would never wittingly have subscribed to the agreement as the French had worded it.[79]

Furious at the advantages the French had taken, Bolingbroke determined to "knock" their scheming "immediately on the head."[80] He strongly urged Prior to make use of the confidence Torcy had in him: "Make the French ashamed of their sneaking chicane. By Heaven they treat us like pedlars, or, what is worse, like attorneys."[81]

Prior acted promptly and succeeded in adjusting the two troublesome articles to the satisfaction of the ministry. The French agreed to abide by the original interpretation of the commercial treaty, by way of concession; but held firmly to their demand for Cape Breton and the Newfoundland fishing rights, the latter a recurrent subject of dispute until its final settlement in the reign of Edward VII. Prior was much chagrined to be caught napping and wrote to Bolingbroke, "I shall not be satisfied with myself or the world, till I know from you that I am not blamed."[82] Bolingbroke dismissed the matter generously—chicanery was a little artifice which always fixed a certain degree of infamy on those who tried it; the affair was now over and there was no need to say any more about it; he was sorry it had given Prior much concern.[83]

The only word of censure seems to have come from Strafford, who spitefully aired his opinions of Prior. No doubt the English

---

[79] *Ibid.*, 388, Prior to Bolingbroke, Paris, February 2/13, 1712/13.

[80] *Ibid.*, 335, Bolingbroke to Shrewsbury, Whitehall, January 25/February 5, 1712/13.

[81] P. R. O. *State Papers, France* 105/266, Bolingbroke to Prior, January 11/22, 1712/13.

[82] Bolingbroke, *Letters and Correspondence*, III, 394, Prior to Bolingbroke, Paris, Feb. 5/16, 1713.

[83] *Ibid.*, 445, Bolingbroke to Shrewsbury, Whitehall, Feb. 18, 1712/13.

Plenipotentiaries at Utrecht had cause to be jealous of Shrewsbury and Prior and to resent playing a minor role in the peace
negotiations. Strafford circulated the story that Prior had come
over to Paris to oppose him and Robinson; that he was a pensioner of the French Court; that he was fond of doing everything
alone, and that he wearied everyone who had business with him
with delays and ambiguous answers. As for the recent chicane
on the part of the French, Strafford charged that Prior was
much to blame. Later Strafford had the temerity to beg Oxford
and Bolingbroke to appoint him Ambassador to Paris, openly
declaring that Prior was incompetent. The two ministers, who
by then had troubles enough on their hands, tactfully persuaded
Strafford that he could not be spared in Holland.

The unpleasant experience with the French ministers over the
commercial treaty caused Prior to redouble his efforts to guard
against any signs of further trickery. Increasingly often Torcy
grumbled about Prior's being *opiniâtre*. Though he admired
Shrewsbury's manner of treating—his suavity, his dignity, and
his courtly demeanor—and so informed Gaultier, he added:
"Je réserve les querelles pour Matthieu avec qui je ne suis pas
toujours d'accord. Cependant quelque opiniâtre qu'il soit, nous
n'avons plus aucun sujet de dispute."[84] Torcy really enjoyed
diplomatic skirmishes and when Prior was temporarily away
from Versailles, missed him, saying that he preferred his "scold-
ings" to his absence.[85]

The chicanery on the part of the French and their innumerable
delays provoked the English ministry to issue an ultimatum to
the French Court threatening a renewal of war if the Queen's
demands for her own nation and for her allies were not complied
with. It brought results. Louis acceded to the English demands.
"Though we were forced to yield to Matthieu's vehemence, I

[84] Paris, Archives . . . , *Correspondance Politique, d'Angleterre*, 243, fo. 196, Torcy to Gaultier, Marly, Feb. 25, 1713.
[85] *Ibid.*, 243, fo. 122, Torcy to Prior, Versailles, Feb. 5, 1713.

do not grudge him the victory that has settled the peace between us," Torcy said.[86]

On March 31/April 11 the peace negotiations at Utrecht were brought to a close. England, Holland, Savoy, Prussia, and Portugal signed treaties with France, and for these nations the War of the Spanish Succession was over. But in spite of the eleven treaties that were signed, there was as yet no universal peace. The Emperor still stubbornly held out for his extravagant claims, and Holland and Portugal had not come to terms with Spain.

It was a Tory peace, dictated by Tory ministers who had succeeded where the Whigs had failed. It embodied their nationalistic ideals. England emerged as the most powerful nation in Europe and so remained for many years. Particularly on the sea was her strength increased by the retention of Gibraltar and Minorca. All her demands recognized in the preliminaries were granted. Louis was not humbled as the Whigs had desired, but his grandson's territories provided spoils for the Allies. To Austria went the Spanish Netherlands and territories in Italy. The Dutch were given a stable barrier against France, but not the generous one promised by the Whigs in return for their support of the War. Though the Whigs might cavil against the treatment of the Allies, there was little excuse for their accusation that England's interests had not been safeguarded.

Prior could be justly proud of the results, if not of the methods of the treaty-making, although he did not join in the chorus of poets who celebrated the peace in verse, and on two later occasions he commented disparagingly on it when writing for the benefit of Whig eyes. On Easter Day he congratulated Oxford "on this great and good thing which you have done for your Queen and country."[87] More metaphorically he saluted Bolingbroke:

[86] Bolingbroke, *Letters and Correspondence*, III, 446, Torcy to Bolingbroke, Versailles, Feb. 7, 1713.

[87] Strong, *Letters . . . at Welbeck*, App. VI, p. 288, Prior to Oxford, April 5/16, 1713.

I congratulate you most sincerely upon the birth of your beautiful daughter, the peace, after all the pangs you have so long time suffered, from the ignorance of some of your Englishmen-mid wives.[88]

Felicitations went the rounds. Gracefully hiding his disappointment over France's failure to drive a better bargain, Torcy congratulated Prior and Bolingbroke, declaring that he rejoiced as much as they upon the peace. By way of a private celebration the Torcys gave a family dinner party—evidently a hilarious affair, for Prior records: "We played the fool as much as people might well do." All Paris rejoiced over a peace that left the boundaries of France, except in North America, practically intact. At Notre Dame a magnificent Te Deum was sung. At Versailles there was the most heartfelt thanksgiving. Louis responded to Prior's compliment by sending one to Queen Anne "with all respect and civility imaginable." Even Madame de Maintenon, in an unusual outburst of gaiety, grew loquacious in praise of Queen Anne.

The celebrations taxed Prior's none too vigorous constitution, and he suddenly fell ill at Versailles with pleurisy and another attack of cholera morbus. Fortunately a Scotch physician was at hand, whose good care brought the penitent Matt back to health. As his health mended, he resumed his gaiety. He felt better than he had done in many years and prognosticated that he might live to become a devouter man. Such a prediction was not to be taken too seriously. Soon almost himself again, he was advising Bolingbroke with worldly wisdom on a matter of gallantry. Bolingbroke had expressed anxiety over gaining the favor of a certain coquette with whom he had become enamored at one of the masquerade balls which the Duke d'Aumont, the new French Ambassador, had introduced to London society, and Prior held out to his friend this cheering advice:

Your huntress will be caught, if you have breath enough to follow

---

[88] Bolingbroke, *Letters and Correspondence*, IV, 75, Prior to Bolingbroke, Versailles, April 7/18, 1713.

her, and so will every huntress, from Atalanta and Diana, to Cloe and Nannette; it is only want of lungs that will distance you in the chase, so go tay-ho, tay-ho! And when you cough like me, hang up your hunting spear and shrill horn, and sit like me too, to write politic letters, and to think of nothing else, but performing the bare duties and obligations of life. Adieu, I love to talk with you, and am ever, etc.[89]

When Shrewsbury made his official entry as Ambassador Extraordinary, Prior was sufficiently recovered from his illness to appear, though he was still weak enough to feel the "fatigue of three days battle in a ceremonial war" in which he had served as the Duke's "aide-de-camp".[90] For some months he had been troubled over his status at the ceremony. As early as February, he had foreseen the situation and had broached the subject to Oxford: "What am I to do or how to behave myself; pray, my Lord, one word of direction." Knowing Oxford's habitual procrastination, he sent similar inquiries to the two Secretaries of State, avowing that while their decision was a matter of indifference to him he must appear, or be recalled, or be ill.

The response Prior received from each of the three ministers is characteristic. Oxford left the perplexed Matt to worry along as best he could. The cold and prudent Dartmouth thought he should appear as a private gentleman, on the ground that the commission of Plenipotentiary did not give him a "representing character." Indignant at Dartmouth's rebuff, Prior appealed to a more sympathetic ear, that of Bolingbroke:

Do me justice, my dear Lord, did I ever desire to be a lion in Arabia, any more than to be Ambassador at Paris?—and could it be supposed that I should think I had a representing character by asking for a coach? As to a private gentleman, are there not of these animals of all sorts from those who have six Flanders horses to others who drive in a *vinegrette*?[91]

---

[89] *Ibid.*, 108, Prior to Bolingbroke, Paris, May 2/13, 1713.

[90] P. R. O. *State Papers, France*, 105/28, fo. 154, Prior to Dr. Arbuthnot, Paris, June 4/15, 1713.

[91] Bolingbroke, *Letters and Correspondence*, IV, 7, [n. d.]

In his reply Bolingbroke made sarcastic comment on Dartmouth's letter, from which Prior had sent him the choicest bits, and then gave him this definite direction:

Ask no more orders from hence; but as you have credit at Paris, use it to put yourself into that equipage which becomes the Queen's servant in such a station at such a time.[92]

The entry took place on May 31/June 11, and a solemn and splendid occasion it was. Prior rode in a coach drawn by six horses, preceded only by Shrewsbury and the Princes of the Blood.[93] His pleasure in the entry was spoiled by his indisposition and the previous annoyance over his official standing. But after all, the entry of an English Ambassador in Paris was no new spectacle for him. It is to be remembered that he had participated in three similar ceremonies—at the entries of Jersey and of Manchester and at the most splendid of all, that of Lord Portland.

Prior's lack of enthusiasm over the entry implies no distaste for ceremony. He loved it, and realizing that his commission as Plenipotentiary would expire with the signing of the peace, he promptly applied to Oxford to send him as Ambassador Extraordinary to present the Queen's compliments to the Duke of Savoy at Turin. Or if such a plan did not suit the Lord Treasurer, Prior ingeniously suggested that Edward Harley, Oxford's son and heir, might be sent in the role of Ambassador, with Matt himself acting as coadjutor.[94] This, we may observe, is the first mention that Prior makes of the young man who became his best friend and patron during the last four years of his life. Again, in September, Prior congratulated Oxford on the recent marriage of his son to the only daughter and heiress of the rich Duke of Newcastle, declaring that he loved Ned Harley as much as if he were a brother.

[92] *Ibid.*, 9, Bolingbroke to Prior, Whitehall, March 26, 1713.
[93] *Le Mercure Galant*, July, 1713.
[94] Strong, *Letters . . . at Welbeck*, 89, Prior to Oxford, Paris, Jan. 7/18, 1713.

The diplomatic mission to which Prior aspired was not only one of compliment but of importance. The Duke of Savoy, who was the favored stepchild of the Tory ministry, would inherit Spain if Philip and his line failed. Bolingbroke had insisted that all the Duke's territories seized by France during the War should be returned, and had handed Sicily over to the Duke against the wishes of Louis XIV, who had wanted to give the kingdom to his ally, the Elector of Bavaria. Another interest that Bolingbroke had in this prince was that the Duke of Savoy had a younger son[95] whom he was ready to educate as an Anglican and as a rival claimant to the throne of England, should Bolingbroke desire to upset the succession as established by law in favor of George Lewis of Hanover and ignore the nearest claimant, the young Stuart Pretender. The claim to the English throne of the Savoyard Prince,[96] great grandson of Charles I, might appeal to Tories disinclined to favor either Catholic James or Lutheran George Lewis.[97] Shrewsbury seconded Prior's bid for the appointment at Turin. Bolingbroke likewise approved it while admitting that the selection was "one of those *arcana imperii nostri*," about which he could say nothing positive.[98] Oxford remained silent; Edward Harley went off on his honeymoon; and the volatile Peterborough, who would cut a figure on account of his social rank, was chosen for the honor which Prior had hoped might justly go to himself.

Prior took his disappointment with resignation. He had a deep affection for the Lord Treasurer, who though neglectful, was still his best friend.

[95] The Duke had already given one of his daughters to be Dauphiness of France, another to be Queen of Spain.

[96] Through his grandmother, "Madame Henriette d'Angleterre," sister of Charles II.

[97] That the possible succession of the Savoyard prince was taken seriously may be seen from the following letter, Gaultier to Torcy, London, Dec. 15, 1713. Paris, Archives . . . , *Correspondance Politique, d'Angleterre*, 247, fo. 138: Prenez garde, je vous supplie, Monseigneur au Peterborough, qui, sous l'ombre de vous faire des confiances, tâchera de pénétrer vos véritables sentiments. Je sais qu'il vous dira qu'il hait le roi de Sicile; mais ne le croyez pas; car il vous mentira, et je suis sur qu'il est dans les intérêts du dernier fils de ce prince.

[98] Bolingbroke, *Letters and Correspondence*, IV, 72, Bolingbroke to Prior, Whitehall, April 20, 1713.

As you please, my Lord, I am always submissive to what may be easiest and best to you, and hopefull you are persuaded that in the Execution of your commands I shall act upon a principle much nobler than that of Self-Interest, however sometimes I may have dunn'd you between Jeast and Earnest.[99]

» 5 «

Peace between the nations permitted freedom of travel and communication which had been limited for a decade or more. Englishmen began to flock to Paris and sooner or later they all hunted out Mr. Prior. His hospitality during 1713 was extended to such varied personalities as Lady Jersey, Jacob Tonson, Sim Harcourt, George Berkeley, and Lord Peterborough.

Harcourt—"Little Sim" to his friends—as secretary of the Brothers Club, had much literary gossip to unfold, the choicest tale being about Addison's *Cato*. The now well-known story of turning a Whig rally into a Tory triumph was pleasing to the ears of Prior, for he and Addison had long been politely hostile to each other. At the climax of the play, Sim related, when the audience at Drury Lane was wildly applauding Booth, the actor, who had delivered himself of much Whig bombast, Bolingbroke called Booth to his box, handed him fifty guineas, and congratulated him on defending the cause of liberty so ably. Thus Bolingbroke by one clever stroke "rescued Cato from Whigism." Addison, for some strange reason, perhaps a temporary inclination to forswear party prejudice, had intrusted "Little Sim" with a presentation copy of *Cato* for Prior. And so in the midst of his rejoicing over the turning of the tables, Prior had to sit down to write a gracious acknowledgment of the gift. The letter, we think, is masterfully noncommittal:

I have received the Tragedy you were pleased to send me by Mr. Harcourt, it can certainly receive no greater commendation than that all

---

[99] Strong, *Letters . . . at Welbeck*, App. VI, p. 294, Prior to Oxford, Fontainebleau, Sept. 18/29, 1713.

parties like it and everybody fancies his friend to be Cato. I know you are so tired of Encomiums that to spare you upon the subject is the best compliment one can make you. I hope you will accept my sincere acknowledgment for your kind remembrance of me at this distance, and do me the justice to believe that no man desires more to cultivate the Honour of your Friendship.[100]

But Prior had not heard the last of *Cato*. Several months later the post brought a copy of John Dennis's withering criticism of the play[101]—a gift from the doughty old critic himself. In view of his effort to remain neutral in the fight, Prior found it difficult to compose a fitting acknowledgment of this somewhat unwelcome gift. His skill, however, did not desert him.

I am obliged to you for your Remarks on *Cato*, which I received. As you designed, and as I have been concerned in the general Peace, I could heartily wish we were all friends at Parnassus, and particular articles stipulated in that behalf. A man plunged in political prose and at his leisure entertained only with some niceties in this Delicate Language, as they call it, may be pardoned if he does not reflect upon the noble Errors of some English Poems and the great strength and judgment of the criticisms upon them. My return to London will, I hope, soon allow me some leisure hours to talk with you upon this subject, and to improve my acquaintance with you. In the meantime you will do me great justice in believing that I have a high esteem for your merit and learning, and desire of embracing all occasions by which I may testify to my being very truly, etc.[102]

Lord Peterborough ran up to Paris frequently from Savoy—sometimes on diplomatic business but more often in search of pleasure. During one of his longest visits there he was often entertained with Prior at the Ferriols, where he shone in the presence of the three charming ladies, but was more especially bewitched by Aïssé. In the intervals between visits Prior and Peterborough carried on a lively correspondence, partly official

---

[100] P. R. O. *State Papers, France*, 105/28, fo. 146, Prior to Addison, Paris, May 11/22, 1713.

[101] *Remarks upon Cato, a Tragedy.*

[102] P. R. O., *State Papers, France*, 105/29, fo. 87, Prior to John Dennis, Paris, March 13, 1714.

and partly personal. Aïssé figures in the letters as the "fair infidel" or the "Mahumetan"; and Prior dubs Peterborough the "Christian Knight." Does Prior seek to fan the flame of jealousy by writing—"I shall see Madame de Ferriol today, and I shall not fail to let her know how far the fair infidel has prevailed upon the Christian Knight"?[103]

More significant is this note:

As to your private commands, the Christian as well as the Mahumetan are your servants and will tell you so themselves very soon. The Christian desires her brother may be made a bishop. I have already nuncupated him the Bishop of Peterbrow as thinking him properly of your own making, and the only one of the order whom you wil! ε ver make; upon which condition the Mahumetan will, I presume, resign her body for her soul. You know as she is a slave it is not at her disposal.[104]

To read too much between the lines here would be idle, for both Prior and Peterborough enjoyed giving their imaginations wide range. In fact, Peterborough was such a habitual fabricator that Swift characterized him as the "ramblingest lying rogue on earth." Peterborough, having made a hazardous voyage from Genoa to Sicily during the winter of 1714, could not resist sending Oxford a much embellished description of it. Oxford, incredulous, passed the letter on to Prior, who tersely commented on his friend's broad strokes:

Lord Peterborough is gone from Genoa in an open boat—that's one; 300 miles by sea, that's two; that he was forced ashore twenty times by tempests and majorkeens to lie among the rocks—that's how many, my Lord Treasurer?[105]

Prior gave a kindlier and probably fairer estimate when he said:

[103] *Ibid.*, fo. 40, Prior to Peterborough, Paris, Jan. 4/15, 1713/14. See also letter, *ibid.*, fo. 69, Feb. 15/26, 1713/14.
[104] *Ibid.*, fo. 107, Prior to Peterborough, Paris, April 3/14, 1714.
[105] Pope, *Works*, ed. Bowles, VIII, 266, Prior to Oxford, Paris, Feb. 10, 1714.

Peterborough's ideas are like those of painters in fresco, bigger than life. If you see them at a certain distance, some of them are pretty enough; but if you look at them near, they are confused.[106]

The freer use of the post, Prior's recovery from his illness, and his lightened work permitted the renewing of long-neglected correspondence with many friends—Swift, Dr. Arbuthnot, and Halifax among them. Life at the Embassy was pleasant during these days, and Prior wrote eagerly and lightheartedly. "Little Sim" was the "joy and life of the Embassy," he told Arbuthnot, fellow member of the Brothers Club, when he was sending inclusive regards to all the Brethren, the Sisters, and other relatives that might be proper.[107] Prior found in Arbuthnot a kindred spirit to whom he could write as freely and foolishly as he pleased:

When you have nothing else to do, pray write to me, but who is a knave or who is a cuckold will make your letter too long; and births and burials I have from the weekly Bill: yet write something. I know not what, and if you don't know, advise with Jonathan. Give my kind love and friendship to our Brother and believe me with very great truth and respect.[108]

This casual mention of Jonathan is puzzling in view of the restraint with which Prior was writing to Swift just then. Hastily he concluded a note while the messenger waited after the packet had closed:

Hang me, if I know how to go on, although I am in a country where everybody does not only write letters but prints them.[109]

Of more significance, however, is a letter of introduction for a Mr. Rosengrave who was going to Ireland. It indicates a temporary disinclination to cry *vive la bagatelle*, quite in con-

[106] Bickley, *Life of Matthew Prior*, p. 199, quoted from Prior Papers at Longleat, XXI, fo. 138d.

[107] P. R. O., *State Papers, France*, 105/28, Prior to Arbuthnot, Paris, June 4/15, 1713.

[108] *Ibid.*, 105/29, fo. 81, Prior to Arbuthnot, Paris, March 9/20, 1714.

[109] Swift, *Correspondence*, II, 18, Prior to Swift, Paris, March 28/April 8, 1713.

trast to the happy spirit of the Arbuthnot correspondence. Probably it is only a subconscious response to Swift's own dark temper:

I have writ letters now above twenty-two years. I have taken towns, destroyed fleets, made treaties, and settled commerce in letters. And what of all this? Why nothing; but that I have had some subject to write upon; But to write a letter only, because Mr. Rosengrave has a mind to carry one in his pocket, to tell you that you are sure of a friendship, which can never do you a three-penny worth of good, and to wish you well in England soon, when I do not know when I am likely to be there myself. All this, I say, is very absurd for a letter, especially when I have this day written a dozen much more to the purpose. If I had seen your manuscript; if I had received Dr. Parnell's poem;[110] if I had any news of Landen being taken, why well and good; but as I know no more than the Duke of Shrewsbury designs for England within three weeks; that I must stay here till somebody else comes, and that brings me necessarily to say, good Mr. Dean, that I am like the fellow in the *Rehearsal*,[111] who did not know if he was to be merry or serious, or in what way or mood to act his part. One thing only, I am assured of, that I love you very well, and am most sincerely and faithfully, dear Sir, your servant and brother.[112]

As much of a surprise as Addison's overture of friendship was a message from Halifax.[113] The post was now open, he wrote Prior, and he would like to begin a correspondence about matters which in no way concerned the state. His Lordship wished Prior to obtain for him from Frère François, author of *Le Jardinier Solitaire*, advice about trees for his garden at Bushey and his orchard at Apscourt. With pathetic eagerness, Matt sought out Frère François and immediately shipped the trees.[114] When notifying Halifax that the plants were on their way, Prior tactlessly commented on the conclusion of the peace at Rastadt:

---

[110] On Queen Anne's Peace.
[111] Buckingham, *The Rehearsal*, Act I, Scene 1.
[112] Swift, *Correspondence*, II, Prior to Swift, Aug. 15/26, 1713.
[113] *Longleat Papers*, III, 443, Halifax to Prior, Dec. 23/Jan. 3, 1713/14.
[114] P. R. O. *State Papers, France*, 105/29, fo. 76, Prior to Halifax, Paris, Feb. 20, March 3, 1713/1714.

Once more we are freed from the weight of foreign stipulations and in estate to become a happy nation if our own follies and divisions will not hinder it. This, my lord, is worth your speculations while you are planting your trees ——.[115]

The peace was a Tory measure, and since Halifax was a vigorous Whig, he was in no mood to discuss politics. Curtly he demanded the bill for the trees, saying that he could not allow Prior to go to so much trouble and expense upon the score of ancient friendship. He also desired some seeds for "salating"; in return for this favor he suggested sending Prior something from England, a malt drink perhaps.[116]

Prior sent the salad seeds, and refrained this time from offering any gratuitous praise of Tory diplomacy. The price of the seeds was negligible, but, since his Lordship demanded an account, Prior asked that the costs of these purchases be credited against his own debt of long standing. Hurt by Halifax's rebuke, he refused the offer of the drink, and concluded the letter stiffly: "Your Lordship may always correspond with me upon what terms you please, and a very light friendship may serve to produce a crop of chicory or lettuce . . ." [117] Upon this distant note the correspondence stopped, only to be renewed after the Queen's death when Prior was forced to ask the Whigs for bread.

[115] *Ibid.*, fo. 85, Prior to Halifax, Versailles, March 2/13, 1713/14.

[116] *Longleat Papers*, III, 444, Halifax to Prior, March 20/31, 1714.

[117] P. R. O., *State Papers, France*, 105/29, fo. 101, Prior to Halifax, Paris, April 2/13, 1714.

CHAPTER X

"Bannisons la Mélancholie"

» 1 «

DURING the spring of 1713 Shrewsbury was suffering from nostalgia—either real or imagined—and longed to be back among his pictures, his books, and his beloved gardens at Heythrop. His second association with Prior was drawing to a close. They had been congenial friends. Shrewsbury had set a good example for his subordinate in many ways, and had even mildly influenced his verse. Although the Ambassador does not figure in the Augustan age as a literary critic, he was possibly the first man of his time to voice a dissatisfaction with the heroic couplet and a preference for blank verse. As early as 1705 he had said:

I wish we did more generally take up the use of those blank verses, more noble and unconfined than the Gothick monkish fashion of gingling rhime, which serves as a crutch to support lame verses and weak thoughts.[1]

Prior was acquainted with Shrewsbury's preference, for a couplet in "Protogenes and Apelles," as well as the preface to "Solomon," contains a similar sentiment:

> And in our Verse e're Monkish Rhimes
> Had jangl'd their fantastic Chimes:[2]

Moreover, in 1713 he undertook in honor of the Duchess of Shrewsbury a blank verse translation of a tale from Boccaccio. The translation was never finished, but it indicates at least

[1] Kemble, *Papers and Correspondence*, p. 433, Shrewsbury to George Stepney, Rome, March 7, 1705.   [2] *Poems on Several Occasions*, p. 191.

that Prior was then in agreement with Shrewsbury as to the weakness of the heroic couplet.[3]

Shrewsbury fretted through the summer months in Paris, finally turning his face toward home on the last day of August. Prior was left at the Embassy as Her Majesty's sole representative. He was in very much the same plight as when Bolingbroke left him the previous August. Without commission again, he composed himself to wait—an act which he exercised with more grace than formerly. General Ross of the Royal Dragoons, "a man of quality," would soon relieve him, he heard. Furthermore, Bolingbroke sent word that the Queen intended to recompense him at home for his good services and would recall him shortly for that purpose. He had every right to expect a reward. Had not Mesnager, originally only a petty merchant from Rouen, retired from his duties at Utrecht a very rich man, honored with the title of Comte de St. Jean? Moreover, the Abbé Gaultier, though descended from the most poverty-stricken Norman peasant family, was battening on his rewards—an abbaye of ten thousand *livres* a year in France, a pension from King Philip of twelve thousand *livres* annually,[4] and a promise of a thousand pounds from Queen Anne.[5] Could Prior be blamed for envying the lot of the French ministers and wondering what his reward was to be?

[3] The following lines found in *Dialogues of the Dead*, p. 339, indicate Prior's opinion of the heroic couplet:

> But not as heretofore, the line prescrib'd
> To equal cadence, and with semblant Sounds
> Pointed, (so Modern Harmony advises)
> But in the Ancient Guise, free, uncontroll'd,
> The Verse, compress'd the Period, or dilated,
> As close discourse requires, or fine description.
> Such Homer wrote; such Milton imitated;
> And Shrewsbury, candid Judge of Verse, approves.

Other examples of Prior's blank verse are found in his translation of two hymns of Callimachus (*Poems on Several Occasions*, pp. 196–204) and in two minor pieces (*Dialogues of the Dead*, pp. 334, 356). His blank verse has been declared superior to that which Addison or other men of his time wrote. See R. D. Havens, *The Influence of Milton on English Poetry*, Cambridge, Mass., 1922, p. 105.

[4] Marquis de Torcy, *Journal inédit*, p. 347.

[5] Paid to Gaultier on July 20, 1714. See Cobbett's *Parliamentary History*, VII, 122 and 198.

Shrewsbury had pointed out to the Lord Treasurer in July the anomaly of Prior's position:

If your Lordship intends Mr. Prior should stay here any time as her Majesty's minister it is fit he should know it, and have money advanced to put himself in an equipage becoming his character. He lives now in hired lodgings dearer than a house, and not decent if he remains, but in the uncertainty he is left in, he can do no otherwise.[6]

And three weeks later he had written:

The handsome rewards the Abbé . . . has received from the Courts of France and Spain for his pains in the peace makes Prior, I believe, hope he shall not be forgotten.[7]

Shrewsbury in London was just as solicitous as he had been in Paris. He again called Prior's plight to the attention of Oxford, who said indefinitely he had something in mind for Prior, but that he would not divulge it at the time.[8] Prior begged Bolingbroke to find out what the secret was, but Bolingbroke could learn nothing from Oxford.

Time and again Bolingbroke announced that Ross would soon leave for France, and rumor had it that Prior would be transferred to Baden. Although Ross's commission of Plenipotentiary was signed in April, illness delayed him further. Eight months had passed since Shrewsbury left, and Prior was still waiting for his recall. His dilemma seems to have been the result of cross-purposes on the part of the two ministers. One post would bring Torcy a dispatch from Bolingbroke saying that General Ross would replace Prior shortly, while the next would bring word from Gaultier, who was very intimate with Oxford, that Prior would not be recalled. Gaultier once urged Torcy to let Prior know the real situation, but warned him to guard the secret carefully.[9] After weeks of circumspection, Gaultier finally stated frankly:

[6] *Longleat Papers*, I, 235, Shrewsbury to Oxford, Paris, July 7/18, 1713.

[7] *Ibid.*, 237, Shrewsbury to Oxford, Paris, July 31/August 11, 1713.

[8] *Portland Papers*, V, 341, Shrewsbury to Prior, London, Sept. 29/Oct. 10, 1713.

[9] Paris, Archives . . . , *Correspondance Politique, d'Angleterre*, 250, fo. 42, Gaultier to Torcy, London, Oct. 31, 1713.

M. de Bolingbroke veut absolument que Prior soit rappelé et que le général Ross luy succède, et l'on m'assure qu'il l'emporteroit malgré le Trésorier.[10]

Oxford ignored Bolingbroke's written recommendation that Prior be sent to Baden save to make notation on the letter: "He has opposed me about a minister for Baden since the Peace of Rastadt was known to be concluded, and that I proposed one."[11] The following day, Bolingbroke wrote again to Oxford, curtly announcing that he would recall Prior and send Ross; but when Ross had recovered from his illness and was ready to go to France, it was too late to send anyone.

It was useless to wait for orders from Oxford. Prior went ahead on his own initiative as soon as his commission arrived, hired a house, and supplied himself with an equipage in keeping with his station. He had credit in Paris, and began to entertain lavishly; so lavishly that the Whigs in their impeachment articles against Oxford accused the Lord Treasurer of corruptly and scandalously combining with Prior to defraud her Majesty of very great sums, declaring the bills of exchange that Prior drew between August 27, 1712, and July 10, 1714, to have amounted to 12,260 pounds.[12]

Although troubled about the future, Prior was making the most of the present. With an air of importance he notified all the other English ministers in Europe to address their communications to him as acting ambassador.[13] His new dignity and the popularity he enjoyed at the French Court increased his self-esteem, and he wrote pridefully to Bolingbroke:

I have ten horses in my stables, knaves in proportion, and am going to Fontainebleau (having been, by the bye, particularly invited by the Monarch *vivâ voce*) as soon as I shall have arranged my papers.[14]

[10] *Ibid.*, 255, fo. 76, Gaultier to Torcy, London, April 5/16, 1714.

[11] *Portland Papers*, V, 423, Bolingbroke to Oxford, April 20, 1714.

[12] Cobbett's *Parliamentary History*, VII, 118.

[13] Paris, Archives . . . , *Correspondance Politique, d'Angleterre*, 249, fo. 286, Prior to Torcy, Paris, Sept. 5, 1713.

[14] Bolingbroke, *Letters and Correspondence*, IV, 264, Prior to Bolingbroke, Paris, Sept. 5, 1713.

Added to the King's invitation was a most urgent one from Torcy, who desired to have lessons in English now that M. Prior had some leisure:

J'aimerais beaucoup mieux, Monsieur, savoir ce que vous faites à Fontainebleau que d'apprendre à quoi vous passez votre temps à Paris et quelques agréables que soient vos lettres, je donnerai toujours la préférence à votre conversation. Vous entretendrez aussi bien d'ici que de Paris vos ministres dispersés dans les cours de l'Europe; mais, en vérité, Monsieur, je crois que vous ne me dites que la moindre des raisons qui vous empêchent de venir nous voir. J'y perdi de toutes façons et si vous étiez venu ici des les temps que je l'espérais, je saurais peut-être assez d'anglais pour vous répondre. J'aimerais beaucoup mieux m'en servir que du français pour vous assurer que toutes les affaires que vous m'avez remises sont encore au même état et qu'aucune n'est finie. Un habile ministre comme vous, Monsieur, ne sait-il pas que les paresseux comme nous ne font rien s'ils ne sont pressés. Venez donc solliciter et vous aurez tout pouru qu'il ne s'agisse point d'affaires de marine.[15]

Gladly Prior accepted these invitations—one could hardly refuse a king—and spent a month during September and October of 1713 at Fontainebleau. Again we catch a glimpse of life at King Louis's Court such as Prior had described when he had been at Fontainebleau as Lord Portland's secretary fifteen years before:

We are in huntings, comedies, feasts and all that the generality of the world calls pleasure: I am mightily *en odeur*, as we call it: but it is a strange fancy I have, I had rather hear once a month from My Lord Treasurer than be talked to once a day by the Grand Monarch.[16]

The too palpable compliment to Oxford does not conceal Prior's pride in being *en odeur* with the Grand Monarch. This attitude is to be contrasted with the mordant satire that he had formerly leveled at King Louis—in gossip with his friends, of

---

[15] Paris, Archives . . . , *Correspondance Politique, d'Angleterre*, 246, fo. 142, Torcy to Prior, Fontainebleau, September 9, 1713.

[16] Strong, *Letters . . . at Welbeck*, App. VI, p. 292, Prior to Oxford, Fontainebleau, Sept. 18/29, 1713.

course. Now he found the King friendly, gracious, and solicitous about his health. The King's own health and spirits were excellent in spite of his age.

At Shrewsbury's entry Prior had remarked that Louis seemed "more blithe" than ever before. No doubt the declining health of Queen Anne made Louis's vigor the more impressive.

The old monarch, at seventy-five eats and sleeps at Versailles, as if he were your age; and seems less concerned about the Empire continuing a War than you can be about the Scots threatening to break the Union.[17]

Frequently, Prior mentioned the King in his letters to Oxford and to Bolingbroke, and the picture he drew is far from Thackeray's famous caricature of Louis XIV as a wizened old man. Rather is it of the King, more active than ever in his search for amusement, journeying from château to château, hunting the deer in his *calèche*, and killing sometimes as many as fifty pheasants and hares with his own gun. Even shortly after the death of Queen Anne, when war clouds threatened the peace of his remaining days, King Louis continued to hunt and to shoot as he had done in his prime:

We are here at Fontainebleau *sicut olim*; our time divided between prayer and council, hunting and eating; the King killed two staggs yesterday, and was this morning as well as I have ever seen him since I have been in France.[18]

Not all of Prior's observations of Louis portray the King in avid search for amusement. A sympathetic side of his nature is revealed in the following anecdote: The governess to the young dauphin asked Prior how he liked the boy, whom Prior described elsewhere as "a pale child, handsome, with a good deal of spirit." "I said," Prior records, "so well that I wished the Queen had such another." Thereupon King Louis asked how

[17] Bolingbroke, *Letters and Correspondence*, IV, 181, Prior to Bolingbroke, Paris, June 23, 1713.

[18] P. R. O. *State Papers, France*, 105/29, Prior to Bolingbroke, Fontainebleau, Sept. 7, N. S., 1714.

many children Queen Anne had lost, and when Prior replied sixteen, the King said "a very civil thing upon her having sustained so many losses of that kind."[19]

Louis liked Prior. The lonely old King, the most "inamusable" man in France, as Madame de Maintenon called him, was entertained by Prior's ready wit and repartee. On one occasion when conversation turned to the theater, the Duc d'Aumont, who had recently returned from London, told the King that in England they blooded the theater too much, and that he had seen the heads brought upon the stage in a performance of *Titus Andronicus*. "Is this accusation true, Monsieur Prior?" the King asked. "We did it upon an extraordinary occasion," replied Matt, "to divert the Duc d'Aumont by the strangeness of the spectacle because he did not understand the beauty of the words."[20]

In spite of such anecdotes, there is less personal comment about the Court circles in Prior's letters at this period than in those more vivid and less cautious ones of the earlier days when he had been only a secretary, and "un jeune orangiste," to borrow Chateaubriand's phrase. Prior was older, wiser, and a Tory. Louis was now an ally of Queen Anne, no longer the archenemy of the great William. Also, many of the royal personages upon whom Matt had once vented his Whiggish anti-French prejudices had died, several of them from the cruel ravages of smallpox or measles. Gone were the corpulent lazy "Monseigneur," the shallow-pated "Monsieur," the ugly but affable Duke of Burgundy and his Duchess, whose childlike graces and mischief had diverted many a dull hour for Louis and Madame de Maintenon. Philippe, the Duc d'Orléans, soon to be the Regent, was in disgrace, accused of having poisoned the three dauphins. As for Philip of Spain, he was constantly

[19] *Ibid.*, 105/28, fo. 61, Prior to Oxford, Paris, Dec. 29, 1712/13.

[20] Wickham Legg, *Matthew Prior*, App. C, p. 330, quoted from Prior Papers at Longleat, XXI, fo. 139.

quarreling with his grandfather. "Madame" was still living, hearty and vigorous as ever. Bolingbroke brought her a letter from Queen Anne in 1712; and Prior delivered to her one from George I, soon after his coronation, which annoyed her because it was not written in George Lewis's own hand. Characteristically enough, she despised her cousin and favored the cause of James III.

Villeroy—"my governor," Prior had called him formerly— appears only occasionally in Prior's correspondence now. His disgrace at Ramillies, Louis had forgiven on the ground that he could not forget "une amitié de naissance." Another old acquaintance is mentioned just once. This is Tallard—a prisoner of war at Nottingham since Blenheim—for whom Prior was anxious to obtain "a perfect *nunc dimittis,*" not only for his own satisfaction, but because "the King would take Tallard's liberty as a favor."[21]

It is mostly of the Torcys, the Ferriols, the Noailles that we read—families whose chronicles belong more to the eighteenth century than to the closing years of the seventeenth. One person unmentioned was the Duc de Saint-Simon, whose *Mémoires* furnish the most vivid picture of the closing years of the reign of the Grand Monarch. This omission is puzzling in view of the fact that Saint-Simon frequently mentioned Prior, summing him up as if he knew him intimately:

Il etait un homme extrêmement capable, savant d'ailleurs, d'infiniment d'esprit, de bonne chère et de fort bonne compagnie.[22]

Better known to Prior than Saint-Simon was Fénelon, who in 1713 was proposing the speedy completion of a second edition of the French Dictionary. Prior was as enthusiastic an advocate of this project as he had been the previous year of Swift's proposal[23] to establish an academy for fixing the standards of the

[21] Strong, *Letters . . . at Welbeck,* App. VI, p. 271, Prior to Oxford, Fontainebleau, Aug. 29/Sept. 9, 1712.

[22] Saint-Simon, *Mémoires,* XXXVIII, 262.

[23] *A Proposal for Correcting, Improving, and Ascertaining the English Tongue,* 1712.

English language, which he feared he might forget while studying French so intensely.[24] Fénelon pays tribute to Prior's interest in the proposed edition and to his mastery of an adopted tongue:

M. Prior, Anglais, dont l'esprit et les lumières sont connus de tout le monde, et qui est peut-être, de tous les étrangers celui qui a la plus étudié notre langue, m'a parlé cent fois de la nécessité du travail que je propose, et de l'impatience avec laquelle il est attendu.[25]

» 2 «

It should not be inferred that Shrewsbury's departure left Prior at leisure, or that jesting with Louis XIV, coaching Torcy in English, and mixing in the round of pleasure at Fontainebleau were all that occupied the Plenipotentiary's time. He was now in the most important diplomatic position an English minister might wish for. The aim of Bolingbroke's whole foreign policy was a closer alliance with France. For one brief year or so, before the death of Queen Anne, the two nations saw eye to eye upon many of the points in the tangled skein of European politics. The designs of the Austrian Emperor in Italy, the problem of barriers for Savoy and the Empire, the question of a concerted policy towards Sweden—threatened on one side by Denmark, on the other by Russia—all these matters were the subject of long diplomatic letters of instruction from Bolingbroke to Prior, of frequent conversations between Prior and Torcy, of voluminous reports from Prior to Bolingbroke. Finally, in the spring of 1714, came full powers for negotiating a defensive treaty between England, France, Spain, and Sicily, at the very time that rumors of Philip's intentions to revoke his renunciation necessitated Prior's getting in touch with the Duke of Orleans, who, as Regent on the death of Louis XIV, would be the Prince of the Blood most concerned. In fact, the year saw not

[24] Swift, *Correspondence*, II, 18, Prior to Swift, April 8, 1713.
[25] Fénelon, *Oeuvres*, XXI, 147.

only a realization, however imperfect, of an alliance between England and France, but a foreshadowing of a situation which was to influence English foreign policy after the era of good feeling had vanished.

Since the study of these transactions belongs more to the historian than to the biographer, we shall confine our attention to the problems which touched Prior more closely.

With the French ministers of finance Prior's relations were less pleasant than with the minister of foreign affairs. It was with Pontchartrain, the Chancellor, and with Desmarets, the Controller of Finance, that Prior had to fight his most difficult battles. Negotiations for commercial relations between the two countries were continued and occupied the greatest share of Prior's time during the summer and autumn of 1713. A draft treaty of commerce, permitting a restoration of trade, had been signed at Utrecht, but two of the forty-seven articles—those providing for the "most-favored-nation treatment"—required sanction of Parliament, running counter as they did to existing trade relations. When the two articles came up for consideration in the House of Commons, a great outcry arose from the Whig mercantile interests in London. The whole scheme was said to be too visionary, too impractical, too contrary to traditional economic doctrine. Even Hanmer and his Tory squires joined the Whigs, fearing that closer trade with France would increase the number of paupers and decrease the value of land. The Whigs won the day in Parliament. The articles were defeated in the House of Commons, to the keen disappointment of Prior, who had labored incessantly over the treaty and who bitterly described the obstructionists as "those who upon the 'change are called topping merchants, and who have made themselves such by downright monopoly of the trade (which should be national) into their own hands." The reflection has a familiar ring and seems decidedly modern. Thus Bolingbroke's pet project, certainly one of his most progressive schemes, received a serious setback.

Nevertheless, Prior continued to negotiate with the French ministers of finance as before. Commissioners from both nations were to be named to meet in London to settle matters of dispute, but it was not until January, 1714, that Prior could induce the French to appoint their representatives, and not until the following spring that he saw them set out for London. Pontchartrain, dubious of the whole scheme, was as helpful as a Whig, and Desmarets, suspicious of any project that might not bring a bargain to France, proved tiresomely obstructive. Scarcely a letter passed from Prior to Bolingbroke which failed to contain some gibe at Pontchartrain, who was "a quiver, whence we shall never find any arrow pointed with justice or winged with honor." Needless to say, the commercial treaty never went into effect. All such enlightened policies were dropped after the death of Queen Anne, when the general anti-French policy returned with a vengeance, and Pope's rosy picture in *Windsor Forest* of a free intercourse of trade never became a reality.

Although the main negotiations with King Philip concerning the lot of the Catalans went through Lord Lexington's hands, Prior was from time to time directed to obtain from the French government support of the ministry's half-hearted intercession for those unfortunate people in whose welfare Queen Anne seems to have had a genuine concern. In September, 1712, Oxford instructed Prior to gain Torcy's coöperation. It was readily given. A courier was promptly sent to Madrid with a letter demanding "the confirmation of all rights and privileges" to the Catalans.[26] Even Bolingbroke actively espoused their cause. "Your Lordship," he wrote to Strafford, "will continue to insist in those terms that the Catalans be restored to their ancient privileges, and we will carry the point."[27] Alas, when the treaty with Spain

[26] Strong, *Letters . . . at Welbeck*, App. VI, p. 269, Prior to Oxford, Fontainebleau, Aug. 29/Sept. 9, 1712.
[27] Bolingbroke, *Letters and Correspondence*, III, 365, Bolingbroke to Strafford, Whitehall, Feb. 3, 1712/13.

was concluded, Bolingbroke had lost all interest in the Catalans. "It is not for the interest of England to preserve the Catalan liberties," he told the plenipotentiaries at Utrecht, declaring that such "liberties are the power of the purse and sword."[28] As a result of Bolingbroke's indifference, the treaty only required Philip to accord to the Catalans an amnesty for their offences. Their ancient privileges—a special Cortes, certain exemptions from taxation, the appointment of their own judges—he was determined to abolish.

In the autumn of 1713, the Queen, through Prior, again appealed to Louis XIV to intercede with Philip in behalf of the Catalans and, although Louis protested that he had little influence at the Spanish Court, he did write a letter to his grandson. Philip replied that he would spare the Catalans if they would immediately lay down their arms. This they refused to do, insisting upon the restoration of their ancient privileges, guaranteed to them by Stanhope and Peterborough in return for their support of the Allies in the War. By this time no one was inclined to champion their cause. "Their old privileges," Prior told Bolingbroke, were "said by the Duke de Noailles, Marshal de Tessé and others, who should know the thing, to be so extravagant and against all the rules of reason and justice as neither the Queen of Great Britain nor the King could insist upon them if they were explained to their Majesties."[29]

Bolingbroke, with no regard for promises made by a former Whig ministry, sought to convince Queen Anne that he had done all that was necessary for the Catalans, and making light of their demands, he washed his hands of them.[30]

In all Prior's correspondence during the autumn of 1713, when the subject of the Catalans was under discussion, there is no sign that he took a more humane attitude towards them than

[28] Cobbett's *Parliamentary History*, VII, lxxvii.
[29] P. R. O. *State Papers, France*, 78/157, fo. 376. Prior to Bolingbroke, Paris, Dec. 6, 1713.
[30] Bolingbroke, *Letters and Correspondence*, IV, 396, Bolingbroke to Queen Anne, Dec. 17/28, 1713.

did Bolingbroke. After all, the treaty with Spain had been signed. The Catalans were no longer his country's allies. They were turbulent rebels, who should be taught to live "in due subjection to authority." In August, 1714, when Whig clamors forced Bolingbroke again to direct Prior to ask Torcy to intercede for the Catalans,[31] he merely wrote back that their demands "were inconsistent with the safety of Spain in general, and tended only to the mutual destruction of the very people that required them, and in fine to anarchy, murder, and rebellion."[32]

The Catalans were left to the mercy of Philip. Though free trade might be held as good Tory policy, a regard for the rights of small nations was too enlightened, and the injured feelings of the Catalans were left to smoulder, though never to die out, as recent events have shown, when by the Convention of 1931 their old rights and privileges were recognized.

Over the tedious and exasperating problem of Dunkirk, Prior acted with more vigor than Whig historians have given him credit for. That he failed to reckon with French chicane and took French promises too seriously may be charged against him, but when the Whigs came into power in 1714, they were no more successful with the Dunkirk question than their Tory predecessors had been. Stair might bluster and Stanhope grow truculent, but so long as Louis XIV lived, they made no headway. By the eighth article of the treaty of Utrecht, Louis XIV promised to raze within five months and at his own expense the fortifications of the City of Dunkirk, to fill up the harbor, and to level the sluices or moles which served to cleanse the harbor. Queen Anne was in no hurry to press the demolition of Dunkirk until she might force the Dutch to grant her better trade terms in the Spanish Netherlands, but the opposition of the Whigs during the

---

[31] P. R. O. *State Papers, France*, 105/28, Bolingbroke to Prior, Whitehall, Aug. 9, 1714.
[32] *Ibid.*, 78/159, Prior to Bolingbroke, Paris, Aug. 28, 1714.

summer of 1713 compelled the ministry to take up the problem with Louis.[33]

The French ministers, informed by Gaultier of the Queen's illness, began to grow alarmed at the prospect of Dunkirk's remaining any longer in English hands,[34] for, said Torcy, should the Queen die, England would be in the hands of the Whigs, and the Prince of Hanover would give Dunkirk to the Dutch in return for their assistance in putting him upon the throne.[35] The dismantling of Dunkirk, therefore, was begun in September. From the very beginning, Prior met opposition from the French. They told him that the treaty would be literally executed,[36] but soon they began to quibble over the meaning of its terms. Did the words *diruantur, ac solo aequentur*, for example, mean that the very foundations of the work were to be removed, or did they mean only that the fortifications should be razed to the level of the ground? Prior stoutly insisted that the destruction must be entire; no stone must be left standing.[37] The French appealed to the Queen through Lady Masham, but to no avail.[38]

Then "the damned sluices," as Prior called them, gave almost endless trouble. The French wanted to keep them on the pretext that they were needed to prevent the surrounding country from being overflooded.[39] At Prior's refusal to yield this point, Torcy grew impatient. Again he appealed over Prior's head, this time in writing to Bolingbroke, begging him to "silence Matthieu," since neither maps, plans, nor anything else could "subdue his obstinacy."

[33] *Ibid.*, 105/28, Bolingbroke to Prior, Windsor, Aug. 29, 1713. See also *ibid.*, Bolingbroke to Prior, Windsor, Sept. 15, 1713, and Ashdown Park, Oct. 11, 1713.

[34] Paris, Archives . . . , *Correspondance Politique, d'Angleterre*, 247, fo. 31, Torcy to Gaultier, Versailles, Oct. 20, 1713.

[35] Bolingbroke, *Letters and Correspondence*, IV, 320, Prior to Bolingbroke, Fontainebleau, Oct. 9, 1713.

[36] P. R. O. *State Papers, France*, 78/157, Prior to Bolingbroke, Versailles, Oct. 20, 1713.

[37] *Ibid.*, Prior to Bolingbroke, Paris, Nov. 23, 1713.

[38] Paris, Archives . . . , *Correspondance Politique, d'Angleterre*, 247, fo. 156, Gaultier to Torcy, London, Dec. 8/14, 1713.

[39] P. R. O. *State Papers, France*, 78/157, Prior to Bolingbroke, Paris, Dec. 25, 1713.

Matthieu is no less unjust than intolerable upon an article of which he is incessantly speaking to me . . . You, my Lord, and you only, by your orders can recall him to reason, which he has absolutely discarded on this article, and I must say, you should do so, as much out of pity for him, as for the honor of the Queen.

With this underhanded criticism of Prior Torcy set out to flatter Bolingbroke, expressing the hope that "instead of quarrelling with each other we [i.e. Torcy and Prior] may for the time to come, only discourse on your perfections."[40]

Bolingbroke did not rise to the bait, but the French had still another trick up their sleeves: they started making sluices and deepening channels in the neighboring port of Mardyck, which would make it as dangerous as Dunkirk. "They do not intend to make the canal navigable for great ships or to keep the harbor open," Prior wrote hopefully; but he was no engineer—Mardyck was seventy leagues away, and clearly he was being outwitted.[41] King Louis, Prior further announced, was "gallantly" setting nine battalions at work upon the demolition of Dunkirk, to comply with the Queen's demands and wished Her Majesty to be assured that the demolition would be completed by the end of June.[42] On June 5, Prior discovered that the demolition promised by the time appointed was not that of the fortifications but only that of the sluices.[43]

Prior then drew up a convention in which Torcy promised that the fortifications should be pulled down and the harbor filled by the end of July.[44] Again the French resorted to subterfuge. They chicaned, delayed, and quibbled over the meaning of the treaty.[45] Soon afterwards, Queen Anne died, and the new

[40] Bolingbroke, *Letters and Correspondence*, IV, 433, Torcy to Bolingbroke, Jan. 17/28, 1714.
[41] P. R. O., *State Papers, France*, 78/157, Prior to Bolingbroke, Paris, April 2/13, 1714.
[42] *Ibid.*, Prior to Bolingbroke, Paris, May 4/15, 1714.
[43] *Ibid.*, 78/158, Prior to Bolingbroke, June 5, 1714.
[44] *Ibid.*, 78/159, Prior to Bolingbroke, July 6/17, 1714.
[45] *Ibid.*, Prior to Bolingbroke, Aug. 4/15, 1714. See also *ibid.*, Prior to Bolingbroke, Aug. 12/23, 1714.

Whig ministry tried to accomplish with strong language what mere patience and persistence had failed to achieve. Prior's further remonstrances with the French Court over the vexatious problem will concern us later.

» 3 «

Prior's curiosity about the young Stuart prince had caused him, during the days of the Portland embassy, to commit a diplomatic indiscretion. He had ventured, we may recall, to cast a glance at the child in the corridors of Versailles when he should have passed by with eyes averted, as became a loyal representative of the English Court. The young prince, who had dropped completely out of Prior's sight for ten years or more, now reappears in the story. The child had grown up to be a tall slender man of twenty-five, dark and swarthy like his uncle Charles II, but unlike the Merry Monarch, reserved and melancholy. The Prince, variously known as the Pretender, James III, and the Chevalier, having been ordered by the terms of the armistice at Utrecht to withdraw from France, had gone to the nearby duchy of Lorraine where King Louis, his chief benefactor, had found an asylum for him.

This arrangement satisfied the ministers in London for a time. Then the Whigs began to raise an outcry in Parliament against the Prince's remaining longer in Lorraine, and in the autumn of 1713 Prior was directed to tell M. de Barrois, the envoy of the Duke of Lorraine in Paris, that "the residence of the Pretender in Lorraine was inconsistent with the friendship between Her Majesty and the Duke."[46] There the matter was dropped until the following spring when Prior was again ordered to acquaint M. de Barrois of Parliament's continued displeasure with Lorraine. He went to Marly for counsel, where Torcy after consulting Louis XIV reported that His Majesty refused to assume

---

[46] *Ibid.*, 78/157, Prior to Bolingbroke, Paris, Nov. 29, 1713.

further obligation in the matter. Nevertheless, Torcy promised that he would endeavor to effect the Chevalier's removal.[47] Perhaps Torcy had his tongue in his cheek when he made this offer and really meant that he would do his best to set the Pretender on the English throne. By this time, Prior was tired of the maneuvers, which, as observed by Whig historians, he was beginning to think ridiculous:

To say the truth, my dear Lord Bolingbroke, M. de Torcy thinks us all mad. He asked me many questions, which for the best reason in the world I did not answer; as for instance, how can we oblige a man to go from one place to another when we forbid all others to receive him.[48]

A letter found among the Pretender's correspondence (*Stuart Papers*) suggests that Prior was guilty of duplicity in the Lorraine affair. The communication came to James III from Berwick, who reported that while Prior had passed the official word to Torcy that the Pretender must be removed from Lorraine he had written Torcy an unofficial note to the contrary:

M. Talon (Torcy) also told me . . . that M. Pecour (Prior) had writ a note to him telling him there was no more necessity for M. Robinson's (James III) parting with M. Loumaire (Lorraine); he will I suppose tell him when he sees him next.[49]

Such a note—if Prior ever wrote one—is not to be found in the *Archives des Affaires Étrangères*, and it seems probable that Berwick was in error. Another reason for doubting Berwick's statement is that Iberville, now French Ambassador in London, when relaying to Torcy a *sub rosa* scheme of Bolingbroke's by which the Duke of Lorraine could evade Bolingbroke's public demands, cautioned Torcy: "Il [Bolingbroke] vous prie, monseigneur, de garder le secret du but de cette maneuvre même avec M. Prior.[50]

[47] *Ibid.*, 78/158, Prior to Bolingbroke, Paris, April 9/20, 1714.
[48] Bolingbroke, *Letters and Correspondence*, IV, 580, Prior to Bolingbroke, n.d.
[49] *Stuart Papers*, I, 318, Berwick to James II, St. Germain, April 27, 1714.
[50] Paris, Archives . . . , *Correspondance Politique, d'Angleterre*, 251, fo. 156, Iberville to Torcy, March 1, 1714.

No matter how silly Prior may have thought the Lorraine business, he was not guilty, we believe, of trickery, inasmuch as he dutifully pursued Bolingbroke's instructions up to the very eve of Queen Anne's death.

More distasteful, since more risky, were the negotiations Oxford entrusted to Prior—the negotiations over the payment of the dowry which, although promised to Queen Mary of Modena by the treaty of Ryswick, had never been paid to her. The dowry, the Duchess of Marlborough once spitefully remarked, had never got farther than King William's pockets. Prior seems to have been fearful of the consequences of this affair. "As to the dowry," he wrote to Oxford, "I shall not only be dunned to death but hang'd; for the Dowager sends messengers to me which you in England do not think it extremely lawful to receive; but if it is to be paid, pray let it be done in a handsome manner, that it may shew the charity of the Queen and the generosity of her Lord Treasurer."[51]

Bolingbroke, during his visit to France, had promised Torcy that Queen Anne would pay Queen Mary the jointure, but not the arrears. After Bolingbroke departed, Prior was left to negotiate with Queen Mary's advisers, who drew up a memorial setting forth the Queen's claims. Louis XIV, Madame de Maintenon, and Torcy were all consulted about the document: Louis said that "there was no inconveniency in sending such a *mémoire* provided there was nothing in it that could shock Prior or hurt others."[52] A letter from Berwick to Queen Mary suggests that Shrewsbury was to be kept in the dark about the transaction and that Prior himself was wary of handling it:

I also desired M. de Torcy to tell Prior not to speak with anybody, and he has assured me that he would, and that he was sure Prior would willingly comply with your commands, for he is very shy, so for the

---

[51] P. R. O., *State Papers, France*, 105/28, Prior to Oxford, Dec. 29, 1712.

[52] *Stuart Papers*, I, 247, Queen Mary of Modena to William Dicconson, Chaillot, Oct. 1, 1712.

future I think you may depend upon it all will pass through M. de Torcy's hands.[53]

Nothing more was said to Prior about the dowry until after the peace negotiations were concluded. Then, in order to witness Queen Mary's signing the procuration, he and Torcy went in June to the convent at Chaillot, where the Queen had lived as a royal patroness since the death of her daughter, the Princess Marie Louise.[54]

Negotiations were still pending at the end of 1713 when Oxford sent over the final papers, and asked Prior to witness the signature. Although Oxford wrote that the papers were "such as our forms of law require," he mentioned no stipulations.[55] Characteristically, at the very time he was insisting in his secret negotiations with the son upon the one point to which James would not agree—a dissimulation or a change of religion —Oxford put into the papers two provisions to which the mother would not agree, namely that she renounce her arrears and recognize Anne as Queen. A memorial, worded so as to avoid angering either Queen Anne or Oxford, was given to Prior. It did not contain a flat refusal, but it set forth the unreasonableness, from Queen Mary's point of view, of insisting that she give in on these two points.[56] In June Torcy was dunning Prior for the dowry and almost tearfully urging not only the justice of the demand but also the dire necessity of Queen Mary.[57] The death of Anne, however, found the dowry still unpaid and the promises of both King William and Oxford unfulfilled—obligations for which the Hanoverians felt no responsibility.

From the records which deal with Prior's handling of these two matters, we now turn to the more important question—was or was not Prior implicated in the secret intrigue to overthrow

[53] *Ibid.*, 256, Berwick to James III, Feb. 24, 1713.
[54] *Ibid.*, Berwick to James III, Feb. 24, 1715.
[55] *Longleat Papers*, III, 444, Oxford to Prior, Jan. 16/27, 1713/14.
[56] *Stuart Papers*, II, 527, Mémoire, dated Feb. 1714.
[57] Strong, *Letters . . . at Welbeck*, p. 299, Prior to Oxford, Paris, June 1/12, 1714.

the Act of Settlement and restore the Pretender? In other words, was Prior a Jacobite? Certainly his well-remembered friendship with Jersey, his almost daily intercourse with Torcy, and his acquaintance with the other French notables, were all construed as presumptive evidence of friendliness toward the Pretender by the Whigs, who in 1715 hoped to find damaging proof in Prior's papers, not only against Prior but also against Oxford. They had even sent Jacob Tonson over to Paris in 1713 to spy on Prior.[58] But in all the correspondence which passed between Prior and his employers in London, there is no reference to the Pretender except that pertaining to his removal from Lorraine. For any mention of Prior in connection with Jacobite activities, we must turn to the *Stuart Papers* and to the documents in the Archives of the Ministry of Foreign Affairs in Paris.

From these papers we learn that as early as 1711, when Prior was at Fontainebleau, Richard Hamilton, Master of the Robes to the Pretender and young brother of the more famous Anthony Hamilton,[59] sounded him out on the attitude of the Tory ministry toward James. Prior spoke guardedly of the "good intentions" of the ministry, but assured Hamilton that "jamais on ne se fieroit à Mid[dleton.]"[60]

In retaining Middleton as Secretary of State—he had held the same office under James II—the Pretender antagonized the Jacobites in England, who thought Middleton responsible for the young Prince's tenacity to his religion. At the very end of December, 1712, Gaultier urged James III to dismiss his Secretary of State and substitute his Master of the Robes on the ground that Oxford and the English ministers distrusted Middleton and would not disclose their plans so long as he remained. James at once suspected that Gaultier's proposals emanated from

[58] Paris, Archives . . . , *Correspondance Politique, d'Angleterre*, 262, *Supplement*, Hooke to the Marquis d'Argenson, Versailles, May 2, 1714.

[59] Anthony Hamilton was court poet at Saint-Germain in the days of James II and was the author of *Mémoires de Grammont*.

[60] Paris, Archives . . . , *Correspondance Politique, d'Angleterre*, 248, fo. 35, James III to Torcy, Chalons, Jan. 5, 1713.

a cabal whose chief object was to elevate Hamilton at Middleton's expense. Middleton was willing to resign, but neither James nor his mother would permit him to do so. James then asked Torcy to find out through some channel other than Gaultier, whom he imagined to be too friendly to Hamilton, what Oxford and the English Jacobites really thought of Middleton, and further requested that Oxford send over from England someone worthy of confidence to act as his adviser if Middleton must go. James was resolved not to give the honor to Hamilton—in fact he had already dismissed Hamilton from his service. In consequence of Torcy's enquiries, the Duchess of Buckinghamshire wrote to Berwick, her brother, to ask if it were really true that James had rashly dismissed Hamilton and to state that the Protestant Jacobites in England were very much displeased, because they "could not suffer my Lord Middleton."[61] Whether or not Prior was implicated in any of these secret maneuvers to oust Middleton and place Hamilton in the chief post of influence is not at all clear. That Prior shared the general disapproval of Middleton is evidenced by his remark to Hamilton in 1711; furthermore, Gaultier twice alluded cryptically to Prior's antipathy to Middleton as expressed in conversations with Torcy during the winter of 1713.[62]

When Gaultier came over to Paris the following May, he consulted Prior about certain questions which the Pretender wanted reopened with Oxford only to find him loath to aid the Chevalier's cause:

Mr. Prior thinks it would not be proper for me to inform the treasurer of what Montgoulin [James III] has done in consequence of the memorandum I sent him on my arrival two months ago nor the orders which he sent to Scotland.[63]

D'Aumont, with ill-considered judgment, thought that Prior

[61] *Stuart Papers*, I, 260, Berwick to James III, Saint-Germain, March 19, 1713.
[62] Paris, Archives . . . , *Correspondance Politique, d'Angleterre*, 240, fo. 193, Gaultier to Torcy, Feb. 16, 1713, and *ibid.*, 248, fo. 225, Gaultier to Torcy, Feb. 28. 1713.
[63] *Ibid.*, 246, fo. 39, Gaultier to Torcy, Paris, July 12, 1713.

was dying of impatience to have Gaultier return to London lest Gaultier should learn too much; he also thought that Prior was imposing on Torcy's honesty by feigning zeal for the interests of the Pretender:

Mr. Prior, que vos connaissez meurt d'impatience que l'abbé Gaultier soit ici, non qu'il l'estime ni que l'abbé Gaultier l'aime mais il le croit susceptible des impressions qu'on voudra lui donner, pendant que de son côte il cherche à abuser de vos bontés se couvrant d'un zêle spécieux pour les intérêts du Chevalier de St. George . . .[64]

Torcy's explanation of Prior's attitude toward the Pretender is the more penetrating:

J'ajouterai que je ne vois nul empressement de la part de Prior pour faire retourner Gaultier en Angleterre, encore moins de démonstrations de zêle pour les intérêts du Chevalier de St. George. Je crois pour vous dire la vérité qu'en bon anglais il songe principalement à lui-même.[65]

After all, Prior had to look after his own neck. He might sympathize with the wretched plight of the Pretender, who could not go from Bar-le-duc to Nancy without setting astir all the ministers of Europe, but he was cold to any suggestions that he risk his fortunes in such a doubtful cause. From his position in Paris he could see the Pretender and his odd motley of followers—the adventurers, the priests, the women, the Irish, the Scotch—all at close range, and there was little to arouse his enthusiasm. Had James III possessed the personal magnetism of his uncle, Charles II, or even that of his own son, the Bonnie Prince, all might have been different. He was merely a good young man, too honest to dissemble or to change his religion, too obtuse to see through the duplicity of the ministers in London, who would not risk their heads in his cause. Living in exile from England, he was totally ignorant of the psychology of his people. When warned by Oxford and Torcy against his

---

[64] *Ibid.*, fo. 54, D'Aumont to Torcy, July 21, 1713.
[65] *Ibid.*, fo. 66, Torcy to D'Aumont, Marly, July 31, 1713.

favorite counselors, he rode a high horse, utterly failing to comprehend their motives.

In October, 1713, Prior spoke more freely than usual with Torcy concerning the Pretender, but it is plain that he was not to be drawn into any conspiracy. The Pretender found little satisfaction in Prior's counsels, which, like Oxford's spelled delay—he was advised to be patient and was reminded that time and his enemies (the Whigs) were on his side.[66] Again Prior counseled delay, when in March, 1714, Berwick, disgusted with Oxford's "dark and incomprehensible ways," made a proposal to go himself to England to work for James III. Prior put Berwick off by promising to think it over and by suggesting that he defer his journey until Parliament should be prorogued[67]—certainly most unfavorable advice, since Queen Anne did not prorogue Parliament until July 9, just three weeks before her death.

From the very beginning, Prior had avoided identification with the Pretender's supporters. At Fontainebleau in 1711, while that most ardent of all Jacobites, Jersey, was still living, Gaultier had warned Torcy not to mention the Pretender to Prior, from which admonition we conclude that Prior did not share his friend's Jacobite leanings.[68] Thereafter all secret communications with James III passed through the hands of Gaultier and Torcy. Gaultier continued to urge Torcy not to mention Jacobite intrigue to Prior. Thus when Gaultier first announced that Bolingbroke had begun to work in the interest of the Pretender, he took care to inform Torcy:

Il ne faut pas s'il vous plaist que M. Prior sache rien de tout cecy, car il me semble que M. de Bolingbroke luy en veut faire un mistère.[69]

Furthermore, when the secret communications were at their

---

[66] *Ibid.*, 250, fo. 23, Torcy to James III, Versailles, Oct. 29, 1713.

[67] *Stuart Papers*, I, 307, 308, Berwick to James III, March 13, 1714, March 18, 1714.

[68] Paris, Archives . . . , *Correspondance Politique, d'Angleterre*, 233, fo. 47, Torcy's memorandum, dated July 21, 1711.

[69] *Ibid.*, 240, fo. 82, Gaultier to Torcy, London, October 12, 1712.

height, when Oxford was laying down the indispensable condition that James must either dissimulate or change his religion, Gaultier warned Torcy: "Matthieu doit absolument ignorer tout cecy."[70] And when after James had sent his refusal, and all hopes for a Stuart Restoration were dashed to the ground, Gaultier in despair sought confirmation of his fears from Prior:

Prenez s'il vous plaist la peine, Monseigneur, de demander à M. Prior ce qu'il en pense et s'il croit que le Chevalier demeurant Catholique pourra jamais monter sur le Trosne.[71]

Prior's reply to this query is not recorded. But in January, 1715, when the Whigs had taken everything from him, even his position in the Customs, and he might be pardoned for sympathizing with the Jacobites, Prior evaded their approaches by maintaining that James must embrace Protestantism—a contingency most improbable.[72]

Further evidence that Prior was no Jacobite is to be found in a comparison of the respective attitudes of Bolingbroke and Oxford towards him. Bolingbroke, impatient with Oxford's vacillation in the Stuart cause and determined to man the government with Jacobites, desired, as we have seen, to replace Prior with Ross, a devoted Jacobite whom the Pretender characterized as "mon unique soutien après Dieu." Bolingbroke's impatience was warranted, for, from the beginning, misfortunes had befallen the cause. The Duke of Hamilton's sudden death removed one of the Pretender's most influential followers. Before accepting the post of Ambassador, Hamilton had asked and obtained the Pretender's sanction.[73] Then the Duke of Shrewsbury,

[70] *Ibid.*, 253, fo. 268, Gaultier to Torcy, London, Feb. 5, 1714.

[71] *Ibid.*, 254, fo. 229, Gaultier to Torcy, March 19, 1714.

[72] *Stuart Papers*, I, 342, Berwick to James III, St. Germain, Jan. 6, 1715: "I had a long discourse with M. Pecour [Prior], but he insisted so much upon M. Robinson's [James III] making up with M. Pery [? Protestantism] that I could bring him to no conclusion favorable for this present time."

[73] Paris, Archives . . . , *Correspondance Politique, d'Angleterre*, 239, fo. 3, Gaultier to Torcy, London, July 2, 1712. The secret object of Hamilton's embassy, so the Jacobites affirmed, was to treat for James's succession to the throne, provided that Queen Anne were left in possession during her lifetime. Martin Haile, *Queen Mary of Modena*, p. 436.

in the face of Bolingbroke's opposition,[74] was appointed. Since Lady Middleton was Shrewsbury's aunt, the Jacobites at Saint-Germain hoped to win the Duke over to their side, but they were disappointed. Shrewsbury scrupulously refused to see any of the leading Jacobites in Paris, not even Berwick or his own aunt, lest he might "give the least suspicion of an inclination to that Court."[75] Then, upon Shrewsbury's resignation, Oxford, playing his double game of pacifying the Jacobites at home while hindering their activities in France, retained Prior in Paris despite Bolingbroke's protest.

Oxford's confidence in his "véritable ami, Monsieur Prior"[76] was not misplaced. During two difficult years Prior firmly but tactfully repulsed all efforts to draw him into Jacobite intrigue. To be a Tory was not necessarily to be a Jacobite, and we believe that Prior, no matter how violently he hated the Whigs, would have agreed with Swift that the coming of the Pretender would be a "greater evil than we are likely to suffer under the worst Whig ministry that can be found."[77] Also we have Matt's own word that he would as soon "be thought a Mahumetan as a Jacobite."[78]

» 4 «

In the midst of his worries of state, Prior had to give ear to exasperating importunities of the companions of his light moments. The beauties, it seems, formed a conspiracy against poor Matt, since each day produced a woman with a whim, which no one but the Plenipotentiary could satisfy. The Duchess of Noailles teased him to get her an Irish greyhound, even appealing to King Louis to speak to Prior about it. She wheedled

[74] Cobbett's *Parliamentary History*, VII, xciv. Lord Oxford's Letter to the Queen, June 9, 1714.

[75] Duke of Shrewsbury, *Life and Character*, p. 12.

[76] *Catalogue of the Morrison Collection of MSS*, 148, Oxford to Torcy, London, August 12, 1712.

[77] Swift, *Correspondence*, II, 349, Swift to Archbishop King, Dec. 16, 1716.

[78] P. R. O., *State Papers, France*, 105/29, Prior to Halifax, Paris, Oct. 12/23, 1714.

and wheedled until Prior, though vexed over the expense and the trouble, requested Shrewsbury, now Lord Lieutenant of Ireland, to procure a dog for her.[79] The Tencin sisters, who wanted their brother made a bishop, insisted that Prior's influence would be indispensable to their cause. Lady Oxford's plea was different but just as strong—Prior must purchase for her a scarf, of which Madame de Maintenon had "the fellow"; and several unnamed admirers besought him to order English fans for them. To add to these petty bothers, there was a bit of gossip to be checked. A rumor about Prior's relations with a nun was spread abroad by a certain ship captain, who had evidently heard gossip about the friendship with Madame de Tencin. Irritated over the rumor, Prior communicated with Bolingbroke, asking him to inform the Queen that her Plenipotentiary in Paris knew not "one word of nuns, blue, grey, or any colour whatever."[80]

More annoying was the decision of the Duchess of Portsmouth to visit England. Over forty years had passed since Charles II had become enamored with one of his sister's maids of honor, a young Breton girl with a "pretty baby face," and had set her up as a reigning sultana at Whitehall. In the letters which passed between Prior and Bolingbroke neither spoke in terms of gallantry of the former reigning beauty, nor did they encourage her visit.

The Duchess of Portsmouth thinks she is mightily beloved in England, not remembering that an Anachronism of forty years, makes a great difference as well in love as politics. She plagues my soul out about her coming to England, and I believe you will have your share of her importunities by her proxy there.[81]

The spoiled old woman was persistent, but Prior was firm with

---

[79] *Ibid.*, 105/29, fo. 50, Prior to Shrewsbury, Paris, Jan. 15/26, 1714.

[80] *Ibid.*, fo. 93, Prior to Bolingbroke, Paris, March 19/30, 1714.

[81] Bolingbroke, *Letters and Correspondence*, IV, 376, Prior to Bolingbroke, Nov. 12/23, 1713.

her, and it was not until the beginning of the Hanoverian régime that she made a journey to England.

The troubles Prior had with the aforementioned ladies, however, were mere trifles compared with the disturbance that Lady Jersey caused him. News of an impending visit from her reached Prior's ears, and the distraught Plenipotentiary immediately passed on his fears to Bolingbroke:

I hear by chance that little widow Jersey designs to come to France; cela ne vaut pas; le diable, empêchez-la, my lord, de le faire autant que vous pouvez.[82]

The "little widow" refused to be balked in her plans, even by Lady Masham, or by Lord Bolingbroke, who took a special interest in the affair, since he was related by blood to the Villiers family. According to rumor, she had sold all her late lord's effects, seized every farthing that should have been used to pay his heavy debts, and had run away to France with her youngest son, Henry Villiers, brother to the "Child of Quality" and a scholar at the Westminster School, whom she aimed to make a Roman Catholic priest. At once there was a furor among the Whigs; the news even reached Hanover, where it was regarded as an open manifestation of the ministry's adherence to the cause of the Pretender. The Whigs were ready to introduce a law preventing Jacobite women from taking their children to France. For these reasons a considerable amount of diplomatic correspondence in the Public Record Office in London and the *Archives des Affaires Étrangères* in Paris is concerned with an affair which appears today to have been of only slight significance.

Lady Jersey reached Paris, unhindered—"shot like the brisk lightning in the *Rehearsal*,"[83] to quote Prior. At once Prior tried to see her, but she avoided him entirely. Every day she

---

[82] *Ibid.*, 323, Prior to Bolingbroke, Paris, Oct. 6/17, 1713.

[83] P. R. O., *State Papers, France*, 78/157, fo. 327. Prior to Bolingbroke, Paris, Oct. 16/17, 1713. Cf. *The Rehearsal*, Act I. Scene I: *Thunder*: I am the bold Thunder. *Lightning*: The brisk Lightning.

took the boy into the country to the house of an abbé, under the pretext of caring for his health. Such conduct threw Prior into a panic. Sooner or later, he was certain, she would become involved in Jacobite intrigue, and the conversion of the son of his close friend Lord Jersey would prove an embarrassment to him:

You say right that you imagine this Medea will give us all trouble, nothing can give more: She sighs and cries; but I know her sighs to be wind, and her tears to be water. The little devil! Her husband had once a knife in his hand to go and kill her; what a puppy was I to hinder him. Adieu, my dear Lord. God keep us all from such wives, and above all, from such widows.[84]

Day after day Prior attempted to see the Countess, but she refused to see him, or Drift, or any other member of his household. When she went to the King's supper, Prior stayed away, since she was in France without the Queen's leave. On two occasions, he saw her in the company of others, but she would not converse with him alone. At last, after frequent calls on her when she was "not at home, or at table, or *en campagnie*," he broke down her resistance and told her he must see her privately, because his duty to the Queen, his orders from the ministry, his long and real friendship with her family obliged him to.

Prior did not find her in a conciliatory mood. She was ready to combat him as an enemy rather than treat with him as a friend and gave evasive answers to all his questions. Shaken out of her denials, she declared between her tears that she would accuse no one, was sorry that the Queen was angry with her, and that she could not imagine that "such a poor woman as herself was worth all this bustle." Still Prior could not swerve her from her purpose—to throw herself upon the French Court and to make her son a Roman Catholic.[85]

[84] Bolingbroke, *Letters and Correspondence*, IV, 373, Prior to Bolingbroke, Paris, Oct. 20/Nov. 1, 1713.
[85] P. R. O., *State Papers, France*, 78/157, Prior to Bolingbroke, Nov. 1, 1713.

Finally Prior decided that pressure must be brought upon the French Court. Both Oxford and Bolingbroke must write to Torcy, every Lord of the Cabinet must protest to Iberville, and Sir Thomas Hanmer must warn Iberville that every Roman Catholic in England might "suffer for the sake of the silliest woman that ever told a pair of beads."[86]

While he waited for action in England, Prior spoke to Torcy about the child. He had himself seen the boy "baptized in the Church of England" when "the late King, the late Earl of Rochester and the Duchess of Somerset stood witnesses to it"; the lad was confirmed in the religion of his country, and had been educated at Westminster, a school founded by a Queen of England. "Reflect," Prior admonished Torcy, "how it will look if any attempt should be made upon his religion, and what consequences it may produce to those of your religion in England."[87] Torcy was embarrassed when Prior insisted that the child must be sent back to England. A devout Catholic, he was wholeheartedly inclined to encourage Lady Jersey and to sympathize with her in her encounters with Prior, whom she now called "mon plus grand ennemy." Furthermore, Lady Jersey had given him to understand that the Queen was not aroused, and that it was Prior who had stirred up all the trouble against her.

Unjustly, although naturally enough, Prior suspected Gaultier of "tampering in this Jersean flight, for which he ought to be hanged,"[88] and wrote to the abbé hinting at his suspicion. Very soon a reply from the abbé, sternly disapproving of the lady's conduct, satisfied Prior that his suspicions were wrong.[89]

Armed with the letters that he had received from England, Prior was determined to prove to Torcy that he was not the

[86] Bolingbroke, *Letters and Correspondence*, IV, 450, Prior to Bolingbroke, Versailles, Jan. 21/Feb. 1, 1714.

[87] P. R. O., *State Papers, France*, 78/157, Prior to Bolingbroke, Paris, Nov. 1, 1714.

[88] Bolingbroke, *Letters and Correspondence*, IV, 374, Prior to Bolingbroke, Paris, Nov. 1, 1713.

[89] Maggs Bros. *Catalogue*, 547, Prior to Gaultier, Paris, December 14, 1713. The letter is in response to one from Gaultier, London, Nov. 20.

boutefeu that Lady Jersey had represented him to be. Since his last interview with Prior, Torcy had himself received a letter from Gaultier, telling of the displeasure of both the Queen and of Oxford with Lady Jersey. The Lord Treasurer, Gaultier said, was convinced that Lady Jersey was "fausse, fourbe et menteuse," and that if Torcy did not take care, she would make mischief between him and his friends. As for himself, Gaultier was chagrined to speak evil of a woman in whom he had thought all virtue and purity resided.[90]

Finally Torcy was convinced that Lady Jersey had stirred up an international problem. He promised Prior to see her, to learn if the child wished to return to Westminster School, and, if so, to arrange for his return.

Again Prior saw Lady Jersey, and after a battle which lasted three hours—"the most tragi-comical encounter I ever sustained"—he left the "poor woman" in a flood of tears, rather terrified than convinced by all he had said. The particulars, he confided to Bolingbroke, must be reserved to be related personally, for it was impossible for him to describe them. The mother still refused to let the child out of her sight, but Prior cleverly managed to have a secret message given to him, telling him what to say in the interview with Torcy. He was to say that he thought France a very fine country, but he would go to no school but Westminster; that he loved Lady Jersey as his mother, but that he had a higher duty to the Queen, who was the mother of his country; in short that he would go home.[91]

Prior has been accused of seeking to undermine the mother's influence. Perhaps, but the boy received from that freethinker, Bolingbroke, a letter similar in tone and content though more unctuous: "You owe something to yourself, and infinitely more . . . to God; You will find a way of saving yourself easy, and

[90] Paris, Archives . . . , *Correspondance Politique, d'Angleterre*, 247, fo. 167, Gaultier to Torcy, London, Dec. 22, 1713.

[91] P. R. O., *State Papers, France*, 78/157, Prior to Bolingbroke, Paris, Dec. 14, 1713.

you will in such manner as Mr. Prior shall direct, escape to his house, from which care will be immediately taken to bring you home. Mr. Prior has the Queen's orders to this effect."[92]

At last, Torcy, having received orders from Louis XIV, saw the boy, who glibly repeated what Prior had outlined for him. Lady Jersey had to surrender. The child was no longer a "prisoner." Prior, who was allowed to "converse with him and to show him Paris," not only bought him a new wardrobe but also supplied him with "a Common Prayer Book in French, a Latin Bible, and a Mons Testament," resolved to send him home a good "little Church of England man."[93] The conclusion was that Prior joyfully returned to the ministers in London "our little Westminster Scholar, who is the bravest boy alive."

After the departure of Henry Villiers for England, Prior often invited Lady Jersey to dinners given for the English nobility and gentry in Paris. Now that she had "humbled herself to the Queen," Prior declared that he and Lady Jersey "were the greatest friends alive." But without his knowledge she became involved in Jacobite intrigue. In May she applied to him for a passport to return to England with the expectation of carrying messages from James III to Hanmer and Queen Anne. There was a hint that she might try to persuade Bolingbroke and other Jacobite leaders "not to insist so peremptorily" on the Pretender's changing his religion.[94] Although Prior urged that she be allowed to make the trip on the grounds that the French were tired of her,[95] permission was not granted her, and Berwick seems to have concluded that she was not the best agent to use. She stayed on in Paris after the accession of George I, "always dining and supping with the top people," ambitious to be

[92] Bolingbroke, *Letters and Correspondence*, IV, 416, Bolingbroke to Henry Villiers, Windsor Castle, Dec. 31, 1713.

[93] P. R. O., *State Papers, France*, 78/158, Prior to Bolingbroke, Feb. 16/27, 1714.

[94] *Stuart Papers*, I, 314, Berwick to James III, St. Germain, April 8, 1714.

[95] Bolingbroke, *Letters and Correspondence*, IV, 546, Prior to Bolingbroke, Paris, May 7/18, 1714.

thought knowing and useful,[96] boasting of her imagined influence in England, and hating Prior to the very end.

» 5 «

News of the serious illness of the Queen and of the growing dissensions between Oxford and Bolingbroke at the beginning of 1714 so filled Prior with apprehensions and misgivings that he became panic-stricken and was in a state similar to that visualized by Thackeray in *Esmond* in the famous chapter on the Wits: "Mr. Prior, I saw, and he was the earthen pot swimming with the pots of brass down the stream, and always and justly frightened lest he should break in the voyage." But there is a bit of self-analysis which is more significant:

So much do my own fears naturally outweigh my joys, or plainer, so much am I rather a coward than a hero. Good God! what a thousand things have I thought since I received your letter; if that should happen which one hates to think of, what is to become of us? What sort or set of men are to be our taskmasters? And what sluices are we provided with to save Great Britain from being overflowed? After what would become of us all? The thought I grant you is very mean, what would become of me? But humanity is frail and querulous: if the prospect, therefore, of this evil (though I hope far removed) be dreadful to the masters of Mortemar Castle, Hinton St. George, Stanton Harcourt, or Bucklebury, what must it be to friend Matt . . .[97]

Other rumors, still more disquieting, led Prior again to appeal frantically to Bolingbroke: "For God's sake, my Lord, how do you all do, in your enchanted island? for the stories we have here, of your irresolutions and misunderstandings are monstrous."[98] Meanwhile, *bannisons la mélancholie!* He must "dissemble, under a face, not handsome but seemingly pleased enough, a heart melancholy enough" so that the French Court

[96] *Stuart Papers*, VI, 525, Sheldon to the Duke of Mar, Paris, June 14, 1718.

[97] Bolingbroke, *Letters and Correspondence*, IV, 446, Prior to Bolingbroke, Paris, January 7/18, 1714.

[98] *Ibid.*, 463, Prior to Bolingbroke, Paris, January 29/February 9, 1714.

would be convinced that Gaultier's alarms and their own apprehensions were groundless—a strategy not easy to accomplish
when such a skeptic as Buys, now Dutch Ambassador to Paris,
showed plainly by his incredulous smile that he did not believe a
word Prior said.

By way of keeping up the illusion of cheerfulness, Prior entertained lavishly and often. To a brilliant dinner, he invited the
Torcys, Torcy's mother and sister, other members of the Colbert
clan, Cardinal Polignac, the Princesse d'Espinay, the Duchess of
Portsmouth, and Lady Jersey.[99] He arranged for Albergotti,
then the rage of Parisian society, to sing, and everything passed
off "a l'honneur de l'Angleterre." On the Queen's birthday—her
last—fifty-two of the English gentlemen in Paris joined Prior
in honoring the occasion; and the entertainment, as fully described in the social columns of the *Mercure Galant*, was magnificent. The entire day was devoted to the celebration, the
principal healths being drunk to the accompaniment of English
trumpets and timbals. There were three tables of guests presided
over by Richard, Karnworth, and Prior, respectively. Following
the dinner there was a fine concert by Albergotti, who was again
the star attraction. When it grew dark, illuminations and bonfires were lighted; and just before the party broke up, a light
supper was served, at which toasts were drunk to the Queen, to
the peace, to Parliament, and, as a final flourish, to an eternal
correspondance between England and France.

Prior's zest for entertainment seemed unlimited—no holiday
was overlooked. On St. George's Day the English nobility and
gentry were again lavishly feasted; on St. Andrew's, the Scot-
tish. The recent death of the Duke of Berry made the merrymaking on St. George's Day less noisy, for violins and English
trumpets were dispensed with out of respect for the royal family,
but in every other way the affair was "all very magnificent and

---

[99] P. R. O., *State Papers, France*, 105/29, Prior to Oxford, Paris, March 7, 1714.

perhaps . . . too expensive."[100] Qualms concerning the cost of all this entertaining were not unwarranted, because in due time the Lord Treasurer would be hearing from Cantillon, the Paris banker. Heedless of his own misgivings and of the increasingly alarming news of the Queen's illness, Prior continued to conceal his heavy heart by throwing himself into these social duties, as well as into the business, of an ambassador.

That he was sincerely tired of the folly of it all and longed to be released is only too evident in a letter to Oxford:

I really am ashamed and weary of spending the Queen's money, reckoning only upon the day when you will be pleased to recall me from this Midsummer Night's Dream, in which amidst all my parade and attendance, a prince to every man else, to myself I look so like the cobbler of Shakespeare's describing—but I submit myself to you, my Lord, observing only that you are wanting to your service, till you make some provision for that life, which most certainly must be dedicated to your commands.[101]

And so the winter months passed and early spring came bringing no change in Prior's fortunes but ever increasing anxiety. By May new rumors spread about the French Court that Monsieur Prior would soon return to England. As he received no official message to confirm the report, his position was most embarrassing. His personal affairs, he realized, were but a mere bagatelle compared to the difficulties the ministers were experiencing in England, but he could not help dwelling on his own fate. Must he go back, after all, to St. John's College and his fellowship? Bitterly he complained of Oxford's neglect to provide for him:

Torcy put me quite out of countenance the other day by a pity that wounded me deeper than ever did the cruelty of the late Lord Godolphin; he said he would write to Robin and Harry about me; God forbid my Lord, that I should need any foreign intercession, or owe the least

---

[100] Bolingbroke, *Letters and Correspondence*, IV, 539, Prior to Bolingbroke, Paris, April 24/May 5, 1714.

[101] P. R. O., *State Papers, France*, 105/29, fo. 59, Prior to Oxford, Jan. 29/Feb. 9, 1714.

to any Frenchman living, besides decency of behavior, and the returns of common civility.[102]

Prior begged Torcy not to communicate with Oxford in his behalf; instead he himself sent a plea calculated to get action from anyone less phlegmatic than the Lord Treasurer:

. . . before I leave France you will please to confer on Me what Her Majesty's Goodness and your choice think proper for Me, and that when I take my leave of the King and Court I may convince them that I have not behaved my Self so here, as to be look't upon as a Cast-away at home: and that those who have employed Me do at least dare to own Me: this, if it were in any body's case but my own, I would affirm to be for the Queen's Interest, and your honour; and as the report of my being shortly to be recalled is gott abroad, I own to you I begin to look very simply already that mons^r. Prior, the English Plenipotentiary, my Lord Treasurer's *supposed* Friend can only say he is going back again to the place from whence He came,—if you would not have Me confounded to death, my Lord, you will enable Me to give the Curious with whom I must converse here a more positive Answer: you know I am your Servant for life, why therefore will you defer to make that life easy to Me?

. . . oncè more I begg you that I may be enabled to say and to prove here that I am not disgraced nor abandoned but called home to SOMETHING.

Adieu, my Lord, that God may bless you and yours for ever is the prayer of your at present very melancholy and dejected Servant.[103]

Daily the relations between the ministers in England grew more strained. Bolingbroke wrote less frequently and in a cold businesslike tone, while Oxford wrote not at all; there were, however, always the *Gazettes*, as well as the dispatches from Iberville and Gaultier, to paint the picture as black as possible. The "properest person"[104] for reconciling the two ministers,

---

[102] Bolingbroke, *Letters and Correspondence*, IV, 542, Prior to Bolingbroke, Paris, May 1/12, 1714.

[103] Strong, *Letters . . . at Welbeck*, p. 85, Prior to Oxford, Paris, May 1/12, 1714.

[104] *An Enquiry into the Behavior of the Queen's Last Ministry*, Swift's *Works*, Temple Scott Edition, V, 445.

Swift declared, was Prior had he not been absent in France. All that Prior could do from a distance was to write diplomatically to both men telling them that the breach between them was the subject of much talk in Paris; that his duty to the Queen and his sincere friendship for them obliged him to give warning that the Queen's service and their honor were suffering in consequence of their actions. "Who is in the wrong, or who is in the right is not in my power at this distance to determine,"[105] was the tactful conclusion of his epistle to Bolingbroke.

Such remonstrance, at this late date, was of no avail. Oxford gave up the White Staff on July 27 and left the field to his enemies, whom he accused of corruption. The Queen's health rapidly grew worse. Prior lived in a constant state of suspense, for every report from England brought increasingly disturbing news. He admitted that he was distraught, that he could not write common sense, that he was woefully upset over the Lord Treasurer's dismissal—yet all was "swallowed in the cruel contemplation of the Queen's death."[106]

As we have seen, Prior had avoided taking sides in the quarrel between his two friends, although he owed everything to Oxford, who had sent him to Paris, and practically nothing to Bolingbroke, who had become exceedingly distant during the previous few weeks. But when Bolingbroke forced Oxford out of office, Prior was only too willing to declare fealty to the new power. If Prior's ethics seem dubious, it must be remembered that one's loyalties are often confused when self-interest is at stake. Hence while "still in the sad incertitude or rather mortal apprehension" of what was happening in England, Prior pledged himself to Bolingbroke with these extravagant and somewhat incoherent words:

While you continue to act, as you have hitherto done, for the safety

---

[105] Bolingbroke, *Letters and Correspondence*, IV, Prior to Bolingbroke, July 27/Aug. 7, 1714.

[106] P. R. O., *State Papers, France*, 78/159, Prior to Bolingbroke, Paris, Aug. 13, 1714.

and honour of your country, I will abandon you and life at the same time.[107]

Prior's eagerness to support the Secretary was not put to the test, as Bolingbroke's victory lasted only two days.

During Queen Anne's last days Iberville had written almost hourly bulletins of her condition to dispatch to the French Court. Slowly these reports began to come through the mails, and finally official announcement of her death on August the first arrived. Through Torcy, Prior learned with a sinking heart all that had happened during those last days: of the landing of Marlborough, of the appointment of the urbane but ineffectual Shrewsbury as Lord Treasurer, of the proclamation in favor of the Elector of Hanover, of the triumph of the Whigs and the downfall of the Tories, of the appalling inability of the panic-stricken Bolingbroke to grasp his opportunities.[108]

Matt's worst fears were realized. The "best of Queens" had died. A Whig ministry had come into power, and he was left in Paris in a very uncomfortable situation. Moreover, he knew that this was no ordinary change of ministry. There would be reprisals.

[107] Brit. Mus., *Stowe MSS*, 242, fo. 160, Prior to Bolingbroke, Aug. 17, 1714.

[108] Paris, Archives . . . , *Correspondance Politique, d'Angleterre*, 257, fo. 277, Torcy to Prior, Versailles, Aug. 6/17, 1714. Torcy concluded his letter by saying, "Je vous prie d'etre persuade qu'independamment de l'intérêt public je prends beaucoup de part à ce qui vous touche en cette occasion et je suis très parfaitement, etc."

CHAPTER XI

The Secret Committee

» 1 «

PHYSICALLY weary from the long strain and heartsick over
the sad news, Prior set out for Versailles on Monday morning
of August 9/20 to make formal announcement of the "death of
the Queen of ever blessed memory and of the happy accession"
of His Majesty George I.[1] He found King Louis in a receptive
mood, warm in his expressions of sympathy for the loss of the
Queen, and ready with assurances of his desire to keep the peace
which he had made with her and which she had labored to accomplish. Soon after this visit Prior was touched to see the old
monarch wearing lavender bands—mourning *en violet* it was.

On the same Monday Prior sent to King George a congratulatory epistle, couched in an appropriately elegant style and containing an avowal of loyalty to the new sovereign.[2] The King,
reluctant to leave his beloved Hanover and somewhat loath to
take up his new responsibilities, did not hasten to England.
Prior continued to send letters to the King at Hanover.[3] This
move was somewhat unwise in that it offended certain persons
in London who thought that the dispatches should have been
sent to them first.[4] King George, however, saw nothing amiss,
and acknowledged the communications in so "gracious and
benign" a manner that Prior was emboldened to send him news

[1] *Gazette de France*, Aug. 25, 1714.
[2] P. R. O., *State Papers, France*, 78/159, Prior to George I, Aug. 9/20, 1714.
[3] See *ibid.*, for letters dated August 12/23, Sept. 10/21, and Sept. 17/28, 1714; also *ibid.*,
105/29, for letters dated Sept. 2/13, and Sept. 5/16, 1714.
[4] *Portland Papers*, V, 493, News letter, Sept. 4, 1714.

of the Pretender's movements since the death of Queen Anne. The Pretender had come incognito to Paris, Prior said, but King Louis had refused to see him. Torcy had been commissioned to tell James that Louis considered such conduct extraordinary, that he would not take a single step calculated to plunge Europe into another war, and that he advised James's immediate withdrawal. Crestfallen, the Chevalier had retired at once.[5] If this letter raises again the question of Prior's Jacobite sympathies, it may be cited, we think, as one more proof of his innocence.

One of the first moves of the Lords Regents, who were in control of affairs until the King should arrive, was to appoint Addison as their secretary. He was directed to begin an examination of the foreign correspondence for months past. The Regents, or Lords Justices, were bent on gathering evidence for the reprisals Prior had foreseen. Addison very soon discovered that there had been on foot a proposal for the alliance between England, France, Spain, and Sicily. This the Whigs interpreted as a design against their old allies—the Emperor, the Dutch, and the "most serene House of Hanover."[6] Prior was ordered to suspend all negotiations relating to this alliance,[7] while Bolingbroke, who was now taking orders from the irate Lords Regents, was requested to submit his letter books. Since Bolingbroke had, however, either hidden or destroyed all correspondence of a compromising nature, Addison wrote peremptorily to Prior:

I am commanded by the Lords Justices to acquaint you that their Excellencies are very much surprised to find from you such a very imperfect intelligence of what has passed in the Court of France since the Death of the late Queen, and do not know how to account for it. Their Excellencies have therefore ordered me to send one of Her Majesty's messengers express to you with this letter in which I am commanded to signify their pleasure that you acquaint them at what time you

---

[5] P. R. O., *State Papers, France*, 78/159, Prior to George I, Aug. 12/23, 1714.

[6] *Political State of Great Britain*, VIII, 141, London, 1714.

[7] P. R. O., *State Papers, France*, 105/28, Bolingbroke to Prior, Whitehall, Aug. 3/14, 1714.

received the news of her Late Majesty's death and that you deliver to him the copies of such letters as you have written to the Secretaries of State or to any others in the Ministry since the eighth of August N. S. that they may be laid before the Lords Justices for their information in points which are of so great consequence to the peace and safety of these kingdoms.[8]

Prior was stunned and bewildered by this reprimand. Why did they accuse him of having sent "imperfect intelligence" to the home office? He had written frequently and copiously to Bolingbroke and had no way of knowing that the fallen secretary might be withholding the dispatches from the proper authorities of the new régime. The more Matt pondered the matter, the more he was puzzled; but he hastened to appease the Regents by replying to Addison's letter on the very day he received it. As soon as he could make them, he assured Addison, he would send copies of the five letters which he had addressed to Bolingbroke, the two to Shrewsbury, the one "rather jovial than serious" to Oxford.[9] Two days later the copies were on their way.[10] Prior breathed more easily and turned his attention to a minor difficulty, a bit of negligence on the part of the Paris *Gazette*.

In the *Gazette*'s announcement of the death of the Queen, mention of the Elector of Hanover as King of Great Britain had been omitted. Prior blamed the omission on the Introductor, St. Jost, whose duty it was to report to the journals the substance of all audiences between the King and the envoys from foreign countries. St. Jost, moreover, had been especially requested to give the editor of the *Gazette* an accurate account of Prior's very important audience with Louis on that unhappy Monday morning.[11] The editor gladly made amends in the issue of the

---

[8] Brit. Mus., *Add. MSS*, 40, 621, fo. 244, Addison to Prior, St. James's, Aug. 14, 1714.
[9] P. R. O., *State Papers, France*, 105/29, fo. 181, Prior to Addison, Paris, Aug. 18/29, 1714.
[10] *Ibid.*, Prior to Addison, Paris, Aug. 20/31, 1714. On the same day he wrote Bolingbroke that he had sent copies of all letters since August 8 to the Lords Regents as directed.
[11] *Ibid.*, fo. 186, Prior to the Lords Regents, Paris, Aug. 20/31, 1714.

following week, and Prior punctiliously sent to Addison a corrected copy of the *Gazette* containing the proper announcement[12]—another evidence that he was eager to set himself right with the Lords Regents even though the price was subservience to Addison, for whom he had a decided aversion.

Prior's correspondence with Addison and the Lords Regents terminated when "a good Protestant wind" carried George I across the channel to be duly crowned at Westminster on September 20, at which time the Regents relinquished their powers.[13] Addison, who had expected that the honor of being secretary to the Regents would herald for him a Secretaryship of State—he had nearly killed himself with hard work, he complained—now had to stand aside and see the two secretaryships go to men of sterner stuff—the blunt, gruff, hot-tempered Stanhope and the brusque, arrogant, stubborn Townshend.

With such men, Louis's protestations of eagerness to abide by all treaties went for naught. They distrusted Louis and were determined to undo Bolingbroke's alliance with France. Much irresponsible talk of war was in the air. Rumors spread that Marlborough would soon set out for Vienna to patch up the old alliance between England, Holland, and Austria.[14] The French were inclined to trust George I, but were convinced that he was governed by a group of Whigs whose chief aim was another war with France.[15] "The conflagration seems to increase," wrote Torcy to the Princesse des Ursins. "I know not to what point it will attain if the British government remains any longer in the hands of people animated against France."[16] Nor was his alarm dispelled when Prior presented new demands from his Whig masters concerning the treatment of the Catalans, the ex-

12 *Ibid.*, Prior to Addison, Paris, Aug. 21/Sept. 1, 1714.

13 Prior's last letter to Addison is dated from Fontainebleau, Sept. 10/21, 1714.

14 Paris, Archives . . . , *Correspondance Politique, d'Angleterre*, 259, fo. 20, Iberville to Louis XIV, Oct. 1, 1714. It was Stanhope, not Marlborough, who undertook the errand on Oct. 21.

15 *Ibid.*, fo. 82, Iberville to Torcy, Oct. 16, 1714.

16 Tremoille, *Madame des Ursins*, VI, 221, letter dated Aug. 23, 1714.

pulsion of the Pretender from Lorraine, the demolition of Dunkirk—those important matters about which the Whig ministers felt that Bolingbroke had been too negligent.

Although Louis pretended that he was resolved to maintain peace with the new King of England, he solemnly protested to Prior that he had done all that the treaties required of him. About one matter, he was adamant. When Iberville, after Stanhope had threatened war if the Dunkirk question were not settled to his satisfaction, reported to his royal master that the "port of Mardyck is at present the *grand cheval de bataille* of the Whigs,"[17] Louis replied with a touch of his old spirit, "Si l'on cherche en Angleterre des prétextes frivoles pour renouveler la guerre, je saurai trouver les moyens de la soutenir."[18]

Consequently Prior's frequent demands made at Fontainebleau during the autumn of 1714 met with no success. After a tiresome repetition of conferences with Torcy, who always put him off with evasive answers, Prior drew up a memorial which he presented to King Louis on October 23, declaring that "when ships can go to Dunkirk by the old canal . . . or by the new . . . Dunkirk will in the same manner be a fort, and be equally incommodious and dangerous to the commerce of Great Britain. In either of these two cases the treaty of Utrecht will be violated." This document, along with the French King's answer, was widely published, not only in England but also in France and Holland.[19] It prompted in London the publication of a six-penny pamphlet, *Reasons for War with France*, a mischievous attempt to fan the flames of ill feeling between the two nations. Again, in Novem-

---

[17] Paris, Archives . . . , *Correspondance Politique, d'Angleterre*, 259, fo. 12, Iberville to Louis XIV, London, Oct. 3, 1714.

[18] *Ibid.*, fo. 57, Louis XIV to Iberville, Oct. 17, 1714.

[19] It is to be found not only in *ibid.*, fo. 175, but also in *La Gazette d'Amsterdam, Le Mercure historique et politique* and in the *Political State of Great Britain* (Nov. 1714) as well as in pamphlet form both in Holland and in England. A rare collector's item is A Memorial Delivered by Mr. Prior, Envoy-Extraordinary of His Brittanick Majesty, to His Most Christian Majesty against the Fortifying the Ports and Harbours of Dunkirk and Mardike. London; printed, and sold by J. Harrison; A. Dodd; and E. Burleigh. 1715.

ber, Prior attacked Torcy about Dunkirk. Torcy countered that all cause for complaint had been remedied; whereupon Prior retorted that he was "perfectly weary of these sort of answers" and that he was impatient to have the substance of his demands laid before King Louis.[20] By December, there came a lull in the negotiations, partly because Stanhope was away in Vienna, and partly because it was expected that the next move would be made by Stair, already named as Prior's successor. As a matter of fact, when Stair, who belittled Prior's efforts, presented his own memorial, he made no more progress than Matt had made. So long as Louis XIV lived, none but evasive answers were received. Not until 1717, when at Hanover Stanhope met Dubois, the French Regent's secretary, did France yield this much disputed point. Even then the fortifications of Dunkirk—the pride and glory of the great engineer Vauban—were not entirely destroyed. These same sluices which had been built in 1680 were used by engineers during the World War to close the frontiers of France, thus affording protection to the French armies.[21]

» 2 «

Prior had realized when the new ministry was formed at the end of September that he must make his peace with his new Whig "taskmasters." He was alone in Paris, without commission, appointment, or regular allowance. But worst of all, he was heavily in debt. In accordance with Oxford's unbusinesslike methods, Prior had drawn bills upon Cantillon, who then forwarded them to his correspondent in London to have them honored by the Lord Treasurer. A bill for two thousand pounds, dated July 15, had been accepted by the Lord Treasurer, and payment ordered; but, after Oxford's dismissal, someone prevailed upon the Queen to defer these drafts. At the death of the Queen many such drafts, Prior's among them, were labeled as

[20] New York Public Library, *Hardwick Papers*, Vol. 137, fo. 105.
[21] Daniel Halévy, *Vauban, Builder of Fortresses*, p. 241.

her Majesty's debts for deferred payment. This ruling worked a hardship upon Prior, for Cantillon was chary of advancing more money. The Court was at Fontainebleau, "the most expensive place on earth except Paris itself," and with "eleven horses, thirteen servants, and all the expenses of mourning for the Queen," Prior saw the debtor's prison yawning before him. Hoping that Shrewsbury as head of the Treasury would help him, Prior poured out his troubles to the Duke, who replied disappointingly that he would not be able now to issue any money without a sign manual from the Lords Regents, "who reasonably declined any distribution of money but what directly tended to the preserving the peace in Britain." Even after King George's arrival in England the matter was further deferred, pending an examination of the late Queen's debt.[22] Poor Matt, playing hide-and-seek with his creditors, was about to renew his wailing to Shrewsbury when that gentleman, true to his old habits, pleaded ill health and was relieved of the post of Lord Treasurer.

With Shrewsbury gone, Prior scanned the remaining ministers and planned a campaign of ingratiation. Townshend and Stanhope, as we have already mentioned, were the Secretaries of State; Devonshire was the Lord Steward, and Nottingham, Lord President. Halifax, who had confidently expected to be named Lord Treasurer, had to content himself with the title of First Lord of the Treasury.

The outlook was not very promising. With none of these men except Halifax had Prior ever been friends, and twelve years had elapsed since these two had been on good terms. Further, all of these statesmen, during the last four years of Queen Anne's reign, had been defenders in and out of Parliament of what they regarded as "Revolution principles." They looked upon Prior as a Jacobite, perhaps a pensioner of Louis XIV. Moreover they could not forget that he had deserted the Whigs and joined their

[22] *Portland Papers*, V, 497, Shrewsbury to Prior, London, Oct. 4/15, 1714.

enemies. All this Prior, of course, knew. He could not pretend to a sudden conversion to Whiggism even if he so desired, for they would doubt his sincerity. Tory supremacy, of course, had expired with the death of Queen Anne. Consequently Prior fell back upon the attitude he had once assumed, that of the moderate, or the man above party, and reiterated to each of the five ministers the hope he had already expressed to the Earl of Dorset, "that Whig and Tory are buried in the same grave and that henceforth we shall have no other contention but who shall love with most zeal the person of the sovereign and the laws and liberties of their country."[23]

Such fine sounding sentiments, coming from a man who, for the last four years, had been one of the hottest of Tories, were not likely to receive hearty approval. Certainly Prior knew that most of the Whigs now in power, having smarted from the attacks of their rivals, were determined to give the Tories a taste of their own medicine. Yet there is evidence that an attempt was made to bring into the ministry men from both parties, and Prior, out of touch with the sudden shifts of the political barometer in London from day to day, may have magnified the possibilities of the success of such a plan. Halifax, it is said, proposed the formation of a motley ministry, recommending, among others, Hanmer and Bromley from the Tory ranks.[24] If such a plan had been accepted, Prior's troubles would have been over, and the remaining years of his life would have been much brighter.

In his letter to Townshend, Prior deliberately set out to flatter that staunch Whig:

I had rather you had the seals than any man in England, except myself . . . I need not ask you for your favour; for, taking it for granted

---

[23] P. R. O., *State Papers, France*, 78/159, Prior to Dorset, Versailles, Aug. 9/20, 1714.

[24] William Coxe, Memoirs of Sir Robert Walpole, London, 1798, I, 60. That Prior clung long to the hope that his friend Hanmer would be a member of the ministry may be seen in a letter he wrote to Hanmer, Jan. 3, 1714/5. See Hanmer, *Correspondence*, pp. 170–73.

that you think me an honest man, I assure myself of everything from you that is good-natured and generous . . . Pray, my Lord, do me all the good you can; and if, as we say here, the names of party and faction are to be lost, pray get me pricked down for one of the first that is desirous to come into so happy an agreement . . . I cannot presume to hope for the happiness of seeing you very soon; for though I should be recalled to-morrow, I shall savour so strong of a French court that I must take my quarantine in some Kentish village before I dare come near the Cock-pit.[25]

"General Jim" Stanhope, Prior addressed in terms of military metaphor, laying the compliments on with a trowel:

As I am a soldier in the State Militant, and His Majesty has been pleased to make you his captain, I most heartily congratulate you upon that honour assuring you that as with all cheerfulness I expect your words of command, I shall obey them with all zeal and duty . . . I have always had the justest esteem imaginable of your great honour as to your own conduct and ability in business. I shall industriously seek every occasion that may recommend me to your friendship.[26]

The letters to Devonshire and to Nottingham were of similar tone, conveying the same quixotic dream of an end of party distinctions. Stanhope, surprisingly enough, encouraged Prior's hopes of burying the party axe. Matt therefore felt that he was making some progress.[27]

Although Stanhope and Townshend as the two Secretaries of State were the men whose good will Prior must have so long as he remained in Paris, it was the support of the First Lord of the Treasury he must win else he could not return home. Despite the fact that Halifax had coldly retired six months earlier from the abortive correspondence reopened with Matt over the purchase of fruit trees and salad seeds, the harassed Plenipotentiary pocketed his pride and again appealed to the man whom he had some fourteen years past been wont to salute as "My dear

---

[25] P. R. O., *State Papers, France*, 105/29, fo. 235, Prior to Townshend, Fontainebleau, Oct. 1/12, 1714.

[26] *Ibid.*, fo. 234, Prior to Stanhope, Fontainebleau, October 1/12, 1714.

[27] *Ibid.*, 78/159, Stanhope to Prior, Cockpit, Oct. 7/18, 1714.

Master." The tenor of his epistle was much the same as that of the communications to Dorset, Stanhope, Townshend, and the rest; but in handling the question of party he varied his language, reverting to a metaphor from the New World, heard years earlier at the Board of Trade. He understood, he said, that "the hatchet of discord is to be buried under the highest tree in the forest and the Calumet of good will to be carried from Susquehanna to the Pemaquid." These preliminaries over, Prior sought to work upon the feelings of Halifax by recalling their childhood friendship:

I have nothing more at heart than to live in the strictest rules of duty and respect with those whom his Majesty pleases to employ in his ministry, and with you, my Lord, to renew that friendship which, as it began when we were children, ought to be continued to our graves. Has it not been uneasy sometimes to you to have suspended the operation of it? And have you not punished yourself in refusing me your favour? Fourteen years, my Lord, is long enough for you to have borne other people's resentments against your old friend, Matt. Let your kindness to me for the time to come make amends for the coldness of the past. I would not beg your favour, but I would have you give it to me, and put me in the wrong, if by my future actions I do not merit it . . .[28]

For eleven days Prior waited impatiently for some sign that Halifax had buried the hatchet. Receiving no answer, he sent a second appeal to the Lord of the Treasury setting forth his dire financial condition and begging that "the plenipotentiary of England should not be left for debt in the Chatelet at Paris." Despite his concern for his own affairs, Prior did not neglect to solicit for his friends, urging that Adrian Drift be retained as under-secretary to the Board of Trade and that Dick Shelton be continued as Commissioner in the Stamp Office. The letter further contains an eloquent self-justification and a denial of Jacobitism:

The answering my last Letter is a point referable only to your own

Goodness. Friendship can no more be forced than Love, and those persons sometimes are the Objects of both our Indulgences in this kind who may least have deserved our favour. I have, however, the Satisfaction to believe that you think me an honest Man and an Englishman: for my having acted as the Queen's Orders given me by Her ministers enjoined me to do. My Dispatches sent to the Court of England, the Copies of my Letters here . . . and all I have to do with; and my own *mens conscia recti* will abundantly justify me . . . and as to any underhand doings, before God, Angels and Man, I shall stand cleared: and You, My Lord, may pass your word and honour upon that Account. I will only add that few men alive have more merit in this regard than myself, and as long as the fourth article either of Ryswick or of Utrecht remain legible, I may as well be thought a Mahumetan as a Jacobite; but as these are little reflexions raised by the underlings who had a mind to justify some of their masters being angry with me, so they will all fall half an hour after you are pleased to be my Friend. Pray let that be within half an hour after you receive this letter . . .[29]

Still Halifax did not reply; but the far more amiable brother, Sir James Montague, wrote announcing Halifax's intention of renewing his friendship with Matt. The present turn of affairs, said Sir James, had brought him in office again—Sir James was now Baron of the Exchequer—and had hindered him from writing sooner. He stated that his brother had expressed great concern upon finding that no better care had been taken of Matt and was "uneasy to find people so little disposed to do anything" for him.[30]

Here was an encouraging message from the friend of Channel Row days. Matt replied promptly, eager to follow up any opportunity of restoring himself in the good graces of Halifax, who not only had charge of the purse strings, but who, as Prior had heard, would shortly be made an Earl and Knight of the Garter:

You will easily believe me, my dear Jemmy, how agreeable your letter was to me since it assured me of the continuance of your friendship,

[29] *Ibid.*, fo. 246, Prior to Halifax, Paris, Oct. 12/23, 1714.
[30] *Longleat Papers*, III, 445, Sir James Montague to Prior, Oct. 17/28, 1714.

and of Lord Halifax's generous intentions to renew his favour to me. I was always truly sensible of your good wishes towards me, and of your kind concern in my behalf, but never had so much reason as at present to thank you upon that account. The future satisfaction of my life will be to live with my master as the most obliged and most faithful of his servants ought to be, and if I do not expatiate upon that subject it is because my interest is so visibly concerned in the thing that whatever I may say would look as flowing from a less noble principle than that of a sincere and pure friendship . . .

In this vein the ingratiating epistle goes on for more than five hundred words.[31] Since Jemmy was so friendly, perhaps the Master needed only a little more coaxing to bring him around. That Matt thought this was true is indicated in a note to Shrewsbury: "My Lord, give me leave to tell you that my Lord Halifax will never pardon you except you make him and I [*sic*] friends as *in principio*."[32]

Finally there came from Halifax a letter, cold and disappointing. The great lord stated that he disagreed on certain points in the two letters which he had received from Prior, that he did not wish to have these matters mentioned again, that he did not desire to be disagreeable to anyone he wished well, but that he had no intention of being misled or imposed upon. Furthermore, he regarded Prior's expenses as excessively large. As a final blow, he announced that Prior had been dropped from the Commission of Customs: "I doubt in that you will think you might have been favored," Halifax concluded, "but if I may have credit with you, it was impossible."[33]

Disheartened by this blow, which now left him only the emolument from his fellowship at St. John's, and rebuffed by the whole tenor of the letter so unlike what he had expected, Matt composed a third communication. Omitting all appeals to old friendship, he gave a brief explanation of his monthly

---

[31] Quoted in full by Bickley, *Life of Matthew Prior*, p. 221.
[32] P. R. O., *State Papers, France*, 105/29, Prior to Shrewsbury, Fontainebleau, Oct. 19/30, 1714.
[33] *Longleat Papers*. III, 445, Halifax to Prior, Nov. 4/15, 1714.

expenses which Halifax had questioned. His expenses had been large, but no larger than diplomatic etiquette imposed. Mourning for Queen Anne, as well as celebrations on the coronation of the new monarch, had made his bills soar. Foreign ambassadors and ministers in Paris, and also the English nobility and gentry resident there had to be entertained. Less an explanation than a justification is the letter:

I acknowledge, my lord, that I have lived here like an Ambassador. I have had the respect and honour from this Court very near to that of an Ambassador: and my table has been as open and handsome as that of an Ambassador: this as well—the French as British Nobility and All the Gentlemen of our country that have been here can testify: this, I say, my lord, was allowed and I thought judged necessary for the honour and dignity of the Nation; and the Moment I received your Commands or that I understand your pleasure to be that I should live in less Compass, I am selling some of my horses and putting off some of my servants: as to my own part, God knows I am so far from having taken pleasure in this noise and magnificence that I have been incumbered with it: but so it was, my Lord and Patron, I was minister from a great Monarch to the most Expensive Court in Europe, as every man who has been here and had an Estate, my lords Jersey, Manchester and Shrewsbury can testify, and as I, who have no estate, must testify by lying in Jail except your candour . . .[34]

While Prior awaited a response to the above letter, he heard that the Earl of Stair would soon come to Paris and take his place. Thereupon Matt implored Townshend in the name of humanity to urge the immediate payment of the 4,458 pounds indebtedness, lest the day of his recall find him in a debtor's prison.[35]

Before the year closed, a more cordial letter came from Halifax. He had read Prior's explanations to King George and had tried to present Matt's plight sympathetically. The difficulty was that Prior's bills far exceeded the allowance of either pleni-

[34] Here the MS ends. See Brit. Mus., *Add. MSS*, 15, 947, fo. 7, Prior to Halifax, Paris, Nov. 12/23, 1714.
[35] P. R. O., *State Papers, France*, 78/159, Prior to Townshend, Paris, Nov. 19/30, 1714.

potentiary or ambassador. The King, however, had ordered the payment of a plenipotentiary's allowance from August 1 to December 1, together with a bill of extraordinaries, amounting in the whole to 1,176 pounds; the bills dating from the Queen's time were to be paid in due course out of the Queen's arrears. Somewhat apologetically Halifax said he hoped the plan would meet with Prior's approval.[36]

Prior was far from satisfied. His debts amounted to more than 5,000 pounds. The Treasury was sending him 1,176 pounds and the 2,000 from the Queen's arrears would eventually be paid to him. Even after that he would still be about 2,000 pounds in debt. He felt disconsolate. Cut off from all his old friends, who were now out of office, he declared that he knew as little of what was happening in London as in Mexico. Although he had scrupulously carried out all the orders of the Lords Regents and had received assurances from the King himself of satisfaction with his services, he had been dismissed from the Customs, his expenses objected to at the Treasury, and he was held as a kind of political prisoner in Paris, where his affairs were descanted upon with varying degrees of compassion by everybody from dukes and duchesses to the *petit bourgeois*. He now began to have fears that his public career was over—an eventuality that he had refused to face hitherto. If so, he would have to sell his house in Duke Street and return to his fellowship at Cambridge.[37] Even in the days of ambassadorial splendor, he had refused to relinquish the fellowship, thinking that when all else failed, and assuredly all else was precarious, it would be bread and cheese at the last.

» 3 «

The last three months of Prior's long stay in France were the most harassing of all. Stair came at the end of January and re-

---

[36] *Longleat Papers*, III, 447, Halifax to Prior, Dec. 2/13, 1714.
[37] Hanmer, *Correspondence*, 170, Prior to Hanmer, Paris, Dec. 23/Jan. 3, 1714/15.

lieved Prior of his diplomatic duties. Prior should, of course, have been allowed to return to London at once, but two more months passed before he could leave Paris. Deprived of his diplomatic rank, he was compelled to wait until the Whig ministers agreed to send him enough money to pay his creditors in order that he might make a decent departure for home. True, the French were ready with expressions of sympathy, and Torcy was voluble in his animadversions against the procrastinating ministers, but Prior was not thus to be comforted. He had never asked from the French more than "decency of behavior and the returns of common civility." In "public character . . . the most proud" and in "private capacity . . . the most humble," he felt keenly his difficulties.[38] Patriot that he was, he resented the injustice that his government was making him suffer. Moreover, he had neither friend nor colleague to whom he might pour out his troubles.

Prior did not immediately make friends with Stair, who was of different mold from Jersey, Shrewsbury, and Bolingbroke— fine gentlemen with a taste for literature and the arts. John Dalrymple, second Earl of Stair and son of the "Butcher of Glencoe," belonged to the same breed as Stanhope, Townshend, and Walpole. Like Stanhope he had derived most of his diplomatic training on the battlefield and applied military tactics to all his problems—even that of courtship. Determined to win a widow who had declared she would never remarry, Stair concealed himself in her house, compromised her by appearing at her bedroom window, and compelled her to marry him to save her reputation.[39] Here is the person who stepped boldly on the scene in January, 1715. Arrogant and reckless by nature, he promptly quarreled with Torcy, and soon they were not on speaking terms. He had no inclination to meet anyone halfway, certainly not the French, but was cocksure of his ability to

---

[38] See his letter to Townshend, Paris, Nov. 9, 1714, P. R. O., *State Papers, France*, 78/159.
[39] D. N. B., John Dalrymple, second Earl of Stair.

bring them to terms. He was at first inclined to be as haughty to Prior as to Torcy, but unlike the French minister, Prior responded with a disarming humility. Thereupon, Stair adopted a friendlier tone, and, after discovering how high was the cost of living in Paris, he sympathized with Prior's financial straits and urged his colleagues to expedite the payment of Prior's debt.

Orders for Prior to deliver all his papers to Stair came on February 1 from the King. At once Stair demanded the papers and the following day sent to Stanhope a fairly detailed account of the success of his errand. Prior had delivered to Stair two folio letter books and a book of memorials, and had promised to give him later all the loose letters referred to in the letter books, as well as any other papers relating to the negotiations. Since there were among all these papers numerous letters of a private nature, Prior asked that the parts of his correspondence which related to public affairs be copied so that his letter books might be returned to him. Stair was pleased with Prior's prompt compliance and felt that he was acting very fairly in the matter. Therefore he wrote to Stanhope, "I believe you will think it [the request] very reasonable and be the more ready to oblige him that he has so frankly complied with the King's commands." [40]

A short while after, Stair sent to Stanhope another packet of Matt's papers, which had been numbered "so that nothing might be taken out." [41] Stair directed Stanhope's attention to several "curious things" in the letters, remarking that the Queen's ministers gradually "grew sensible that France, after it had got them into its power, kept none of the promises it had made in order to draw them in."

Bolingbroke, ignorant of the ministry's demands upon Prior, but growing nervous about his own safety, now made through Iberville and Torcy the unreasonable request that Prior should

[40] P. R. O., *State Papers, France*, 78/160, Stair to Stanhope, Feb. 2, 1715.
[41] *Ibid.*, Stair to Stanhope, Feb. 9, 1715.

leave in Paris their mutual correspondence of a public nature
and all private letters which contained any reference to the
peace negotiations. A recent example of Whig technique had
aggravated Bolingbroke's uneasiness. When Strafford, upon his
return from Holland, refused to turn over his papers to Townshend, he was examined before the Council, censured, and punished. Not only were all his papers removed from his house, but
even those which were still at the Custom House and on ship-
board were sealed by his Majesty's command.[42] In order that
Prior might be forewarned against a similar mishap, a courier
with a note hidden in his saddle was dispatched to Calais to
meet him there in the event that he should be returning to
London.[43] Bolingbroke's request about the correspondence seems
to have been delayed in reaching Versailles. Torcy knew only
that Prior had received orders to surrender his papers. The ever
useful Gaultier, who was now back in France, went, at Torcy's
behest, to see Prior and learned that Prior had already given up
his papers to Stair. Torcy immediately passed this word on to
Iberville in London with the additional information that the
papers contained nothing which would be used against either
Prior or the preceding ministry.[44] This intelligence came direct
from Prior, who also wished to have some keys delivered to a
friend at home. With them Torcy sent this explanation:

The keys which I send you belong to M. Prior. I pray you give them
from him to M. Richard Shelton, whom you will seek at the home of
Madame Stacy in Berry Street, and you will give him the commission
mentioned in the following letter.

The enclosure indicates that Matt had worked himself up into
a fine state of fright:

Look in the drawers of the green table in the study. Burn a ballad
which you will find in these drawers, or in those of my escritoire, or

[42] *Political State of Great Britain*, IX, 75.
[43] Paris, Archives . . . , *Correspondance Politique, d'Angleterre*, 266, fo. 77, Iberville to Torcy, London, Jan. 24, 1715.
[44] *Ibid.*, 266, fo. 125, Torcy to Iberville, Versailles, Feb. 6, 1715.

in the table in the little study, and remove all other papers which you may judge capable of giving offense. Take the silver which you will find in the escritoire and guard it until I return. When you write me in order that I may know what you have done, only say that your cousin is better.[45]

What poem it was that Prior was so anxious to have burned will probably never be known. It must have been one written before August, 1712, since after that time, except for a few weeks, Prior had been in France.

By the end of February Stanhope and Halifax were promising Matt an early payment of his debts, now that he had been obedient and given up his papers. Stanhope had read Prior's letters—and what plaintive ones they were—to the King, who had directed that Halifax make certain reimbursements. Halifax's letter regarding the matter indicates such an about-face that it should be quoted:

'Tis with great pleasure that I can now let you know that upon reading my Lord Stair's letter, giving an account of your readiness to obey His Majesty's orders, the King has directed us to pay you 2408£ for the two bills of extraordinaries which you demanded, which together with what is due to you yet on your ordinary allowance shall be dispatched with all the favour and civility we can show you. 'Twill be a great pleasure to me in particular to hasten your return from an unhappy and uneasy station to your own country and friends, in which number I desire you will rank me.[46]

How profoundly relieved Matt was to escape the debtor's yawning prison may well be imagined. Stair, who rejoiced with him, wrote to Stanhope: "I am exceedingly glad that His Majesty has acted so generously with Mr. Prior. It's impossible for me to describe to you the joy and gratitude he shows upon it."[47] But Matt's happiness was short-lived. The new ministers,

---

[45] *Ibid.*, fo. 143, Torcy to Iberville, Versailles, Feb. 11, 1715.

[46] *Longleat Papers*, III, 447, Halifax to Prior, Feb. 7/18, 1715. Halifax's letter was a reply to a fourth "dunning letter" from Prior, written on the eve of Stair's arrival and dated Paris, Jan. 11/22, 1715. See *Calendar of Treasury Papers*, 196, fo. 16.

[47] P. R. O., *State Papers, France*, 78/160, Stair to Stanhope, Paris, Feb. 24, 1715.

now firmly intrenched in power and flushed with success at the recent parliamentary elections, were resolved to bring their predecessors to account.

The paying of Prior's debts was not due to generosity on the part of the Whig ministry. Their attitude is perhaps best explained by an item found in a periodical of that date which stated that the ministers were unwilling for Prior to have any pretense for staying in France "when his presence may be necessary in England towards the detection of mismanagements."[48] The idea that Prior might remain in France is not far-fetched, for Dick Shelton advised deferring return to London until the gathering storm cloud should blow over. Shelton feared that Prior, who had no influential kinsmen as did the titled ministers, would be the victim of the fury of the Whigs.[49] It was even rumored that Prior had rented a house in the country near Paris.[50] We learn from Torcy that Matt, justly alarmed over news from England, had resolved not to return and was making arrangements to have his pictures, books, and plate removed from his London home for safekeeping.[51] More significant is the message Matt sent to Bolingbroke, by way of Iberville, saying that he would absent himself until the skies should clear.[52]

In spite of the advice of Shelton and others, Prior changed his mind abruptly and decided to go to England. This sudden change called forth many surmises. It was suggested that he thought it expedient to follow after his correspondence, which had been so summarily demanded that he had had no opportunity to revise it. If we may take Iberville's word for it, Bolingbroke was determined that Prior should come home to speak in his, that is, Bolingbroke's defense.[53] The strongest motives, as Torcy knew,

[48] *Political State of Great Britain*, IX, 145, London, 1715.
[49] Paris, Archives . . . , *Correspondance Politique, d'Angleterre*, 266, fo. 227, Iberville to Torcy, London, Feb. 18, 1715.
[50] *Ibid.*, 267, fo. 10, Iberville to Torcy, London, March 4, 1715.
[51] *Ibid.*, fo. 31, Torcy to Iberville, Versailles, March 13, 1715.
[52] *Ibid.*, fo. 32, Prior to Iberville, March 13, 1715.
[53] *Ibid.*, fo. 194, Iberville to Torcy, London, April 4, 1715.

were Prior's love for England—Matt was always restless to get home—and his desire to face his critics as a point of honor.

His debts having been settled, Prior was free to leave Paris after making the customary round of calls upon friends and the members of the royal household. When he paid his farewell call at Versailles, he was presented with a picture of Louis XIV in a frame set with diamonds as a token of the monarch's high regard. In asking permission of Stanhope to keep the gift, valued at 900 pounds, Prior with self-pity uppermost in mind, said, "If I had never seen the original [i.e. King Louis], it might possibly have been as happy for me"—a sentiment calculated to please those in power.[54]

One evening late in March Prior set out for London, armed with a message from Stair to Stanhope: "I write this by Mr. Prior, who desires to be recommended to your favour and protection. You won't find him disposed to defend what has been done amiss, or to meddle with anything. In that case I have assured him that you won't incline to hurt him."[55] By the time he had reached Boulogne, Prior was so ill that he had to break the journey. He sent his servant on to Calais with the dispatches for the London office and a personal note of explanation to Stanhope: "I set out from Paris Monday evening, not having been in any state of health for some time before. I was taken here very ill with a violent colic, vomiting and something worse. This, Sir, is strange stuff to entertain a secretary of state with—I wish I had better. . ."[56] This may have been a convenient illness—Iberville thought it was feigned[57]—to give Matt time to receive replies to certain letters, among them, perhaps, a reassuring one from Harcourt, of whom he had asked legal advice.[58]

[54] P. R. O., *State Papers, France*, 78/159, Prior to Stanhope, Paris, March 10/21, 1715.

[55] *Ibid.*, 78/160, Stair to Stanhope, Paris, March 13/24, 1715.

[56] *Ibid.*, 78/159, Prior to Stanhope, Boulogne, March 18/29, 1715.

[57] Paris, Archives . . . , *Correspondance Politique, d'Angleterre*, 267, fo. 225, Iberville to Torcy, London, April 9, 1715.

[58] *Harcourt Papers*, II, 69, Prior to Harcourt, Paris, March 13/24, 1715.

Eleven days after departing from Paris, Prior arrived in London and made haste to "wait upon" the Earl of Dorset. Matt was weak and sick and in sore need of the Earl's protection. The very next day Prior was introduced by Dorset and Townshend to the King, "who received him very graciously"; that evening he was invited to dine at Townshend's with many important people—Dorset, Stanhope, and several other of the new ministers were present.[59] While Prior was dining bravely with his examiners, Bolingbroke took fright and fled in disguise for Paris to throw himself into the cause of the Pretender and into the arms of Mme. de Tencin. Ever since Prior had surrendered his papers to Stair, Bolingbroke's position had become increasingly perilous. Bolingbroke unjustly blamed all the evil upon Matt, and falsely argued that neither misconduct nor high treason had been mentioned until those fateful papers had arrived.[60] When Stanhope began to examine Bolingbroke's papers Bolingbroke looked on with shattered nerves, which gave way completely when he learned that impeachment proceedings and the charge of treason were in store for him.

Prior soon learned that the surrender of his papers had provoked a storm of criticism by the Tories. They hotly accused him of pursuing his own interest and of succumbing to seductive promises of the Whigs. He defended himself for handing over the letters without removing those which might incriminate Bolingbroke on the ground of the summariness of the order to produce them. As for the likelihood of his serving as witness against the deceased Queen's ministers, he would refuse to; nor could he give any evidence, he said, which would make the least trouble for them.[61] Prior's dilemma was a real one. Quite

[59] *Political State of Great Britain*, IX, 226, London, 1715. Cf. Horatio Walpole's letter to Stair, Hague, April 16, 1715: "It is conjectured here that Mr. Prior's arrival in England hastened his lordship's flight. . . We hear that honest Matt is merry, has been received very well by the King, dined with the Ministers of State . . . and is resolved to tell the truth." (*Stair Annals* I, 274.)

[60] Paris, Archives . . . , *Correspondance Politique, d'Angleterre*, 267, fo. 242, Iberville to Torcy, London, April 11, 1715.   [61] *Ibid.*, fo. 225, Iberville to Torcy, April 9, 1715.

naturally, if he hoped to receive another diplomatic post, he must be *persona grata* with the ruling party. He had, in fact, told Torcy that he had no choice but to win favor with the government of his country, and that he was not a person to defy his King.[62] His loyalty to his old associates precluded any desire to betray them. Thus he was trying to follow a middle course and may sometimes have intentionally misled the Whigs into thinking that the payment of his debts would be the price of his testimony. Prior's perturbation of spirit had distressed Torcy, who remarked that Prior was so agitated before his departure for England and was so anxious that everyone should be pleased with him there that he himself would not be surprised at any decision which Matt might make. With penetration Torcy summed up Prior's temper: "He so loves his country that I am persuaded that if the government should change, he would change likewise, sooner than that he should lose from sight London and the University of Oxford [*sic*]."[63]

» 4 «

Even in his most troubled moments Prior never anticipated the harsh treatment that was in store for him. Perhaps he expected that he would be able to conciliate the most hostile of the Whigs just as he had already gained the good will of Stanhope and Stair, and that in any event he could count on the protection of Dorset, Halifax, and Shrewsbury, all of whom stood high in the councils of George I. Dorset seems to have been an indolent and cautious man, certainly a less colorful personality than his vigorous father. Himself no poet, he felt no obligation to continue his father's patronage of poets; therefore he left Matt to shift for himself. Shrewsbury, conveniently ill with the gout and unsympathetic with the new ministry's

---

[62] *Ibid.*, 266, fo. 276, Torcy to Iberville, March 6, 1715.

[63] *Ibid.*, 267, fo. 240, Torcy to Iberville, Versailles, April 13, 1715. Torcy obviously mistook the University of Oxford for the University of Cambridge.

rancor toward his old colleagues, absented himself from Court and threatened to resign from the post of Lord Chamberlain. Whigs of a younger generation like Walpole ignored him or talked of impeaching him for his part in the making of the Treaty of Utrecht. Prior's best hope lay in Halifax, who by means of splendid dinners at Bushey Park, won the King's consent to a general amnesty for all Tories. By one of those strange ironies of fate, Halifax was taken ill of pneumonia on May 15 and died a few days later. Walpole, having examined the diplomatic papers of Prior, Bolingbroke, and Strafford, soon influenced the King to change his mind, and demanded that a committee be appointed to investigate the Tory ministry. Stanhope, who had also read the documents, seconded the suggestion, declaring that the late ministry was "the most corrupt that ever sat at the helm."

The sudden death of his oldest friend and the complete inadequacy of the others left Prior in a world hostile to him. All his movements were watched. He dared not go near Iberville, and, except when ordered to report before the ministers, he did not venture very far from Duke Street. When strolling one evening at about five o'clock in St. James's Park, Matt was accosted by a Captain St. Ledger. The captain had a grievance which he thought worthy of a challenge to a fight. Matt refused the challenge, and what followed was variously reported, some saying that Prior's nose was wrung and others that only a few uncouth epithets were bestowed upon him.[64]

Stanhope was indefatigable in his preparations for the investigation, and on April 8 he presented to the House of Commons fifteen volumes of papers relating to the Treaty of Utrecht, which more than forty copyists had laboriously transcribed. Since the papers were too many and too voluminous to be examined by all the members, it was voted that a Secret Committee should be appointed to study them and to report the findings.

[64] *Political State of Great Britain*, IX, 300.

The Committee numbered twenty-one, and the relentless Walpole was its chairman.

The Committee was ready to report by the first of June. As a preliminary, one of the members, Boscawen, assured the House that they had found "sufficient matter to impeach of high treason, several lords and some commoners." Walpole oratorically pronounced that "he wanted words to express the villainy of the late Frenchified ministry," and Stanhope deplored "that men who were guilty of such enormous crimes had still the audaciousness to appear in the public streets." Then before proceeding further, the Committee deemed it advisable to apprehend certain persons who were to be examined. The "certain persons" were none other than Mr. Matthew Prior and Mr. Thomas Harley. The report came next, and the reading of it took up the best part of two days. With its appendices it fills over two hundred columns of fine print in Cobbett's *Parliamentary History*.[65] Immediately after the reading, impeachment proceedings were ordered against Oxford and Bolingbroke, and later against Ormonde and Strafford.

Prior and Thomas Harley were arrested and confined in the custody of messengers in their own homes, which happened to be situated two doors apart in Duke Street. On June 16, a week after his arrest, Prior was summoned to appear before the Secret Committee. This order occasioned much comment. Addison, who delighted in Prior's misfortunes, wrote that "several wish that it had been made much sooner," for it was rumored that on the night before Prior was examined Oxford and Ned Harley had talked with Prior and had prearranged his testimony to be given before the Secret Committee.[66]

Prior's own account of his examination before the Secret Committee[67] is readable and witty, but since it has been previ-

---

[65] Volume VII.
[66] Addison, *Works*, VI, 671, Addison to Charles Delafaye, London, June 18, 1715.
[67] First printed in *History of His Own Time*, pp. 286–302.

ously published in full we shall here give only the high lights. We picture a group of pompous and bewigged M. P.s, many of them poorly informed on the evidence in the fifteen volumes of letters and state papers, but eager to intimidate Prior into confessing more than he knew. They grew irritable with him and irascible with each other, frequently asking him to retire while further information was dug out. On occasion when doors were left ajar, Prior scornfully observed his examiners wrangling unbecomingly. There is ample testimony in his story as to the unbusinesslike conduct of the whole affair. To begin with, Prior was told with "affected eloquence" by Mr. Lechmere that as he had served in "a very high employment and with great applause" the Committee was relying upon his "candour and probity." He was reminded that this investigation was for the King's service and that what he answered would be for his own honor. First, vague questions as to how much he knew of the negotiation and how long he had known the Abbé Gaultier were thrown at him. Prior reminded the gentlemen that his books and papers containing all such information were before them; the Committee acquiesced and passed on to the matter of Prior's expenditures, always a troublesome business.

An explanation of his drawing out 200 pounds from the Treasury in 1711 was demanded. When Prior could not recall which French banker he had credit with at that time, although four years had elapsed, the Committee was displeased and asked him to retire. When he returned to the room, the same question was put again and the same answer given, Prior adding that he hoped those bills and others had been paid, else he would find himself a beggar. At this point he was told that the King had particularly directed that what he might say to the Committee "should not be of any prejudice" to himself, a contingency of which Prior was fearful, for he was appearing without counsel and had to depend upon his memory. Again he was told to withdraw, and upon his reappearance, a battery of confused questions was put to him. Coningsby, sadly muddled, spoke of Prior's having been sent to France by Lord Oxford. Prior reminded him, haughtily, that he had gone to France on the Queen's especial appointment and that a copy of her instructions was to be found in the records at hand.

After this divagation the interrogation reverted to the subject of Prior's banker in Paris, M. Cantillon. "Was he not a Papist?" Boscawen asked suggestively. Prior admitted that he was, cleverly countering, "Else, sir, he could not have been a banker at Paris." At this there was much frowning and nodding, and Prior was sent out while the lords conferred.

The Committee was glowering again when Prior faced them. Stanhope told him that the members of the Committee were not satisfied with his behavior toward them; they could not understand why, although there was much correspondence on Prior's side to the Lord Treasurer (Oxford), they could find no answers to these letters. Strange, they said, inasmuch as practically all of Bolingbroke's answers to Prior had been produced. An explanation was in order. Briefly, Prior said that whereas what he wrote to Oxford was for Oxford's information, Oxford usually sent necessary answers and directions to him by the Secretary of State. The Committee was sure that Prior could produce letters which contained the secrets of the negotiation, but the reader will recall that Prior often complained that the Lord Treasurer did not write to him frequently. Coningsby raved and threatened, but Prior maintained that he knew of no such letters, and that if such letters existed his Lordship (meaning Oxford) must produce them. To Coningsby he said, spitefully, "You know, my Lord, that your countryman is no very exact correspondent," knowing that Coningsby, who had "troubled great men . . . with letters," had often been snubbed.

Coningsby withdrew in a passion, while Stanhope proceeded to the next point—how much Prior knew of the meeting at his house in Duke Street of the lords with Mesnager and Gaultier when the preliminaries were signed. Matt had been forewarned that the Committee had consulted the law and planned "to fix upon that meeting . . . as an accusation of treason." When questioned as to which lords were present at this meeting, he unhesitatingly answered that the two Secretaries of State were there (this much was in the instrument itself which the Committee had before them). The chairman then asked, "Was my Lord of Oxford there?" Prior replied, "I cannot recollect it. One of the lords was absent; whether the Duke of Shrewsbury or the Earl of Oxford I cannot tell. In all sincerity and honour this is truth." This convenient forgetfulness angered the cross-examiners, and Matt was sent out to "recollect if both these lords were not present." He, however, either could not or would not recall the meeting clearly, and since it could not be determined which lord was present and which was absent, the effect was the same as if both had been absent. Certainly Matt had his back to the wall. The Committee was trying to extort from him evidence in order to "bring to the scaffold" persons who were his former friends and patrons; moreover, he feared that he might prove himself a traitor by admitting his own presence at the meeting. The old epigram, "every man who is a partner is a principal in treason," was ringing in his ears. Wisely, or not, he confessed that he was present.

A week had elapsed since Prior had been taken into custody. The Committee now wished to know if he had seen Lord Oxford during that time. While dining with Thomas Harley, likewise in custody, Prior had seen Oxford but only to exchange greetings and this in the presence of a messenger, he answered. Before the simple explanation was finished, the Committee stopped him, seizing upon the admission that he had seen Oxford and his cousin. As usual, Prior was asked to retire while the Committee planned its next move.

Upon the resumption of the questioning, a mutilated piece of paper, containing almost illegible handwriting, was presented to Prior for identification. Matt claimed it, explaining that it was a *brouillon*. The use of the French word was unfortunate; some members of the Committee immediately pounced upon him, demanding a definition. That a *brouillon* was a rough draft was accepted, but what signified the French, "My Lord Tr. ne doute point que la Cour de France n'y trouve point de remède"? Avidly the Committee had assumed that this meant that the Lord Treasurer would give up Tournai to France, "whereas," Prior wrote in the report, "the whole hint was meant to renew to the ministers at that Court that Tournai was to be given to the Allies." This interpretation was found to be in keeping with Bolingbroke's letter, of which the *brouillon* was partly an abridgement and partly a verbal translation. Stanhope held Bolingbroke's letter while Prior translated the *brouillon*. There was no denying that the sense of the two papers was the same. Coningsby, foiled again, grew violently angry, and Prior was sent to the anteroom. For nine hours Prior had been subjected to this incoherent and confused examination. The Tournai affair was reopened after a short recess. Upon Prior's stating that so far as he knew the negotiations had proceeded according to the Queen's instructions that the Dutch were to have Tournai, Walpole and Stanhope grew "mightily perplexed," and Coningsby "raved outright." Since the Committee had already based the charge of high treason against Oxford upon the articles of Tournai, Prior's testimony was more than disconcerting.

Prior's comment on the *brouillon* misunderstanding is well made:

To shew the justice, as well as the good judgment of these men, it must certainly appear not only extravagant, but ridiculous to all who think righter than the Committee, that is, to all men living, that an article of high treason should be founded against an English minister upon Tournay, which was not given to the French, and no mention ever made of Lisle, which actually was given up. This by the way. It may be further observed, that at that time not one third part of the Committee themselves did know upon what point the accusations either against the Earl of Oxford or any man else, were to be grounded; several of them having since told me themselves, that they never drew up or read the report; but that those things came to them, as they merrily expressed it, ready cut and dried.

The less hostile members of the Committee were now bored. Two of them had left early in the day, ashamed of the whole performance. Walpole grew weary of the bickering, but Stanhope urged him to see the examination through.

After a last recess, Prior was asked to set down answers to some hastily drawn-up questions. He demurred, for he felt that he could not answer some of them in as direct a manner as their wording demanded; others required facts, whereas he was dependent upon his memory only; and still others had already been answered. For instance, he challenged the statement in the report that he "confessed" having conversed with Lord Oxford and his nearest relations, because "confession" supposed a crime. Again he tried to tell his little story of the accidental meeting with Oxford on the stairway in Harley's home, but Coningsby broke out saying, "Jesus! How perjured is this man!" Seeing that the Committee were all against him, Prior finally signed the paper; he knew that if any of his three friends—Shrewsbury, Oxford, or Bolingbroke—should be brought to trial he would then have an opportunity to explain what he had said and how he had been used by the Committee.

At once news of the examination got abroad. Some said that Prior had betrayed Oxford; others that he had not, but that the author of the *Thief and the Cordelier* was in danger of sharing the fate of his hero if he would not yield to pressure and make further revelations. By his prevarication, and his convenient forgetfulness, Prior had shielded his friend and foiled the Secret Committee. The Committee was sure that an attempt had been made to restore the Pretender, and had expected that Prior's papers would furnish evidence to that effect. The papers failing, the Committee had tried to drag the desired testimony from Prior. Had not these same men sent Jacob Tonson to Paris the previous year to spy upon Prior? That Oxford had written occasionally to Prior was certain, inasmuch as several of Prior's letters in the hands of the Committee were obviously replies to Oxford's. The contents of the letters which Matt had so mysteriously destroyed will never be known. Perhaps the Lord Treasurer had again only been writing of his vague policy towards the Jacobites. Hence though such correspondence would have been inconclusive evidence, it would have proved at least that some contact had been established between Oxford and James III. Yet Stanhope in his fishing for information about these letters was on the wrong track. The really incriminating evidence was the correspondence that had passed between Oxford and the Pretender by way of Gaultier. It was now safely filed away in the French foreign office out of reach of the Secret Committee, and Gaultier himself had slipped quietly home several months previously without even being questioned by the watchful Whigs. Prior was not hanged as rumor said he might be, but was kept under lock and bar in the home of the Sergeant-at-arms of the House of Commons for more than a year.

CHAPTER XII

"Non sum qualis eram"

» 1 «

ON JUNE 9, 1715, Prior was remanded to the custody of Thomas Wibergh, Sergeant-at-arms, whose home was in Brownlow Street, Longacre. No person was allowed to visit him except by permit of the Speaker of the House of Commons. Every day the Messenger, Mr. John Hollingshead, kept guard over his prisoner. Every evening after his duties at the House of Commons were over, Mr. Wibergh relieved the Messenger and took the prisoner for a constitutional,[1] probably a turn about St. James's Park. Prior would hardly have been human had he not recalled with bitterness those other strolls when, before repairing to the Smyrna for a convivial evening he, with the great Lord Oxford or the puissant Swift, would circle this same park while engrossed in discussions of Tory affairs.

Now all was changed. The great days of the Tory Wits were gone forever. The Brothers were widely dispersed. Oxford was in the Tower under charge of high treason; Swift, an exile in Ireland; Bolingbroke, in France, dancing attendance upon the Pretender. Even in France conditions were decidedly altered— the long reign of the Sun King had come to a close, and a five-year-old child sat on the throne of the great Louis. In this new order Prior realized that there was no place for him. His public

---

[1] *Calendar of Treasury Papers*, 1714–1719, Vol. CCXIV. On May 8, 1718, Thomas Wibergh submitted to Paul Jodell, Clerk of the House of Commons, a memorial for fees amounting to 517 pounds. In reply, Mr. Jodell informed Wibergh that since Prior had been committed for no offense, he should pay no fees, and therefore the Chancellor would order the Sergeant to apply to the Treasury for satisfaction.

career was over, and he had little to look forward to. Had he been as cautious, as acquisitive as Addison, he might have saved enough from his earnings to retire comfortably from this new Whig world; but he had always been improvident and in debt from his college days. Slightly over fifty, he was prematurely old, and his cough did not diminish.

Since he was forbidden to write or receive friendly letters, information concerning him during the months of his confinement is meager—we rely chiefly on the London journals for intelligence of him. He was, we know, in good hands. The Sergeant and the Messenger were both gentlemen, and the Sergeant's home was in what was then a good neighborhood, inhabited by genteel families. Matt was not one to accept the loss of freedom without protest, however, and at the end of two months in his Longacre prison he addressed a letter of inquiry into the circumstances of his confinement to the Speaker of the House of Commons.[2] The letter was duly read before the House and referred to the committee of which Walpole was chairman. After three weeks had elapsed, Walpole reported on behalf of the committee that Prior's confinement was in accord with precedent and that it was a proper way for the House to redress grievances and bring "great offenders to justice." With more acrimony than justice, the chairman advised against setting Prior at liberty or making the confinement any easier, for he declared that Mr. Prior had been guilty of contemptuous prevarication during the examination before the Secret Committee. Furthermore, he argued, it was necessary to hold Prior as a material witness against high offenders.[3]

After six months of virtual imprisonment—in January, 1716, to be exact—Prior took the oath of allegiance to the government.[4] On his appearing in public for its administration, the

[2] On August 27, 1715. See *Political State of Great Britain*, X, 184.

[3] Sept. 20. See *ibid.*, 292; House of Commons *Journal*, XVIII, 324; Cobbett's *Parliamentary History* VII, 215.

[4] Baker, *History of the College of St. John the Evangelist*, I, 533.

Whig lampooners marked him for their own. In broadside satires they attacked his sincerity and even circulated verses purported to have fallen from his pocket as he emerged from the Court of Laws:

> Our Fathers of old took Oaths, as their Wives,
> To have and to hold for the term of their Lives;
> But we take the Oaths, like a whore, for our Ease,
> And a whore and a rogue may part when they please.[5]

Other attacks appeared in print from time to time; one enterprising printer reissued Maynwaring's portentous verses on "Matt's Peace" in a new edition.[6] The obnoxious Curll brought out a second pirated collection of Prior's poems. The eight poems in the volume were really his own, but Prior chose to repudiate the edition in the London *Gazette* of March 20–24, 1716.

To such a busy, active man as Prior, the monotony of confinement proved almost unbearable. For occupation he again turned to writing, and soon after his removal to Brownlow Street began his *Answer to the Secret Committee*,[7] which proves to be an admirable justification of Tory procedure up to a certain time. Like the account of his examination, which is an eloquent self-justification, the *Answer* is clear, readable, and lively. It might have become a chief source of information about the whole peace negotiation, but it goes no further than the Barrier Treaty and the Treaty of Gertruydenberg, where it suddenly breaks off. Perhaps Prior took up the story again in later years. At any rate, Dr. Freind stated in his inscription on Prior's monument that Prior was at the time of his death collecting materials for a history of the transactions of his own times. A misreading of Dr. Freind's Latin brought forth an ill-natured outburst from Pope: "What a simple thing was it to say upon his [Prior's] tombstone, that he was writing a history of his own times! He

---

[5] *London Post*, Jan. 14, 1716.   [6] Advertised in the *Daily Courant*, Sept. 10, 1715.
[7] *History of His Own Time*, pp. 436–58.

could not write in a style fit for history, and I dare say he never had set down a word toward any such thing."[8] Prior was not an historian, but an account of the complicated transactions of which he knew many secrets would be invaluable.

Tiring of prose, Prior turned to poetry, only to produce another fragmentary work—"Alma: or, the Progress of the Mind." The poem is a purported dialogue in facile Hudibrastics between the poet and his friend Dick Shelton upon the location of the soul. The subject might presuppose a serious interest, but Matt in his prison chose to laugh at philosophers. In place of the systems of Aristotle and Descartes as taught in the Universities, which after all were "only form'd to disagree," Prior proposed "a healing scheme" based, he said, on an absurd Spanish conceit to the effect that "as we are born our Mind comes in at our Toes, so goes upward to our Leggs to our Middle, thence to our heart and breast, Lodges at last in our head and from thence flies away."[9] But Prior either had forgotten his source or was deliberately hoaxing his reader. As Professor Barrett has shown, the major conceit of the poem came directly from Montaigne, from whom Prior also took suggestions for some of his best passages.[10] The poet rambled on, ridiculing all philosophical systems. All systems, he claimed, have unsound foundations: if one questions the premises of any philosopher's theory, then one is rendered helpless; deny to Descartes his subtle matter, and he has nothing left; refuse to accept the elastic force of matter, and Sir Isaac Newton would be discredited; disprove the existence of the philosopher's stone, and our "chymic friends" would be undone.[11] Then to cap off his skepticism, Matt placed on the title page of the poem the old Greek epigram:

$$\Pi \acute{\alpha}\nu\tau\alpha\ \gamma \acute{\epsilon}\lambda\omega\varsigma,\ \kappa\alpha\grave{\iota}\ \pi \acute{\alpha}\nu\tau\alpha\ \kappa \acute{o}\nu\iota\varsigma,\ \kappa\alpha\grave{\iota}\ \pi \acute{\alpha}\nu\tau\alpha\ \tau\grave{o}\ \mu\eta\theta \acute{\epsilon}\nu$$
$$\Pi \acute{\alpha}\nu\tau\alpha\ \gamma\grave{\alpha}\rho\ \grave{\epsilon}\xi\ \grave{\alpha}\lambda \acute{o}\gamma\omega\nu\ \epsilon\sigma\tau\grave{\iota}\ \tau\grave{\alpha}\ \gamma\iota\gamma\nu \acute{o}\mu\epsilon\nu\alpha.$$

[8] Spence, *Anecdotes*, p. 129.

[9] "Essay upon Opinion," in *Dialogues of the Dead*, p. 191.

[10] W. P. Barrett, "Matthew Prior's Alma," in *Modern Language Review*, XXVII (October, 1932), 454–58. [11] *Poems on Several Occasions*, p. 240.

Two anecdotes of the period indicate clearly that Prior thought lightly of this excursion into metaphysics. He once asked Pope how he liked "Solomon." Whereupon Pope responded, "Your *Alma* is a masterpiece." Prior replied with asperity, "What do you tell me of my *Alma*, a loose and hasty scribble to relieve the tedious hours of imprisonment while in the messenger's hand"?[12] The second story concerns the making up of the subscription volume of Prior's poems for which two of his friends, Lord Bathurst and Lord Edward Harley, were largely responsible. While reading and selecting the pieces for the volume with Prior, Lord Bathurst asked Prior if he had other poems to offer. Prior replied that he had no more which he thought good enough. "What is that?" asked Bathurst, pointing to a roll of paper, which was "Alma." "A trifle," answered Prior, "that I wrote in three weeks, not worthy of your attention."[13]

The eighteenth-century reader agreed with Prior in preferring the finished couplets of "Solomon" to the hasty Hudibrastics of "Alma." Likewise most modern readers prefer the earnestness of the former poem to the burlesque philosophy of the latter. Probably Mr. David Nicoll Smith was deferring to contemporary taste when he included a passage from "Solomon" in the *Oxford Book of Eighteenth Century Verse* and omitted one from "Alma." Yet Austin Dobson thought that "Alma" was most readable because of its "delightfully wayward digressions, its humor and its good-humor, its profusion of epigram and happy illustration." Further, Dobson pronounced Prior "second to none" in his mastery of Hudibrastic or octosyllabic verse.[14]

Despite the light mockery of "Alma" something of the poet's dejection during his imprisonment crept into at least one passage:

[12] Ruffhead, *Life of Pope*, p. 482.
[13] J. H. Burton, *Life and Correspondence of David Hume*, London, 1846, II, 501.
[14] Prior, *Selected Poems*, ed. Dobson, p. lvii.

Now Alma, to Divines and Prose
I leave Thy Frauds, and Crimes, and Woes:
Nor think To-night of thy Ill-Nature,
But of Thy Follies, Idle Creature,
The turns of Thy uncertain Wing,
And not the Malice of Thy Sting:
Thy Pride of being great and wise,
I do but mention, to despise.
I view with Anger and Disdain,
How little gives Thee Joy, or Pain;
A Print, a *Bronze*, a Flow'r, a Root,
A Shell, a Butter-fly can do't;
Ev'n a Romance, a Tune, a Rhime,
Help Thee to pass the tedious Time,
Which else would on thy Hand remain:
Tho' flown, it ne'er looks back again.
And Cards are dealt, and Chess-boards brought,
To ease the Pain of Coward-Thought.[15]

There were hours, as Matt confessed, when neither cards nor
chess could "ease the Pain of Coward-Thought"; when he was
plunged into a melancholy even to stupidity; when to write to a
friend was utterly impossible, for although he could sometimes
amuse himself for ten hours at a time, he could not bring himself to set down one idea; and though he might think of a
friend all day, he could not gather up courage to tell him so in a
letter that might be written in a quarter of an hour. And who
indeed, he mused, should have a greater abhorrence of writing
letters than he? Since letter writing was forbidden during his
confinement, these retrospections were not set down on paper
until the autumn of 1716 when as a free man he was communicat-
ing with Hanmer. The world, the town, he fretted, was a desert,
though there were many wild beasts (Whigs) in it. Therefore he
cautioned his friend to keep to his sheep and hounds, and,
meaning no reflection on any other species, to esteem them **very**
good companions. Hanmer had invited Matt to visit him, and

[15] *Poems on Several Occasions*, p. 251.

this Matt said he would do as soon as he had attended to his affairs, one of which, he feared, would be the selling of his house in Duke Street. He would then be more like the philosopher: *omnia mea mecum porto*.[16]

After a sojourn of nearly thirteen months at the home of Mr. Wibergh, Prior was given his freedom on June 26, 1716, when Parliament was prorogued;[17] but he remained "under a cloud" for the rest of his life. By Royal Act of Grace, July, 1717, pardon was extended to a number of political prisoners, but Prior, Oxford, and Thomas Harley were not among them.[18] It is known that Oxford was excepted on a motion made by the Earl of Stanhope,[19] whose vindictiveness may have extended to Prior. Certainly Prior thought that this was true, and he never forgave Stanhope. Several years later when Stanhope's nephew solicited Prior for a subscription to a biography of the Earl, recently deceased, Prior acidly advised him to employ himself on a life that would better recompense him for his pains.[20]

» 2 «

Immediately after his release Prior began receiving messages from friends in many quarters who wished not only to congratulate him upon being free once more but to express their indignation over his punishment. Edward Harley, Oxford's cousin, declared that Mr. Prior's treatment at the hands of the Secret Committee was one of the most villainous outrages ever made upon the liberty of an Englishman.[21] And Swift from Dublin wrote with characteristic vigor that Prior was "the first person in any Christian country that ever was suffered to starve

[16] Hanmer, *Correspondence*, p. 178, Prior to Sir Thomas Hanmer, Oct. 11, 1716, and 179, Prior to Hanmer, Nov. 10, 1716.

[17] *Political State of Great Britain*, XI, 763.

[18] An Act for the King's Most Gracious, General, and Free Pardon. See *ibid.*, XIV, 59–72.

[19] Basil Williams, *Stanhope*, p. 174.

[20] *Longleat Papers*, III, 501, Hugh Stanhope to Prior, April 6/17, 1721.

[21] *Portland Papers*, V, 664, *Memoirs of the Harley Family, especially of Robert Harley*, by Edward Harley, Auditor of the Exchequer.

after having been in so many great employments. . . . But amongst the Turks and Chineses it is a very frequent case, and those are the properest precedents for us at this time."[22] The most heart-warming message came from Paris from the "fellow traveller" of a happier day, the Abbé Gaultier:

We often remember you, the glass to the hand, and I shall never cease to cherish and to love you. . . You deserve a better treatment after all the great services which you have rendered to your country. . . Your old friends, among whom is my great patron, M. le Marquis de Torcy, always love you; all his family do likewise, and never change in their regard for you.[23]

More than sympathy, however, Prior needed financial assistance. Consequently the plan of publishing the aforementioned subscription edition of his works was launched, and Bathurst and Lord Edward Harley divulged the scheme to a group of friends who met with Erasmus Lewis one evening in January, 1716/17 when Prior, Pope, Gay, and Arbuthnot were present. While the guests discussed the enterprise, Lewis withdrew to write to the one absent person who would be most interested, Jonathan Swift. He appointed Swift as chief solicitor of subscriptions in Ireland and set forth Matt's plight:

Our friend, Prior, not having had the vicissitude of human things before his eyes, is likely to end his days in as forlorn a state as any poet before him if his friends do not take better care of him than he has done himself. Therefore to prevent the evil which we see is coming very fast, we have a project of printing his *Solomon*, and other poetical works by subscription; one guinea to be paid in hand and the other at the delivery of the book.

No advertisements in the London journals were to be published, Lewis explained, because the friends wished to manage the whole affair in such a manner as should be "least shocking to the dignity of a plenipotentiary."[24]

[22] *Ibid.*, 561, Swift to Harley, Dublin, May 17, 1718.
[23] *Longleat Papers*, III, 461, Gaultier to Prior, Paris, Oct. 9/20, 1718.
[24] Swift, *Correspondence*, II, 360, Erasmus Lewis to Swift, January 12/23, 1716/17.

Thus, in the most distinguished company of literary men who ever assembled for such an occasion, was launched the project which Prior had promised the Earl of Dorset eight years earlier when, in the dedication of the 1709 volume, he pledged himself to bind up a "fuller sheaf"—the product of his "severer studies."

Swift proved to be an invaluable canvasser, securing seventy subscriptions in Ireland. But in spite of the efforts of the committee the work progressed slowly, and more than two years passed before the volume was distributed to the subscribers. Six months after the meeting at Lewis's, when Prior had received four letters from Swift about the subscriptions, he could hardly bring himself to reply, for fear that government agents might open his letters.[25] Here is not the fearless Prior of old, but a man broken in spirit, unequal to a task to which willing friends were lending every assistance. His health was fairly good except for his "whoreson cough" and a deafness which was creeping upon him. Swift advised a change of scene, and in August Prior accepted an invitation to visit the Duke of Shrewsbury at Heythrop in Oxfordshire.

During this summer Lord Oxford was released from the Tower, acquitted without trial but forbidden the Court. He turned greedily to Prior for companionship. From this time on Matt spent much time either with Oxford or his son Lord Edward Harley, or with other members of the Harley clan, who adopted Matt as one of their own. When Lord Oxford was in London, he monopolized Matt completely—a monopoly which Matt faintly protested but which secretly flattered him and did much to restore his waning ego.

The real benefactor of Prior's last days, however, was Lord Edward rather than his father. Lord Oxford soon retired to his country seat, and although Prior visited him at Benington he found as time went by that his life was becoming more closely interwoven with that of the son than that of the father. Lord

[25] *Ibid.*, 398, Prior to Swift, Westminster, July 30, 1717.

Edward Harley is a dim figure beside his more illustrious father. Indolent and unambitious, he did not enter politics nor did he take an active part in the life of his time. He spent his and his wife's fortunes so lavishly on books, manuscripts, and estates that when he died in 1741 he was deep in debt. Loyally Prior celebrated his friend's knowledge of books in an epigram which he scribbled one morning among the vast treasures in Harley's library at Wimpole:

> Fame counting thy books, my dear Harley, shall tell,
> No man had so many and knew them so well.[26]

That Prior exaggerated his friend's knowledge of books may not be disputed. While Harley could not have known the contents of half his books or of even a third of them, he knew books as a collector knows them—by their editions and their value. Bolingbroke made a gross mistake when he remarked after Prior's death that Matt should have addressed himself to his young patron as Aristippus did to Dionysus: "You have money, which I want. I have wit and knowledge, which you want."[27] As a matter of fact, Harley was kind and generous to Prior, and it was due to him more than to anyone else that Matt's last years were spent in dignified ease commensurate with his high merits. Lady Harriett Harley has gone down in history as dull, stupid, worthy. Though not clever enough to appreciate Pope, she admired Prior and was as loyal a friend to him as was her husband. In keeping with his custom of choosing endearing epithets for his friends, Matt tagged Lord Edward and Lady Harriett as "amabilis" and "adoranda."

But the greatest attraction for Matt in the Harley family was little Margaret Cavendish—"dearest daughter of two dearest friends," as Prior addressed her. Born in 1714, she was only seven when Prior died, yet no one watched over her with more

---

[26] "Written in the Library at Wimpole, Dec. 2, 1720." See *Dialogues of the Dead*, p. 364.
[27] Swift, *Correspondence*, III, 112, Bolingbroke to Swift, Dec. 21/Jan. 1, 1721/2.

fond pride during her early years. He rarely failed to mention her in letters to her father, mother, or grandfather; always he would send his love—"a very pure and innocent passion"—to "little Margaretta." "La petite ange," "little Pearl," "Chara Infantula"—almost numberless were the pet names that the lonely old bachelor lavished upon the baby girl. And Lady Margaret returned Prior's affection, bestowing on him her most graceful curtsies and winning smiles. Artless beyond her years, she paid him the compliment of learning the library epigram. "I was never in my life better pleased with my own verses," said Matt, "than to hear little Mademoiselle Harley repeat them the next morning with the prettiest tone and manner imaginable."[28] On her sixth birthday, Prior wrote for her one of the most charming children's poems in any language:

> My noble, lovely, little PEGGY,
> Let this, my FIRST-EPISTLE, beg ye,
> At dawn of morn, and close of even,
> To lift your heart and hands to heaven:
> In double beauty say your pray'r,
> *Our father* first, then *notre pere*;
> And, dearest CHILD, along the day,
> In ev'rything you do and say,
> Obey and please my LORD and LADY,
> So GOD shall love, and ANGELS aid, Ye.
>
> If to these PRECEPTS You attend,
> No SECOND-LETTER need I send,
> And so I rest Your constant Friend,
>   M. P.[29]

To her Prior bequeathed a miniature copied from his Rigaud portrait which had been done in Paris in 1699.[30] Years later, when Peggy had become Duchess of Portland, she remembered the poet as one who "made himself beloved by every living

---

[28] *Portland Papers*, V, 610, Prior to Oxford, Wimpole, Dec. 23, 1720.

[29] *Dialogues of the Dead*, p. 131.

[30] The copy is by Charles Boit. See Goulding, *Welbeck Abbey Miniatures*, p. 143.

creature in the house—master, child, and servant, human creature or animal.''

Refreshed in mind and spirit as well as in health, Prior returned to Duke Street in the autumn of 1717 from summer visits at Heythrop, Wimpole, and Cambridge and settled down to prepare his volume for the press, though writing a book, he confessed to Lord Edward Harley was the thing in the world he most hated.

Tonson was to publish the poems. Subscription editions were, of course, not a new thing to Jacob. Sponsor of the subscription *Paradise Lost* in his early days as a publisher, he had also, it may be recalled, brought out Dryden's *Aeneid* and a collected *Tatler* under similar arrangement. It is true that a rival bookseller, Bernard Lintot, had outbid Jacob in the latest success, Pope's *Iliad*; moreover, Tonson was a Whig dog, but he had been Prior's official publisher since The Hague days—it was too late to change. There were, no doubt, business reasons more compelling than loyalty.

Probably because of the success of the *Iliad*, Prior sought Pope's advice:

If Mr. Pope be not engaged for Tomorrow Night He will do me a great favour in meeting Mr. Lewis at my house about Seven to confer upon the premises with Jacob Tonson and finish a piece of friendship which Mr. Pope has very generously begun to his humble servant.

M. Prior[31]

Prior's inability to settle down to work, his prolonged visits in the country, his fondness for social life were not the only causes for his failure to complete the volume until long after the subscribers grew impatient. His magnificent ideas about the book brought on a clash with Tonson. Prior desired that the book be printed on vellum. This was "impracticable, improbable, impossible," Tonson stormed; but of some of the other demands, he was not so scornful. It was finally agreed that the

[31] Fitzwilliam Museum, Cambridge. For a transcript of this letter, I am indebted to Professor George Sherburn.

edition should be published on "paper imperial and the largest in England."[32]

While these matters were being arranged, copies of "Solomon" and "Alma" were circulated among friends, who passed pretty compliments on the poems and affected a reluctance to return them. Thus the Duke of Buckinghamshire returned "Solomon" "with all the thanks imaginable for so agreeable an entertainment" and with apologies for "fear of wearing out the poem with reading it so often."[33] Bathurst at length returned "Alma" though he could not see why Prior would not suffer him to keep her a little longer—verily he was in love with her; the lady might safely be left with him since she was "immaterial and all spirit."[34] Atterbury sent "Alma" and "Solomon" home on New Year's Day accompanied by a whimsical though involved compliment:

I make you a better present than any man in England receives this day —two poems composed by a friend of mine with that extraordinary genius and spirit which attends him equally in whatever he says, does, or writes. I do not ask your approbation of them; deny it if you can, or if you dare; the whole world will be against you; and should you therefore be so unfortunate in your judgment, you will, I dare say, be so wise and modest as to conceal it, for, though it be a very good character and what belongs to the first pens in the world, to write like nobody, yet to judge like nobody has never yet been esteemed a perfection.[35]

Swift was not so flattering. He called the plan for the subscription volume a "sorry, wretched business." In replying to Swift, Prior took the cue and adopted a patronizing tone toward his editing: "A pretty kind of amusement I have been engaged in: commas, semicolons, italics, and capitals to make nonsense more pompous, and furbelow bad poetry with good printing."[36]

[32] *Longleat Papers*, III, 450, Prior to Harley, Nov. 30/Dec. 11, 1717.
[33] *Ibid.*, 458, Buckinghamshire to Prior, Sept. 1718.
[34] *Ibid.*, Bathurst to Prior, [Sept. 1718?].
[35] *Ibid.*, 451, Atterbury to Prior, New Year's Day, 1717/18.
[36] Swift, *Correspondence*, III, 4, Prior to Swift, May 1/12, 1718.

A few more weeks dragged by before Prior announced that two friends—Drift and Shelton, we surmise—were helping him read proof: "I have two colon and comma men. We correct and design to publish, as fast as the nature of this great sorry work as you [Swift] call it, will bear; but we shall not be out before Christmas."[37] For advice as to the typography, Prior had the expert assistance of Humphrey Wanley, Lord Oxford's librarian, who found fault with the printer for his "filthy hooks, meagre letters and unequal lines." Further delays occurred so that the volume was not ready until the middle of March, 1718, or, as we reckon it today, 1719, more than two years after it was proposed.[38]

A noble volume was this subscription edition, measuring thirty-six inches by twelve, and weighing from nine to ten pounds. On account of its ungainly size it is not a favorite with collectors, but it is a fine specimen of the typography of the period, the type "flowing as a rivulet in a meadow of paper" through its five hundred pages. Looking down the pages which contain the subscribers' names, one finds that there were 1,445 persons who took 1,786 books, for which, along with the copies Tonson sold in his bookshop, Prior received some four thousand guineas. The subscription list reads like a social register of the period. Here are all the grand lords and ladies of that by-gone day; literary men like Pope, Swift, Congreve, and Steele; artists like Jervas and Kneller. And if Walpole and Bolingbroke are conspicuous by their absence, there are Stanhope, Craggs, and Stair—the latter, down for not one but five copies. But the reader of this impressive list should not fail to note the presence of the names of hosts of Cambridge dons and Dorsetshire vicars, and of the few still living friends of early days—Sir James Montague, Dorothy Stepney, and Katherine Harrison, the favorite cousin.

The tall book contains all the poems that appeared in the

[37] *Ibid.*, 8, Prior to Swift, May 29, 1718.
[38] Advertised in the *Daily Courant*, March 19, 1719.

authorized edition of 1709, arranged in a slightly different order, and some additional material, chief of which is, of course, the "Alma" and the "Solomon." The same dedication to the Earl of Dorset is here, and the same preface, to which was added a postscript bringing the poet's compliments to his benefactor down to date. About sixty new short pieces, ranging in length from a two line epigram to the two hundred line translation of the "Second Hymn of Callimachus," comprise another section of this vast volume.[39] Here for the first time are several of the best Cloe poems, such as "Cloe Jealous," "The Dove," "Lisetta's Reply," "A Lover's Anger," "The Garland," "A Better Answer"—poems which were mentioned in an earlier chapter, where Cloe was discussed. Almost as good as these are tales like "Protogenes and Apelles," "The Thief and the Cordelier." Of the epigrams, "A Reasonable Affliction," "The Lady Who Offers Her Looking Glass to Venus," and "The Converse" are not only among the best that Prior ever wrote but are ranked among the best in the language.[40] The six brief lines of "Democritus and Heraclitus" we single out for prominence because they seem eminently expressive of Matt's mood as he approached his fifty-fifth birthday:

> DEMOCRITUS, dear Droll, revisit Earth,
> And with our Follies glut Thy heighten'd Mirth:
> Sad HERACLITUS, serious Wretch, return,
> In louder Grief our greater Crimes to mourn.
> Between You both I unconcern'd stand by:
> Hurt, can I laugh? and Honest, need I cry?[41]

---

[39] "It is, of a surety, one of the vastest volumes of verse in existence." Prior, *Selected Poems*, ed. Dobson, p. xii.

[40] We quote at this point the following "Epigram" never included in any edition of Prior's works but attributed to Prior in *Amaryllis: Consisting of such Songs as are most esteemed for Composition and Delicacy and Sung at the Public Theatres or Gardens*, London, c. 1750, II, 63.

To heal the Smart a Bee had made	Pleas'd I obeyed and from the Wound
Upon my Cloe's Face	Imbib'd both Sweet and Smart
Honey upon her Cheeks she laid	The Honey on my Lips I found,
And bid me Kiss the Place.	The Sting within my Heart.

[41] *Poems on Several Occasions*, p. 194.

But little can be said for the majority of the other short pieces as poetry. Many are merely complimentary verses addressed to friends or are otherwise purely fugitive in character. A few of the epigrams like "A Critical Moment,"

> How capricious were Nature and Art to poor Nell!
> She was painting her Cheeks at the time her Nose fell.

cater to the popular taste which regarded dyed hair, detachable eyebrows, glass eyes, and other artificialities of my lady's dressing table as the proper butt of satire. Such "mean and stale" epigrams, says a certain critic, "cannot be redeemed by mere smartness or mere versifying skill."[42] Equally bad are the tales attempted "in Chaucer's stile" despite the fact that Prior and Chaucer had something in common as poets, as was pointed out by Professor Minto while he was drawing a parallel in their careers as men of affairs.[43] No doubt Prior would have found in Chaucer a kindred spirit had his interest in Chaucer been as real as his interest in Spenser. The inclusion of these poor pieces is regrettable, as is that of an early and feeble poem like the "Picture of Seneca Dying in a Bath"—wisely excluded from the 1709 edition—when there were tucked away in the poet's escritoire such superior poems as "The Secretary," "Daphne and Apollo," and "To a Child of Quality."

Undoubtedly Prior set the greatest store upon "Solomon": he beamed when his friends admired it and was shocked when Pope perversely claimed to prefer "Alma." More convinced of the pessimistic philosophy of "Solomon" than when he first conceived the poem a dozen years earlier, the embittered Matt looked back over his life and found no refutation of his theme, echoing Montaigne's Essay, *Coustume de l'isle de Cea*, that "the pleasures of life do not compensate the miseries" but, rather, found much to establish the certainty that "Age steals upon us

---

[42] Hamilton, *The Soul of Wit*, XV.
[43] Article on Prior in the *Encyclopedia Britannica*, Ninth Edition, Edinburgh, 1885.

unawares; and Death, as the only Cure for our Ills, ought to be expected but not feared."

Prior's affection for "Solomon," which Pope thought due to a critical blind spot, Dr. Johnson considered natural. Much has been made of Dr. Johnson's dictum that the poem is tedious. This criticism, the Doctor explained, was made because he found "Solomon's" long, uninterrupted speeches tiresome rather than the subject matter boring. The author of *The Vanity of Human Wishes* read much in "Solomon" that satisfied him, and his comments, on the whole, are favorable:

Prior infused into it much knowledge and much thought; and often polished it to elegance, often dignified it with splendour, and sometimes heightened it to sublimity: he perceived in it many excellencies, and did not discover that it wanted that without which all others are of small avail—the power of engaging attention and alluring curiosity. . . Yet the work is far from deserving to be neglected. He that shall pursue it will be able to mark many passages to which he may recur for instruction or delight; many from which the poet may learn to write, and the philosopher to reason.[44]

In view of Dr. Johnson's pronouncement, no more need be said in justification of Prior's pride in his self-styled masterpiece. After all, "Solomon" is not in the same category with "Alma," which was included in the volume only after the insistence of friends, but should be considered with those other poems upon which equal labor was lavished. The carefully polished society verse and "Solomon" represent respectively the Democritus and Heraclitus sides of Prior's nature—the gay and the grave, the waggish and the philosophic—which maintained such fitful ascendencies in his breast. Much reading in divers literature is reflected in "Solomon." In Prior's Duke Street home there was a library far more extensive than that of any of his literary contemporaries and that ran to several thousand volumes.[45] Beside the many lovely and rare Aldines and Elzevirs

---

[44] "Life of Prior," Birkbeck Hill Edition of Johnson's *Lives of the English Poets*, II, 206.
[45] W. Roberts, "Matthew Prior as a Book-Collector," in *The Athenaeum*, June 19, 1897,

and the volumes of English and of French literature and history, there reposed on his shelves scores of treatises on philosophy and religion—Anglican, Catholic, and Nonconformist—which had been collected in England and abroad. Milton and the Old Testament jostle Lucretius and Theognis in "Solomon," but there is to be found in a final analysis of the poem the philosophy of the man Prior, who was, like Dr. Johnson, a pessimist by temperament.

The subscription volume did not mark a cessation of writing for Prior. During the less than three years that remained to him, he wrote some of his best works and planned others, which progressed no further than the outline. Among the works actually completed, there is much of his best prose—"Essay upon Learning," "Essay upon Opinion," and the four *Dialogues of the Dead*.[46] It is a pity that these pieces, known to Pope, Joseph Warton, Beattie, Malone, and probably to other literary celebrities of the eighteenth century, were not given to the world until Mr. Waller published them in 1907. Since then they have not received the recognition which they justly deserve. The two essays, from which we have drawn from time to time for biographical information, are charmingly personal. They achieve that conversational mood so happily described else-where—"the man you talk with is Mat. Prior."

The "Essay upon Learning" contains much sensible advice on such allied topics as misapplied learning, useless study, the art of quotation, conversational wit, the advisability of cultivating some secondary interest in addition to one's vocation. As we have said in a preceding chapter, Prior bestowed the highest praise on his first patron, Dorset, in the field of conversational

---

p. 810. Mr. Roberts wrote: "In his *Journal* to Stella we get many delightful glimpses of Swift as a book-hunter. Pope was a book-lover and owned a fairly good library, and even the great Mr. Addison could not have denied the soft impeachment of bibliomania. But greater in this way than all these was Matthew Prior, the genial wit and wily diplomatist."

[46] *Dialogues of the Dead*, pp. 177-270.

wit. For examples of excellence in the art of quotation, he turned to three eminent bishops then living, Atterbury, Smalridge, and Gastrell. These divines, he declared, "placed texts of Scripture as advantageously as expert jewellers would set precious stones." Reverting to the subject of wit, he cited the "writers of the Bible" as supreme in wit as well as in truth and loftiness of thought. Since the essay is undated, we can only place it approximately as having been written after 1718 and before the death of Smalridge, in September, 1719.

The "Essay upon Opinion" deals with a more difficult subject than the previous treatise: it is less chatty, and its illustrations are drawn not so much from the writer's reminiscences as from his wide reading in history. We follow Prior by a somewhat devious course as he discusses the relation between opinion and the "passions which subjugate our opinion." Preëminent among these passions are ambition and love—"the first makes us think too well, and the latter too meanly of ourselves." He goes on to argue that these passions—better called "natural fire or impulse" —may be guided by our judgment and understanding into a great variety of channels of expression. Next he makes a distinction between the man of passions, opinion, genius, and the common herd or majority of mankind who have no opinions and hence "go to the next coffee house to be informed of their own sentiments."

Even better than these essays are the *Dialogues of the Dead.* While Prior does not invite comparison in this literary form with Lucian, Fontenelle, and Landor, he excelled all writers of Dialogues during his century. A well-stored mind, an eye for the contrasts of character, an intense realism, an ability to set down dialogue in a pert and nimble style were Prior's assets for this type of composition. The dialogue between Charles the Emperor and Clenard the Grammarian represents a gay and witty colloquy on the age-worn question of greatness, which, according to Prior, is purely relative. The dialogue between Montaigne and Locke is the most interesting of the four. Prior's undoubted admiration for Montaigne, his prejudice against philosophy furnish the keynote to the dialogue. What first strikes the reader is the unfairness toward Locke and the success with which Prior reproduces the very manner of Montaigne. In this achievement, as Professor Barrett says truly, "he is assisted by a certain skill in parody, but more particularly by a remarkable sympathy of temper."[47] Not so weighty is the dialogue between Sir Thomas More and the Vicar of Bray—the one an idealist, the other, an opportunist. The fourth and last of these pieces, where Cromwell converses with his porter, portrays the Protector unfavorably. It suggests Prior's Tory bias and indicates less careful workmanship than the other three.

Pleased with these efforts, Prior planned three more dialogues which would have offered themes of even greater controversial interest. There was to be a dispute between Ximenes and Wolsey, one between Wolsey and Cranmer, one between Luther and Loyola. These conversations promised Prior an opportunity to draw upon his knowledge of doctrinal subjects as well as to point sharp contrasts in character, but the actual writing was never begun. Still more exciting would have been the contemplated dialogue with Jane Shore and the wife of Edward IV on the stage. This, we believe, Matt would have handled with a dexterity similar to that shown in "Daphne and Apollo," in "Protogenes and Apelles," and in the other poems where sprightly nymphs of charming impertinence proclaim themselves true sisters to the Olivias, the Melanthas, the Millamants, the Florimels of Restoration comedy.

One might wonder why Prior never attempted comedy, and is surprised to find that he seriously undertook to write tragedy. Among the Longleat MSS Mr. Waller found several notebooks labeled "Minutes for a Tragedy," which outline Prior intended

[47] W. P. Barrett, "Matthew Prior's Alma," in *Mod. Lang. Rev.*, XXVII (October, 1932), 454–58.

to develop into a drama to be called *Britanicus* [*sic*]. The notes were too imperfect, the editor thought, to be printed.[48] In these same notes there was the long "Argument of Ladislaus," another tragedy in outline only. There were also many observations, even more fragmentary, on Homer and Ovid, besides the mere jottings down of a number of projected works in prose and verse—some in Latin and some in English. All these fragments indicate a fertile brain but an absence of tenacity. Had they been completed, the bulk of Prior's work would be greater; of its quality, one may only speculate.

Finally we come to "Jinny the Just," that very delightful character sketch, from which we quoted when discussing the identity of Prior's mistresses. The poem, never published until 1907, barely escaped publication in a volume of Pope and Swift miscellanea that Pope was sponsoring in 1727, Harley having refused a request for it.[49] The date of composition of the poem has never been determined. The fifth of the Dryden Miscellanies (1703/4) may contain the secret, for here is a poem, "An Epitaph," anonymous to be sure, but unmistakably "Jinny the Just" in embryo:

> Here lies little . . . a Yard deep and more,
> That never lay silent or quiet before,
> Her Head always working, her Tongue always prating,
> And the Pulse of her Heart continually beating,
> To the utmost Extreams of Loving and Hating.
> Her Reason and Humour were always at Strife;
> And yet she perform'd all the Duties of Life:
> An excellent Friend, and a pretty good Wife.
> So indulgent a Lover, that no Man could say
> Whether *Patty* or *Minta* did Rule or Obey:
> For the Government chang'd some ten times a day.
> At the Hour of her Birth, some lucky Star gave her
> Wit and Beauty enough to have lasted for ever;
> But Fortune, still froward when Nature is kind,

---

[48] *Dialogues of the Dead*, p. 355.

[49] Pope, *Works*, ed. Elwin and Courthope, VIII, 232, Pope to Harley, Dec. 26, 1726.

A narrow Estate maliciously join'd,
To a vast Genius, and a noble Mind.

Her Body was built of that superfine Clay
That is apt to grow brittle for want of Allay:
And, when, without shew, it was apt to decay,
It began by degrees to moulder away.
Her Soul, then, too busy on some Foreign Affair,
Of its own pretty Dwelling took so little Care,
That the Tenement fell for want of Repair.

Far be from hence the Fool, or the Knave,
But let all that pretend to be Witty or Brave,
Whether gen'rous Friend or amorous Slave,
Contribute some Tears to water her Grave.[50]

An unnamed manuscript among the Prior papers at Welbeck is
almost identical with "An Epitaph." Certain lines are smoother,
but the main difference is that the subject of the epitaph is
named, so that the first line reads, "Here lies little Lundy a
yard deep and more." One familiar with "Jinny the Just"—a
title bestowed by Mr. Waller—can come to only one conclusion
—that Jinny and Lundy are one and the same person and that
"An Epitaph" is a hasty effort which Prior intended to improve before publishing over his own name. Jinny ironically
outlived her immortalizer and hence her eulogy lay unprinted
these many years.

The first printings of various of Prior's works that found their
way into single-sheet folios, miscellanies, and unauthorized or
pirated editions have brought the criticism that Prior was a
careless writer. It is true, as might be expected of one who used
the anapaestic triplet and the octosyllabic couplet with such
ease, that he wrote very rapidly. A careful comparison of the
first drafts of the poems with those which Matt got ready for
publication would indicate that he was rarely satisfied with his
original inspiration and spent many hours in painstaking re-
vision.

[50] *Poetical Miscellanies*, Part V, p. 292.

» 3 «

With no political office to absorb his attention, and his writing, always done fitfully, easy to postpone or to leave unfinished, Matt was free to flit about the town. He dined with the Harleys in Dover Street, with Oxford in Lincoln's Inn Fields, he entertained the Virtuosi or other friends at his own home, attended the theatre, and read the latest English and French books. Nevertheless he was a man living in retirement. Subject to colds or to his old complaint, cholera morbus, he was confined for days at a time to his house, where in the good company of "that great philosopher Dick" or "that ingenious person, Adrian," he would drink the healths of absent friends or dictate chatty letters to them, Adrian holding the pen. Out of touch with Court and ministry which had dealt so harshly with him, he had little knowledge of government affairs except what he picked up at the Smyrna or from the daily news sheets. The collapse of the South Sea Bubble, in which he lost an uncomfortable amount of money, made him rue having lent an ear to the "conversation of pick-pockets and stock jobbers" and to wonder, with Dick Shelton, if one could expect better from a "conjunction of scoundrels at Court with sharpers in the city."

Most of his companions were Tories, but he still kept in touch with old friends of the opposite side: he visited the Earl of Dorset, now rewarded for his attachment to the new régime with a dukedom; he drew up the preamble for the patent to the Duke's title; and dedicated *The Conversation* to the son of his old patron. When, for old times' sake, Sir James Montague requested him to write an inscription for the tomb of Lord Halifax in Westminster Abbey, Matt complied with a long and impressive eulogy.[51]

On the other hand, he was resentful towards the Walpoles,

[51] *Longleat Papers*, III, 470, Sir James Montague to Prior, Oct. 27/Nov. 7, 1719. For the epitaph, see Prior's *Poetical Works*, ed. by R. B. Johnson, 307.

the Stanhopes, and the Coningsbys, who, he thought, might have helped him to emerge from the cloud of the trial a happier man instead of a discomfited one. Nor did time soften his feelings for Addison, for even after Addison's death he cast another stone in this letter to Swift: "I do not know why you have not buried me as you did Partridge, and given the wits of the age, the Steeles and the Addisons, a new occasion of living seven years upon one of your thoughts."[52]

Prior renewed relationships with his few surviving kinspeople. He could sympathize with Cousin Katherine Harrison, who had also been a victim of the South Sea catastrophe, and he not only helped her to disentangle her affairs but often enjoyed her informal hospitality, when she would ask him over for "something between a dinner and a supper" and cards. Of the more distant relatives, we know little save that he always asked Swift to "remember" him to Cousin Pennefather and that he bequeathed a ring each to the Colonel and his lady.

Many of Prior's hours were idled away in sitting for his portrait, a favorite eighteenth-century pastime. Dahl painted him several times, and two other Swedish painters, Boit and Richter, each put his likeness on canvas at least once. The best of the Dahl portraits is the one at Knole, in which "the elegant statesman and poet stands leaning his left hand on a table while with the right he proudly points to the works of Spenser."[53] In London there are paintings enough of Matt's sharp countenance and lank, hollow-chested figure. A likeness by Kneller hangs in Stationer's Hall; one by Jonathan Richardson, bearing a strong resemblance to portraits of Pope, is in the National Portrait Gallery; one by an unknown painter, in the South Kensington Museum. The portrait by Alexis Simon Belle (frontispiece), made at Louis XIV's order and for a fee of a hundred pistoles, Prior left to St. John's College, Cambridge. The best of all the portraits—

[52] Swift, *Correspondence*, III, 50, Prior to Swift, Westminster, May 4, 1720.
[53] Wilhelm Nisser, *Michael Dahl and the Contemporary Swedish School of Painting in England*, p. 122.

at least Lord Edward Harley and Drift thought it the best, and probably Prior himself thought so—is the one by Rigaud which Matt willed to Lord Edward Harley. It now hangs along with portraits of countless other ladies and gentlemen of the long ago in Welbeck Abbey among the Portland treasures inherited from the distaff side. It is a half-length, life-size profile of the poet-secretary at the age of thirty-five. Characteristically, he was posed with a book, which he held open in the left hand and rested on a table. He was attired in a greyish purple velvet coat, opened carelessly at the throat to display the shirt; across the right shoulder a russet-colored cloak was draped, and he was topped off with a black dressing cap, encircled by a blue ribbon. The interesting shadow effect appears to have been cast by candle-light although no taper is seen in the picture.[54] Unquestionably, some of the other painters portrayed a handsomer man, and Prior's partiality to the Rigaud likeness may be explained only on the grounds that it recaptured for a disillusioned man something of the promise and vigor of his youth.[55]

Soon after the distribution of the subscription edition of Prior's poems, Tonson put on sale some small engraved copies of the Richardson painting. Tonson also continued to publish Matt's current poems, usually in single sheet folios. Thus were brought out *The Conversation, A Tale*,[56] the *Prologue to the Orphan*,[57] and two poems in honor of Lady Harley—*Verses Spoke to the Lady Henrietta-Cavendish Holles Harley in the Library of St. John's College* and *Colin's Mistakes*.[58] Anything belonging to Prior published elsewhere was probably done without his permission. None of these poems adds anything to his reputation, but he seems to have felt proud of the verses he had recited in

---

[54] *A Catalogue of the Pictures . . . at Welbeck Abbey, and in London*, p. 67.

[55] Other portraits of Prior are at Oxford and at Cambridge. Three Richardsons are at Oxford: one, presented by Harley, is in the Bodleian Library, and two others, also thought to have been presented by Harley, are the property of Christ Church College. A reproduction of an excellent one at Cambridge by Sir Godfrey Kneller faces p. 150, above.

[56] Advertised by Tonson in the *Daily Courant*, Feb. 10, 1720.

[57] *Ibid.*, March 10, 1720. [58] *Ibid.*, Feb. 15, 1721.

cap and gown to Lady Harley in the academic halls of his own college. The occasion restored something of the sense of self-importance which he had lost since he was no longer His Excellency, the Plenipotentiary in Paris.

With his book out of the way and an income assured for the rest of his life, Prior felt a sense of security. He could return to that society of literary men which his employment in France and resulting misfortunes had denied him. The Brothers Club, which was flourishing so agreeably at the time of his departure for Paris, gradually gave way to the Scriblerus Club, of which Matt was not a member, owing to his prolonged absence from London. Even the Scriblerus, whose purpose was solely literary, whereas the Brothers had mingled literature with politics, was now inactive, probably on account of the absence of Swift. Yet the other members, Pope, Gay, and Arbuthnot were in London and were the brightest lights in the literary galaxy of the moment. Arbuthnot, Prior had known in the Brothers Club, but it is not recorded just when he became acquainted with Pope, and therefore with Gay, since to know one was to know the other. He may have met Pope by May, 1712, the date of the publication of Lintot's famous *Miscellany*, in which three of Prior's poems were included,[59] for Pope is generally conceded to have been the editor of the collection. It seems significant that Dorset's verses, "To all you Ladies now at Land," made their *première* in this *Miscellany*; our conjecture is that Prior suggested their inclusion to Pope. If, however, Prior did know Pope as early as 1712, it is strange that there is no mention of him in any of Matt's letters from France. Moreover, although Prior's name appears on the subscription list of the *Iliad* among the "First Names of the Age," it is not included in the pretentious list of the "most distinguished Patrons and Ornaments of Learning"

[59] They were *"Gaulterus Danistonus ad Amicos,* Imitated by Mr. Prior," p. 67, "Horace, *Lib.* I, *Epist.* IX" and "To the Right Honourable R-H Esq., by the same Hand," p. 74, and "An Imitation of Chaucer, By the same Hand," p. 74.

in Pope's proud preface. Further, Prior's note, already quoted, inviting Pope to join in the conference with Tonson and Lewis, suggests that the acquaintance between the two poets was not of very long standing. We may be sure that whenever they met, Prior made haste to annex the rising young Mr. Pope as a friend. The handsome compliment on Pope's *Eloisa to Abelard*, an interpolation amounting to eighteen lines in "Alma," is plainly a bid for favor:

> O ABELARD, ill-fated Youth,
> Thy Tale will justify this Truth:
> But well I weet, thy cruel Wrong
> Adorns a nobler Poet's song,
> *Dan* POPE for thy Misfortune griev'd,
> With kind Concern, and Skill has weav'd
> A silken Web; and ne'er shall fade
> It's colors: . . .[60]

These lines were used as a motto in a later edition of the *Eloisa*. Bathurst, who seems to have been responsible for some of the choicest bits of information about "Alma," told Joseph Warton that Pope did not like that part of Prior's compliment,

> He o'er the weeping Nun has drawn,
> Such artful Folds of Sacred Lawn, . . .

which implies palliation of Eloisa's guilt.[61] This statement we hardly believe, because several other editions of *Eloisa to Abelard*, which Pope himself saw through the press, also carried the passage from "Alma" prefixed. Had Pope really been displeased, he would have dropped Prior's lines from the pages of the poem without ceremony.[62] We may recall that Pope preferred "Alma" to "Solomon." May not this bit of flattery explain his preference?

Throughout the years 1717 to 1721, Prior and Pope, belonging as they did to the same literary circle, must have met frequently,

[60] *Poems on Several Occasions*, pp. 231–32.
[61] Pope, *Works*, ed. by Elwin and Courthope, II, 218.   [62] *Ibid.*, 218*n*.

although documentary evidence of their meetings is slight. From *Mr. Pope's Welcome from Greece*, written by Gay in 1720, we take a line which indicates Prior's high standing in that inner circle:

Dan Prior next, belov'd by every Muse[63]

In February, 1720, Prior asked Pope to give him an opinion on *The Conversation, A Tale*, then only in manuscript form.[64] Frequently the two poets met at Buckingham House to dine with the seventy-two year old Duke of Buckinghamshire, who was demonstrating to Pope how advantageous it was to consort with dukes.[65] Old John of Bucks, as he was familiarly called, had scribbled verses to be prefixed to the 1717 edition of Pope's poems. Mediocre though the verses were, Prior seized his pen and introduced in "Alma" a compliment to the crotchety old gentleman:

Happy the Poet, blest the Lays,
Which BUCKINGHAM has deign'd to praise.[66]

In gratitude the Duke added Prior to the circle of Wits already admitted to Buckingham House. But in spite of the good companionship of Pope, Gay, Charles Ford, and Buckinghamshire, there was little to remind Prior of the *camaraderie* of the Brothers. Pope was no substitute for Swift; in fact, Prior never became intimate with Pope.[67] The successful young poet, starting out on a brilliant social career, could not use the older poet in furthering his ambitions—indeed he had no need of Matt, who doubt-

---

[63] Gay, *Poetical Works*, I, 211.   [64] Pope, *Works*, X, 105.

[65] One occasion is referred to when Prior wrote Lord Edward Harley, June 16/27, 1720, that he was "going to dine with Buckingham as a sort of *convivium poeticum*, for Pope and Gay are the other two guests." *Longleat Papers*, III, 482. Pope was probably speaking of the same gathering in an undated letter to Charles Ford: "I write this to give you timely notice that the Duke of Buckingham having heard of Mr. Prior's and our meeting desires it may be at his Grace's house . . . I beg you to pre-ingage Mr. Gay, as for my own part, I shall goe to London on purpose that day." (Pierpont Morgan Library, Swift MSS.).

[66] *Poems on Several Occasions*, p. 232.

[67] The two brief letters from Prior to Pope, to which we have referred, dealt purely with literary matters. Prior mentioned Pope only twice in seventy-two letters to Lord Edward Harley, and both times only casually. In his letters to Swift, and others who were acquainted with both poets, he never referred to Pope, nor did any of these men ever speak of Pope in their letters to Prior.

less proved a bore with garrulous tales of the proud days when he had jested with Louis XIV, danced with the beautiful Mademoiselle de Charolais, or outwitted the famous Pontchartrain.

Pope early showed that he considered himself a better poet than Prior and did not hesitate to match his verse with Prior's. For instance, he once sent to a friend three versions of the *Adriani Morientis ad Animam Suam,*—Flatman's, Prior's and his own,—asking for an opinion as to which of the verses were "best written."[68] Then, it is said on good authority, Pope first thought of writing the *Epistle from Eloisa to Abelard* after perusing Prior's *Henry and Emma.*[69] Grub Street's version of the story was that Pope wrote his poem "in opposition" to Prior's.[70] Whether this story is true or false, Pope undeniably borrowed some of his very best lines from Prior. This borrowing was never acknowledged, nor was the gracious compliment in "Alma" reciprocated. Shenstone wondered if Pope's failure to repay such poetical obligations might not be attributed to selfishness.[71]

Most of Pope's waspish remarks about Prior are recorded in Spence's *Anecdotes*; some are based on fact and some on fiction. The famous slur relative to Matt and his mistress was probably warranted, but the reflection upon Prior's business acumen was so contrary to fact that Dr. Johnson felt moved to contradict it at length.[72] However carping Pope was in his conversations with Spence, he was liberal enough with his praise when he was asked to examine Prior's literary remains:

I now not only desire but want, and long to read the remains of Mr. Prior. My respect for him living extends to his memory, and it gives me leave to say in this I resemble your Lordship [Harley], that it dies not with his person.[73]

---

[68] Pope, *Works*, ed. Elwin and Courthope, IV, 408, Pope to John Caryll, June 12, 1713.
[69] Dr. Johnson quotes Savage to this effect in his "Life of Pope," Birkbeck Hill edition of the *Lives of the English Poets*, III, 105.
[70] See James Ralph, *Sawney, An Heroic Poem, occasion'd by the Dunciad*, London, 1728.
[71] Shenstone, *Men and Manners*, p. 43.
[72] In his "Life of Prior," Birkbeck Hill edition of the *Lives of the English Poets*, II, 198.
[73] Pope, *Works*, ed. Elwin and Courthope, VIII, 193, Pope to Harley, Aug. 24, 1723.

Our conjecture is that Pope's caustic remarks about Prior were the result, in part at least, of his later intimacy with Bolingbroke. It is quite safe to wager that Prior never had a line from that mercurial gentleman after the eventful night when, blaming Prior for all his troubles and terror-stricken lest Prior should testify against him, he had fled to France. Never afterwards did Bolingbroke mention Prior in his correspondence except to profess "great indifference" to a volume of Prior's *Works*, which had been sent to him by mistake instead of a copy of Pope's *Iliad*, which he was "impatient to see."[74] We might add that Pope was no less eager to have the exiled Viscount receive this presentation copy, for Pope had a habit of cultivating men of position who had been friends of Prior's—Trumbull, Halifax, Dorset, Shrewsbury, Swift, the Harcourts, the Harleys —but not one of them would have been so eager to pour into the willing ears of Pope poison about Prior as that erstwhile crony, Bolingbroke.

While tracing Prior's friendships during these years of leisure, it might be interesting to note his relationship with Bishop Atterbury, his schoolmate at Westminster. We know that Prior and Atterbury renewed their acquaintance from time to time in after years. In 1704 Matt lent to Atterbury what must have been a manuscript copy of *A Tale of a Tub*, which was being passed around among their little circle. Again, in 1712, Prior spent a congenial evening—from six until one in the morning—with Atterbury and Swift at the home of Dr. Robert Freind, recently appointed headmaster of Westminster School. Ever ready with congratulatory epistles, Prior did not neglect Atterbury when he simultaneously became Bishop of Rochester and Dean of Westminster. To go into Atterbury's Jacobitism would be a digression; suffice it to say that the Bishop was willing to overlook Matt's coldness towards the cause and even urged Prior to come

---

[74] Pierpont Morgan Library, *Bolingbroke MSS*, Bolingbroke to Charles Ford, January 29, 1720.

down to Bromley for an extended visit. Since the invitation came while Prior was away in Dorsetshire, the Bishop was kept waiting for an answer. The summer wore on, and the peaches and the nectarines hung on the trees at Bromley until they rotted. Atterbury, suffering from impatience and gout, expostulated with Prior in a deluge of Latin and Greek, which was concluded in English with characteristic vigor:

Today, tomorrow, always; at Bromley, at Westminster, everywhere; in Greek, in Latin, in English; and which is more, in good earnest, I am your faithful humble servant.[75]

It is a pity that these friends of such long standing were soon to turn against each other. Atterbury had many quarrels in the course of his career. The quarrel of the moment was one with Dr. Freind, the still popular headmaster of Westminster, who had on his side three old Westminsters—Stratford, Lord Harley, and Prior. It centered on the building of a new dormitory at the school.[76] The old one, once the granary of the monks, was falling into ruins. Atterbury, determined to have a new building, went ahead on his own initiative and commissioned Sir Christopher Wren to draw up plans. As funds were needed, the bishop solicited far and wide, even pocketing his Jacobite sympathies to beg subscriptions from George I and the Prince of Wales. When he chose a site for the dormitory it was found that the building would encroach upon Dr. Freind's private garden on one side and upon the college garden on another.

In the eyes of these loyal Westminsters—all Tories as well—Atterbury was guilty of a darker deed than disturbing the hallowed atmosphere of the old school, that of making his peace with the Whigs. He had been so outspoken an enemy of the Hanover régime that his overtures to them seemed the

---

[75] *Longleat Papers*, III, 456, Atterbury to Prior, Aug. 27/Sept. 7, 1718.
[76] For Atterbury's dispute over the college dormitory, see Lawrence E. Tanner, *Westminster School*, pp. 24–25.

worst form of infidelity. On Atterbury's conduct, Matt commented to Swift:

Roffen [Atterbury] is more than suspected to have given up his party, as Sancho did his subjects, for so much a head, *l'un portant l'autre*. His cause, therefore [the contest over the dormitory] which is something originally like that of Le Lutrin is opposed or neglected by his ancient friends, and openly sustained by the ministry. He cannot be lower in the opinion of most men than he is.[77]

Matt further expressed his impatience with Atterbury by writing and circulating an anonymous epigram:

> Meek Francis lies here, friend! without stop or stay.
> As you value your peace, make the best of your way,
> Though at present arrested by Death's caitiff paw,
> If he stirs, he may still have recourse to the law.
> And in the King's-bench should a verdict be found,
> That by livery and seisin his grave is his ground,
> He will claim to himself what is strictly his due,
> And an action of trespass will straightway ensue,
> That you without right on his premises tread,
> On a simple surmise that the owner is dead.[78]

The authorship did not long remain secret; the epigram undoubtedly bore Matt's earmarks. It was only good fun, and Atterbury could not take serious offense at it.

Prior, however, did not stop with this piece of waggery but used his skill with more deadly results in an affair that indirectly affected Atterbury. It may be recalled that the Earl of Mulgrave had once been the butt of some of Matt's collegiate satire. When, however, the Earl as the Duke of Buckinghamshire became a man of great influence, a favorite with Queen Anne, Prior repudiated the early poems which Curll had published. The Duke, as we have seen, had affected of late years an interest in poets, entertaining them at Buckingham House, and Prior had often been invited there. In February 1720/1721 the pompous old

[77] Swift, *Correspondence*, III, 75, Prior to Swift, April 25, 1721.
[78] *Dialogues of the Dead*, p. 172.

gentleman died, leaving an epitaph in Latin to be inscribed on his tomb. On the day of his funeral an imperfect version of the Latin lines appeared in the London newspapers. Hastily Prior turned off a mischievous epigram:

> "I have no hopes," the Duke he says, and dies;
> "In sure and certain hopes," the Prelate cries:
> Of these two learned Peers, I pry'thee, say, man,
> Who is the lying knave, the Priest or Layman?
> The Duke he stands an infidel confest,
> "He's our dear brother," quoth the lordly priest.
> The Duke though knave, still "Brother dear," he cries;
> And who can say the Reverend Prelate lies?[79]

Atterbury did not regard this trifling as a mere joke. Prior, he thought, had traduced the memory of his dead friend by calling him "an infidel confest," but worse still he had reflected upon the bishop himself. Atterbury was not to forgive this insult immediately; however, he regretted that he was too ill to attend Prior's funeral, because he would have done it, he told Pope, to show that he had "forgiven and forgotten" what Prior had written about him.[80]

Another friend of former days whom Prior now saw frequently was Harcourt, son of the former Lord Chancellor. It was young Sim who had brought to Paris a copy of *Cato* for Prior. The Plenipotentiary and his young guest had had a gay time, it may be recalled, and Sim as a token of esteem had presented his portrait to Matt. Sim occasionally wrote friendly epistles in couplets, but the few extant verses published in *Harcourt Papers* would never lend support to a claim that he was a poet. "To Mr. Pope on the Publishing his Works" and "To Mr. Prior upon his Invitation to Town"[81] are typical of his verse. In spite of his slender output, two poems of real merit, "The Female Phaeton" and "The Judgment of Venus," which from their first publication

---

[79] *Dialogues of the Dead*, p. 172.
[80] Pope, *Works*, ed. Elwin and Courthope, IX, 29, Atterbury to Pope, Sept. 27, 1721.
[81] *Harcourt Papers*, II, 164.

date were attributed to Prior, were from time to time credited to Harcourt. An advertisement of the former poem in the *Daily Courant* on April 8, 1718, uses the original cumbersome title:

This day is published Verses on the Lady Katherine H—de's first appearing at the Play-house in Drury Lane. By M—w P—r, Esq. Sold by W. Graves at the Black Spread Eagle in Paternoster Row and J. Graves in St. James Street. Price 2d.

The text of the poem in this first edition is as follows:

I

Thus *Kitty*, beautiful and young,
And mad as Colt untam'd;
Bespoke the Fair from whom She sprung,
With little Rage enflam'd.

II

Inflam'd with Rage at sad Restraint,
Which wise *Mamma* ordains,
And sorely vex'd to play the Saint,
Whilst humbler Beauty reigns.

III

Shall I thumb Holy Things confin'd,
With *Abigails* forsaken!
Kitty's for something else design'd,
Or I am much mistaken.

IV

Must Lady *Jenny* frisk about,
In Visits with her Cozens?
At Masques and Balls make all the Rout,
And bring home Hearts by Dozens?

V

What has She better, pray, than I?
What hidden Charms to boast,
Then all Mankind for her should die,
Whilst I am scarce a Toast?

VI

Dearest *Mamma* for once let me
 Unchain'd my Fortune try;
I'll have my *Earl* as well as She,
 Or know the Reason why.

VII

I'll soon with Jenny's Pride quit Score,
 Make all her Lovers fall;
They'll grieve I was not loose before,
 She, I was loos'd at all.

VIII

The Mother's Fondness soon gave way,
 Kitty at Heart's Desire,
Obtain'd the Chariot for a Day,
 And Set the World on Fire.

Sometime during the same year Curll brought out a single sheet folio edition of the poem under the title by which it has since been known, i.e., "The Female Phaeton." The author's name was omitted, but a statement, "The Copy before publish'd, has not one stanza printed right," was given a prominent place. Curll greatly exaggerated the superiority of his version, although at least two improvements were made in it, which have been adopted in all subsequent texts of the poem. He substituted *wild* for *mad* in the second line, and the twenty-ninth line, "The Mother's Fondness soon gave way," was amended to read "Fondness prevail'd, Mamma gave way." Within a few months Curll was advertising what he called a third edition of the poem together with a hitherto unpublished song of Prior's.[82] Then in April, 1720, came Curll's *The Court Miscellany in Prose and Verse*, which included "The Female Phaeton" and named the author as M. Prior, Esq.

From 1720 until 1907 "The Female Phaeton" and "The Judg-

[82] In the *Post Boy*, Feb. 28, 1719. The song was the "Horace and Venus, Set by Monsieur Galliard," which under the title "Cantata" Prior had published in the subscription volume, p. 266.

ment of Venus" were repeatedly published over Prior's name in editions of his works and in various miscellanies and anthologies,[83] but when Mr. Waller in 1907 published Prior's poems from the Longleat MSS there was among them a hitherto unknown piece, entitled "Answer to the Female Phaeton.[84] In not very good verse and with labored humor, Prior chided old Curll for having ascribed "The Female Phaeton" to him. Just what are we to believe about the poem? It was written early enough to have been included in the subscription volume but was not. This is not *prima facie* evidence, however, that Matt did not write it, for he held back rather inexplicably some of his best poems from publication during his lifetime. The fact that there is no copy of it at Longleat is perhaps the strongest argument against Prior's authorship. On the other hand, are we to believe in the unfinished "Answer," which the author never even troubled to send to the offending Curll? Had Prior done so, should we feel justified in accepting the denial in the face of his several repudiations of poems that were known to be his? Our conjecture is that Matt wished to let whatever praise the little poems merited go to Harcourt, but that Sim's untimely death in June, 1720, robbed the gesture of its meaning.

A figure of the world of letters in this second decade of the century, and one to be reckoned with, was John Dennis. We may recall that Dennis had sent a copy of his *Remarks on Cato* to Paris to Prior, whom he undoubtedly recognized as a kindred critic of Addison. He had openly expressed admiration for *Henry and Emma* in the past, and it is not surprising that he should address one of his *Letters Familiar, Moral and Critical* (1721) to Prior.[85] Its theme was that of the relative merits of

---

[83] With music by Dr. Arne it was sung at the close of the third act of a performance of *All for Love* in Dublin, May 5, 1756, and was published the following year with Dr. Arne's music in *A Favorite Collection of English Songs Sung . . . . At Ranelagh Gardens.* See W. H. Gratton Flood, "Dr. Arne's Visit to Dublin," *The Musical Antiquary,* July, 1910, I, 230.

[84] *Dialogues of the Dead,* p. 335.

[85] *Longleat Papers,* III, 494, John Dennis to Prior, Jan. 10/21, 1720/1. This "Letter"

Horace and Juvenal, a topic of never failing interest to these men who had conned their classics almost from the cradle. The tone of the letter indicates that the two were not new friends. It is reasonable to suppose that Prior had simply renewed his acquaintance with Dennis and that the letter was but a continuation of some of their debates when the learned arguments of Rigaltius and Scaliger, the Elder, champions of Juvenal, and of Heinsius and La Bruyère, partisans of Horace, were batted back and forth with great agility. If Prior was a silent instigator of any of the serious squabbles that Dennis had with the other writers of the time, we can find no record of it. It is to be hoped that he was not involved.

Other writers less important than Dennis clamored for Prior's patronage, hoping to make capital of his intimacy with Lord Harley. Giles Jacob, a Grub Streeter, dedicated a volume of poems to Prior in appreciation of financial assistance recently rendered.[86] Later, when Jacob published the *Poetical Register*, Prior furnished the date for the sketch of himself. Jacob presently presumed too far. He began to brag all over town about Prior's approbation of the aforementioned poems and to circulate the malicious rumor that Prior was affronted by one of the letters in Dennis's newly published book. Dennis, we are glad to learn, turned the "vile scribbler" ignominiously from his door.[87] Another hack writer of the same stripe was Charles Gildon. He once sent Prior the manuscript of a tragedy in hopes that it would find its way to Lord and Lady Harley.[88] Prior ignored this bid, and Gildon, becoming ill-tempered, sent him a nasty, insulting note, which, ironically enough, followed Prior to Wimpole where he was visiting the Harleys.[89] This too was ignored, and the Grub Street chapter was closed.

---

was reprinted by Samuel Humphreys in his life of Prior prefixed to the third edition of Prior's *Works*, London, 1733, pp. xi–xv.

[86] *Longleat Papers*, III, 493, Giles Jacob to Prior, Jan. 6/17, 1720/1.

[87] *Ibid.*, 501, John Dennis to Prior, April 11/22, 1721.

[88] *Ibid.*, 496, Gildon to Prior, Feb. 15/16, 1720/1.

[89] *Ibid.*, 506, Gildon to Prior, July 21/Aug. 1, 1721.

Prior had in his early days been a confirmed Londoner—as much so as Lamb or Dr. Johnson—and his friends could hardly hold him to his promises made in all good faith to pay visits outside the city. After his release from custody, however, he lost his urban preference and spent a great deal of time in the country. Of all of the country estates which he visited, Wimpole was his favorite, and on one occasion he found it so hard to tear himself away that he prolonged a visit for four months. London, he told one friend, no longer had allurements for him; it was an "abominable place," a "sink of inquity and sea coal"—strange words from the man whose *summum bonum* had been a seat at the Smyrna, a desk at the Cockpit, and who had seldom viewed nature except from a round in St. James's Park or a stroll in the gardens of Versailles or Fontainebleau. Yet a desire for a cultivated retreat in the country is the theme of lines penned twenty years earlier in Paris on the flyleaf of Robbe's Geography. Now he was ready for his "garden, house, and stable." Fortunately the opportunity to become a landholder came shortly after the subscription volume appeared, when Lord Harley furnished Prior with the sum of four thousand pounds necessary for the purchase of Down-Hall, an estate in Essex, three miles from Harlow on the road to Hatfield Heath. A condition of the purchase was that the property should revert to Harley at the poet's death.

The purchase of Down-Hall was effected through that great land-jobber of the time, John Morley of Halstead, who as Harley's agent was reputed to have negotiated for Lord Edward his marriage to the heiress of the Duke of Newcastle. For that deal Morley is said to have received ten thousand pounds. Shrewd, keen, and bluff, Morley stands out as a picturesque character. He amassed a fortune with very little trouble and, although brought up to the trade of a butcher, he achieved easy meeting terms with the leading poets of the time—Prior, Gay, and Pope. Prior frequently visited Morley at Blue Ridge, and while there in 1717 he conveniently supplied verses for a commemorative tablet which Morley wished to place in the chancel of the Halstead Church.[90] Contemporary opinions of Morley are conflicting. Undoubtedly he was tricky. Swift remembered him as a "rascally butcher and knave" and laid the blame for Harley's financial embarrassments in later years to his weakness and credulity in trusting his estates to Morley's management.[91] Although in the "Ballad of Down-Hall," Prior calls the agent "soft Morley, mild Morley," he had reason later to regard him in a less kindly light.

The "Ballad of Down-Hall"[92] describes vividly and humorously Prior's first visit to the estate, made toward the close of 1719. Unlike those sorties from The Hague, so jauntily made in a "little Dutch-chaise," this journey was taken in state in an elegant chariot, with no nymph at his side, alas, but with Squire Morley as companion, and Matt's servant Jonathan pacing along beside on the good steed Ralpho. The poem, which we should like to quote in full were it not too long, recounts in mock heroic style the exploits of two British heroes, Matthew and John

> And how they rid Friendly from fine London Town
> Fair *Essex* to see, and a place they call Dᴏᴡɴ

Matthew begins to expound his ambitions to his companion,

> And now in this *Journey* of Life, I wou'd have
> A place where to Bait, betwixt the *Court* and the *Grave*
> Where Joyful to live, not unwilling to Die —

---

[90] *Poems on Several Occasions*, p. 206.

[91] Swift, *Correspondence*, VI, 92, Swift to John Barber, Aug. 8, 1738.

[92] *Down-Hall; a Ballad. To the Tune of King John and The Abbot of Canterbury.* First published by Roberts in 1723. In some of the editions of Prior's *Works* in the eighteenth century it was wrongly dated 1715. Morley urged Prior to write a second part to the ballad, but Prior, though flattered, never complied.

but Morley characteristically interrupts,

> *Gadzooks*, I have just such a Place in my Eye
> There are Gardens so stately and Arbors so Thick,
> A *Portal* of Stone, and a *Fabrick* of Brick.

At nightfall the realtor, to use modern jargon, and his client arrive at the Bull Inn at Hoddesdon in Hertfordshire. At this point a serious note is injected into the story. After supper when the travelers join the landlady for ale, they relapse into that pensive, reminiscent mood so often induced by wholesome fatigue, appeased appetites, and the brimming cup. Prior makes inquiry after "Sisley, so cleanly and Prudence and Sue," as well as for other acquaintances of bygone days:

> And where is the Widow that dwelt here below?
> And the Hostler that Sung about Eight Years ago?
>
> And where is your Sister so mild and so dear?
> Whose Voice to her Maids like a Trumpet was clear,

He sorrowfully hears of the many changes that have taken place since last he passed that way:

> Why now let me Die, Sir, or live upon Trust,
> If I know to which Question to answer you first,
> Why Things since I saw You, most strangely have vary'd,
> And the Hostler is Hang'd, and the Widow is Marry'd.
>
> And Prue left a Child for the Parish to Nurse;
> And Sisley went off with a Gentleman's Purse;
> And as to my Sister so mild and so dear,
> She has lain in the Church-yard full many a Year.

In unadorned but "cantering anapestics" Prior has recited with humor and pathos a tale of the vicissitudes that are the common lot of man; it contains the stuff of life—the *sine qua non* of all good narrative whether it be extemporized by pilgrims on their way to Canterbury or to Down or recounted by travelers as fireside tales at the Tabard or the Bull.

Early the following morning, the two wayfarers resume the journey to Down. Presently the object of their quest comes in view, and alack and alas, Prior discovers that Morley has deceived him. The "fabrick of brick" turns out to be "a low ruin'd white Shed" built of plaster and lath. Prior is angry, but Morley tosses the matter off lightly by saying that his business is land and by advising Prior to see an architect about the house. As a final sally the agent cries,

> I wish you cou'd tell, what a duce your head ails:
> I show'd you *Down-Hall*; did you look for *Versailles*?

Prior easily fell in love with Down; however disappointing the house might be, its situation on a rise of ground was delightful, and it commanded a fine prospect. The ideal pastoral scene reminded him of his favorite Latin poets: "I have read Horace and Virgil above forty years, but I never understand two passages of them until I saw Down."[93] Matt was bent upon making the house more habitable. To help him in this undertaking he appealed for advice to his friends, the Virtuosi. This society numbered among its members the leading practitioners of the arts—Michael Dahl, James Thornhill and John Wootton, all painters; George Vertue and Charles Christian, engravers; James Gibbs, architect, and Charles Bridgeman, landscape gardener. At the meetings of the society, Prior would steer the conversation in the direction of his new interest, airing his plans and receiving suggestions. Gibbs, who had designed St. Martin's-in-the-Fields and St. Mary-le-Strand, the Radcliffe Library at Oxford and King's College Library at Cambridge, lent a hand and drew up plans and specifications for a new house at Down. Bridgeman, "virtuoso grand jardinier," also became

---

[93] *Dialogues of the Dead*, p. 404. The passages were Horace:
> O rus! quando ego Te aspiciam quandoq; Licebit
> Ducere Sollicitae jucunda oblivia vitae

and Virgil:
> Oh! qui Me gelidis submontibus Emi
> Sistat et ingenti ramorum protegat umbra?

interested in Matt's landscaping and sketched a garden to accompany the proposed house.

The building plans (which may be seen in Gibbs's *Book of
Architecture*), called for a spacious mansion built around a court
ninety feet wide and seventy-eight feet deep, from which the
main entrance, an arched portico, led into a reception hall
twenty-five feet square. Opening off the hall were a parlor, a
withdrawing room, and a library. The ample bedrooms would
occupy the upstairs, and servant quarters in the rear were to be
connected with the house by an arcade.[94] Certainly these were
no mean plans. The extravagance of Matt's dream may easily
be accounted for when we consider his attendance at the French
Court, his associations with the wealthy, both at home and
abroad, his love of show. How proudly he would conduct his
visitors around the estate, and how agreeable it would be to
drink in their compliments on the excellence of the scene both
indoors and out! As for the gardens, Prior's taste was heroic,
colored by his long familiarity with the artificial regularities
and symmetries of Dutch and French landscape.

The house as it stood was adequate, and during clement
weather very comfortable—comfortable enough for Pope, at
any rate, who, when he spent the Christmas of 1725 there with
Harley, advised against making any changes.[95] Little did Prior
realize that all these plans were destined to be merely paper ones.
He ran back and forth between Down and London during the
summer of 1720, looking eagerly forward to September, when
Gibbs had promised to come to Down with the completed design for the house, and Bridgeman had agreed to lay out the
garden. It was not until 1780, long after both Prior and Pope
had ceased dabbling in architecture and gardening, that the
rambling lath and plaster structure was replaced with brick
and mortar—but that is another story.

[94] Gibbs, *A Book of Architecture*, Plate LV.
[95] Pope, *Works*, ed. by Elwin and Courthope, VIII, 216, Prior to Harley, Jan. 22, 1725.

During the years of retirement Prior contemplated only once a return to public office. In April, 1719, Dr. Jenkin, successor to Gower as Master of St. John's College, asked Prior if in the event of the death of Dr. Pasch, one of the University members of Parliament, he would care to become a candidate. Dr. Jenkin, a Tory like his predecessor, was certain that Prior would be acceptable to the university, his only fear being that Prior's exception from the Act of Grace might debar him from being seated. Matt replied eagerly that he should like to become a candidate; he believed that his mistreatment by the Whigs would be a good talking point with a Tory constituency; he understood that a second Act of Grace to include those excepted from the former Act would shortly be passed. Further, he reasoned that Lords Oxford and Harcourt exercised their rights in the House of Lords as though under no cloud; also he knew that more than one corporation was waiting for an opportunity to elect Thomas Harley, who was in the same boat as far as the Act of Grace was concerned. Prior did not fail to inform Dr. Jenkin that he had already been urged by many members of the House of Commons to seek election. In the autumn of 1720 Pasch accommodatingly died, and Prior journeyed up to Cambridge to offer himself for election; but he found the Whig element strong and the Chancellor unfriendly. Furthermore, it was bruited about that the election of Mr. Prior would be prejudicial to the university. He therefore withdrew his name. Apropos of of Prior's near candidacy some friend wrote Lord Edward Harley that Prior had not a ghost of a chance and advised Harley to use his influence in behalf of an "honest Tory." The last word about the affair is found in a letter that Matt sent to Lord Oxford from Wimpole, voicing his keen and not unnatural disappointment:

I have stayed here [Wimpole] long enough to see the popular folly of our neighbouring University. . . The farce acted there has just the same exit which you foretold. Annesley was beaten out of the pit, ill-supported by his new acquired friends, and everybody denying that they had had any hand in bringing him down; my own college, a little ashamed of the usage they gave their own fellow, whose friendship they have and may yet have further occasion for, but we pass that. . . This is the world, My Lord, and the same tricks are played in courts and camps, universities and hospitals, and so men act and have acted, for the proof of which your Lordship and your humble servant need not read much history.[96]

From Wimpole Prior returned to London for the winter and buried his disappointment in plans for further improving Down, which had become his hobby, one which, he feared, might even "turn" his brain. Shortly after Christmas he and Drift drove to Down to supervise the laying out of squares, rounds and diagonals and the planting of quincunxes, without which no formal eighteenth-century garden was complete.[97] He described for Chesterfield[98] in detail the walks that he was cutting through a little wood, the fish pond that would hold "ten carps," and asked triumphantly what a Cicero, a Pliny, or a Chesterfield could enjoy more than the "same thing in a larger volume."[99] This congenial task was soon interrupted by cold weather, and Matt went back to London to nurse his cough in warmer quarters. Furthermore he was feeling his years. "Age, I find comes on," he wrote Swift, "and the cough does not diminish—

> Non sum qualis eram bonae
> Sub regno Cynarae.[100]

By March he was feeling more fit and was off again for Down to see the results of his plantings and mayhap to build a grotto.

Did he ever resume correspondence with friends in France? At least once, when he wrote a letter introducing William Sherard,

[96] *Portland Papers*, V, 610, Prior to Oxford, Wimpole, Dec. 23, 1720.
[97] *Longleat Papers*, III, 492, Prior to Harley, Jan. 9/20, 1720/1.
[98] Philip Stanhope, third Earl of Chesterfield, who, deaf and crippled with rheumatism, lived in retirement at Bretby. In *Longleat Papers* are six letters from Chesterfield to Prior, in reply to letters from Prior.
[99] Pope, *Works*, ed. Elwin and Courthope, VIII, 193, n.
[100] Swift, *Correspondence*, III, 73, Prior to Swift, Feb. 28, 1720/1.

the botanist, to that scholarly antiquarian, the Abbé Bernard de Montfaucon. In the days when he had been Plenipotentiary, Prior had often visited the Benedictine abbey at Saint-Germain-des-Prés, where he was known as "un érudit fort distingué," and where, in search of relief from burdensome diplomatic duties in scholarly conversation, he often envied the "tranquillity of spirit" of his friend and hoped that something of that spirit might some day be his. The letter to Montfaucon is too long to quote in full, but we cannot spare the last part of it, which throws some light upon Prior's temper during the last few months of his life: ". . . Depuis que jai eu l'honneur de m'entretenir avec vous, jai senti tous les troubles qui accompagnent ordinairement le changement d'une haute fortune, *pericla, damna, carceres*, mais grâce à Dieu, sans inquiétude ni crainte me contenant de réfléchir que pour ce qui regarde la *publica Res*, j'ai toujours agi en honnête homme et bon sujet, et pour le reste, me réjouissant quelquefois avec mes amis du mépris de la grandeur, et d'autres fois me trouvant retiré dans mon jardin et avec mes livres dans une vie fort particulière, et presque aussi solitaire que la vôtre!"[101]

A slight ripple in the political world which Prior may or may not have been cognizant of, reached London in the spring of 1721. The English Jacobites in France were mentioning Prior for the Secretaryship of State to the Pretender, whom Whig diplomacy had forced to seek refuge in Rome. James had commissioned one of his agents to procure for the English party two names for his consideration; the ones proposed were those of Prior and Lord Lansdowne.[102] The agent reporting on these sug-

---

[101] Broglie, *Bernard de Montfaucon et les Bernardins*, I, 138–39, Prior to Montfaucon, London, May 12, 1721. The original is in the Bibliothèque Nationale, MS 17711, fo. 142. It is surprising that the Royal Historical Manuscripts Commission did not see fit to publish in their volume of Prior papers at Longleat the copy of this letter and Montfaucon's reply, dated July 11, 1721, both of which are at Longleat.

[102] On March 20, 1721, Sir Henry Goring wrote to the Duke of Ormonde: "You are not ignorant that the King hath sent for a Secretary—the two persons in question at present are Ld. Lansdowne and Mr. Prior." He added that personally he thought Prior would

gestions, believed that the appointment of Prior would be injurious to the Pretender's cause inasmuch as he had learned that
the Pretender's "best and principal" friends in England would
not be willing to correspond through Prior. No doubt the agent
had conferred with an influential Jacobite or two who had
found Prior as lukewarm to the Pretender's cause as in earlier
days.

In June Prior was again at Down-Hall, so busy with his
husbandry that the days seemed short and his health better.
The place which he loved "more than Tully did his Tusculum or
Horace his Sabine Field" absorbed all his thought and he filled
his correspondence with details of the homely tasks to which he
had accustomed himself.[103] A stile was made at the end of Great
Hilly Field—he had named all the pastures and meadows—
where trespassing cattle had done great damage; an old gate was
stopped with brushwood to keep the "plaguey" pigs out of the
pease close; salating was planted, and even the setting of the
miller's hen was recorded.[104] Since water for the gardens was a
pressing problem, Matt was impatient to confer with Morley
about locating a well on the place. That his preoccupation with
things rural should amuse his friends ruffled Matt, or so a note,
penned in a somewhat strutting mood, on the subject of the
well would indicate:

I have a great deal to say to my friend and countryman Morley about

---

not do. Later Goring wrote a letter to Dillon, James's agent in Paris, which deciphered
reads as follows: "You are not ignorant that the King hath sent for a Secretary. The persons in question at present are Ld. Lansdown and Mr. Prior. If the last goes I am afraid
it will wrong the King's affairs for to my knowledge his best and principal friends in
England will not keep correspondence by that Canal." Dillon then wrote to James on May
5 telling him that his friends in England would not agree in the choice of Secretary, some
being for Prior, though the majority wanted Lansdowne. In July Lansdowne wrote to
James offering to take the post and was accepted. For information concerning this correspondence, I am indebted to Miss Elizabeth Handasyde, author of *Granville the Polite,
the Life of George Granville, Lord Lansdowne*, and for a transcript of the letter from Goring
to Dillon (in the unpublished Stuart Papers at Windsor), to Mr. M. Mackenzie, Registrar
of the Royal Archives, Windsor Castle.

[103] *Longleat Papers*, III, 504, Prior to Harley, Down, June 8/19, 1721.
[104] *Ibid.*, 505, Prior to Harley, Down, June 14/25, 1721.

sinking a well and splashing a quickset, by which discourse I may happen to prove that I am not so ignorant of country affairs as some people may imagine.[105]

The well was duly sunk, and our country gentleman with his magic watering pot envisioned for his little Eden greener lawns, more umbrageous shrubs, hardier blossoms. But Prior did not live to see the fulfillment of his dreams.

During July he returned to London for a brief stay. August found him at Wimpole, where he was always welcome. While in a very sober mood he began a "brouillon" of what was to have been a long poem on predestination. Rapidly he wrote off nearly two hundred couplets, leaving some of them in imperfect form. In view of the heretical statement in the preface to "Solomon" that "he that writes in rhimes, dances in fetters," this return to the "rocking horse" is surprising but may be attributed to the influence of Pope and his circle. In these last few weeks of his life when his health was far more precarious than his friends realized, Prior was not unnaturally preoccupied with the fate of his own soul. We may regard the poem as a sequel to "Solomon," for, if in that poem he gave utterance to pessimistic sentiments, in "Predestination" he gave utterance to religious convictions just as strong. Prior called his poem "Predestination," but he gave equal attention to the opposite doctrine of free will. Predestination, he thought, involved the acceptance of such abhorrent beliefs as that "we are machines" and that "our good endeavors signify nothing." Equally repugnant was the teaching of the Apostle that "we are clay in the hands of the Potter," for that meant that man is "no better than inanimate objects." No less objectionable was the solution that "God foresaw and permitted," for that was the equivalent of predestinating. Turning to free will, Prior argued that unless man possess liberty of will, why are his acts "imbued with good and ill," why must there be judgment, punishment,

[105] *Ibid.*, 506, Prior to Harley, Down, June 22/July 3, 1721.

or reward, and why must the Son of God die to save the World. Unfortunately, he could not dismiss the problem so dogmatically as Dr. Johnson did in an epigram: "All theory is against the freedom of the will, all experience for it." Neither belief satisfied Prior; he intended to find some middle means by which "destin'd sentence and free will agree." It is at this point that the poet hinted at an escape from his dilemma but did not present it.

Certainly throughout the poem, interspersed as it is with prayers for guidance and for forgiveness of sin, there is a ring of genuine sincerity. Nowhere can we find any evidence that Prior was, like many of his contemporaries, an agnostic deist. Here is no attack upon accepted beliefs but an earnest effort to think his way through conflicting doctrines. "Predestination" merely concludes a long series of poems of piety, of which the Exodus ode, the poem on the 88th Psalm, the Epistle to Dr. Sherlock, and "Solomon" are the most conspicuous examples.

While wrestling with this troublesome subject, Matt decided that it was time to make his will. True, he had little property, but he wished to remember appropriately those friends who had stood by him through thick and thin. There was that honest old Westminster, faithful secretary of diplomatic days and companion of his last years, Adrian; there was impulsive Dick, playfellow of many an idle hour and no more provident than Matt himself; there was the "well beloved and dear Cousin Katherine," his nearest relative and the only survivor of the Channel Row Priors. Also to be considered were his servants, John Newman and Jane Ansley.

He thought of his medals, his pictures, his maps, his manuscripts and diplomatic papers, the thousands of books not only in his study but lying on shelves all over the place. From these he would make bequests of intrinsic value, leaving his little substance to friends in real need. He had been a collector of almost everything except a fortune. To his college, in spite of the recent political snub, he would leave the portrait Belle had painted of him in his ceremonial wig and ambassadorial dress of rich brocade; likewise to St. John's he would leave the portrait of the Earl of Jersey over which he had haggled with Rigaud so many years ago. These two portraits, together with books to the value of two hundred pounds and a copy of the tall *Poems*, were to be placed in the library—a lasting monument to the joiner's son upon whom the Grand Monarch had bestowed favors.[106]

As for the rest of the pictures, Lord Edward Harley might choose the six he liked best; Lady Harriett would be given the portrait of Queen Elizabeth by Marcus Gheeraats the elder; Peggy, the oval miniature in the gold case. Harley could have three hundred of his books,[107] and then the rest of the library, the remaining pictures, considerably over a hundred in number,[108] the medals, the silver plate, etc. should be sold to provide funds for the cash bequests he would name.[109]

Harley and Drift should be the executors. There would be a thousand pounds for Adrian. And Dick, who had borrowed from him as he had borrowed from others, should have all bonds remitted. Three hundred pounds would do for Dick's son George— it would be sufficient to send him to the university or to start

[106] These books, selected by Dr. Bedford of St. John's College included many volumes of Continental history, richly bound and bearing Prior's crest. Among them is a volume of 43 French pamphlets, entitled *Recueill de diverses pièces*, 1612–1666; another volume, called *pièces touchant Mazarin* contained 105 French pamphlets, 1649.

[107] Lord Edward Harley's selection of books, to the value of 71 pounds, included the Bordeaux edition of Ausonius, 1575; the Aldus *Commentary* of Aristotle, 1504; Blackwood's *Martyre de la Rayne d'Ecosse, Douairière de France*, 1587; the *Apologie ou Defense de Marie Stuart*, 1588; two editions of Ovid, *his invective against Ibis*, 1577 and 1658; the Etienne edition of Horace, 1577; and other rare volumes.

[108] The pictures which Lord Edward Harley chose included a Veronese, a Titian, a Guido Rheni, a Claude Lorrain and two Poussins. In addition he purchased about seventy others from Prior's collection. Among them were three pictures by Rubens, a Tintoretto, a Rembrandt, a Van Dyke; also an original portrait of Dryden by Kneller, one of Lord Dorset by the same painter, and Belle's portraits of Simon Harcourt and the Abbé Gaultier. See Richard Goulding's *Catalogue of the Pictures . . . at Welbeck Abbey and London*, p. xxxii.

[109] Prior's library, after the bequests were deducted, was valued at 375 pounds, a very large amount for his time.

him in a suitable employment. Cousin Katherine should receive
one hundred pounds for mourning. His servants should receive
mourning and one year's wages, Jane and Jonathan coming in
for fifty additional pounds each.

Finally, there were Betty and Anne—back-street companions
of whom Matt was strangely unashamed. To Anne Durham,
whom he had set up in business, he would leave three hundred
pounds "to be employed in the enlargement of her stock." To
Betty Cox, he desired to give a thousand pounds for the purchase
of an annuity, payable solely to her order and not to "any husband she might marry." In an earlier chapter we identified these
two women of easy virtue as subjects of several of the Cloe
poems, but, as Prior mentioned them so rarely elsewhere, we
must depend on gossip for further gleanings as to their place in
his life. Rumor had it that Betty Cox's husband died about a
month before Prior and that it was death alone that saved Matt
from having to marry her. It was even rumored that her wedding
clothes had been ordered, and it was said that she grew so
"humoursome and imperious" with Prior that his friends remarked upon it. To their remonstrances, Matt replied that long
familiarity with her "humours" made them tolerable. He preferred Betty with all her faults to a new mistress who would
"bring a new temper" and the trouble of conforming there-
with.[110]

In spite of all this tittle-tattle and of Prior's manifest interest
in Mrs. Cox's welfare, it is unlikely that he would have married
Betty. As he was no man's fool, he was no woman's either, and
knew how to dally with the fair sex without becoming entangled. From John Wesley's comments on the poet we take a
story which was told to John by his elder brother Samuel, head
usher at Westminster School.[111] One day there came to Samuel's
quarters in Dean's Yard a Miss Taylor. She wanted advice.
"Sir, I know not what to do," she said. "Mr. Prior makes large

---

[110] *Biographia Britannica*, V, 3446.   [111] From 1713 to 1733.

professions of his love; but he never offers me marriage." Samuel advised her to bring the matter to a point at once; whereupon she went directly to Matt and asked him plainly if he intended to marry her. The poet responded with many "pretty sayings," to which she replied, "Sir, in refusing to answer, you do answer. I will say no more." She never saw Matt again, but after his death spent many hours weeping at his tomb.[112] Wesley used this story to confute the testimony of Pope, Spence, and others as to the low character of Prior's women. With that matter we are not concerned, but the story does seem to indicate that if Prior could not be cajoled into matrimony by the more scrupulous Miss Taylor, he certainly would have eluded the unspeakably common Betty Cox.

Snobs have scoffed at the wish of the joiner's son that he be buried in Westminster and at his "last piece of human vanity" in setting aside in his will five hundred pounds for that purpose. To us his ambition seems only natural. Born and reared within sound of the Abbey bells, educated within its gates, employed as a trusted diplomat by two monarchs, Prior had as much right to pomp and circumstance as did Stepney and Halifax. The will provided that Gibbs should draw plans for the monument which was to be surmounted by the Coysevox bust, a gift from Louis XIV. Not one of the three epitaphs Prior himself had written, half gay, half cynical, should be inscribed on the monument—he had made Atterbury promise him that. Dr. Freind, the best Latin scholar of the day, should write a fitting epitaph enumerating all the public employments Prior had held. Lastly Matt wished to lie near his favorite English poet, Spenser, whose public services had been even less rewarded than his own.

The will made, Matt's thoughts again turned to Down, where he planned to stop on his return to London in the autumn. In London he hoped to see Lord Oxford, if the health of the latter permitted him to journey to the city. It was barely possible

[112] John Wesley, *Works*, VII, 421.

that Swift might arrive from Ireland for a visit; Matt had frequently urged the Dean to come to Duke Street where "a book, a bell, and a candle" always awaited him.

But none of these plans materialized. Prior was never to see either Down-Hall or Duke Street again. On September 11, 1721, he was stricken with a violent attack of cholera morbus. Two days later he felt better and thought that his illness was over. Suddenly it returned with extreme violence, and exactly one week after he had first been taken ill, he died.[113] From Wimpole his body was carried to Jerusalem Chamber, Westminster, to lie in state until placed in a tomb at the feet of Spenser in the Poet's Corner.

Within a few days after the funeral, several of the faithful friends gathered to hear the reading of the will, the contents of which provoked considerable comment. To satisfy their curiosity, Dr. Arbuthnot and Erasmus Lewis visited Betty Cox's ale-house in Long Acre. There over a bowl of punch the proprietress, the "brimstone bitch" as Arbuthnot called her, bragged to her guests of her relations with the deceased poet and rejoiced over his generosity.[114]

Prior's death was genuinely mourned by both friends and fellow poets. Scores of panegyrics were fittingly written about one who had himself always been ready with the panegyric pen. Allan Ramsay apostrophized Prior in a pastoral dialogue: "Dear sweet-tongued Matt! thousands shall greet for thee!" Pope and Swift both asked for copies of the Rigaud portrait; Sir James Montague wrote the memoirs from which we have quoted frequently. Swift, on learning the sad news, broke off a letter to a friend: "I am just now told from some newspapers that . . . my excellent friend, Mr. Prior is dead; I pray God deliver me from many such trials. I am neither old nor philoso-

---

[113] *Portland Papers*, V, 625, Harley to Humphrey Wanley, Wimpole, Sept. 19/30, 1721.
[114] *European Magazine*, XIII, 8, Extracts from original letters from Dr. Arbuthnot to Henry Watkins, Sept. 30 and Oct. 14, 1721.

pher enough to be indifferent at so great a loss; and therefore I abruptly conclude."[115]

The London friends inserted a notice in the *Post Boy* which recited all of Prior's public employments and concluded with this tribute: "He was a person of universal learning and the most refined turn of wit; a pleasing and instructive companion, a kind master and a dear friend. He had a great soul, but cloathed with humility and good nature: He was an able minister, and an admirable poet, a generous benefactor, and what adds to his praise, an honest and sincere man."[116]

---

[115] Swift, *Correspondence*, II, 103, Swift to Archbishop King, Sept. 28, 1721.

[116] *The Post Boy*, Thursday, Sept. 21, to Saturday, Sept. 23, 1721. On Nov. 27, the *Boston Gazette*, in far away New England, reprinted from the London *Loyal Mercury* of Sept. 21, the following announcement: "We hear that on Friday last the immortal Mr. Prior expired at one of the seats of the Lord Harley.

> Ye melting Muses mourn around his Hearse,
> And sooth his gentle Shade with Melancholy Verse."

On March 12,1721/2, the same paper reprinted from the London *Weekly Journal*, Sept. 30, 1721, the following news of the burial: "On Monday in the evening the corpse of Matthew Prior, Esq. was carried from the Jerusalem Chamber and splendidly interr'd in Westminster Abbey." With this announcement the *Boston Gazette* printed twenty-five lines of "melancholy verse," "On the Death of Mr. Prior," by Lucius. French and Dutch papers also copied reports of Prior's death from the London journals.

Bibliography

MANUSCRIPT SOURCES

Bodleian Library
  A286.198; A450.22; Rawlinson, D739; SC 25427 (MS. Montague); 29558.
British Museum
  Add. MSS., 7,121; 12,112; 15,947; 21,508; 28,644; 29,589; 37,361; 40,621; 40,771–40,773.
  Harleian MSS., 378; 4042.
  Lansdowne MSS., 1236.
  Sloane MSS., 655; 1786.
  Stowe MSS., 222; 227; 242; 755; 970.
Middlesex Guildhall
  Hearth Tax Accounts, 16 Charles II, City and Liberties of Westminster, No. 7.
New York Public Library
  Hardwick Papers.
Paris: Archives du Ministère des Affaires Étrangères
  Correspondance Politique d'Angleterre, Vols. 190–204; 230–67.
Pierpont Morgan Library
  Prior MSS.
Public Records Office
  State Papers, France, 78/154–78/160; 105/27–105/29 (Prior's Letter Books); Stepney Papers, 87/11, 105/50–105/89.
  State Papers, Holland, 84/221–84/223.
  Subsidy Rolls, E 179: 143/366; E 179: 353/25.
Rush Rhees Library, University of Rochester (N. Y.)
  R. B. Adam Collection on loan to the Library.
St. Margaret's Westminster
  Baptismal Records.
Somerset House
  Prerogative Court of Canterbury: 158 Pembroke; 62 See; 62 Pitt.

Stowe Hall, Kings Lynn, Norfolk
  Hare Papers.
Welbeck Abbey, Worksop, Notts
  Prior Papers.
  Prior MSS.
Wellesley College Library
  Lady Winchilsea MSS.
Windsor Castle
  Stuart Papers.

PUBLICATIONS OF H.M. GOVERNMENT

Calendar of State Papers, America and the West Indies, 1700–1708. Ed. by Cecil Headlam. 1910–1916.

Calendar of State Papers, Domestic, 1697–1704. Ed. by W. J. Hardy and R. P. Mahaffy. 11 vols., 1895–1924.

Calendar of Treasury Papers, 1696–1719. Ed. by Jos. Redington and W. A. Shaw. 5 vols., 1868–1883.

Baker Papers, 1871 (MSS. of W. R. Baker, Esq.) H.M.C. Second Report.

Buccleuch Papers, Vols. I–III, 1889–1925 (MSS. of the Duke of Buccleuch and Queensbury).

Dartmouth Papers, 1887 (MSS. of the Earl of Dartmouth).

Journal of the Commissioners for Trade and Plantations, 1704–1715. 2 vols., 1920–1925.

Longleat Papers, Vols. I–III, 1904–1908 (MSS. of the Marquess of Bath at Longleat, Wiltshire).

Marlborough Papers, 1881 (MSS. of the Duke of Marlborough)— H.M.C. Eighth Report.

Polwarth Papers, 1911 (MSS. of Lord Polwarth).

Portland Papers, Vols. V and VI, 1899, 1901 (MSS. of the Duke of Portland at Welbeck Abbey, Worksop, Notts).

Stuart Papers, Vols. I–VI, 1902–1923 (MSS. at Windsor Castle).

Trumbull Papers. Vols, I and II, 1924 (MSS. of the Marquis of Downshire, at Easthampstead Park, Berks).

OTHER PRINTED SOURCES

Addison, Joseph, Works. Ed. by Richard Hurd. 6 vols., London, 1856.

A[glionby], W[illiam] F. R. S., The Present State of the United Provinces of the Low Countries. London, 1669.

Aitken, G. A., "Matthew Prior," *Contemporary Review*, Vol. LVII, 1890.
——"Notes of the Bibliography of Matthew Prior," *Transactions of the Bibliographical Society*, Vol. XIV, 1916.
Allegations for Marriage Licenses issued by the Dean and Chapter of Westminster, 1558–1699. Publications of the Harleian Society, XXIII, London, 1886.
Allen, John, Article on Bolingbroke, *Edinburgh Review*, Vol. LXII, No. CXXV, 1835.
Ancezune, Madame la Marquise d', "Abrégé de la vie de M. le Marquis de Torcy," *Revue d'histoire diplomatique*, Vols. XLVI, XLVII. Paris, 1932, 1933.
Baker, Thomas, History of the College of St. John the Evangelist. Ed. by J. E. B. Mayor. 2 vols., Cambridge, 1869.
Ball, F. Elrington, Swift's Verse. London, 1928.
Barrett, W. P., "Matthew Prior's Alma," *Modern Language Review*, XXVII, 1932.
Bastide, C., "Un Secrétaire d'ambassade anglais à Paris sous Louis XIV," *Revue des sciences politiques*, Vol. XLVIII. Paris, 1925.
Bertrand, Louis, Louis XIV. Paris, 1923.
Bickley, Francis, Life of Matthew Prior. London, 1914.
——The Shorter Poems of Matthew Prior. London [1923].
Biographia Britannia. 6 vols., London, 1747.
Boileau-Despréaux, Nicolas, Œuvres. Ed. by M. Agar. Paris, 1848.
Bolingbroke, Lord, Authentic Memoirs of the Conduct and Adventures of Henry St. John, Late Lord Bolingbroke. London [n.d.].
——Letters and Correspondence. Ed. by Gilbert Parke. 4 vols., London, 1798.
Bowen, Marjorie, Luctor and Emergo, Being an Historical Essay on the State of England at the Peace of Ryswick, 1697. Newcastle-upon-Tyne, 1925.
Boyer, Abel, History of the Reign of Queen Anne, Digested into Annals, Vols. I–X, London, 1703–1712.
Broglie, Emmanuel de, Bernard de Montfaucon et les Bernardins, 1715–1750. 2 vols., Paris, 1891.
Cambridge University, Historical Register of the University of Cambridge. Ed. by J. R. Tanner. Cambridge, 1917.
Capefigue, M., La Comtesse de Parabère et le Palais Royal sous la régence. Paris, 1863.

Catalogue of the Pictures belonging to His Grace, the Duke of Portland, at Welbeck Abbey, and in London. 1893.

Celebrated Authors, the Works of. [Dorset, Halifax, Stepney, and others]. 2 vols., London, 1740.

Character of a Tavern, The. With a brief Draught of a Drawer. London, 1675.

Clark, G. M., The Dutch Alliance and the War against French Trade, 1688–1697. Manchester, 1923.

Cobbett's Parliamentary History, Vol. VII.

Cole, Christian, Memoirs of Affairs of State. London, 1733.

Collins-Baker, C. H., Lely and the Stuart Painters. London, 1912.

Committee on Secrecy, *See* House of Commons.

Cooke, George Wingrove, Memoirs of Lord Bolingbroke. 2 vols., London, 1836.

Correspondentie van Willem III en van Hans Willem Bentinck eersten Graaf van Portland. 2 vols., The Hague, 1927, 1937.

Court Miscellany in Prose and Verse, The. London, 1719.

Coxe, William, Memoirs of Marlborough. 6 vols., London, 1820.

Coynart, Ch. de, Les Guerin de Tencin, 1520–1758. Paris, 1910.

Dangeau, Philippe de Courcillon, Marquis de, Journal. 19 vols., Paris, 1854–1882.

Davenant, Charles, A Discourse of Grants and Resumptions. London, 1699.

Defoe, Daniel, The Consolidator. 1705.

Dennis, John, Original Letters, Familiar, Moral and Critical. London, 1721.

Dickerson, Oliver M., American Colonial Government, 1696–1765. A study of the British Board of Trade in Its Relation to the American Colonies. Cleveland, Ohio, 1912.

Documents Relative to the Colonial History of the State of New York. Albany, N. Y., 1853.

Doughty, Oswald, The English Lyric in the Age of Reason. London, 1922.

Dryden, John, Miscellany Poems: Third Part, (London, 1693); Fourth Part, (London, 1694); Fifth Part, (London, 1704).

——Poetical Works. Ed. by G. R. Noyes. Boston, 1908.

Eagle, The, a Magazine Supported by Members of St. John's College, XLIV, 1924.

Elliott, Hugh, Life of Sidney, Earl of Godolphin. London, 1888.

Elstob, Elizabeth, Rudiments of Grammar. London, 1715.

Examiner, The. London, 1710–1711.

Feiling, Keith, History of the Tory Party, 1640–1714. Oxford, 1924.

Fénelon, François de Salignac de la Mothe, Œvures, Vol. XXI. Paris, 1824.

Fieldhouse, H. N., "Oxford, Bolingbroke, and the Pretender's Place of Residence, 1711–1714," *English Historical Review*, April, 1937.

——"Bolingbroke's Share in the Jacobite Intrigue of 1710–14," *English Historical Review*, July, 1937.

Firth, Sir Charles, "Two Poems Attributed to Prior," *Review of English Studies*, Vol. I. London, 1925.

Gay, John, Poetical Works. Ed. by John Underhill. 2 vols., London, 1893.

Gazette de France. Volumes for 1711–1715.

Gentleman's Journal, The; or the New Monthly Miscellany. London, 1692–1694.

Gentleman's Magazine, The. New Series, II, London, 1834.

Gibbs, James, A Book of Architecture, Containing Designs of Buildings and Ornaments. London, 1728.

Gosse, Sir Edmund, French Profiles. London, 1905.

Goulding, Richard, Catalogue of the Pictures belonging to his Grace the Duke of Portland at Welbeck Abbey. . . . Cambridge, 1936.

——Welbeck Abbey Miniatures . . . A Catalogue Raisonné. Walpole Society Publications, Vol. IV. Oxford, 1915.

Grew, Marion E., William Bentinck and William III. London, 1924.

Grimblot, Paul, Letters of William III and Louis XIV and of their Ministers, 1697–1700. London, 1848.

Guthkelch, A. C., "A Review of Francis Bickley's *Matthew Prior*," *Modern Language Review*, Vol. X, 1915.

Haile, Martin, Queen Mary of Modena: Her Life and Letters. London, 1905.

Halévy, Daniel, Vauban, Builder of Fortresses. Trans. by Major C. J. C. Street. New York, 1925.

Hamilton, G. R., The Soul of Wit, A Choice of English Verse Epigrams. New York, 1925.

Hanmer, Sir Thomas, Correspondence. Ed. by Sir Henry Banbury. London, 1838.

Harcourt Papers. Ed. by Edward William Harcourt. 13 vols., Oxford [n. d.].

Harrop, Robert, Bolingbroke, A Political Study and Criticism. London, 1884.

Hazlitt, William, Lectures on the English Poets. Vol. V in the Centenary Edition of his Complete Works. London, 1930.

Hills, Alfred, "Matthew Prior in Essex," *The Essex Review*, Vol. XXXVII, 1935.

House of Commons, Journal, 1701, 1715–1717.

——Report from the Committee of Secrecy, Appointed by Orders of the House of Commons. London, 1715.

——Observations on the Report of the Committee of Secrecy. Edinburgh, 1715.

House of Lords, Journal, 1715–1717.

Journal de l'ambassade extraordinaire de son excellence My Lord Comte de Portland en France par rapport an ceremonial. Ed. by G. D. J. Schotel. The Hague, 1851.

Kemble, John, Papers and Correspondence Illustrative of the Social and Political State of Europe from the Revolution to the Accession of the House of Hanover. London, 1857.

Kerr, William, Restoration Verse. London, 1930.

Klopp, Onno, Fall des Hauses Stuart. 14 vols., Wien, 1875–1888.

Lamberty, Guillaume de, Mémoires pour servir à l'histoire du XVIIIme siècle. La Haye, 1724.

Legg, L. G. Wickham, Matthew Prior, a Study of his Public Career and Correspondence. Cambridge, 1921.

Legrelle, A., La Diplomatie française et la succession d'Espagne. 4 vols., Paris, 1888–1892.

Legrelle, H., Notes et documents sur la Paix de Ryswick. Lille, 1894.

Letters of Denization and Acts of Naturalization for Aliens in England and Ireland, 1603–1700. Publications of the Huguenot Society of London, XVIII, 1911.

Lexington Papers . . . Extracts from the Official and Private Correspondence of Robert Sutton, Lord Lexington. Ed. by H. Manners Sutton. London, 1851.

Liber scholasticus; or an Account of the Fellowships and Exhibitions at the Universities of Oxford and Cambridge. London, 1829.

Lister, Martin, An Account of Paris at the Close of the Seventeenth Century. London, 1699.

Locker-Lampson, Frederick, Lyra Elegantiarum. Revised edition, London, 1891.

Lovering, Stella, L'Activité intellectuelle de l'Angleterre d'après l'ancienne "Mercure de France" (1672–1778). Paris, 1930.

Luttrell, Narcissus, A Brief Historical Relation, 1678–1714. 6 vols., London, 1857.

Macaulay, Thomas Babington, History of England from the Accession of James II. Ed. by T. F. Henderson. 5 vols., Oxford, 1931.

McKnight, Thomas, Life of Henry St. John, Viscount Bolingbroke. London, 1863.

Macky, John, Characters of the Court of Great Britain. London, 1732.

MacPherson, James, History of Great Britain from the Restoration to the House of Hanover. 2 vols., London, 1775.

MacLean, Kenneth, John Locke and English Literature of the Eighteenth Century. New Haven, 1936.

MacPherson, James, History of Great Britain from the Restoration to the House of Hanover. 2 vols., London, 1775.

Marlborough, Duchess of, Private Correspondence. 2 vols., London, 1837.

Marlborough, Duke of, Letters and Dispatches. Ed. by Sir George Murray. 5 vols., London, 1845.

Marriage, Baptismal and Burial Registers of the Collegiate Church or Abbey of St. Peter. Ed. by Joseph Lemuel French. Publications of the Harleian Society, Vol. X. London, 1876.

Masson, Maurice, Madame de Tencin. Paris, 1909.

Memorials of St. Margaret's Westminster: The Parish Registers, 1539–1660. Ed. by Arthur Meredyth Burke. London, 1914.

Mercure de France, 1694–1700; 1721–1774.

Mercure galant, 1711–1715.

Mercure historique et politique, 1711–1715.

Michael, Wolfgang, England under George I, Vol. I. London, 1936.

Minto, William, "Matthew Prior," Encyclopædia Britannica. Ninth ed., Edinburgh, 1885.

Miscellany Poems and Translations by Several Hands. London, 1712.

Moestissimae ac laetissimae Cantabrigiensis affectus decedente Caroli II succedente Jacobi II. Cambridge, 1684/5.

Montague, C., The Works and Life of C. Montague, the late Earl of Halifax. [Ed. by John Oldmixon?]. London, 1715.

Montaigne, Michel de, Essais. Ed. by Jean Plattard. 6 vols., Paris, 1931–1932.

Musical Miscellany, The; Being a Collection of Choice Songs. By the Most Eminent Masters. London, 1729/30.

Nisser, Wilhelm, Michael Dahl and the Contemporary Swedish School of Painters in England. Upsala, 1927.

Oldmixon, John, Life and Posthumous Works of Arthur Maynwaring. London, 1715.

Osgood, Herbert L., The American Colonies in the Eighteenth Century. New York, 1924.

Poems on Affairs of State, Vols. II, III. London, 1703, 1704.

Political State of Great Britain, Vols. I–XXII. London, 1711–1721.

Pope, Alexander, The Iliad of Homer. London, 1715.

—— Works. Ed. by William Lisle Bowles. 10 vols., London, 1806; Ed. by Elwin and Courthope. 9 vols., London, 1871–1886.

Prior, Matthew, Dialogues of the Dead and other Works in Prose and Verse. Ed. by A. R. Waller. Cambridge English Classics, 1907.

—— Eighteen Canzonets for Two and Three Voices. . . The Words chiefly by Matthew Prior. Set to Music by John Travers. London [1745?].

—— Henry and Emma, a New Poetical Interlude . . . with alterations and a new air and chorus, the Music by Dr. Arne. London, 1744.

—— The History of His Own Time, Compiled from Original Manuscripts. Ed. by Adrian Drift. London, 1740.

—— Lyric Poems; Being Twenty-four Songs (Never Before Printed) by the late Matthew Prior, Esq. Set to Music by Several Eminent Masters. London, 1741.

—— Miscellaneous Works. London, 1740.

—— Poems on Several Occasions. 1709.

—— Poems on Several Occasions. 1718.

—— Poems on Several Occasions. . .Volume the third. . .to which is prefixed the Life of Mr. Prior, by Samuel Humphreys. London, 1727.

—— Poems on Several Occasions. 2 vols., London, 1766.

—— Poems on Several Occasions. Ed. by A. R. Waller. Cambridge English Classics, 1905.

    Unless otherwise specified, this is the edition referred to in the footnotes.

—— Poetical Works, with Memoir and Critical Dissertation. Ed. by G. Gilfillan. Edinburgh, 1869.

—— Poetical Works. Ed. by R. B. Johnson. 2 vols., London, 1907.

—— Selected Poems. Ed. by Austin Dobson. The Parchment Library, London, 1889.

Registers of St. Margaret's, Westminster, London, 1660–1675. Publications of the Harleian Society, LXIV, London, 1935.

Roberts, W., "Matthew Prior as a Book-Collector," *Athenaeum*, June 1897.

Rowe, Elizabeth, Miscellaneous Works in Prose and Verse. 2 vols., London, 1739.

Ruffhead, Owen, Life of Alexander Pope. London, 1769.

Sackville-West, Victoria, Knole and The Sackvilles. New York, 1922.

St. Léger, A. de, La Flandre maritime et Dunkerque sous la domination française, 1659–1789. Paris, 1900.

Saintsbury, George, The Peace of the Augustans. London, 1916.

Saint-Simon, Duc de, Mémoires. Ed. by A. de Boislisle. 42 vols., Paris, 1879–1928.

Salomon, Felix, Geschichte des letztens Ministeriums Königin Annas von England. Gotha, 1894.

Shenstone, William, Men and Manners. Ed. by Havelock Ellis. London, 1927.

Shrewsbury, Duke of, Life and Character of the Duke of Shrewsbury. London, 1718.

Sichel, Walter, Bolingbroke and His Times. 2 vols., London, 1901–1902.

Sourches, Marquis de, Mémoires sur le Règne de Louis XIV. 13 vols., Paris, 1882–1893.

Spence, Joseph, Anecdotes, Observations, and Characters of Books and Men. Ed. by S. W. Singer. London, 1858.

Stanhope, Earl. History of England Comprising the Reign of Queen Anne until the Peace of Utrecht, 1701–1713. 2 vols., 1889.

—— History of England from the Peace of Utrecht, 1713–1783. 7 vols., 1858.

Strong, S. Arthur, A Catalogue of Letters and Other Historical Documents Exhibited in the Library at Welbeck. London, 1903.

Suckling, Sir John, Works in Prose and Verse. Ed. by A. H. Thompson. London, 1910.

Swift, Jonathan, Correspondence. Ed. by F. Elrington Ball, 6 vols., London, 1897–1908.

—— Journal to Stella. Ed. by George A. Aitken. London, 1901.

Tanner, Lawrence E., Westminster School, a History. London, 1934.

Tatler, The. London, 1709–1710/1711.

Thackeray, William M., The English Humorists of the Eighteenth Century. London, 1858.

Thayer, Harvey W., "Matthew Prior, His Relation to English *Vers de Société*," *Sewanee Review*, Vol. X, 1902.

Thomson, Mark, The Secretaries of State, 1681–1782. Oxford, 1932.

Torcy, Jean Baptiste Colbert, Marquis de, Journal inédit. Ed. by Frédéric Masson. Paris, 1884.

—— Memoirs. 2 vols., London, 1757.

Trémoille, Duc de la, Madame des Ursins et la succession d'Espagne. 6 vols., Nantes, 1902.

Trent, William P., Longfellow and Other Essays. New York, 1910.

Trevelyan, George M., England under Queen Anne. 3 vols., London, 1930–1934.

—— "The Jersey Period of the Negotiations Leading to the Peace of Utrecht," *English Historical Review*, January, 1934.

Turell, Ebenezer, The Life and Character of the Reverend Benjamin Colman. Boston, 1749.

Vertue, George, Notebooks, I–IV. Publications of the Walpole Society, Vols. XVIII, XX, XXII, XXIV. Oxford, 1930–1936.

Vocal Miscellany, The, A Collection of Four Hundred Songs. London, 1734.

Ward, Ned, The Secret History of Clubs particularly the Kit-Cat. . . . London, 1709.

Weber, Ottocar, Der Friede von Utrecht. Gotha, 1891.

Wentworth Papers, 1705–1739. Ed. by J. J. Cartwright. London, 1883.

Wesley, John, Works. London, 1782.

Whitley, William T., Artists and Their Friends in England, 1700–1799, London, 1928.

Williams, Basil, Stanhope, a Study in Eighteenth Century War and Diplomacy. Oxford, 1932.

Williams, Marjorie, William Shenstone. A Chapter in Eighteenth Century Taste. Birmingham, 1935.

Winchilsea, Anne, Countess of, Poems. Ed. by Myra Reynolds. Chicago, 1903.

Wise, Thomas J., The Ashley Library, A Catalogue of Printed Books, Manuscripts and Autograph Letters. 10 vols., London, 1922–1930.

Wolseley, Garnet Joseph, Viscount, The Life of John Churchill, Duke of Marlborough, to the Accession of Queen Anne. 2 vols., London, 1894.

Wright, Thomas, Isaac Watts and Contemporary Hymn-Writers. London, 1914.

Yart, Antoine, Idée de la poësie angloise, ou traduction des meilleurs poëtes anglois. 8 vols. in 12, Paris, 1749–1771.

Index